William James

The Essential Writings

William James

The Essential Writings

BRUCE W. WILSHIRE

with a Preface by

James M. Edie

State University of New York Press
Albany

To
June Withington Wilshire Ford

The Essential Writings of the Great
Philosophers are published under the
editorship of Charles M. Sherover.

Published by
State University of New York Press, Albany

© 1984 State University of New York

For information, address State University of New York
Press, State University Plaza, Albany, N.Y., 12246

Library of Congress Cataloging in Publication Data
James, William, 1842-1910.
    William James: the essential writings.

    1. Philosophy — Addresses, essays, lectures.
I. Wilshire, Bruce W. II. Title.
B945.J21 1984   191   84-8848
ISBN 0-87395-935-3
ISBN 0-87395-934-5 (pbk.)

10   9   8   7   6   5   4

CONTENTS

Sight of elephants and tigers at Barnum's menagerie whose existence, so individual and peculiar, yet stands there so intensely and vividly real, as much so as one's own, so that one feels again poignantly the unfathomableness of ontology, supposing ontology to be at all. They are, eodem jure *with myself, and yet I, with my pretensions or at least aspirations to adequately represent the world, can never hope to* sympathize *in a genuine sense of the word with their being. And the want of sympathy is not as in the case of some deformed or loathsome human life, for their being is admirable; so admirable that one yearns to be in some way its sharer, partner or accomplice. Thus their foreign-ness confounds one's pretension to comprehend the world— while their admirableness undermines the stoic or moral frame of mind in which one says the real meaning of life is* my *action. The great world of life, in no relation with my action, is so real!*

WILLIAM JAMES (1873)

I, for my part, cannot escape the consideration, forced upon me at every turn, that the knower is not simply a mirror floating with no foot-hold anywhere, and passively reflecting an order that he comes upon and finds simply existing. The knower is an actor and coefficient of the truth on one side, whilst on the other he registers the truth which he helps to create. Mental interests, hypotheses, postulates, so far as they are bases for human action—action which to a great extent transforms the world—help to make *the truth which they declare. In other words, there belongs to mind . . . a spontaneity, a vote. It is in the game, and not a mere looker-on; and its judgments of the* should-be, *its ideals, cannot be peeled off from the body of the* cogitandum *as if they were excrescences. . . .*

WILLIAM JAMES (1878)

Preface

At the present time in American philosophy, there are three major ways of interpreting and assessing the value of the philosophy of William James. The first—perhaps the most widespread, though also the most lethargic, unimaginative, and unproductive— is based on the belief that the thought of William James now belongs to the history of philosophy exclusively and has nothing but historical interest for the contemporary philosopher. This view is most authoritatively presented in *The Encyclopedia of Philosophy*, edited by Paul Edwards in 1967. In that extremely important but very one-sided and occasionally narrow-minded series of essays on contemporary philosophy, William James Earle takes responsibility for a critical discussion of the early thought of William James on the explicit assumption that its "main philosophical significance" lies solely in its historical influence on the "subsequent movement in philosophy typified by Whitehead and his disciples."[1] There are quite a number of other American philosophers who might situate James somewhat differently, according to their various philosophical persuasions and predilections, and depending on which period of his thought they personally favor, but who would not challenge this viewpoint as such; namely, that James's thought is no longer of importance in itself but only as it has worked itself out in the various schools which it fathered.

A second view, almost as widespread as the first, takes its point of departure from the attempts which began almost before James's death to domesticate his thought by making him into a kind of culture-hero. Such a move, by elevating James to the status of an

1. William James Earle, "William James," *The Encyclopedia of Philosophy*, Paul Edwards, ed. (New York and London, 1967), IV, 244.

institution, would cut him off from any effective engagement in the give-and-take of ongoing philosophical debate. Within a year of James's death, Josiah Royce—one of his true philosophical enemies, an honest Hegelian—eulogized him for his ability to give full verbal expression to certain latent and culturally operative ideas "which are characteristic of a stage and an aspect of the spiritual life of this people."[2]

One of the best exponents of this viewpoint at the present time is John J. McDermott. He writes:

> If James's originality constituted a stage of the national self-consciousness in his time, his vision now replies to the needs of man today, who confronts an endless but increasingly controllable cosmos. An analysis of the life history and thought of William James involves us in the three great mooring points of human experience: self-consciousness, national culture, and cosmic setting. By virtue of his spirit, his concerns, and even the direction of his unfinished technical thought, William James places us at a vantage point, from which we can attempt to reconstitute the human endeavor in a way that is creative and honest.[3]

Though this way of approaching James is much more vital and challenging than the first, since it at least recognizes the current relevance of James's philosophical thought, it suffers from a kind of Hegelian historicism: James's life and thought are inextricably bound up with American culture and the philosophical awakening to self-consciousness of *this* people. McDermott here gives expression to the quasi-universal attitude toward James which is currently found in American studies programs, in American history courses, in American literature and criticism, and even in many courses in American philosophy. James's Yankee practicality, his insistence on the "cash value" of ideas, his "pragmatism," his "pluralism," his "scientific" no-nonsense attitude toward outmoded metaphysical theorizing, even his "radical empiricism" (which is as badly misunderstood by cultural and intellectual his-

2. Josiah Royce, *William James and Other Essays on the Philosophy of Life* (New York, 1911), p. 7.

3. John J. McDermott, ed., *The Writings of William James* (New York: Random House, 1967), pp. xvii-xviii.

torians as by his own philosophical progeny) —all these are sufficient as global titles under which it is deemed possible to sum up
the whole of James's thought in encapsulated, mythical form. In
this way, James's philosophy is certainly not relegated to the past;
it is an essential component of the dominant myths and the still-
creative cultural institutions of our national existence, and its
study will provide us with continued and renewed insights into
our present and future existential predicament as citizens and
participants in this specifically "New World" culture.

But a third attitude toward William James is still theoretically
possible: namely, to treat him as a philosopher. What both of
these first two attitudes toward the thought of William James lack
is any true appreciation of his contributions to philosophy in the
strict sense, and it is to the strictly philosophical study of James
that Professor Wilshire, the editor of this volume, has up to now
made his most important personal contribution.[4]. In so doing,
Professor Wilshire occupies an honorable place among a restricted
but important number of contemporary philosophers, such as Aron
Gurwitsch, Alfred Schutz, Herbert Spiegelberg, Hans Linschoten,
John Wild, and others, who have begun to develop the strictly
philosophical implications of a number of James's truly creative
and innovative doctrines. This movement toward a complete re-
evaluation of James's thought began in the discovery of his pivotal
importance for Edmund Husserl and, thus, for the foundation of
phenomenology as a method of philosophical reflection and as a
body of substantive conclusions on the nature of experience,
thought, reality, the body, the self, and the world. Here it is not
James's importance for American culture, undeniably important as
this is, but James's contribution to universally acceptable philosophical theory which is the focus of attention. It is in this strictly
philosophical renewal of his thought that James now emerges as

4. Bruce Wilshire, *William James and Phenomenology: A Study of "The
Principles of Psychology"* (Bloomington: Indiana University Press, 1968) . See
my review of this book in the *Review of Metaphysics* (March, 1970) , pp. 481 ff.,
which also lists the other recent contributions to the James renaissance which
can now be said to be well under way.

one of the giants of contemporary philosophy, and, with Husserl, as the founder of a new phenomenology.

The importance of the present collection of readings from James lies in the fact that it has been arranged so as to provide a systematic introduction to his major *philosophical* discoveries, and precisely to those doctrines and theories which are of most burning current interest. This is not, therefore, another haphazard assemblage of texts, chosen to give some "flavor" of the American intellectual frontier to the student of philosophy, sociology, history, or cultural anthropology, but a series of philosophical arguments on some of the most "obscure and head-cracking problems" in contemporary philosophy: the relation of thought to its object; the interrelationships between meaning and truth; the levels and structures of experience; the degrees of reality; the nature of the embodied self; the relation of ethics, aesthetics, and religious experience to man's strenuously and "heroically" active nature; and, above all, the structurization of the experienced life-world as the validating ground and origin of all theory. Professor Wilshire has provided an introduction to William James's thought on these and other related points which is at once both substantial and subtle; there is no need for me to repeat the outline or summarize the content of his arguments here.

But let me point out two things. Professor Wilshire has already produced a philosophical commentary, referred to above, on James's first major work of philosophy, *The Principles of Psychology,* in which he has continued and developed the work of earlier phenomenological commentators on James's epistemological and metaphysical thought. His is beyond doubt the best commentary on the *Principles* which has yet been written, and it has done more than anything else in recent philosophical literature to rescue this *chef d'oeuvre,* one of the "classics" of contemporary philosophy, from the oblivion into which it was cast by James's immediate disciples. Like Dewey, Wittgenstein, and Husserl, Wilshire considers this work to contain, in germinal form, all the ideas which James later on orchestrated for a popular audience in his

pragmatist essays. This is an extremely important, and recent, reconstruction of James's thought. Moreover, Wilshire sees—correctly, I believe—that James's second great book is *The Varieties
of Religious Experience,* and it is to the phenomena of risk, adventure, heroism, sanctity, the possibility of failure, the inescapa-
bility of commitment, as these are illustrated in this final work,
that he is now turning his attention. Like John Wild,[5] Wilshire
sees that James's whole philosophy is an "ethics," not in the sense
of just another sublimated version of utilitarianism (as Ralph
Barton Perry argued), or in the sense of the pan-moralism of a
Tolstoy, but in a sense which integrally flows from the epistemological doctrines of the *Principles.*

James's theory of the relations between meaning, truth, and
reality culminated in the famous chapter (21) on the orders of
reality in the second volume of the *Principles* in which the various
levels and kinds of "reality" were found to be strict correlates, in
their relations to lived time and to lived space, in their relations
to the primary perceptual situation (the "paramount" reality) of
the experiencing ego—to the purposes, intentions, and "practical
powers" of the lived self as the *fons et origo* of all reality. But this
epistemological-metaphysical conclusion is not to be understood in
the sense of the subjectivistic and relativistic theory of truth with
which superficial readers have taxed his pragmatist essays. It is to
be understood, in a deeper and truer sense, as the ultimate "ethical" foundation of all practical and theoretical human cognition
and life-action. It is the basis of James's theory of freedom and
responsibility. In this, James does not at all appear to be the
Yankee optimist which we see described in the frontier-myth of
which he is supposed to be the first philosophical expression. He
appears, rather, as the philosopher of the "twice-born," of heroic
risk, the strenuous life, and the possibility of tragedy, of the limit-
consciousness of the "morbid" and "pathological," as these are
described in *The Varieties of Religious Experience.* "Naturalistic

5. John Wild, *The Radical Empiricism of William James* (New York:
Doubleday & Co., 1969).

optimism," he writes, "is mere syllabub and flattery and sponge cake." There is, within human life, the intrinsic possibility that the human condition does not allow for a completely happy and triumphant conclusion. But, insofar as the world and history will not be accomplished without each individual effort, there is the possibility of limited success. On this possibility we unhesitatingly act, no less in our epistemological distinctions, in our "sense of reality," than in our moral choices. This ability to contrast what *could be* with what *is*, to distinguish our moral acts and intentions from *what we are*, from the factually given and determined situation in which we find ourselves, is, according to James, the deepest root of human specificity.

I am, therefore, completely in agreement with Professor Wilshire that most of the traditional criticism of James's pragmatic theory of truth misses the point. It is the merit of the phenomenological interpretation of James, in fact, to provide us with a means of making sense of James's popular essays on pragmatism and of incorporating them into a systematic account of his philosophy as a whole. If we fully understand the sense in which "to know" is not merely to passively copy reality or to take the disinterested attitude of divine contemplation toward it, but is rather a specific form of the ability to act, to structure, to gear into the world, we will be able to understand the underlying unity which ties James's epistemology and metaphysics to his ethics and provides us with a means to systematize and clarify his thought as a whole in terms of its inner logical coherence and methodological unity. With Husserl and Merleau-Ponty, James would say that consciousness (in the most fundamental sense of an operating intentionality in the world) is much less an "I know that such and such is the case" than an "I can do." The contemplative constatation of facts is a derived and late faculty of consciousness, a "founded" operation, which presupposes a more primordial contact with the real. To speak of the real *in itself*, minus consciousness, minus the experiencer, is not to speak of anything that, for us, ever could *be*. The solution is not to hypothesize metaphysical theories about the *in-itself*, but to describe the experienced life-world in all the fullness of its various orders of reality in their various correlations to the experiencing self.

To give such an interpretation to James is, admittedly, to accept him as a proto-phenomenologist, and there is no question about the fact that Wilshire, and a number of other philosophers who share the broad lines of his interpretation of James, is here joining issue with a whole tradition of interpretation and professional scholarship. But since I think that the working out of these issues in the next few years will be one of the most exciting aspects of contemporary American philosophy, for this reason alone, though there are many others, I most enthusiastically recommend this selection of James's writings, and this introduction to his thought, to the interested student of philosophy.

James M. Edie
Northwestern University

Introduction

Although William James is a world-renowned thinker and as close to being an American culture-hero as any academic philosopher could be, the actual influence of his thought upon academic philosophy in this country is not great. We have the pragmatic tradition, to be sure, but it has usually been other pragmatists who have set the dominant tone and leading problems—at least within the confines of academic thinking. One might be tempted to dismiss this thinking as just confining, but in a world atomized by professionalism, the departmentalized university has a sizable impact on our culture. Besides, some important thinking goes on there. We should seek out the reasons for James's oddly peripheral position.[1]

The understandable reserve and caution with which most of us deploy ourselves around the problems of philosophy involves an effacement of personality. Indeed so great may be the feeling of awe that the effacement is pushed to the point of inverted, defensive impersonality or pomposity (or at least dullness, whether ponderous or mincing). But James's personality is intrusive and irrepressible. His style is by turns inspirational and dramatic, blunt and colloquial. He is present as a person in his writing. The tacit question which runs through so much professional response to James in this country is, I think, How could such a vivacious writer and personality possibly be a great thinker? The assumptions and resonances of this question are disturbing.

Second, there is James's not wholly reasonable expectation that professional philosophers would sincerely try to understand what

1. Concerning James's attitude toward the academic, see "The Ph.D. Octopus" in this volume.

he was saying, and that they could understand it. This faith that he would be followed and understood, even if he took leaps in his thought and stretched the senses of terms (not always consistently) in order to catch his vision whole, is perhaps due in part to his early family experience. His gifted father practically took as his vocation the education of his children, and William's brother, younger by less than two years, the novelist Henry, though quite different from William in temperament, was one of the most sensitive and perceptive men to live in the modern world. Indeed, it is almost as if James believed in an Oversoul of mutual understanding. And why might he not? When he was a boy at his own table, he occasionally heard Emerson himself speak of such things, and perhaps he was there to hear that man say once again that mere consistency is the hobgoblin of little minds.

But the most important reason for the faulty recognition of James is just that his thought is a new vision of the philosophical enterprise which overwhelms traditional distinctions and terms. The reader firmly ensconced within any tradition will only be confused or angered by him if he allows himself to be moved at all. With a certain pre-Socratic naïveté about him, James saw central philosophical problems as if for the first time. Sometimes James is tripped by his vocabulary—when he cannot jump clear of received philosophical usage. Yet the inconsistencies, wrenchings, and vagueness of certain of his terms cannot conceal a vision of the world which is much more comprehensive and revealing than one would expect in thought of recent times; and it is a vision which has a center. Through a reading of such European thinkers as Husserl, Bergson, Heidegger, Merleau-Ponty, and Wittgenstein, we are, somewhat ironically, helped to capture the centered vision of the American philosopher.

James undercuts and reverses the tradition of modern epistemology regnant in various forms since Descartes. The father of modern philosophy (as he has aptly been called) had thought that mind knows immediately only its own mental bits or sensations, and that it is up to judgments like those of mathematical physics to tell us what is out there in the external world. Philosophically important truths are established by clear and distinct ideas interlocked with conceptual necessity—a position developed by the Continental rationalists. As the tradition developed in Britain—

particularly with Hume—only passively received discrete sensations were thought to supply a halfway reliable basis for judgments about the so-called external world.

James repudiates all this. He claims this tradition rests on a blindness to everyday experience of the world as we actually live through it. The tradition plasters over this experience with distinctions that are not true. First, James claims that we do not, in the life we actually live, experience the world as mental; and what the experience is experienced *as* is what the experience *is*. Second, he claims that we do not experience discrete bits of things, but whole "fields" irreducible in their wholeness. Third, our most fundamental experience and knowledge of the world is not in the form of clear and distinct ideas, but rather of ones which are vague to various degrees. (That ideas can be important and true but vague is an extraordinary thought.) Fourth, knowledge of the world requires constant, active interpretation in terms of values or standards set within an ever-present and vague world-horizon, with temporality an essential dimension; thus that sensations are allegedly passively received is not a criterion of objectivity. Fifth and finally, there is no internal or strictly subjective realm inhabited by sensations, feelings, and values which is set over against a realm of brute fact ascertained by the dispassionate methods of mathematical physics; hence there is no fundamental gulf dividing science from ethics or thought from life.

It is the intent of James's theory of knowledge to do justice to, and to build upon, pre-theoretical experience (in the sense of theory as deliberate theorizing). James thinks it bootless and misleading to construct a theory of truth in ignorance of what the truth is true about—being or reality—and the initial grasp of this is the world experienced pre-theoretically. His theory of knowledge emerges from the center of a putatively pre-theoretical view of reality which also generates from its center an aesthetics, an ethics, a philosophy of religion, and a kind of philosophy of science. It is as pointless to seek for neatly compartmentalized specialties in James as it would be in Heraclitus, Pythagoras, Anaxagoras, or Plato: all is entwined in a single world vision. Hence, the all too common approach to James by way of his late statement of his theory of knowledge (*Pragmatism*) is inimical to understanding that theory, for this requires a grasp of his whole vision, a grasp which is impossible when James is approached from within the assumptions of modern theory of knowledge. Even certain eminent pragmatists ignore or repudiate James on this point; e.g., C. I. Lewis restricts the term "cognition" to theoretical formulations which refer to experience, with the latter a bare "given" which is neither true nor false.[2] This is a bow to the autonomy and priority of science and theoretical thought which James does not usually make; for him there is a knowledge by acquaintance (and truth) which is presupposed by descriptive or theoretical knowledge.

Critics ignorant of the pragmatic tradition have fumbled into gauche suggestions such as that James is a mere popularizer of the thought of C. S. Peirce.[3] In the same month in which Peirce published his notable "How to Make Our Ideas Clear" (January, 1878), James published a seminal article portending his whole view, which contains in germ his own version of both the pragmatic theory of meaning and of truth.[4] The truth is just "the fate of thought," given an experienced world in which events fall out as the thought predicts, with what it predicts being its meaning.[5] But without an understanding of the center of James's vision —the structures of the experienced world—his later talk about thoughts "verifying themselves" and being true because they "satisfy" must inevitably be misconstrued in terms of Cartesian subjectivism, the very position his philosophy of experience rejects. James does not epistemologize truth so much as ontologize it. To be sure, he thinks that truth pertains to mind, but mind cannot be spoken of independently of the world experienced by it; hence, he rejects traditional empiricism and rationalism, as well as realism and idealism, because they all speak of mind "in itself" as a domain or agency for the cognition of the empirical world. His

2. See John Wild's illuminating book, *The Radical Empiricism of William James* (New York: Doubleday & Co., 1969), p. 369. James himself at some points in his later work suggests the same thing as Lewis. See Intro., p. 1 fn.

3. James's talk about his work is much less reliable than the work itself. Thus his words of praise for Peirce ("the founder of pragmatism") do much to conceal his own work in theory of truth. Of course, James was not only impressed by Peirce's work but was trying to boost Peirce's ill-starred career. That important philosopher could not get a regular appointment in a university.

4. "Remarks on Spencer's Definition of Mind as Correspondence," included in this volume.

5. With this proviso: p. xxi.

words comprising the twin epigraphs of this volume are not inconsistent—realism in the first, idealism in the second. Minds are
those of embodied beings, and they are in the world and act upon
it; the world is knowable only insofar as it falls within their ideal
and, in some degree, spontaneous projects. But we embodied minds
find ever more and more meaning in the world than we can at any
one time predict we will find, and we experience the world as that
which exists independently of, and prior to, our projects.

One of the best routes to the center of James's thought is to
develop John Dewey's insight[6] that James attempted to reconcile
"nature lore" (science) with "individual fate lore." James was
convinced that science had generated a nightmare of alienation
for man. In the ordinary nightmare we have motives but no
powers; in the scientific nightmare we have powers but no
motives.[7] By that he means that the world as construed by science
and by much philosophy since Descartes—i.e., as predictable but
purposeless forces describable in the non-human terms of mathematical physics—answers in no way to our desires and emotions.
There is no reverberation; we wander detached, our emotions
merely subjective. Despite our powers and scientific accomplish-
ments, we often ask, So what? Yes, we have done such and such—
we have gone to the moon or whatever—but what's new? Our
headlong pace—our dead run—crowds out consummatory experiences. How can life be significant and activity worth the bother if
human dreams and emotions are nothing but by-products of
systems that are describable, predictable, and controllable without
any reference to them at all?

The center around which James's philosophy develops is the
conviction that this scientific assumption is not just demoralizing
but false. Though there appear no references to human emotions,
valuations, and purposes in the formulations of science, that is due
merely to the special interests and constricted viewpoint of science
itself. Any complete account of what is going on when men do
science—any adequate philosophy of science—will reveal a ubiquitous reference to the human element, and in the most significant, though special, sense of reference: as presupposition of

6. *The Problems of Men* (New York: Philosophical Library, 1946), p. 390.
7. *The Principles of Psychology* (New York: Henry Holt & Co., 1890), II, 313.

scientific descriptions. As banal a description as "precipitation is occurring" presupposes for its sense the use of a standard involving human expectation and sensuous experience; to wit, if one were to walk outside and he were not hysterical, i.e., bereft of selective and purposive attention, he would feel sensations of water drops. Though there be no reference within the scientific description itself to human experience—though only the most technical, abstract, or quantitative notations appear—still these make sense only as progressive refinements of, and abstractions from, a world experienced by all of us in none other than sensuous, valuational and purposive terms. This experienced, or lived, world is the foundation without which human activities—e.g., scientific ones—would be impossible.

Before developing this central point further, we should note that James's terminology sometimes impedes its understanding. For example, he writes that a philosophy "will not be accepted that essentially baffles and disappoints our dearest desires and most cherished powers," and "for a philosophy to succeed on a universal scale it must define the future *congruously with our spontaneous powers.*"[8] But it is the spontaneous powers of the reader that may be baffled. Does James mean by "will not be accepted" a fact of intellectual history, or is he doing philosophy, and saying that it is not acceptable because not true? In fact, he is doing both at once, but not bothering to make the distinction. He is saying that such a philosophy will not be accepted and that it is not acceptable because not true; i.e., not only are our spontaneous powers a part of the world and must be understood if it is to be, but the world is understood in terms of these powers—and the interactions they involve—whether we like it or not. Because he does not always make these distinctions, he may give the impression of being a mere huckster of ideas—concerned with the question of which ideas will sell—and with this conceal the serious and unsentimental position which lies at the bottom of his thought. Is the failure to make these distinctions due to mere haste and carelessness on James's part? No, because he is trying to work out an incipient and still inchoate ethics which is rooting itself at the cen-

8. "The Sentiment of Rationality," a portion of which is included in this volume, pp. 25 ff.

ter of his view, and which he will not ignore for fear of losing touch with it. This is an ethics which allows for the tragic elements of human life, and which identifies good with personal struggle and self-realization in history.

The best vantage point on James's philosophy as a whole is gained from reading his *The Principles of Psychology*, a two-volume work written at the height of his powers (1890) which is not ostensibly philosophical at all. His aim was to develop psychology as a natural science untrammeled by the questions and perplexities of metaphysics; e.g., is there a soul substance existing beyond the range of sense experience? The pleasant irony of his attempt is that he lays out a vast and fertile breeding ground for his own radically experiential philosophy.

James hoped to protect the autonomy of psychology as a science by adopting a dualistic view of mind and matter. He "supposes two elements, mind knowing and thing known, and treats them as irreducible. Neither gets out of itself or into the other, neither in any way *is* the other. . . ."⁹ He presumed that mental states could be specified and identified independently of any philosophical commitment to the nature of the world known by them, and that they could then be correlated contingently to the brain. As it turned out, his attempt to specify mental states involved him in far-flung inquiries into the nature of the world as experienced—the world as presented to mind—an incipient phenomenology. Mind turned out to be non-substantial, and understandable only in terms of relations between objects experienced, with the thinker's own experienced, expressive, and active body a ubiquitous term. Hence an assumed dualism of mental and physical substances becomes an impossibility. Likewise undercut are the presumptions of science to be independent of philosophy.

The best first stroke to sketch James's radically experiential philosophy is to recount Edmund Husserl's acknowledgment that reading James's psychology helped him find his way out of psychologism.¹⁰ That confining view held that since all thought is psychical, what thought is about is subject to psychological laws, and hence the ultimate account of the world is to be given by

9. *Principles*, I, 218.
10. *Logische Untersuchungen*, 3rd ed. (Halle: Niemeyer, 1922), II, 208.

psychology. James observed that because of psychologists' typical presuppositions they tended to systematically misdescribe what is presented in thought—thought's object, what it is about. Unwittingly they substitute what they know about the thought for what the thought knows; e.g., since they know, or think they know, that each thought is psychical and caused by a sequence of intra- and interorganic events linking stimulating object and stimulated brain, they infer that the thought knows (has as its object) its own psychical nature juxtaposed against the particular stimulating object. Nothing could be farther from the truth: the object of ordinary non-reflective thought includes nothing of a psychical nature, and much more than any *particular* object. It always includes objects related in a field which shades off from a focus of sharply defined objects and relations to a margin of those vaguely presented, and which includes the thinker's own lived-body experienced as actively involved and inserted in some way in the world. Psychology properly pursued, then, reveals a world experienced which is not subject exclusively to psychological laws. Psychology is shown to depend upon a phenomenological philosophy—an account of the world-experienced *as* it is experienced, and this includes within itself, for example, a sphere of relations properly studied by physics.

Just as there is no thought or experience which is of a single thing and nothing else (there must always be relations and a background), so there is no experience which is locked into a discrete moment of time, a "now," and experiences only it. What is given is a "specious present," a field of duration or continuity, in which the just past is present as the just past, and the anticipation of the future is present as the anticipation. Nor is this just a psychical matter of slowly expiring sensations or images. A feeling of succession is not a succession of feelings, he writes, and just as there are relations in *rerum natura*, so there are relations in thought by which they are known. That is, physical things really are temporal, what we mean by them is what we take their temporality to be; i.e., a knife really is that which *will* cut if given operations are performed, and thunder really is that which breaks in upon silence. When James says that things *are* their most important characteristics relative to our concerns and purposes, he does not subjectivize the world experienced and leave another world unknown, or in itself; for our concerns and purposes *are* only relative to the world experienced. Purposes are no mere psychological impertinence. What is given is the mind-world relationship, not one or the other by itself. Hence James's pragmatic theory of truth is rooted in his pragmatic theory of meaning, which is rooted in turn in his philosophy of experience.

Each realm of the world is experienced in terms of temporal standards native to it; e.g., standards of mathematics are peculiar precisely because of their ideal and eternal objects, and the mode of time peculiar to operations upon them; music likewise has its own indigenous standards, etc. These criteria are not derived from mind alone or world alone, but from the relationship which is experience. Experience is a "double-barreled" term: an experiencing *of* an experienced world. James's metaphysics of radical empiricism emerges directly and explicitly from the discoveries of his *Principles of Psychology,* long before the appearance of the essays bearing that title.[11] The essential point is that mind and self cannot be specified independently of the world which appears to mind, and world cannot be specified independently of its modes of appearance to mind.[12] Appearances or phenomena are, then, "neutral" between mind and world, the difference between the two being nothing but a difference in the arrangement or context of the experiences. Above all, as we shall see, it is the body which is neutral: as actively lived, or body-subject, it is the non-focal center of the mental context; taken as just another organic object subject to physiological and physical laws (as a physician would take it), it is part of the context which is the physical world.

Concepts for James are "teleological instruments."[13] That is, the world is sorted into kinds on the basis of the sorts of consequences things are taken to produce in the active train of human experience. But thought for James is not all deliberate and theoretical. Most of it is non-reflective, non-deliberate, and unable to

11. *Essays in Radical Empiricism.* See pp. 162 ff.
12. James obviously thinks in a milieu influenced by Kant. Yet James sanctions no sweeping deduction of necessities of thought which are necessities of the phenomenal world. It is up to experience itself to decide which "brain-born," non-inductively learned necessary truths apply to experience; knowing which apply is piecemeal work and always incomplete. See below, p. lviii ff.
13. See "The Sentiment of Rationality" and chap. 12 on conception in *Principles,* portions of which are included below.

give an articulate account of the conditions of its application. Knowledge by acquaintance, as he calls it, is a wash of non-deliberate thought and experience, habitually and essentially vague and ill defined, which is the current which bears our existence, and out of which all deliberate thought takes rise. Moreover, there is always more to any real thing than any set of concepts has as yet revealed, and what will be revealed may correct our previous ideas of the thing.

Real things, for James, are obdurate and inexhaustible. (Even when we destroy a thing, we do not thereby know it through and through.) Water, say, is no more essentially H_2O than it is a slaker of thirst, or an object for a painter, and so on endlessly.[14] Any abstraction is a miserable substitute for the world's concrete richness.[15] We are lodged in a world of facticity (to use a contemporary term) the being of which is not ultimately explainable. We cannot answer why there is any being at all and not rather nothing, James says.[16] And we come upon ourselves as beings opaque at the center, in need of being known.

For James, the self is not identifiable in isolation from the sense and image of self, and this sense of self derives from care and interest in matters which owe nothing to a reflective source.[17] That is, experience is absorbed in objects of the world that are not deliberately chosen as objects of thought, and this absorption, whether friendly, hostile, or matter-of-fact, elicits from us incessant plays of our spontaneity. At least three times, James quotes the aphorism of Kierkegaard, "We live forward but understand backwards,"[18] and it is clear that he wishes to enlarge the boundaries of understanding so as to grasp life as it is lived.

James is involved in a reinterpretation of consciousness and self along non-dualistic lines. When thought reflects and attempts to

14. No doubt James agrees that a painting of water cannot exist unless water does or did exist (or some matter did exist), while the water can exist without the painting. But for him there is no reference to existence without a notion of existence, and the notion is no more essentially a product of research in physics than it is of the expressiveness of painters. Nor is existence exhaustively expressed in any finite set of notions.

15. *Principles*, II, 319 ff. Included in this volume, "On 'Essence.'"

16. See James's *Some Problems of Philosophy* (New York: Longmans, Green & Co., 1948) and "The Sentiment of Rationality," pp. 1 ff. and 25 ff. below.

17. See "The Consciousness of Self," pp. 82 ff., N.B. p. 95.

18. See, e.g., "Is Radical Empiricism Solipsistic?," p. 220.

"catch itself in the act," it finds not itself, James writes in one passage, but organic feelings of adjustment in the head and throat. A man's self is "remembering and appropriating thought incessantly renewed"; i.e., the self is all that is appropriated and taken as mine, with the body occupying a peculiarly constant and intimate position, even though vague. But the implication of this passage of James's *Principles* is that thought never does find "itself," but only more object, or total field, with the body given, even if peripherally, as present, and given in this case in the peculiar stance of memory (eyes rolled up or unfocused, perhaps, and the body disengaged from tasks in the present world). It is to this body given as present that the body given as past is tied and appropriated. Hence consciousness or thought "itself" is empty—exhausted by its multi-relational object. The implication is that the continuity which is the self requires no inherently subjective seat or source—that one *is* an acting, thinking, remembering body.

James regards attention and will as the core of the self. That is, the kind of person I am is a matter of my behavior, and this is a matter of the patterned turnings of my attention; what I do is a matter of what I "hold before me" as objects of thought. And James is willing to construe will and attention in terms of the experienced body: for example, the consent to an object or project is a release of breath through the glottis—though not just the release of breath, of course, but the-release-of-breath-in-conjunction-with-this-object.

James's discoveries in the *Principles* shock him, and he shies away from the indicated conclusion that the feeling of subjectivity or selfhood is nothing but a feeling of "the whole cubic mass of the body which we feel all the while."[19] But room is left for such a conclusion, and indeed it must be seen to follow, I think, when a mode of reflection is developed which does not freeze, atomize, and hence distort the pre-reflective flow of experience, but which grasps the body as lived forward in time; which grasps it as inserted in a world which is systematizable and experienceable only with "reference to a focus of action and interest which lies in the body; and the systematization is now so instinctive (was it ever not so?) that no developed or active experience exists for us at all except in that

19. *Principles*, I, 333. See below, p. 102.

ordered form."[20] The body must be grasped as it is actually lived;
e.g., as a rehearsal of action in subvocal speech, or a consummating
of it in gestures and acts.

Such a mode of reflection must not turn directly upon the body
to objectify it, as would one playing his own physician, but must be
an enlargement of consciousness which participates in the flow of
experience of the body-*subject*—the body as actually lived, as
intentionally related to the rest of the world (cf. the work of
Merleau-Ponty). Such participant observation would see as intimately related to the lived-body (or what James calls the spiritual
self or "self of selves" with its turnings of attention) the other
elements of the world which are mine, other "selves" of our self, as
he puts it, the social and material selves. Because other people who
are in some way mine—my friends or my rivals, or objects of my
sight or my thought—carry with them images of me which I
construe in some way and which comprise my social self. And
possessions into which I have poured my labor or concern are
mine, a part of me, the material self. The *Principles* indicates the
need to relate more thoroughly the manner in which our body is
involved in, and treated by, others and other things.

Precisely the reverse of what might be expected, the view of the
self as the lived-body opens up for James new vistas for the comprehension of spirituality, autonomy, and freedom. Since James
considers consciousness functionally, he regards it as a phase in a
cycle of interaction with the world which inevitably tends to result
in action unless other thoughts, confusing or contrary, cancel each
other and prevent it. Hence self-initiated activity—control of
action by self, which is the essence of freedom—is comprehensible
if one can explain how a thought, possibly unpleasant, can be held
before consciousness in a sufficiently enduring and believable way
to trigger action. The secret of freedom is the secret of control of
mental effort.

Now, James in the *Principles* first tries his programmatic natural scientific and dualistic analysis of the problem. In typical
scientific fashion, he poses the question of freedom as whether we
can at any time act differently from the way we do in fact act. But
how could we ever determine that the amount of mental effort

20. "The Experience of Activity." See p. 211 fn.

actually exerted (which by hypothesis is decisive of action) was all that could have been exerted, given a chain of prior causes extending back indefinitely in time and out indefinitely in the world? He can conceive of no experiment which would confirm this, hence "indeterminism or freedom" is at least not disproven.

But James is on the verge of a wholly new and much more fruitful analysis of the problem: consciousness and self cannot be understood as a sequence of mental events emerging from the past and unrolling parallel to, or as resultants of, a sequence of neurological events. True, as he says, consciousness brings "a reservoir of possibilities" and ends which were not there prior to its emergence, and which cannot be explained in non-mental or neurological terms.[21] But it does not follow that what must be thus described is a mental event, stuff or state. That is, the body as an object in the physiological context cannot be spoken of as having ends,[22] but the *lived*-body requires another analysis entirely, and is precisely that to which ends can and must be ascribed. Moreover, the conscious, active body must inevitably emphasize or "select" certain aspects of the world and relegate others to the background, if for no other reason than the structure of its functioning organs.

James indicates that the self is a lived-body poised on the brink of several possible futures (appealing or unappealing precisely as futures) which experiences itself as speaking, attending, literally gritting its teeth, perhaps, and commanding one into existence: Be thou my future![23] Physiological talk about conditions of behavior is not so much untrue as utterly irrelevant and misleading. He suggests that in human existence a rock bottom of conditions has been reached, a kind of unconditioned. The first act of freedom, he says, must be the belief in freedom itself. It is anomalous to think evidence for *freedom* can be *forced* upon us.[24] To be free, James decides, is just to act as if one were free: this releases that confidence, initiative, and fitness of action to situation—together with certain unexpected results or novelties which productively

21. "Remarks on Spencer's Definition of Mind as Correspondence." See pp. 22 ff.
22. See *Principles,* I, 140–141.
23. Not just any of the possible things we cannot do counts against freedom. The only possibilities that count are those that we want or need to do.
24. See "The Will," pp. 42–43.

enlarge and enrich the situation—which is simply all that we mean by freedom.[25] There are no other conditions requisite for the application of the term, so belief in freedom conditions its own emergence. To the extent that it is not further conditioned, it is unconditioned. Existence is grounded in itself as freedom.

This, now, is at the heart of James's philosophical vision. It is not systematically developed in the sense of axioms or theorems or even extended argumentation, but as in the work of many creative thinkers it is there nevertheless, and without it the rest of James's philosophy does not make sense. His treatment of self-identity and freedom is the locus of his ethics, epistemology, aesthetics, metaphysics, and philosophy of religion. He writes,

When your ordinary Brooklynite or New Yorker, leading a life replete with too much luxury, or tired and careworn about his personal affairs, crosses the ferry or goes up Broadway . . . he [does not] realize at all the indisputable fact that this world never did anywhere or at any time contain more of essential divinity, or of eternal meaning, than is embodied in the fields of vision over which his eyes so carelessly pass. There is life; and there, a step away, is death. There is the only kind of beauty there ever was. There is the old human struggle and its fruits together. There is the text and the sermon, the real and the ideal in one. . . . And that very repetition of the scene to new generations of men *in secula seculorum,* that eternal recurrence of the common order, which so fills a Whitman with mystic satisfaction is to Schopenhauer, with the emotional anaesthesia, the feeling of 'awful inner emptiness' from out of which he views it all, the chief ingredient of the tedium it instils.[26]

There is no perception of the world without the imposition of teleological standards of interpretation and selection; all perception is art-like, though the perceiver himself be unaware of this. There is no perception without a perceiver to be molded by the total act of perception, whether the perceiver know he is thus molded or not. We help create the truth of the world which we come to know, and we cannot help that. In certain areas—particularly those relating to knowledge of what we can and cannot accomplish in the world and of who we are—the way we choose to know determines what is true and what is known. To believe

25. *Some Problems of Philosophy* (Longmans, Green & Co., 1948) , p. 213.
26. See "On a Certain Blindness in Human Beings," pp. 326 ff.

that one can do something often is all that enables one to do it; the belief creates the evidence that verifies it.[27] Truth will always involve satisfaction of the *thought* (to think that there is a thief in the hall, and to go out and find him, is to satisfy the thought that predicts it, though not necessarily the *thinker*, in any but the narrowest portion of his rational nature), but in ethics, aesthetics, and religion part of what we *mean* by the *objects* of belief is that they do have the characteristics which satisfy the *thinker* as well; hence he must be satisfied if his thought be true.

For James, the good life is the progressive realization of "that strange union of reality with ideal novelty" which is possible in the person's situations and in respect to his capacities. James denies that there are any actualities, knowable in advance, which set a clear and determinate limit to human potentialities. Man's ability to reflect with (and upon) signs and to manipulate them in dream, art, and hypothesis involves him in open-ended situations, and developments, and to deny this is to suffer a kind of death in life, a premature crystallization; one becomes an "old fogey at twenty-five."[28] The "originals" of value presupposed by all articulable judgments of value are feelings of "excited significance" attending upon encounter with people and Nature, and involving pre-reflectively experienced ideals. These experiences are fundamental, "They tingle with an importance that unutterably vouches for itself."[29] (The provocative and beautifully metaphorical example he uses is children walking about in the dusk with lanterns concealed underneath their coats. The excitement of knowing that they each have one is an original of value which vouches for itself.) But this is "the excitement of reality," for as we live it, life is the lived union of real and ideal (if we can but see it), together with the motivating power of the as yet unrealized ideal: moral, aesthetic, cognitive, or whatever. That is, what the world is, is what it is experienceable as being, and it is experienceable only in terms of standards and norms of expectation which are ideals. Hence fact is inseparable from value

27. See "The Will to Believe," pp. 309 ff.
28. *Talks to Teachers on Psychology and to Students on Some of Life's Ideals* (New York: Dover Books, 1962), p. 81.
29. "On a Certain Blindness . . . ," pp. 326 ff.

in this minimal sense, and the significance of a life is a matter of freeing the mind to new perspectives on the world (new employments of the ideal) which make possible creative and constructive action, instead of pipe dreams. Still, all values are based on "feelings of excited significance" which magnetize our attention and thus form the core of our lives; it is the reality of which only poets are equipped to speak—hence the "haunting and spectral unreality of 'realistic' books. . . ."[30]

The strongest behavioral motivation, according to James, is the drive for the heroic. There is something wild and heroic at the center of us. Man's "common instinct for reality" regards the world as "a theatre for heroism" in as yet undecided struggles with evil. "Naturalistic optimism is mere syllabub and flattery and sponge cake."[31] For James, most of our problems stem from our inability to cope with this drive: either we try to blink it out of existence or gloss it over with crypto-sophistication in our modern institutions—e.g., educational ones—or we allow it rampant, superstitious, and destructive expression as in wars. Our greatest need, then, is to find a moral equivalent for war.[32] The grand, the holy, and the heroic—even if it be only heroic pessimism or skepticism—excite us; this is a fact and we must learn to deal with it. What is our motivation, beyond mere survival, for dealing with it? The dignity of fact.[33]

Because James grounds the heroic so basically in the human affective, cognitive, indeed metaphysical, situation, there is an element of universalism in his ethics—a rethinking of natural law. The drive to struggle to realize his capacities in the light of the ideal "slumbers in every man." James was particularly incensed at the behavior of Americans in the Philippines during the Spanish-American War. We suffer from a certain blindness in all human beings which renders us incapable of sympathetically participating in the life as it is lived—basically similar to our own—of foreign peoples. "Little brown men" are only objects for us, not embodied subjects living forward in the light of their future. "They are too

30. *Ibid.*
31. Quoted in Wild, *op. cit.*, p. 320.
32. See pp. 349 ff.
33. Variations on this theme occur over and over in James.

remote from us to be realized as they exist in their inwardness."[34]

He writes of his philosophy,

> The practical consequence of [it] . . . is the well known democratic
> respect for the sacredness of individuality—is at any rate, the outward
> tolerance of whatever is not itself intolerant. These phrases are so famil-
> iar that they sound now rather dead in our ears. Once they had a
> passionate inner meaning. Such a passionate inner meaning they may
> easily acquire again if the pretension of our nation to inflict its own
> inner ideals and institutions *vi et armis* upon Orientals should meet with
> a resistance as obdurate as so far it has been gallant and spirited. Reli-
> giously and philosophically, our ancient national doctrine of live and let
> live may prove to have a far deeper meaning than our people now seem
> to imagine it to possess.[35]

Above all, we must not interpret James's ethics in a Cartesian
subjectivist fashion—a manner still ascendant, and by now worked
into the underpinnings of popular culture. Human embodiment
in a world socialized by language and institutions like the family
determines the form that satisfaction in the struggle for the realization of capacity takes. Though he contends that "the facts and
worths of life need many cognizers to take them in. . . . there is no
point of view absolutely public and universal. Private and incommunicable perceptions always remain over . . ."[36]; still, satisfaction is no mere personal whim or vagary. James rejects full scale
cultural relativism and emotivism. The heroic drive is launched
within a world characterizable by generic attributes, and out of a
human existence the natural propensity of which is continuity
and unity.[37] Not just any choice really tempts us, nor is worthy
to be considered when considering human freedom, but only those
choices which open up in line with the continuous maturation
of our powers, in a world in which self-identity is possible for
embodied beings of the human type. He advises teachers to utilize
their capacity to reproduce sympathetically in their imagination

---

34. R. B. Perry, *The Thought and Character of William James* (Boston:
Little, Brown & Co., 1935), II, 311.
35. *Talks to Teachers*, p. vi.
36. *Ibid.*
37. See John K. Roth's introduction to his *The Moral Philosophy of William
James* (New York: T. Y. Crowell Co., 1969).

the mental life of their pupil as the active unity which he feels himself to be.[38] Like Nietzsche, James makes sense of an asceticism which puts off short-range satisfactions for long, and like Kierkegaard, who observed that freedom is quietness in continuity, James rejects the equation of freedom and libertinism. Freedom involves novelty, to be sure, and an element of contingency, but freedom is that track on which we cannot help but do what is right for us to do in view of our creative human gifts and constructive capacities. We become selves through synthesizing our past, present, and future. The self requires consciousness of self, and this consciousness requires conscience—a keeping of promises to oneself.[39]

Given James's philosophical view, there is room enough for the tragic. It is quite inadequate to read the first pages of "The Moral Philosopher and the Moral Life" in which James writes of good as *prima facie* the satisfaction of demand, and to conclude that he adopts a leveling sort of utilitarianism which equates good with trying to satisfy the greatest number of persons' demands. For as James discusses at the end of the essay, the philosopher's job must be to show the priorities of demands in a world in which we must live together in realizing our capacities, and in which not all demands can—nor should—be satisfied. James then concludes that the moral universe he strives for is really possible "only in a world where there is a divine thinker with all-enveloping demands," not only for reasons of establishing priority of demands, but because only here would "every sort of energy and endurance, of courage and capacity for handling life's evils [be] set free in those who have religious faith." But how can an empiricist like James, who roots the self so tightly in the lived-body and space-time, talk intelligently about the existence of God? At this point in his thought, James postulates a Divine Being and then "prays for the victory of the religious cause." He postulates a God and then prays to Him that his postulation is correct. There is an element of the tragic in this, I suppose, or at least the ironic, but it is not the absolute absurdity that the formalist and logician might take it to be. For the resources of James's metaphysics and theory of truth

38. *Talks to Teachers*, p. v.
39. Perhaps certain promises should not be made. James suggests that we can go against our own grain.

are peculiarly applicable to this kind of apparently hopeless inquiry.

In being taxed to their uttermost, his philosophical resources are displayed to their fullest, and this brings us to his second major work, *The Varieties of Religious Experience*. The most obvious feature of James's worldview is its open-ended character, and this is nowhere more important than in his treatment of concepts. He denies that any exhaustive set of concepts adequate to the world is even in principle deducible from a framework of pure thought or logic. The ground of meaning for James, hence the ground of the abstract and fully verbalizable concepts of the intellect, is the vaguely apprehended lived-world, with its pre-linguistic perceptual meanings, its significatory tendencies of expressive motor behavior, and its vast and diffuse unreflected use of signs—functions of partial purposes and private ends. The ground of concepts is thus open, vague, ambiguous, and changing; concepts arise from this ground, only to be amended, aggregated, and deleted as time goes on and our purposes and insights reticulate new areas of meaning. The ground of meaning is a moving ground—a lived-world-forward. Concepts arise, are tested, are found more or less adequate; concepts are eternal in their several meanings, but are not eternal in their applicability to the world actually experienced.

What is religious experience? James cautions the "theorizing mind" against its occupational hazard—the initial oversimplification of its materials. Let us admit at the outset that ". . . we may very likely find no one essence, but many characters which may alternately be equally important in religion."[40] "The pretension, under such conditions, to be rigorously 'scientific' or 'exact' in our terms would only stamp us as lacking in understanding of our task. Things are more or less divine, states of mind are more or less religious, reactions are more or less total, but the boundaries are always misty. . . ."[41] We may have to get at religious experience through seeking "its nearest relatives elsewhere"; e.g., states of chemically induced intoxication.[42] Thus James suggests we return to the ground of meaning in pre-reflective existence, for there we will find those far-flung "familial" relationships which lead us in

40. See "Circumscription of the Topic," pp. 222 ff.
41. *Ibid.*
42. See "Mysticism," pp. 241 ff.

their several ways into the area of religious experience, rather than
getting stuck in an initial concept of "the essence" of religious
experience which pre-judges its nature with a label, and pastes
shut access to the open area in which we actually spend our lives.
James's opening up of the ground of meaning anticipates Wittgenstein's notion of "family resemblance," and may in part explain
Wittgenstein's interest in James.[43]

It is understandable that James subtitles his work on religious
experience "A Study in Human Nature." For his basic point is
that sensory experience is not a passive copying of a world,
mappable and describable in advance either by mathematical
physics or by the pure reason of classical metaphysics, but that it is
an art-like interpretation of a vaguely and incompletely presented
world-horizon, within which interpretation physics and metaphysics arise, and to which they must return for replenishment
and new hypotheses. That is, elemental human life is really
mysterious; a greater understanding of man may lead to an understanding of God. Hence James speaks of "the mystery of fact,"[44]
which is mysterious on several levels: not only is the existence of
the world as a whole a mystery, but also details.

> One need only shut oneself in a closet and begin to think of the fact
> of one's being there, of one's queer bodily shape in the darkness (a
> thing to make children scream at, as Stevenson says), of one's fantastic
> character and all, to have the wonder steal over the detail as much as
> over the general fact of being, and to see that it is only familiarity that
> blunts it. Not only that *anything* should be, but that *this* very thing
> should be, is mysterious! Philosophy stares, but brings no reasoned solu-
> tion, for from nothing to being there is no logical bridge.[45]

That is, a person can be shocked by the shape and existence of his
own body, because he perhaps never bothered to encounter it as
just an object there in space. No knowledge of *what* one is, no
matter how extensive, can substitute for the grasp *that* one is

43. I have heard it argued that Dugald Stewart is another antecedent of
Wittgenstein in this matter. Those interested in intellectual history and tracing
influences should know that James describes himself as at one time "immersed"
in Dugald Stewart. (See his introductory remarks in Lecture I of *The Varieties
of Religious Experience*.)

44. See "Mysticism," pp. 241 ff.

45. See "The Problem of Being," pp. 6 ff.

(although whether there is a grasp of "that" without any "what" is left somewhat questionable by James). It is not *just* one's queer bodily *shape* in the darkness; it is that one has any shape, any being. Familiarity blunts our sense of sheer existence, and conceals whatever pits of insecurity lie at the ontological level of our daily lives. Even if we prescind from the ontological mystéry itself ("from nothing to being there is no logical bridge"), and settle at the level of what an individual is, we find as a corollary that fact is mysterious at this level as well: overflowing in significance and never to be grasped completely—dense and interrelated beyond our imagination—it swims in an ocean of ambiguity, of possible conceptual interpretation. Which interpretation it receives depends in part upon our partial purposes and private ends—purposes which are themselves pre-reflectively generated and incompletely known to us. James's awe in the face of existence, and the reminder he gives us of our finitude, is strongly suggestive of salient aspects of Christianity. In "The Sentiment of Rationality" James writes, "The notion of non-entity may thus be called the parent of the philosophic craving in its subtilest and profoundest sense. Absolute existence is absolute mystery, for its relations with the nothing remain unmediated to our understanding." He continues in *The Varieties* descriptions of events which ignite this awe:

The simplest rudiment of mystical experience would seem to be that deepened sense of the significance of a maxim or formula which occasionally sweeps over one. . . . This sense of deeper significance is not confined to rational propositions. Single words, and conjunctions of words, effects of light on land and sea, odors and musical sounds, all bring it when the mind is tuned aright. Most of us can remember the strangely moving power of passages in certain poems read when we were young, irrational doorways as they were through which the mystery of fact, the wildness and the pang of life, stole into our hearts and thrilled them. The words have now perhaps become mere polished surfaces for us; but lyric poetry and music are alive and significant only in proportion as they fetch those vague vistas of a life continuous with our own, beckoning and inviting, yet ever eluding our pursuit.[46]

In the daily life we live, walking down a path and kicking a stone, let us say, the experienced world is an enveloping, ill-defined

46. See "Mysticism," p. 244.

presence; suggestion, reminiscence, and tendril-like tendency are such that reflective thought cannot stop experience, single out each tendency and suggestion, and give a verbal account of it all. For James, we are beings vastly more vulnerable and dependent than most of us care to acknowledge.

Very similarly to Heidegger's notion that the existentialia of mood and pre-propositional speech are ontologically significant, James writes,

> Religion, whatever it is, is a man's total reaction upon life. . . . Total reactions are different from casual reactions, and total attitudes are different from usual or professional attitudes. To get at them you must go behind the foreground of existence and reach down to that curious sense of the whole residual cosmos as an everlasting presence, intimate or alien, terrible or amusing, lovable or odious, which in some degree every one possesses. This sense of the world's presence . . . is the completest of all our answers to the question, "What is the character of this universe in which we dwell?"[47]

A 'total reaction upon life' is not a comprehension in formula and in extension of the totality of beings in the world, but it reveals that totality which is one's own world-relationship (and perhaps we can say that it reveals the world as a totality, at least as it can be revealed at that point), and this has its own metaphysical importance. James specifies religious experience more exactly: it is the sense of the primal and enveloping reality to which the individual feels impelled to respond solemnly and gravely, and neither with a curse nor a jest. It is a sense of the holy and the overwhelming. We experience a submission which is not dull or grudging, but serene and glad—solemn but glad. It is a special openness in the world.

Now, it is in these moments of submission, when deliberate purposes and plans and verbal formulations have exhausted themselves, that James believes that the subliminal and usually pre-conscious margins of consciousness may bear the traces of a personality continuous with our own (but concealed and sundered from our ordinary consciousness so habitually as to be more than just our own personality) denominatable as Divine. Whatever it is exactly, it is an expansion and unification of the self which can revivify and redirect a life. It gets work done, James says, hence it

47. See "Circumscription of the Topic," pp. 222 ff.

is real, and we needn't know exactly what it is in order to be able to believe with some reason that it is real.[48]

In what was originally intended to be the first paragraph of *The Varieties of Religious Experience,* James wrote,

> Our words come together leaning on each other laterally for support. . . . Life, too, in one sense stumbles over its own fact in a similar way; for its earlier moments plunge ceaselessly into the later ones which re-interpret and correct them. Yet there is . . . something entirely un-paralleled by anything in verbal thought. The living moments—some living moments, at any rate—have somewhat of absolute that need no lateral support. Their meaning seems to well up from out of their very centers, in a way impossible verbally to describe. . . . The moment stands and contains and sums up all things; and all change is within it, much as the developing landscape with all its growth falls forever within the rear windowpane of the last car of a train that is speeding on its headlong way. This self-sustaining in the midst of self-removal, which characterizes all reality and fact, is something absolutely foreign to the nature of language, and even to the nature of logic, commonly so called.[49]

It is only in the light of James's analysis of experience that his later popular lectures on pragmatism can be understood. James says that one can be a pragmatist without being a radical empiricist, and that pragmatism is logically independent.[50] But, as is the case with many creative people, what James says about his own work is often inferior to the work itself and misleading in regard to it. At the heart of his philosophy of radical empiricism is a doctrine of consummatory experience; its distinctly contemplative aspect renders wildly wrong equations of pragmatism and that which "helps us get ahead."[51] Only here at the center of his

48. James regarded the discovery of the subliminal and unconscious dimension of mind as the most important discovery of psychology in his day. But clearly, for James, it has metaphysical and not just psychological significance.

49. Perry, *op. cit.,* II, 328–329.

50. Author's preface to *Pragmatism* (Lowell Institute Lectures, Boston, 1906) . Contrast with his preface to *The Meaning of Truth.* For selections from the latter book see pp. 262 ff.

51. Recall the first epigraph of this volume. They are lines written when James was thirty-one, but as Dewey has wisely pointed out (*The Problems of Men,* p. 395) , the early thoughts and experiences of James are fundamental to understanding the later metaphysics, even though the former undergo some modification.

philosophy can we understand what he means by the truth being
that which satisfies. For example, faced with the possibility that we
experience an immanent God, it is impossible to distinguish
clearly between the *thought* of God (or the belief) being satisfied
and the *thinker* of the thought being satisfied, and for perfectly
good logical reasons. Part of what we mean by an immanent,
personal God is that the thinker will be satisfied and vivified in
encountering Him, hence not to be emotionally involved in the
belief being tested is not to test the belief. By contrast, we do not
mean this by other intentional objects of experience, e.g., a pile of
rubbish. Another part of what we may mean is that a personal
God establishes personal relations with us, hence not publicly
verifiable ones (at least not publicly verifiable as would be pointer-
readings). When a belief is about persons, we should not hope for
facile distinctions dividing logical and psychological consequences
of a belief; it would not be logical. It is just these logical points,
deriving from his metaphysics, that James does not emphasize in
his popular lectures; nor does he reiterate, as he evidently should
have on every page, that the concept of the workability of an idea
as constituting its truth means that when we hold it, we find our
way about in the world rather than colliding in ignorance.

> Woe to him whose beliefs
> play fast and loose with
> the order which realities
> follow in his experience;
> they will lead him nowhere
> or else make false connexions.[51a]

Henri Bergson wrote to James, "I repeat . . . pragmatism is one
of the most subtle and *nuancés* doctrines that has ever appeared
in philosophy (just because the doctrine reinstates truth in the
flux of experience), and one is sure to go wrong if one speaks of
pragmatism before having read you as a whole. . . ."[52] The point
is that James's theory of truth emerges as an integral part of a

---

[51a] *Pragmatism: A New Name for Some Old Ways of Thinking* (New York:
Longmans, Green & Co., 1947), p. 205. Quoted in John J. McDermott, ed., *The
Writings of William James* (New York: Modern Library, 1968), p. xxiv. Mc-
Dermott sees that James's ostensibly prose lines have the quality of Aeschylean
verse, and I follow McDermott's rendering.

[52]. Perry, *op. cit.*, II, 632.

metaphysical view in which the temporality of being and experience is central. James maintains that the traditional "ontological" theory of truth (in which truth is identical with what is the case) is a lazy theory which has the effect of begging most of the important questions in philosophy. It is a simplistic theory which amounts to a superficial equation of reality and truth, and this amounts to a begging of the question of being. For example, according to the theory, the historically real is what has been, so the truth must have been already too: it stands statically in its own realm, awaiting discovery, corresponding point for point with the real. According to James, this ignores the actual situation of inquiry: the progressive but never completed clarification and exposure of an enveloping world which is given vaguely and incompletely in a temporal horizon.[53] Because of this oversight, the thinker's account of reality is vulnerable to whatever uncritical and hubristic elements in his theory of truth project themselves into the account; for example, illusions of completeness, definitive form, ultimate clarity, and exhaustive differentiation.

The anatomy of the world is logical, and its logic is that of a university professor, it was thought. . . . But . . . there are so many geometries, so many logics, so many physical and chemical hypotheses, so many classifications, each one of them good for so much and yet not good for everything, that the notion that even the truest formula may be a human device and not a literal transcript has dawned upon us.[54]

Thought is simply an instrument for illuminating one aspect of the world from one angle and from one point of insertion. It is more or less adequate; it is never completely adequate. It is never an exhaustive literal transcript, and notions of absolute truth amount to fanatical reifications of regulative ideals.

James, then, discards the notion of eternally asserted meanings or propositions which state truly and eternally what has been, is, or will be the case, and which await discovery by our intellects. Since his pragmatic theory of meaning requires that any theoretic difference must be "cashable" in a predicted difference in the course of our experience, the notion of eternally true but as yet undiscovered propositions lacks a full complement of meaning.

53. See "Humanism and Truth," pp. 262 ff.
54. *Ibid.*

That is, the notion is a theoretic difference which makes no difference: it makes no more difference in what we expect from our experience than is already made by actual statements which we understand in terms of what their verifiability by experience would consist in. Hence it is only actual thoughts or statements, so construed, which are true or false.

James is often introduced to readers by way of his theory of truth without any account given of his chief works or his metaphysical position; hence his theory of truth cannot be fully understood. James's later remarks about truth have been so eccentrically emphasized by traditional criticism that Professor James Edie's remark that there is a myth of William James has merit.[55] The typical criticism makes the apparently innocent assumption that truth is what is the case (or what corresponds to the case); from this it follows that the truth is impersonal and eternal, for whatever is or was the case is just the case, and if things were different it would not be the case, so the truth can never be different; and if things are that case then they are that case independently of whatever experience or evidence any knower might think he has about the case.

But for James this is not an innocent assumption at all. It assumes the very thing James denies: that we can talk about the world "in itself," as "what is the case," independently of its experienceability. And James thinks that likewise we cannot speak of truth independently of the experienceability of what is the case. For James, this is a matter of the meaning of truth, and any retort that we can suppose things to be the case which we cannot suppose to be actually verifiable misses his point.[56] All James says is that true statements are verifiable *if* put to the test, not that all true statements actually could be put to the test; this is what we *mean* by truth, and meaning pertains to possibility.[57] (Although, as I show below, James is not sufficiently clear about possible experience.) The truth of his theory of truth is that it is true that we

55. *An Invitation to Phenomenology* (Chicago: Quadrangle Books, 1965), p. 110.
56. For an example of fairly typical professional criticism of James, see George Nakhnikian, *An Introduction to Philosophy* (New York: Alfred A. Knopf, 1967), p. 263.
57. See "A Dialogue" from *The Meaning of Truth*, pp. 281 ff.

do mean this in ordinary language and experience, whether we know that we mean this or not. One's claim to be able to suppose an instance of what is the case which is logically impossible of verification is most revealing of one's own questionable but tacit metaphysical preconceptions. "Suppose," one says, "nobody is immortal. Then all propositions of the form 'S is not immortal' are true but impossible of verification, since no immortal persons could, by hypothesis, be around to do the verifying." But why suppose that only immortal humans could verify their own immortality? Besides, what do we mean, really, by supposing "an immortal human" (let alone "an immortal human using something as evidence for something")? If Martin Heidegger is right, part of what we mean by a human is that he will die and knows he will die. The correspondence theory of truth makes it easy to suppose that we know what it is we are supposing even when we don't know what we are supposing. Also, the equation of truth and what is the case leads unwittingly to the questionable conclusion, as above, that only immortal beings could themselves verify their own immortality. (After all, are not truth and existence one?) But James, like phenomenologists, is concerned with establishing the logical priority of meaning, and to do so on the basis of ordinary, practical experience; sheer facility in making distinctions, the typical Ph.D.'s quasi-formal brilliance, is inimical to this. He is saying in effect that if we have no idea of what it would be to *know* what is the case, we really don't know what we are supposing to be the case (we don't know what our supposition means). The standing body of truths structures our experience and allows us to stand, because it is knowledge of what was supposed and what verified it; candidates for new truth must be integrable with it. To lose touch with our suppositions is to lose touch with ourselves and the world. Far from being innocent, the correspondence theory of truth can be a subtle agency of alienation.

When James said that truth happens to an idea, this caused a scandal amongst those who tended to conflate truth and reality. They assumed that James was saying that determinate states of affairs did not exist until they were discovered, or that the discovery of them created them through a sort of magic of thought. But given James's notion of an ongoing temporal world, much too vast and thick to be equated with any set of formulations, this is precisely what he could not have believed. When, say, the stars in a constellation are counted, the truth about them was not known before—and truth and knowledge of the truth are inseparable for James—but the truth of their number "virtually pre-existed," he says, because every condition of its realization save the condition of the counting and comparing mind was present (hence mind alone can never be a sufficient condition for the truth of the physical world).[58] The stars themselves, James says, dictate the results to the inquiring mind; they are discovered *as* those which we mean to have existed before the grasping of the truth about them.[59] Truth is knowledge of the truth. Either we have it or we do not, and any other position on the matter is a sentimental evasion of. the facts.[60] Of course, it is possible to say or even perhaps believe what is true without knowing that it is true: e.g., without counting, I say there are 281 lemons on a tree, and there are just that many. But James's point is that what we *mean* by saying that I speak the truth is that *if* persons counted, 281 would be all they could consistently get. Actual truth does not pre-exist its discovery, but is added by our meanings and operations which conserve and further connect the world. It is a function both of things-known and the knowing, for it is limited by our ability to mean and to care.

James's ultimate concern is metaphysical: to determine the meanings of "real" and "one" etc. in the light of the structures of experience. In the *Principles,* he writes that when I decide what to do I am deciding in effect what kind of person to be. But human being or reality cannot be determined in isolation of the reality of the world experienced by us; human behavior and human reality is a function of the world intended in it and involved by

58. See "Humanism and Truth," pp. 262 ff.

59. It might be argued that truth happens to an idea in its act aspect, not its object or content aspect. Part of what we mean by an idea of the stars being true is that the stars existed before the idea (*qua* act) existed. Difficulties in his radical empiricism made the proper accentuation of this distinction between act and object impossible. If it is objected that on his own grounds he cannot verify his idea that they existed before he knew them, and that therefore he cannot know truly that they did, the proper Jamesian response is that the idea of ongoing ("having been before") existence, central in knowledge by acquaintance, is pre-supposed as true by all theoretic knowledge by description. One who asserted that the stars did not exist before they were known would have to prove that they did not; e.g., evidence of processes in the stars only as old as the knowing would have to be adduced.

60. Perhaps James should have allowed a use of "true" as "the case," such that the needs of formal logic for a very abstract notion of truth could be met.

it. Hence *The Varieties of Religious Experience* is a study in human nature at the same time that it tries to ascertain the nature of ultimate reality or the Divine. Dewey writes of the book:

> The root idea is that in religious experience the essential individual —call it his soul—stands in communication with the universe at a level more primitive and at the same time more fundamental, in a certain way more veridical, than is attainable at the level of conscious and rational observation and thought. The result is "a kind of experience in which intellect, will and feeling, all our consciousness and all our subconsciousness together, melt in a kind of chemical union." . . . The nub of the whole matter is the problem of the genuine relation of the individual and the universe, and this is the question which is final for philosophy itself.[61]

The metaphysical question—what are the basic facts and what must we think of them?—cannot be divorced from this primary perceptual experience of the ever-present world-margins and their "circumpressure,"[62] because all that we can mean by anything— e.g., mean by calling it "real"—derives ultimately from this experience. It is a founding level of meaning; there is here an unmistakable overlapping with the phenomenological concept of *Lebenswelt*.

The sense of the world's presence is the basic sense of reality for James, and upon this sense other uses of "real" derive their use through abstraction, reduction, or extrapolation. Not a mere entertaining and manipulating of concepts, this sense involves the emotional and volitional orientation of the knower: his presence to the world.[63]

James attempts to capture the notion of actuality and presence in the idea of a "pure experience"—that which is experienced as being (and which is meant as being) neither physical nor mental, nor non-physical nor non-mental, but simply "there"—a "that" in "the instant field of the present."[64] But James admits that only newborn babies or men in semi-comas have the experience in the literal sense of a "that" which is not any definite "what"; "that" is a limiting concept. And yet James insists that it is an essential

61. *The Problems of Men*, p. 392.
62. "Humanism and Truth," p. 269.
63. See the crucial "The Perception of Reality," pp. 132 ff.
64. See "A World of Pure Experience," pp. 192–193.

concept, because we mean by "that" something more than any set of "whats." We mean that which is ready to be apprehended as "all sorts of whats"—that which can "boil over" in "whats" inexhaustibly, with the inexhaustibility not itself just another "what." We mean that which is both "oneness and manyness but in respects that do not appear . . . its phases interpenetrate and no points either of distinction or identity can be caught . . . [but] it tends to fill itself with emphases, and these salient parts become identified and fixed" and finally "abstracted."[65]

This is the moving, open ground of meaning in which intelligibility is reticulated as a function of purpose and concern; and it should not be thought that this "primitive stage of perception" is pure only because a particular "that," apprehended neither as physical nor mental, is apprehended as a pure "that" right there, shorn of all relationships. James seems to mean that part of its purity consists precisely in the fact that that sort of particularizing distinction has not yet been made. Particulars are experienced on the primordial level, but not *as* particulars, not *as* sundered from everything else in the universe. Particulars are experienced not as single ones, but as just there-as-a-part-of-the-field. For example, an experience of motion is not necessarily an experience of a moving particular apprehended *as* a moving particular. "Motion originally *is;* only later is it confined to this thing or to that."[66] (He cites experiences of trains when we do not know whether ours or the other is moving.) So closely tied is the "that" to the "what" in actual experience that when apprehended "pure," the perceptual "that" is involved in characteristics which might be called primitive generic.

James is at his most brilliant when illuminating patterns of the perceptual world which are usually ignored precisely because they are habitual, pervasive, and enveloping. Thunder, he says, is not apprehended pure (in the sense of alone), but as breaking-in-upon-silence.[67] This disclosure may surprise us just because to perceive thunder—to live it, so to speak—is not necessarily to judge about it verbally; i.e., "Thunder breaks in upon silence."

65. "The Thing and Its Relations," p. 198.
66. "The Place of Affectional Facts in a World of Pure Experience," pp. 204–205. See also p. 122 below.
67. See "The Stream of Thought," p. 54.

James is a humanist not only because he is concerned to discover saving truths for men, but because for him concepts of metaphysics must be cashed in a human experience which is surprising and replenishing when brought within the focus of reflective awareness.

Most important, the perceptual object of experience, thunder-breaking-in-upon-silence, is "pure" in that it is neutral between mind and world; i.e., it is the single basis for specifying both mind and world. That is, what we mean by the thunder *itself* is that it is sequential and fringed relationally in our experience in such a manner; and what we mean by the perception itself is that it is *of* such a relational object.[68] To be sure, physics and physiology inform us that thunder is radically different from silence; it is an abrupt disturbance in the air which causes a disturbance in the brain accompanied presumably by a conscious experience which is the polar opposite of silence—noise. But if we did not experience thunder on the primitive perceptual level as the *kind* of thing that is linked with silence (if only through contrast), the more refined meanings of physics and physiology would be impossible. Basic cognition is of the primitive generic.

Turning the tables on those who would charge him with anthropomorphism or animism, James argues trenchantly that the construal of the metaphysical term "cause," for example, in terms of impersonal factors "hidden in the cubic deeps" (which purportedly act upon us to trigger the illusion that our wills are causally effective) is what is really anthropomorphic. For what we mean primarily by "cause" is just the intimate experience within ourselves of initiation of activity and striving, and any theory which projects this sense out of the context in which it is known and into the cubic deeps amounts to an anthropomorphic and logically illicit displacement of human traits into non-human contexts.[69] What is at stake is the clarification of a ground which is not an axiomatically sure source of deductively certain truths about the world, but which is a perpetually opening ground of meaning. "It boots not to say that our sensations are fallible. They are indeed; but to see the thermometer contradict us when we say

68. For a criticism of James's notion of intentionality, see below in this introduction.
69. See "The Experience of Activity," pp. 216–217.

'it is cold' does not abolish cold as a specific nature from the universe. Cold is in the arctic circle if not here."[70] Somewhere the "what" and the "that" must be experienced together, he says.

Meaning is primarily a matter of what things are known as, or experienced as, in primary perception, and it is not the case that things are experienced in a way that the sheer concept of their nature—gleaned through progressive abstraction and refinement —is such that it generates out of itself conceptual linkages that tie it to all the rest of the things of the experienced world in internal and necessarily true relations. Hence James's famous pluralism. According to him, the most effective creative minds refuse to think that the essence of a thing is what can be neatly articulated about it in its definition, and they bring to the focus what most people ignore because it is either too vague or too "obvious." "The great field for new discoveries is always the unclassified residuum. Roundabout the accredited and orderly facts of every science there ever flows a sort of dust-cloud of exceptional observations, of occurrences minute and irregular and seldom met which it always proves more easy to ignore than to attend to."[71]

"Vicious intellectualism" is the cutting of the continuity of perceptual experience into discrete conceptual bits and substituting an artificial continuity (if it can be supplied at all) for the one which is lost. We experience ourselves related to the world, and one thing related to another, in an indefinite variety of ways, none of which relations is an internal bond which relates everything else. Any moment of experience flows beyond itself (and in this sense is its "own other")[72] to connect in relations that may be purposive at one end of the continuum of experiences, or suffered, intrusive, and disruptive at the other. Only a small portion of what occurs is predictable on the basis of pure conceptual or definitional thought, and to say that all events are predictable on any basis is an article of faith which ignores not only the novel thoughts which strike us, together with their novel behavioral consequences, but the simple fact that some things are so loosely bound to others as to be merely "along with"

70. *Ibid.*
71. "On Psychic Research"; quoted in Arthur Koestler, *The Act of Creation* (New York: Dell, 1954), p. 191.
72. See "The Continuity of Experience," pp. 362 ff.

them in the world; e.g., a cloud in China and my thought of the moon as I sit here in America. There are an indefinite variety of conjunctive relations, and many of these at one time or another bind the multiverse into a universe, but no single relation everywhere all the time.

The never fully resolved difficulty of James's metaphysics is to reconcile the pre-reflective flow of our perceptual experiencing, as he penetratingly conceives it, with the structure of the experienced world, which he takes to exist independently of any particular experiencing of it. James must be able to distinguish experiencing from the experienced, and knowing from the known, without relying upon any dualistic conception of mental and physical substances. For example, he must be able to distinguish in a sequence of experience between a sequence in the experienced thing and a sequence in our experiencing of it. Granted, any sequence in a thing is conceivable for James's philosophy only in terms of a sequence in a possible experiencing. Experience, under *some* specification, is the neutral ground of everything; James's pluralism occurs within an overarching and very special monism. But even in perception—for example, looking at an object on the ground in the twilight—we must and do distinguish characteristics of our experiencing from characteristics of the experien*ced* within our experiencing; our perceiving is at first vague and indeterminate, merely of some object, and only later of some definite thing, say, a pen. But we do not think of the pen itself as having just been created; it is experienced in our experiencing as having been a pen before we perceived it to be one. Even if we conceive it to be a magical pen which, in a recurrent cycle, flows into a lump and then re-forms itself into a pen, and even if we visualize it as such, still we do distinguish *this* sequence in our experiencing from the sequence into which we conceive our acts of perception, or modes of perceiving, to fall. Now, how in James's terms is this distinction to be understood?

James says that the perception of a pen is just the "self-same piece of experience taken twice over in different contexts." "Pen" is a pure (or in itself neutral) experience; in one context it is matter (e.g., the chemical processes occurring in it); in another context it is mind (e.g., how it is related to the cumulative career of the embodied being that knows it). Mind or consciousness is just a context. But instead of capitalizing on his own insights into the contextual role played by the marginally experienced lived-body in the *present* moment of perceptual experience (conceived as act of perceptual experiencing) , he says in *Essays in Radical Empiricism* that the only context which counts as conscious mind is a *later* experience which retrospectively appropriates, on the basis of the bodily feelings then associated with it, the pen as object of my perception. Hence he concludes that in perception the percept *is* the reality, and any necessary and internal relation between body margins as act of experiencing and pen as intentional object is submerged.[73] In perception, consciousness and world are simply amalgamated, and how we can look at a pen and take it to be a cigar, say, he does not fully explain. Presumably it is only later, when equipped with further evidence, that I can know that it was really a pen, in the sense of truly know, but James does not explain how I then did take it to be a cigar, in the sense of meant it or intended it to be one, and knew that I so meant it.

The answer to our question, then, is that James in the *Essays* does not properly distinguish act of perception and object perceived. Hence, ironically, his later philosophy takes on a subjectivistic and psychological cast. Indeed, it is the height of irony in view both of his sweeping critique of Descartes and of his own notion of the lived-body—a notion which could, if developed, supply a basis for distinguishing act and object of perception without the taint of subjectivism. Moreover, his idea of concepts as a coordinate realm of reality[74] could, if developed, distinguish the

73. Pure experience becomes a "little absolute," a *mere* that, and knowledge by acquaintance lost sight of. James here plays into the hands of later pragmatists. Moreover, he gets into trouble in theory of truth, e.g., when he writes that "the immediate experience is always 'truth,' practical truth, *something to act on* . . . If the world were then and there to go out like a candle, it would remain truth absolute and objective, for . . . it would have no critic . . ." (see p. 172) . This is an excellent reminder of the worldly *meaning* of prereflective perceptual experience; but it seems he should have added, " 'truth' *which has to be taken* as objective because no further experience could correct it." Because he does not add this we are forced to say, for example, that a person really is guilty because all the evidence that could be collected points to his guilt (e.g., other witnesses have been killed); but this should give us pause. James cannot add this qualifier because he leaves no room for the act of perceiving in a here and now perception; he cannot at this point distinguish meaning and truth.

74. See "Does 'Consciousness' Exist?," pp. 168–171.

reality of a thing in terms of its conceived experienceability (conceptual constructs, if you will) from its suspiciously subjectivistic position as a content of an actual experience.

Non-perceptual knowledge is construed by James either as two "pieces" of actual experience characterizing the same subject with definite tracts of conjunctive experience linking them (e.g., I know the pen because I walk in the room and get it from a drawer), or the known is a *possible* experience (either of that subject or another) to which the present context of experience would lead if followed out.[75] Now, with appearance of the subjunctive case James would be thought to be including an object given as absent, i.e., a species of intentional object. Yet he hastens to add that he thinks the latter type of non-perceptual knowledge can always "formally and hypothetically" be reduced to the former type, hence experiences are "flat," and the referentialness of mind to world is a kind of contingent and external relation.

Of course, it could be objected that the locution "formally and hypothetically reduced" is unclear, but that on the only intelligible rendering it begs the question of intentionality, because it is assumed that later experience *would* verify an earlier experience without explaining what it was—the intentional meaning—that was available to be verified (by someone somehow).

At this point in the *Essays,* James seems to be lumping together theory of meaning and theory of truth, and among the difficulties in which he is landed is that of solipsism; this is a position not at all congenial with the metaphysics he is seeking to develop. According to James, if we think about Memorial Hall,[76] all that is happening is that a sequence of experiences is being initiated which, if followed out, would lead directly to Memorial Hall itself; our meaning is just that very building, i.e., what the sequence terminates in. This doctrine led to the charge that James was solipsistic, and it is not difficult to see why. In the case of actually being led to the building, the difficulties inherent in the doctrine may be obscured; for in one sense of meaning—i.e., the topic or reference—the building itself truly is the meaning. But what if our thoughts of Memorial Hall lead us to a smoking pile of debris? Our experiences do not terminate in the building, yet we

75. See "A World of Pure Experience," pp. 183 ff.
76. *Ibid.*

do know we were thinking about it and nothing else: if we cannot know that we were meaning it (in the sense of "sense" or "Object"), then we cannot know that Memorial Hall has been destroyed, nor that we are now standing where it once was. James's occasional doctrine, it could be charged, not only cuts us off from physical reality but cuts us as well from our own future and past experience. It provides no basis for the person himself to know what he means; it contributes to self-alienation and *Unheimlich-keit*. And, incidentally, not only does being led to Memorial Hall fail to be a necessary condition for meaning it, but it fails as a sufficient condition as well. For if I fell into Memorial Hall from an airplane, we would not say that for that reason I was thinking about it. James was forced to admit in 1905 that in some sense thoughts are self-transcendent—that they are not "flat" but have a "point"—that they are like the "compass needle which points to the pole without stirring from its box."[77] (This, of course, is a position which is found in the *Principles:* the omnipresence of cognition—the view that thought is already about an object, whether a real referent in the world is to be found or not for the topic which the object may contain.) But the difficulties surrounding his treatment of intentionality have at this stage of his career so permeated his experiential philosophy that they are not easily weeded out.

The deepest problem is that while he says that his radical empiricism means that the real must be experience*able*,[78] he does not erect the apparatus which would allow a fully intelligible analysis of things as possible objects of experience. His own notion of concepts as "a coordinate realm of reality" could help fill the need: unexperienced but experienceable things conceived in terms of conceptual constructs. In view of this lack, James must construe his enduring belief that things exist independently of their being known by us as the existence of experiences which, because they form no mental context, are not conscious.[79]

But what does this mean? How can there be an experience without an experiencer? Without the experiencer, construed in

77. See "Is Radical Empiricism Solipsistic?," pp. 218 ff.
78. See "The Experience of Activity," pp. 206 ff.
79. See "How Two Minds Can One Thing," p. 202.

Jamesian terms, James's philosophy loses its center. His only recourse, given his difficulties with intentionality, and the one which he takes in his last writings, is toward pan-psychism.[80] Because of the blurring of intentional act and object, he can ask, Since both your percept and mine are "at" the same place (e.g., I hold you by the arm and my percept of that place is "at" just the point where your percept of it is), why may not the experiences themselves become common also someday?[81] In his late *A Pluralistic Universe,* he denies his earlier view that states of consciousness do not exist as entities and cannot be summed (their whole, as a field, being irreducible and unsummable). He suggests there may be a trans-human mind in which all our several minds are thought together as its fringe and "contained" in some sense.

This is, I think, not the most fortunate turn of philosophical events, and it is not the only way that James's unfinished metaphysics can be developed. The key difficulty in his later view—the lumping of intentional act and object as well as meaning and truth—tends to be concealed rather than rectified. (What is the cash value, to put it in James's own terms, of the theory that your percept of a thing and mine are both "at" it?) Nor is it the only way that James's incipient views on the Divine, to be found in *The Varieties of Religious Experience,* can be developed. Finally, it is particularly unfortunate because James was led to denounce "intellectualism" as a mutilating conceptualization and cutting up of the ever-flowing and growing stream of experience, when it is only some "intellectualism" which does this, and when his own thinking stands in need of certain key conceptual distinctions of his own making.

James never did write the book on metaphysics which he knew he must in order to round out his view. He was left with "too much like an arch built up on one side."[82] The difficulty mentioned relates to his contention that everything real must have an "external environment."[83] One can see what he wanted to say by this, and even some good reasons for his saying so. If basic rela-

---

80. See "The Continuity of Experience," p. 366.
81. See "A World of Pure Experience," pp. 196 ff.
82. See prefatory remarks to *Some Problems of Philosophy,* p. vii.
83. See "Conclusions," pp. 367 ff.

tionships are internal, then they are deducible by conceptual thought, the whole becomes more real than the parts, and James's insights into the structure of perceptual experience and the relative autonomy of the individual go by the boards. But this is the heart of his philosophy. Hence we have a verbal—but, as we shall see, not completely harmless—paradox: James sees *external* relations as essential to that relation of *intimacy* between man and world which is continuity, individuality, openness, and freedom. Though every part of experience hangs together with its very next neighbors in some sort of "inextricable interfusion," as he says, still we experience many of the parts as being at once in many *possible* connections ("the word 'or' names a genuine reality"[84]), some of which we experience as dependent on our own as yet unformulated choices. As for a single source of all being, James says that the existence of the universe must simply be begged and is a mystery; the radically experiential philosophy most naturally begs it bit by bit rather than all at once, and as such can very well conceive different origins of it. "So far as things have space-relations, for example, we are free to imagine them with different origins even. If they could get to *be*, and get into space at all, then they may have done so separately. Once there, however, they are additives to one another, and, with no prejudice to their natures, all sorts of space-relations may supervene between them."[85] This "concatenated" rather than "through and through" unity is how the world is experienced, hence this is the only responsible thing we can say about what it is.

As understandable and essential as this view is, however, James was led by it to the very questionable position that consciousness itself is "a kind of external relation";[86] which suggests that mind can be conceived without a necessary and internal relation between act of thought and intentional object. This led him to (1) a kind of solipsism, (2) the inability to clearly distinguish theory of meaning from theory of truth, and (3) an inability to

---

84. *Op. cit.*, p. 368.
85. *Essays in Radical Empiricism* [1942 ed.], p. 110. For example, it is not necessarily part of what we *mean* by a piece of paper that it is now on the desk instead of on the floor—the paper is not related internally to the desk.
86. See "Does 'Consciousness' Exist?," p. 172.

conceive the world as *meant* in terms of its experience*ability,* and meant as existing independent of particular acts of experiencing.

Even here, however, there are mitigating circumstances. Not without reason did James grow to distrust what he took to be an excessively formal construal of intentionality, as by the scholastics; it violated his sense of life. To say that a thought is meaningful because it refers beyond itself to its intentional object seemed to him so schematic and rigid that it missed the actual content of flowing, burgeoning experience; it seemed an *a priori* leap into another, a logical realm of intentional objects. He was especially impressed by the way feeling and thought burgeon and grow in a way that is not planned, but which nevertheless fits in—a lived-forward flow, filled often with desirable novelties, which falls outside focal intention and explicit will.[87] Above all, James wished to grasp the overflowing, not fully predictable, and never completely transparent nature of our experienced situation. In his view, the traditional doctrine of intentionality slights both the roots and the fruits of our mental life.

If we would round out James's metaphysics, we must return to the *Principles* and develop its key insights into the lived-body and intentionality so that they can be woven through his radical empiricism. To begin to trace the generic traits of the things which are, we must distinguish the structures of the experienced world from those of the act-aspect of experience, the experiencing; to do this, James's appropriation in the *Principles* of Kant's distinction between synthetic and analytic apperception must be developed. That is, things can be together in experience ("subjective synthesis") without having to be thought of as *being* together ("objective synthesis"); it is just the former which the act of thought must be if it is to be conceived in the non-dualistic fashion James's radical empiricism requires; i.e., as in some experiential sense objective, but not objective in the sense that it is what thought is

87. "Since the desire of [the] end is the efficient cause, we see that in the total fact of personal activity final and efficient causes coalesce. Yet the effect is oftenest contained *aliquo modo* only, and seldom explicitly foreseen. The activity sets up more effects than it proposes literally. The end is defined beforehand in most cases only as a general direction, along which all sorts of novelties and surprises lie in wait. These words I write even now surprise me. . . ." (*Some Problems of Philosophy*, p. 213.)

focused on, or what thought is *about,* in any usual sense.[88] Only the lived-body experienced marginally can fill the bill of the mental. In *Essays in Radical Empiricism,* James construes thinking and experiencing largely in terms of the breathing of the lived-body, but he fails to say that it is non-focal; hence he cannot develop the conception of it as act of thought.

When this is done, an account can be given of sequences of experience which are experienced as sequences in the experienced world rather than in the experiencing. The generic traits of the things which are can be sketched without the account being cast necessarily in a pan-psychic mold. Moreover, we can, for example, do credit to James's insight that the sense of our effort is a paradigm of "cause" without generating the conclusion that all causal relations are teleological.[89]

88. For elaboration, see my *William James and Phenomenology: A Study of "The Principles of Psychology"* (Bloomington and London: Indiana University Press, 1968), pp. 146 ff. Notice the partial congruity between A. J. Ayer's and my interpretation of James's theory of self-identity (*The Origins of Pragmatism* [London: Macmillan, 1968]), pp. 256–336. N.B. p. 297.

89. Any reconstruction of James's metaphysics must, of course, establish conditions of identity of individual things. For James, an individual *is* relative to its experienceability; it is context bound. This view affords a great sensitivity and latitude of treatment: even momentary dust-wraiths are individuals of some sort, he says, while, on the other hand, really new and surprising things can happen to individuals of other sorts, and they remain themselves, for merely to identify a thing is not to grasp, even implicitly, all the relations that can qualify it. James's talk of "new occasions" (see the selection below from his *Pluralistic Universe,* p. 368) is a germ of important ideas developed later by A. N. Whitehead and other 'process philosophers.' His general view is congenial with Whitehead's notions of the fallacies of 'simple location' and 'misplaced concreteness.' 'Adjacent minima of experience' are through and through interpenetrated, according to James, and 'things in themselves,' supposedly existing only within the boundaries of their surfaces, are recognized to be high abstractions, for things do not function in that manner in concrete experience. Above all, James's notions that any pulse of experience is a nexus of many more relations than are explicitly and articulately conscious, and that the religious experience is a relationship *qua* totality that reveals the world at a fundamental level (above, xxxviii), both suggest Whitehead's idea that the occasion of experience is an occasion of the whole universe.

But it is hoped that the greater attention given to other traditions in this introduction will suggest modes of completing James's metaphysics through dialectical exchange with the already standing Whiteheadian interpretation (exchanges something of the sort set forth by William Barrett in *What is Existentialism?* [New York: Grove Press, 1964], pp. 31–40). Some basic questions are: Does Whitehead's idea of a human being as a 'super-ject' do justice to the uniqueness of the 'event' which is human self-consciousness? Does Whitehead

It is the lived-body which supplies acceptable content to experiencing, act of thought, or intentionality. As he says, the human body is "the palmary instance of the ambiguous."[90] Taken in one context, it is talking, acting, gesticulating, expressing, i.e., mental; taken in the other, it is the physiological object and process. Although each context may require for its description some unique terms, still the connection between contexts is intimate. One context plays into the other's hands, so to speak. For example, the muscular structure of the abdomen, describable physiologically as a weakness and/or spasticity of cellular structure, may be explained in the other context of configurational expressivity of the body—e.g., the expression of doubt about the world and depression—and this is mental. (It has been observed, not altogether facetiously, that bodies of schizophrenics tend to look like question marks.)

This intimacy of contexts accords with the structure of experience. Much more occurs in consciousness than is aimed at by explicit will and deliberate focusing. "The centre works in one way while the margins work in another, and presently overpower the centre and are central themselves. What we conceptually identify ourselves with and say we are thinking of at any time is the centre; but our *full* self is the whole field, with all those indefinitely radiating subconscious possibilities of increase that we can only feel without conceiving, and can hardly begin to analyze."[91] That is, James appears to be saying that sequences of efficient causation in the living human organism are caught up in contexts which are teleological when experienced on the level of consciousness. One level is not primary and the other derivative; they are complementary. The secret of the connection between efficient and final causality, and with it a sizable portion of the metaphysical secret as a whole, seems lodged in an analysis of the

---

account for apprehension of essence and form in a manner that fully exploits Jamesian ideas, e.g., conceptualization as 'general purpose'? Finally, if we say, following Whitehead, that *every* event, since it is a concrete fact of relatedness, is a kind of perceiving, do we mean it is a kind of perceiving in the act aspect of perceiving, in the object aspect, in both, or what? The Whiteheadian philosophy can throw important light on James's idea of pure experience.

90. See "The Place of Affectional Facts in a World of Pure Experience," pp. 205 ff.

91. See "The Continuity of Experience," pp. 365 ff.

thinker's own body, as that analysis has been initiated by James.

The most promising line of development of Jamesian thought is from its center: the embodied self, in terms of whose activity the world-as-experienceable must be construed. The open ground of meaning is a matter of how the world is systematized relative to a center of action and interest which lies in the acting, ongoing body. It is in part a function of our choices and dreams, full of surprises for reordering and more fully understanding the world experienced and for resituating ourselves within it. Always the lived-body at the center: those places which are the same for ourselves and those who touch and embrace us, and from which, as reference points, further common topics can be indicated by pointing, and common directions and concerns signified.[92]

Thus in front and behind the body become generalized into North and South, and left and right into West and East. But, of course, it is the body as expressive, as ourselves; the body freed from self-description exclusively in terms of its organic shape and geographical locale; the body as spirit, as open to possibility, and as ground of freedom; the body as basis for refashioning the world through art, technique, and work—a world which claims us most when most we change it. For, as James makes clear, we are situated within the world and forever responsible for the consequences of our freedom which pile up around us and structure our lives.

James is a philosopher who has not lost his sense of fact. This is best brought out in his construal of necessary truths as internal relations between ideal objects or concepts of mind which supervene upon experience through free mental play; they are not reproductions of the actual order of our sensory experience. Yet it is up to experience to decide if they apply to the factual world, e.g., *if* there are triangular objects, the sum of their included angles will be 180°, but we must see if there are any such objects. James rejects Kant's distinction between synthetic and analytic *a priori* truths: "It seems to me that the distinction is one of Kant's most unhappy legacies, for the reason that it is impossible to make it sharp. No one will say that such analytic judgments as 'equi-distant lines can nowhere meet' are *pure* tautologies. The predicate is a somewhat

---

92. James seems to suggest at one point that there can be no notion of individual minds or personalities without a notion of the lived-body as a common object of many minds. See "A World of Pure Experience," pp. 196 ff.

new way of conceiving as well as naming the subject. There is something ampliative in our greatest truisms . . ."[93] That is, necessary truths are not simply an intra-linguistic matter of using new names in the predicate for already conceived meanings in the subject; at least not for those important necessary truths which actually "enrich our state of mind." Hence, if concepts exceed the range of verbalization (namelessness is compatible with existence, he asserts, and mere incipient tendencies and directions of thought, whose objects are not named, are as good thoughts as others[94]) and, further, if concepts inform the whole range of our perceptual life ("by these whats we apprehend all our thises"[95]), then we must draw the conclusion that no technique concerned only with our words can ascertain the scope of necessary truths in our experience.[96]

Moreover, James rejects Kant's contention that a limited set of necessary truths legislates for all possible experience. For experience, while being informed by concepts, prompts, overflows and deflects them too, and their usability as teleological instruments is progressively tested.[97] Thus he rejects the idea of a single perfected

93. P. 158 fn.
94. Pp. 59 ff. and 117 fn.
95. *Some Problems of Philosophy*, p. 52.
96. The assertability of both protases is debatable in James: Sometimes he *equates* the verbal and the conceptual, and sometimes he refers to experiences that are mere *thats*, not *whats* (thus suggesting that there is no conceptual component). However, there would still be grounds in James for affirming *perceptual* meanings interlocked as implicit necessary truths, as well as perceptual meanings in the singular, which elude verbalization. He writes, "Philosophy lives in words, but truth and fact well up into our lives in ways that exceed verbal formulation. There is in the living act of perception always something that glimmers and twinkles and will not be caught, and for which reflection comes too late." (p. 253.)
97. This aspect of his thought is not apparent in some of the passages of his chapter on necessary truth in the *Principles*—pp. 148–161 below. (Although he suggests it in his treatment of metaphysical axioms as those whose applicability is only progressively understood—pp. 160–161). These passages are James at his most nearly positivistic, and his allusion to the view that the universe is purposeless, and qualities and values are "illusions of fantasy" which "the eternal cosmic weather will dissipate," shows the influence of Chauncey Wright. That is, he does not consider all that on his own analysis is suggested in affirming—even hypothetically—necessary truths of real things: this is, I believe, that a necessary truth does not tell us *that* any particular such and such actually exists, but that it is *such and such* is explained only on the supposition that some real things coincide in their attributes with some interrelated concepts, some necessary truths—though with which ones, and for how long, may each be problematical

transcendental method which could account for the possibility of, and render intelligible, all possible experience.

For James the question of existence finally comes home to our own. He writes,

> In both existential and attributive judgments a synthesis is represented. The syllable *ex* in the word Existence, *da* in the word *Dasein*, express it. "The candle exists" is equivalent to "The candle is over there." And the *"over there"* means real space, space related to other reals. The proposition amounts to saying: "The candle is in the same space with other reals." It affirms of the candle a very concrete predicate, namely, this relation to other particular concrete things. *Their* real existence . . . resolves itself into their peculiar relation to *ourselves*. Existence is thus no substantive quality when we predicate it of any object; it is a relation, ultimately terminating in ourselves, and at the moment when it terminates, becoming a *practical* relation.[98]

To say that something exists is to say it is in the same space with other things, some of which are over there from me now. If I am to expose the movement of the situation in which I am, and if I am to grasp myself and cease flailing and stumbling, I must find my existence as implicated in that pre-reflective practical relationship to the world. There is no science of the subject in itself, or the object in itself, which left to itself can answer our questions as existing men. For we live within the relationship within which questions emerge to direct themselves at that portion of the world, and that portion only, that our pre-reflectively given purposes and ends (themselves not self-luminous) can at that time illuminate.

---

points. In some passages James foreshadows C. I. Lewis's conception of the pragmatic *a priori* (viz., Some subjects involve in their very identification particular predicates, hence the predication must now constitute a necessary truth. But we may cease to identify them in this manner, since other attributes, either ever-present as additional identifying ones, or newly so, or simply contingently related previously or newly, may come to carry alone the identifying function; hence the original necessary truth may cease to be so without becoming necessarily false; it is perhaps only contingently true, if it is asserted at all.) At other points James does not foreshadow Lewis on this matter of a pragmatic *a priori*, e.g., "whether any two attributes whatever are compatible, in the sense of appearing or not to occupy the same place and moment, depends simply on *de facto* peculiarities of natural bodies and sense organs" (p. 113 fn.). (Although 'appear' may not here carry the force of 'appear to be,' hence the philosophical force of this passage is somewhat problematical.) Cf. pp. 265–268 with their overtones of Kant and Lewis.

98. P. 136 fn.

I must realize that at the end of all technique, no matter how necessary, it is essential that I confront the limitations of it, and myself as standing at just that point of illumination and ignorance. I am left with myself and the world, finally, and either I am open to unforeseeable possibilities of response, insight and action, or I am not. A total reaction from me is called for, as James would put it, not just a professional one.

A scientist's subject matter may require him to forever prescind from his subjectivity, to simply follow his method, and to pass it on together with data so far amassed to the next generation of inquirers. But it is highly questionable if philosophy progresses this way. James would remind us that philosophy requires remarkable individuals willing at some points to take risks in achieving closure in their thought and in locating their existence; merely following another philosopher is usually degenerative. (There is no science of 'science'—to use a Husserlian insight which is remarkably close to James's view—no science which is adequate to its own sources of meaning in subjectivity and inter-subjectivity.) A philosopher is a lover of wisdom, his subject matter is ourselves—and at closest range, and with relentless claim upon him, his own self. At some point he must confront our lived-situation, and try to map it as it is, i.e., as a whole, as that which locates and contains us. He must try to tell us where we are, who we are, and what we are to do. We cannot postpone our existence, and choose not to choose, not to act. Decisions concerning experience as a whole, which we make one way or the other, actively or by default, affect our existence, and they determine, among other things, just what we shall count as evidence. Hence these decisions are themselves beyond conclusive evidence. Philosophy involves engagement, leap and choice; it is intrinsically dramatic.[99]

99. Cf. to "Will to Believe": Julián Marías, *Philosophy as Dramatic Theory* (University Park: Pennsylvania State University Press, 1971), p. 56. James's first lecture from *A Pluralistic Universe* should also be studied on this point. "Either what the philosopher tells us is extraneous to the universe he is accounting for, an indifferent parasitic growth, so to speak; or the fact of his philosophizing is itself one of the things taken account of in the philosophy, and self-included in the description. In the former case the philosopher means by the universe everything *except* what his own presence brings; in the latter case his philosophy is itself an intimate part of the universe, and may be a part momentous enough to give a different turn to what the other parts signify. It

James, I believe, would be dismayed at what many American academic philosophers so pride themselves in—their 'professionalism,' their mastery of technique, their attempt to break off and dispatch philosophical problems as if they were scientific or technological problems, one by one, neatly, all in a row. In their guild, standards of elegance are high and demanding. Each work must be neatly packaged, however miniscule the contents, and be stackable with what the next man on the bench has done. And nearly without exception one must have the academic badge, the Ph.D. It is what James deplored and warned against, "the increasing hold of the Ph.D. Octopus upon American life."[100] Far too infrequently do students of philosophy master techniques as a part of working out their destinies as individual persons. James wrote nearly seventy years ago,

> our universities . . . should never cease to regard themselves as the jealous custodians of personal and spiritual spontaneity. They are indeed its only organized and recognized custodians in American today. They ought to guard against contributing to the increase of officialism and snobbery and insincerity as against a pestilence; they ought to keep truth and disinterested labor always in the foreground . . . and in season and out of season make it plain that what they live for is to help men's souls, and not to decorate their persons with diplomas.

James, without the degree, his work massively untidy, creatively untidy (of the *Principles* he writes: this "loathsome, distended, tumified, bloated, dropsical mass . . ."[101]) —it is a question if work

---

may be a supreme reaction of the universe upon itself by which it rises to self-comprehension. It may handle itself differently in consequence of this event. . . . We can invent no new forms of conception, applicable to the whole exclusively, and not suggested originally by the parts. All philosophers, accordingly, have conceived of the whole world after the analogy of some particular feature of it which has particularly captivated their attention. . . . All follow one analogy or another; and all the analogies are with some one or other of the universe's subdivisions. Every one is nevertheless prone to claim that his conclusions are the only logical ones, that they are necessities of universal reason, they being all the while, at bottom, accidents more or less of personal vision which had far better be avowed as such; for one man's vision may be much more valuable than another's, and our visions are usually not only our most interesting but our most respectable contributions to the world in which we play our part." See also p. 271 below.

100. Pp. 343 ff.

101. Perry, II, *op. cit.*, 47–48.

like his, which A. N. Whitehead ranks with that of Plato, Aristotle and Leibniz, could even be published in the prestigious philosophy journals today.[102]

The greatest contemporary thinkers have, with technique and greatness of person, thought beyond technique. For example, Ludwig Wittgenstein discovered that there is no single rule for following a rule in uses of terms; language goes on indefinitely in its complications. But by pursuing the technique of determining what can be said, and how it can be said, to the point of its exhaustion, we garner at some points the greatest profit of our inquiries: knowledge of what cannot be said, and this signals the rock-bottom shape, the boundaries, of our situation in the world; it is the ethical, in the classical sense of the term.[103] For another example, Edmund Husserl at the end of his life shifted his emphasis to include an historical approach to the understanding of meaning.[104] As modified and radicalized by Merleau-Ponty: all our presuppositions cannot be excavated and reflectively acknowledged (hence a 'presuppositionless' philosophy grounded), because as embodied we can never completely step out of and survey our own situation; existence claims us in too many ways to be reflectively enumerated. William James is another example; he forever transcends his own techniques.

Yet in progressively departmentalized universities in America many students of philosophy have been trained to think that mastering a technique of analysis and cooperating with other journeymen in that specialty is enough, e.g., think that chirping, 'Synthetic or analytic?' 'Contingent or necessary?' is enough to make a career. To turn away in the university setting from a technologized and progressively depersonalized society, but not to keep touch with one's own historical and existential situation, is to fall victim of

102. "In Western Literature there are four great thinkers, whose services to civilized thought rest largely upon their achievements in philosophical assemblage; though each of them made important contributions to the structure of philosophic system. These men are Plato, Aristotle, Leibniz, and William James." *Modes of Thought* (New York: The Macmillan Co., 1938), p. 3.

103. E.g., Stephen Toulmin, "Ludwig Wittgenstein," *Commentary* (England), January, 1969.

104. Husserl, *The Crisis of the European Sciences and Transcendental Phenomenology*, trans. by David Carr (Evanston: Northwestern University Press, 1970).

that very professionalism and depersonalization, but on another level: one which conceals itself from itself with rationalizations that go unchallenged. Experts create experts *ex nihilo ad nihilum*. Linguistic analysis, the most recent mode in technique, has become in the hands of the 'trained' an establishment mentality which more often than not simply ignores 'competing' philosophies, e.g., existentialism and the religious and even humanistic side of traditional American philosophy; this goes on in utter forgetfulness of James's warning.

The recessional movement from personal existence to professional *persona*, the programmatic idea that one can abstract *forever* from subjectivity and lived-situation and reduce it to a formal or quasi-formal schematization, produces the strange emptiness, the phantom-like quality of much of the academic philosophical discussion in this country.[105] It is certainly part of that which settles around us, the "nameless *Unheimlichkeit*" James speaks of, and as more and more persons attend universities, an ever-enlarging part.[106] Insofar as academic philosophy is non-ethical, in the classical sense, it is aesthetic in an oddly narrow sense; and insofar as it still claims to be the love of, and pursuit of, wisdom, it stands exposed to the most pointed questioning.

The general drift of James's thought is toward a conception of aesthetics so profound that it is part and parcel of an ethics. Perception for James is art-like, and perception as involving action figures in the ground of that developmental continuity which is the good life. James's genius as a philosopher is his ability to mate reason with the pre-reflectively experienced world—an activity of mind usually consigned to the dramatist or artist. His work should be regarded as an attempt to mend the breach created by Hume's exhaustive distinction between factually empty truths of reason,

105. As an example of this schematization: the attempt to formalize all verbal communication in a syntactics, pragmatics and semantics. Even formal work of notable significance for self-knowledge, modal and epistemic logics (e.g., the accumulating work of H.–N. Castañeda), is, from a Jamesian viewpoint, not sufficient.

106. According to James the historical tendency is that philosophy be a cross fertilization of poetry, religion, science and logic, within a discipline whose boundaries cannot be neatly marked off. If we follow this view, we must regard philosophy today as deformed, for it lacks notably the first two components, and we must regard it as historically displaced. (See immediately below, "Philosophy and its Critics.")

the domain of logic and formal studies, and truths of fact, the domain of the sciences. Attempts to perpetuate reason by perpetuating this breach excite an irrational corrective reaction which demands instant relevance—irrelevant relevance—from philosophy, and which would like to turn even universities into centers of mere activism and anti-intellectualism. For James, existence and reason are not antithetical. I hope we can recapture his maturity and vision.

Bruce W. Wilshire
University College
Rutgers University

June 23, 1971

William James

The Essential Writings

1.

From *Some Problems of Philosophy*

A. PHILOSOPHY AND ITS CRITICS*

. . . The principles of explanation that underlie all things without exception, the elements common to gods and men and animals and stones, the first *whence* and the last *whither* of the whole cosmic procession, the conditions of all knowing, and the most general rules of human action—these furnish the problems commonly deemed philosophic *par excellence;* and the philosopher is the man who finds the most to say about them. Philosophy is defined in the usual scholastic textbooks as 'the knowledge of things in general by their ultimate causes, so far as natural reason can attain to such knowledge.' This means that explanation of the universe at large, not description of its details, is what philosophy must aim at; and so it happens that a view of anything is termed philosophic just in proportion as it is broad and connected with other views, and as it uses principles not proximate, or intermediate, but ultimate and all-embracing, to justify itself. Any very sweeping view of the world is a philosophy in this sense, even though it may be a vague one. It is a *Weltanschauung*, an intellectualized attitude towards life. Professor Dewey well describes the constitution of all the philosophies that actually exist, when he says that philosophy expresses a certain attitude, purpose and temper of conjoined intellect and will, rather than a discipline whose boundaries can be neatly marked off.

To know the chief rival attitudes towards life, as the history of human thinking has developed them, and to have heard some of the reasons they can give for themselves, ought to be considered an essential part of liberal education. Philosophy, indeed, in one

---

* These three selections are taken from the first three chapters of *Some Problems of Philosophy*, published posthumously in 1911 as *A Beginning of an Introduction to Philosophy* (New York & London: Longmans, Green & Co.). James's footnotes have been deleted.

sense of the term is only a compendious name for the spirit in education which the word 'college' stands for in America. Things can be taught in dry dogmatic ways or in a philosophic way. At a technical school a man may grow into a first-rate instrument for doing a certain job, but he may miss all the graciousness of mind suggested by the term liberal culture. He may remain a cad, and not a gentleman, intellectually pinned down to his one narrow subject, literal, unable to suppose anything different from what he has seen, without imagination, atmosphere, or mental perspective.

Philosophy, beginning in wonder, as Plato and Aristotle said, is able to fancy everything different from what it is. It sees the familiar as if it were strange, and the strange as if it were familiar. It can take things up and lay them down again. Its mind is full of air that plays round every subject. It rouses us from our native dogmatic slumber and breaks up our caked prejudices. Historically it has always been a sort of fecundation of four different human interests, science, poetry, religion, and logic, by one another. It has sought by hard reasoning for results emotionally valuable. To have some contact with it, to catch its influence, is thus good for both literary and scientific students. . . .

In spite of the advantages thus enumerated, the study of philosophy has systematic enemies, and they were never as numerous as at the present day. The definite conquests of science and the apparent indefiniteness of philosophy's results partly account for this; to say nothing of man's native rudeness of mind, which maliciously enjoys deriding long words and abstractions. 'Scholastic jargon,' 'mediæval dialectics,' are for many people synonyms of the word philosophy. With his obscure and uncertain speculations as to the intimate nature and causes of things, the philosopher is likened to a "blind man in a dark room looking for a black hat that is not there." His occupation is described as the art of "endlessly disputing without coming to any conclusion," or more contemptuously still as the *"systematische Missbrauch einer eben zu diesem Zwecke erfundenen Terminologie."*

Only to a very limited degree is this sort of hostility reasonable. I will take up some of the current objections in successive order, since to reply to them will be a convenient way of entering into the interior of our subject.

Objection 1. Whereas the sciences make steady progress and yield applications of matchless utility, philosophy makes no progress and has no practical applications.

Reply. The opposition is unjustly founded, for the sciences are themselves branches of the tree of philosophy. As fast as questions got accurately answered, the answers were called 'scientific,' and what men call 'philosophy' to-day is but the residuum of questions still unanswered. At this very moment we are seeing two sciences, psychology and general biology, drop off from the parent trunk and take independent root as specialties. The more general philosophy cannot as a rule follow the voluminous details of any special science. . . .

Objection 2. Philosophy is dogmatic, and pretends to settle things by pure reason, whereas the only fruitful mode of getting at truth is to appeal to concrete experience. Science collects, classes, and analyzes facts, and thereby far outstrips philosophy.

Reply. This objection is historically valid. Too many philosophers have aimed at closed systems, established *a priori*, claiming infallibility, and to be accepted or rejected only as totals. The sciences on the other hand, using hypotheses only, but always seeking to verify them by experiment and observation, open a way for indefinite self-correction and increase. At the present day, it is getting more and more difficult for dogmatists claiming finality for their systems, to get a hearing in educated circles. Hypothesis and verification, the watchwords of science, have set the fashion too strongly in academic minds.

Since philosophers are only men thinking about things in the most comprehensive possible way, they can use any method whatsoever freely. Philosophy must, in any case, complete the sciences, and must incorporate their methods. One cannot see why, if such a policy should appear advisable, philosophy might not end by forswearing all dogmatism whatever, and become as hypothetical in her manners as the most empirical science of them all.

Objection 3. Philosophy is out of touch with real life, for which it substitutes abstractions. The real world is various, tangled, painful. Philosophers have, almost without exception, treated it as noble, simple, and perfect, ignoring the complexity of fact, and indulging in a sort of optimism that exposes their systems to the contempt of common men, and to the satire of such writers as Voltaire and Schopenhauer. The great popular success of Schopenhauer is due to the fact that, first among philosophers, he spoke the concrete truth about the ills of life.

Reply. This objection also is historically valid, but no reason appears why philosophy should keep aloof from reality permanently. Her manners may change as she successfully develops. . . . In the end philosophers may get into as close contact as realistic novelists with the facts of life.

In conclusion. In its original acceptation, meaning the completest knowledge of the universe, philosophy must include the results of all the sciences, and cannot be contrasted with the latter. It simply aims at making of science what Herbert Spencer calls a 'system of completely unified knowledge.' In the more modern sense, of something contrasted with the sciences, philosophy means 'metaphysics.' The older sense is the more worthy sense, and as the results of the sciences get more available for co-ordination, and the conditions for finding truth in different kinds of question get more methodically defined, we may hope that the term will revert to its original meaning. Science, metaphysics, and religion may then again form a single body of wisdom, and lend each other mutual support.

At present this hope is far from its fulfilment. . . .

B.   THE PROBLEMS OF METAPHYSICS

No exact definition of the term 'metaphysics' is possible, and to name some of the problems it treats of is the best way of getting at the meaning of the word. It means the discussion of various obscure, abstract, and universal questions which the sciences and life in general suggest but do not solve; questions left over, as it were; questions, all of them very broad and deep, and relating to the whole of things, or to the ultimate elements thereof. Instead of a definition let me cite a few examples, in a random order, of such questions:—

What are 'thoughts,' and what are 'things'? and how are they connected?

What do we mean when we say 'truth'?

Is there a common stuff out of which all facts are made?

How comes there to be a world at all? and, might it as well not have been?

Which is the most real kind of reality?

What binds all things into one universe?

Is unity or diversity more fundamental?

Have all things one origin? or many?

Is everything predestined, or are some things (our wills for example) free?

Is the world infinite or finite in amount?

Are its parts continuous, or are there vacua?

What is God?—or the gods?

How are mind and body joined? Do they act on each other?

How does anything act on anything else?

How can one thing change or grow out of another thing?

Are space and time beings?—or what?

In knowledge, how does the object get into the mind?—or the mind get at the object?

We know by means of universal notions. Are these also real? Or are only particular things real?

What is meant by a 'thing'?

'Principles of reason,'—are they inborn or derived?

Are 'beauty' and 'good' matters of opinion only? Or have they objective validity? And, if so, what does the phrase mean?

Such are specimens of the kind of question termed metaphysical. Kant said that the three essential metaphysical questions were:—

What can I know?

What should I do?

What may I hope?

A glance at all such questions suffices to rule out such a definition of metaphysics as that of Christian Wolff, who called it 'the science of what is possible,' as distinguished from that of what is actual, for most of the questions relate to what is actual fact. One may say that metaphysics inquires into the cause, the substance, the meaning, and the outcome of all things. Or one may call it the science of the most universal principles of reality (whether experienced by us or not), in their connection with one another and with our powers of knowledge. 'Principles' here may mean either entities, like 'atoms,' 'souls,' or logical laws like: 'A thing must either exist or not exist'; or generalized facts, like 'things can act only after they exist.' But the principles are so numerous, and the 'science' of them is so far from completion, that such definitions have only a decorative value. The serious work of metaphysics is done over the separate single questions. If these should get cleared up, talk of metaphysics as a unified science might properly begin. This book proposes to handle only a few separate problems, leaving others untouched.

These problems are for the most part real; that is, but few of them result from a misuse of terms in stating them. 'Things,' for example, are or are not composed of one stuff; they either have or have not a single origin; they either are or are not completely predetermined, etc. . . .

C. THE PROBLEM OF BEING

How comes the world to be here at all instead of the nonentity which might be imagined in its place? Schopenhauer's remarks on this question may be considered classical. "Apart from man," he says, "no being wonders at its own existence. When man first becomes conscious, he takes himself for granted, as something needing no explanation. But not for long; for, with the rise of the first reflection, that wonder begins which is the mother of metaphysics, and which made Aristotle say that men now and always seek to philosophize because of wonder— The lower a man stands in intellectual respects the less of a riddle does existence seem to him . . . but, the clearer his consciousness becomes the more the problem grasps him in its greatness. In fact the unrest which keeps the never stopping clock of metaphysics going is the thought that the non-existence of this world is just as possible as its existence. Nay more, we soon conceive the world as something the non-existence of which not only is conceivable but would indeed be preferable to its existence; so that our wonder passes easily into a brooding over that fatality which nevertheless could call such a world into being, and mislead the immense force that could produce and preserve it into an activity so hostile to its own interests. The philosophic wonder thus becomes a sad astonishment, and like the overture to Don Giovanni, philosophy begins with a minor chord."

One need only shut oneself in a closet and begin to think of the fact of one's being there, of one's queer bodily shape in the darkness (a thing to make children scream at, as Stevenson says), of one's fantastic character and all, to have the wonder steal over the detail as much as over the general fact of being, and to see that it is only familiarity that blunts it. Not only that *anything* should be, but that *this* very thing should be, is mysterious! Philosophy stares, but brings no reasoned solution, for from nothing to being there is no logical bridge.

Attempts are sometimes made to banish the question rather than to give it an answer. Those who ask it, we are told, extend illegitimately to the whole of being the contrast to a supposed alternative non-being which only particular beings possess.[1] These, indeed, were not, and now are. But being in general, or in some shape, always was, and you cannot rightly bring the whole of it into relation with a primordial nonentity. Whether as God or as material atoms, it is itself primal and eternal. But if you call any being whatever eternal, some philosophers have always been ready to taunt you with the paradox inherent in the assumption. Is past eternity completed? they ask: If so, they go on, it must have had a beginning; for whether your imagination traverses it forwards or backwards, it offers an identical content or stuff to be measured; and if the amount comes to an end in one way, it ought to come to an end in the other. In other words, since we now witness its end, some past moment must have witnessed its beginning. If, however, it had a beginning, when was that, and why?

You are up against the previous nothing, and do not see it ever passed into being. This dilemma, of having to choose between a regress which, although called infinite, has nevertheless come to a termination, and an absolute first, has played a great part in philosophy's history. . . .

Contemporary philosophers, even rationalistically minded ones, have on the whole agreed that no one has intelligibly banished the mystery of *fact*. Whether the original nothing burst into God and vanished, as night vanishes in day, while God thereupon became the creative principle of all lesser beings; or whether all things

1. Despite James's general praise of Bergson, he was critical of this idea of his. Perry, *op. cit.*, II, 620, letter to Bergson of 6/13/07. See Bergson's *Creative Evolution* (New York: Henry Holt & Co., 1911) chap. 4, "The Idea of 'Nothing.' " [B.W.]

have foisted or shaped themselves imperceptibly into existence, the same amount of existence has in the end to be assumed and begged by the philosopher. To comminute the difficulty is not to quench it. If you are a rationalist you beg a kilogram of being at once, we will say; if you are an empiricist you beg a thousand successive grams; but you beg the same amount in each case, and you are the same beggar whatever you may pretend. You leave the logical riddle untouched, of how the coming of whatever is, came it all at once, or came it piecemeal, can be intellectually understood.

If being gradually *grew,* its quantity was of course not always the same, and may not be the same hereafter. To most philosophers this view has seemed absurd, neither God, nor primordial matter, nor energy being supposed to admit of increase or decrease. The orthodox opinion is that the quantity of reality must at all costs be conserved, and the waxing and waning of our phenomenal experiences must be treated as surface appearances which leave the deeps untouched.

Nevertheless, within experience, phenomena come and go. There are novelties; there are losses. The world seems, on the concrete and proximate level at least, really to grow. So the question recurs: How do our finite experiences come into being from moment to moment? By inertia? By perpetual creation? Do the new ones come at the call of the old ones? Why do not they all go out like a candle?

Who can tell off-hand? The question of being is the darkest in all philosophy. All of us are beggars here, and no school can speak disdainfully of another or give itself superior airs. For all of us alike, Fact forms a datum, gift, or *Vorgefundenes,* which we cannot burrow under, explain or get behind. It makes itself somehow, and our business is far more with its What than with its Whence or Why.

2.

Remarks on Spencer's Definition
of Mind as Correspondence*

As a rule it may be said that, at a time when readers are so
overwhelmed with work as they are at the present day, all purely
critical and destructive writing ought to be reprobated. The half-
gods generally refuse to go, in spite of the ablest criticism, until
the gods actually *have* arrived; but then, too, criticism is hardly
needed. But there are cases in which every rule may be broken.
"What!" exclaimed Voltaire, when accused of offering no substitute for the Christianity he attacked, *"je vous délivre d'une bête
féroce, et vous me demandez par quoi je la remplace!"* Without
comparing Mr. Spencer's definition of Mind either to Christianity
or to a *"bête féroce,"* it may certainly be said to be very far-reaching in its consequences, and, according to certain standards, nox-
ious; whilst probably a large proportion of those hard-headed
readers who subscribe to the *Popular Science Monthly* and *Nature*
and whose sole philosopher Mr. Spencer is, are fascinated by it
without being in the least aware what its consequences are.

The defects of the formula are so glaring that I am surprised it
should not long ago have been critically overhauled. The reader
will readily recollect what it is. In part III of his *Principles of
Psychology,* Mr. Spencer, starting from the supposition that the
most essential truth concerning mental evolution will be that
which allies it to the evolution nearest akin to it, namely, that of
Life, finds that the formula 'adjustment of inner to outer relations,' which was the definition of life, comprehends also 'the entire process of mental evolution.' In a series of chapters of great
apparent thoroughness and minuteness he shows how all the
different grades of mental perfection are expressed by the degree
of extension of this adjustment, or, as he here calls it, 'correspon-

* *Journal of Speculative Philosophy* (January, 1878, 12, 1–18).

dence,' in space, time, specialty, generality, and integration. The polyp's tentacles contract only to immediately present stimuli, and to almost all alike. The mammal will store up food for a day, or even for a season; the bird will start on its migration for a goal hundreds of miles away; the savage will sharpen his arrows to hunt next year's game; while the astronomer will proceed, equipped with all his instruments, to a point thousands of miles distant, there to watch, at a fixed day, hour, and minute, a transit of Venus or an eclipse of the Sun.

The picture drawn is so vast and simple, it includes such a multitude of details in its monotonous frame-work, that it is no wonder that readers of a passive turn of mind are, usually, more impressed by it than by any portion of the book. But on the slightest scrutiny its solidity begins to disappear. In the first place, one asks, what right has one, in a formula embracing professedly the "entire process of mental evolution," to mention only phenomena of cognition, and to omit all sentiments, all aesthetic impulses, all religious emotions and personal affections? The ascertainment of outward fact constitutes only one species of mental activity. The genus contains, in addition to purely cognitive judgments, or judgments of the actual—judgments that things do, as a matter of fact, exist so or so—an immense number of emotional judgments: judgments of the ideal, judgments that things *should* exist thus and not so. How much of our mental life is occupied with this matter of a better or a worse? How much of it involves preferences or repugnances on our part? We cannot laugh at a joke, we cannot go to one theatre rather than another, take more trouble for the sake of our own child than our neighbor's; we cannot long for vacation, show our best manners to a foreigner, or pay our pew rent, without involving in the premises of our action some element which has nothing whatever to do with simply cognizing the actual, but which, out of alternative possible actuals, selects one and cognizes that as the ideal. In a word, 'Mind,' as we actually find it, contains all sorts of laws—those of logic, of fancy, of wit, of taste, decorum, beauty, morals, and so forth, as well as of perception of fact. Common sense estimates mental excellence by a combination of all these standards, and yet how few of them correspond to anything that actually *is*—they are laws of the Ideal, dictated by subjective *interests* pure and simple. Thus the greater part of Mind, quantitatively considered, refuses to have anything to do with Mr. Spencer's definition. It is quite true that these ideal judgments are treated by him with great ingenuity and felicity at the close of his work—indeed, his treatment of them there seems to me to be its most admirable portion. But they are there handled as separate items having no connection with that extension of the 'correspondence' which is maintained elsewhere to be the all-sufficing law of mental growth.

Most readers would dislike to admit without coercion that a law was adequate which obliged them to erase from literature (if by literature were meant anything worthy of the title of 'mental product') all works except treatises on natural science, history, and statistics. Let us examine the reason that Mr. Spencer appears to consider coercive.

It is this: That, since every process grows more and more complicated as it develops, more swarmed over by incidental and derivative conditions which disguise and adulterate its original simplicity, the only way to discover its true and essential form is to trace it back to its earliest beginning. There it will appear in its genuine character pure and undefiled. Religious, aesthetic, and ethical judgments, having grown up in the course of evolution, by means that we can very plausibly divine, of course may be stripped off from the main stem of intelligence and leave that undisturbed. With a similar intent Mr. Tylor says: "Whatever throws light on the origin of a conception throws light on its validity." Thus, then, there is no resource but to appeal to the polyp, or whatever shows us the form of evolution just *before* intelligence, and what that, and only what that, contains will be the root and heart of the matter.

But no sooner is the reason for the law thus enunciated than many objections occur to the reader. In the first place, the general principle seems to lead to absurd conclusions. If the embryologic line of appeal can alone teach us the genuine essences of things, if the polyp is to dictate our law of mind to us because he came first, where are we to stop? He must himself be treated in the same way. Back of him lay the not-yet-polyp, and, back of all, the universal mother, fire-mist. To seek there for the reality, of course would reduce all thinking to nonentity, and, although Mr. Spencer would probably not regard this conclusion as a *reductio ad absur-*

dum of his principle, since it would only be another path to his theory of the Unknowable, less systematic thinkers may hesitate. But, waiving for the moment the question of principle, let us admit that relatively to *our* thought, at any rate, the polyp's thought is pure and undefiled. Does the study of the polyp lead us distinctly to Mr. Spencer's formula of correspondence? To begin with, if that formula be meant to include disinterested scientific curiosity, or 'correspondence' in the sense of cognition, with no ulterior selfish end, the polyp gives it no countenance whatever. He is as innocent of scientific as of moral and aesthetic enthusiasm; he is the most narrowly teleological of organisms; reacting, so far as he reacts at all, only for self-preservation.

This leads us to ask what Mr. Spencer exactly means by the word correspondence. Without explanation, the word is wholly indeterminate. Everything corresponds in some way with everything else that co-exists in the same world with it. But, as the formula of correspondence was originally derived from biology, we shall possibly find in our author's treatise on that science an exact definition of what he means by it. On seeking there, we find nowhere a definition, but numbers of synonyms. The inner relations are 'adjusted,' 'conformed,' 'fitted,' 'related,' to the outer. They must 'meet' or 'balance' them. There must be 'concord' or 'harmony' between them. Or, again, the organism must 'counteract' the changes in the environment. But these words, too, are wholly indeterminate. The fox is most beautifully 'adjusted' to the hounds and huntsmen who pursue him; the limestone 'meets' molecule by molecule the acid which corrodes it; the man is exquisitely 'conformed' to the *trichina* which invades him, or to the typhus poison which consumes him; and the forests 'harmonize' incomparably with the fires that lay them low. Clearly, a further specification is required; and, although Mr. Spencer shrinks strangely from enunciating this specification, he everywhere works his formula so as to imply it in the clearest manner.

Influence on physical well-being or survival is his implied criterion of the rank of mental action. The moth which flies into the candle, instead of away from it, 'fails,' in Spencer's words, to 'correspond' with its environment; but clearly, in this sense, pure cognitve inference of the existence of heat after a perception of light would not suffice to constitute correspondence; while a moth which, on feeling the light, should merely vaguely fear to approach it, but have no proper image of the heat, would 'correspond.' So that the Spencerian formula, to mean anything definite at all, must, at least, be re-written as follows: "Right or intelligent mental action consists in the establishment, corresponding to outward relations, of such inward relations and reactions as will favor the survival of the thinker, or, at least, his physical well-being."

Such a definition as this is precise, but at the same time it is frankly teleological. It explicitly postulates a distinction between mental action pure and simple, and *right* mental action; and furthermore, it proposes, as criteria of this latter, certain ideal ends—those of physical prosperity or survival, which are pure *subjective interests* on the animal's part, brought with it upon the scene and corresponding to no relation already there.[1] No mental action is right or intelligent which fails to fit this standard. No correspondence can pass muster till it shows its subservience to these ends. Corresponding itself to no actual outward thing; referring merely to a future which *may* be, but which these interests now say *shall* be; purely ideal, in a word, they judge, dominate, determine all correspondences between the inner and the outer. Which is as much as to say that *mere* correspondence with the outer world is a notion on which it is wholly impossible to base a definition of mental action. Mr. Spencer's occult reason for leaving unexpressed the most important part of the definition he works with probably lies in its apparent implication of subjective spon-

---

1. These interests are the real *a priori* element in cognition. By saying that their pleasures and pains have nothing to do with correspondence, I mean simply this: To a large number of terms in the environment there may be inward correlatives of a neutral sort as regards feeling. The 'correspondence' is already there. But, now, suppose some to be accented with pleasure, others with pain; that is a fact additional to the correspondence, a fact with no outward correlative. But it immediately orders the correspondences in this way: that the pleasant or interesting items are singled out, dwelt upon, developed into their farther connections, whilst the unpleasant or insipid ones are ignored or suppressed. The future of the Mind's development is thus mapped out in advance by the way in which the lines of pleasure and pain run. The interests precede the outer relations noticed. Take the utter absence of response of a dog or a savage to the greater mass of environing relations. How can you alter it unless you previously *awaken an interest—i.e.*, produce a susceptibility to intellectual pleasure in certain modes of cognitive exercise? Interests, then, are an all-essential factor which no writer pretending to give an account of mental evolution has a right to neglect.

taneity. The mind, according to his philosophy, should be pure product, absolute derivative from the non-mental. To make it dictate conditions, bring independent interests into the game which may determine what we shall call correspondence, and what not, might, at first sight, appear contrary to the notion of evolution which forbids the introduction at any point of an absolutely new factor. In what sense the existence of survival interest does postulate such a factor we shall hereafter see. I think myself that it is possible to express all its outward results in non-mental terms. But the unedifying look of the thing, its simulation of an independent mental teleology, seems to have frightened Mr. Spencer here, as elsewhere, away from a serious scrutiny of the facts. But let us be indulgent to his timidity, and assume that survival was all the while a 'mental reservation' with him, only excluded from his formula by reason of the comforting sound it might have to Philistine ears.

We should then have, as the embodiment of the highest ideal perfection of mental development, a creature of superb cognitive endowments, from whose piercing perceptions no fact was too minute or too remote to escape; whose all-embracing foresight no contingency could find unprepared; whose invincible flexibility of resource no array of outward onslaught could overpower; but in whom all these gifts were swayed by the single passion of love of life, of survival at any price. This determination filling his whole energetic being, consciously realized, intensified by meditation, becomes a fixed idea, would use all the other faculties as its means, and, if they ever flagged, would by its imperious intensity spur them and hound them on to ever fresh exertions and achievements. There can be no doubt that, if such an incarnation of earthly prudence existed, a race of beings in whom this monotonously narrow passion for self-preservation were aided by every cognitive gift, they would soon be kings of all the earth. All known human races would wither before their breath, and be as dust beneath their conquering feet.

But whether any Spencerian would hail with hearty joy their advent is another matter. Certainly Mr. Spencer would not; while the common sense of mankind would stand aghast at the thought of them. Why does common opinion abhor such a being? Why does it crave greater 'richness' of nature in its mental ideal? Simply because, to common sense, survival is only one out of many interests—*primus inter pares,* perhaps, but still in the midst of peers. What are these interests? Most men would reply that they are all that makes survival worth securing. The social affections, all the various forms of play, the thrilling intimations of art, the delights of philosophic contemplation, the rest of religious emotion, the joy of moral self-approbation, the charm of fancy and of wit—some or all of these are absolutely required to make the notion of mere existence tolerable; and individuals who, by their special powers, satisfy these desires are protected by their fellows and enabled to survive; though their mental constitution should in other respects be lamentably ill-'adjusted' to the outward world. The story-teller, the musician, the theologian, the actor, or even the mere charming fellow, have never lacked means of support, however helpless they might individually have been to conform with those outward relations which we know as the powers of nature. The reason is very plain. To the individual man, as a social being, the interests of his fellow are a part of his environment. If his powers correspond to the wants of this social environment, he may survive, even though he be ill-adapted to the natural or 'outer' environment. But these wants are pure subjective ideals, with nothing outward to correspond to them. So that, as far as the individual is concerned, it becomes necessary to modify Spencer's survival formula still further, by introducing into the term environment a reference, not only to existent things, but also to ideal wants. It would have to run in some such way as this: "Excellence of the individual mind consists in the establishment of inner relations more and more extensively conformed to the outward facts of nature, and to the ideal wants of the individual's fellows, but all of such a character as will promote survival or physical prosperity."

But here, again, common sense will meet us with an objection. Mankind desiderate certain qualities in the individual which are incompatible with his chance of survival being a maximum. Why do we all so eulogize and love the heroic, recklessly generous, and disinterested type of character? These qualities certainly imperil the survival of their possessor. The reason is very plain. Even if headlong courage, pride, and martyr-spirit do ruin the individual, they benefit the community as a whole whenever they are displayed by one of its members against a competing tribe. "It is death to you, but fun for us." Our interest in having the hero as he is, plays indirectly into the hands of our survival, though not of his.

This explicit acknowledgment of the survival interests of the tribe, as accounting for many interests in the individual which seem at first sight either unrelated to survival or at war with it, seems, after all, to bring back unity and simplicity into the Spencerian formula. Why, the Spencerian may ask, may not all the luxuriant foliage of ideal interests—aesthetic, philosophic, theologic, and the rest—which co-exist along with that of survival, be present in the tribe and so form part of the individual's environment, merely by virtue of the fact that they minister in an indirect way to the survival of the tribe as a whole? The disinterested scientific appetite of cognition, the sacred philosophic love of consistency, the craving for luxury and beauty, the passion for amusement, may all find their proper significance as processes of mind, strictly so-called, in the incidental utilitarian discoveries which flow from the energy they set in motion. Conscience, thoroughness, purity, love of truth, susceptibility to discipline, eager delight in fresh impressions, although none of them are traits of Intelligence *in se,* may thus be marks of a general mental energy, without which victory over nature and over other human competitors would be impossible. And, as victory means survival, and survival is the criterion of Intelligent 'Correspondence,' these qualities, though not expressed in the fundamental law of mind, may yet have been all the while understood by Mr. Spencer to form so many secondary consequences and corollaries of that law.

But here it is decidedly time to take our stand and refuse our aid in propping up Mr. Spencer's definition by any further good-natured translations and supplementary contributions of our own. It is palpable at a glance that a mind whose survival interest could only be adequately secured by such a wasteful array of energy squandered on side issues would be immeasurably inferior to one like that which we supposed a few pages back, in which the monomania of tribal preservation should be the one all-devouring passion.

Surely there is nothing in the essence of intelligence which should oblige it forever to delude itself as to its own ends, and to strive towards a goal successfully only at the cost of consciously appearing to have far other aspirations in view.

A furnace which should produce along with its metal fifty different varieties of ash and slag, a planing-mill whose daily yield in shavings far exceeded that in boards, would rightly be pronounced inferior to one of the usual sort, even though more energy should be displayed in its working, and at moments some of that energy be directly effective. If ministry to survival be the sole criterion of mental excellence, then luxury and amusement, Shakespeare, Beethoven, Plato, and Marcus Aurelius, stellar spectroscopy, diatom markings, and nebular hypotheses are by-products on too wasteful a scale. The slag-heap is too big—it abstracts more energy than it contributes to the ends of the machine; and every serious evolutionist ought resolutely to bend his attention henceforward to the reduction in number and amount of these outlying interests, and the diversion of the energy they absorb into purely prudential channels.

Here, then, is our dilemma: One man may say that the law of mental development is dominated solely by the principle of conservation; another, that richness is the criterion of mental evolution; a third, that pure cognition of the actual is the essence of worthy thinking—but who shall pretend to decide which is right? The umpire would have to bring a standard of his own upon the scene, which would be just as subjective and personal as the standards used by the contestants. And yet some standard there must be, if we are to attempt to define in any way the worth of different mental manifestations.

Is it not already clear to the reader's mind that the whole difficulty in making Mr. Spencer's law work lies in the fact that it is not really a constitutive, but a regulative, law of thought which he is erecting, and that he does not frankly say so? Every law of Mind must be either a law of the *cogitatum* or a law of the *cogitandum*. If it be a law in the sense of an analysis of what we *do* think, then it will include error, nonsense, the worthless as well as the worthy, metaphysics, and mythologies as well as scientific truths which mirror the actual environment. But such a law of the *cogitatum* is already well known. It is no other than the association of ideas according to their several modes; or, rather, it is this association definitively perfected by the inclusion of the teleolog-

ical factor of interest by Mr. Hodgson in the fifth chapter of his
masterly *Time and Space*.

That Mr. Spencer, in the part of his work which we are considering, has no such law as this in view is evident from the fact
that he has striven to give an original formulation to such a law in
another part of his book,[2] in that chapter, namely, on the associ-
ability of relations, in the first volume, where the apperception of
times and places, and the suppression of association by similarity,
are made to explain the facts in a way whose operose ineptitude
has puzzled many a simple reader.

Now, every living man would instantly define right thinking as
thinking in correspondence with reality. But Spencer, in saying
that right thought is that which conforms to existent outward
relations, and this exclusively, undertakes to decide what the
reality *is*. In other words, under cover of an apparently formal
definition he really smuggles in a material definition of the most
far-reaching import. For the Stoic, to whom *vivere convenienter
naturæ* was also the law of mind, the reality was an archetypal
Nature; for the Christian, whose mental law is to discover the will
of God, and make one's actions correspond thereto, *that* is the
reality. In fact, the philosophic problem which all the ages have
been trying to solve in order to make thought in some way correspond with it, and which disbelievers in philosophy call in-
soluble, is just that: What is the reality? All the thinking, all the
conflict of ideals, going on in the world at the present moment is
in some way tributary to this quest. To attempt, therefore, with
Mr. Spencer, to decide the matter merely incidentally, to forestall
discussion by a definition—to carry the position by surprise, in a
word—is a proceeding savoring more of piracy than philosophy.
No, Spencer's definition of what we ought to think cannot be
suffered to lurk in ambush; it must stand out explicitly with the
rest, and expect to be challenged and give an account of itself like
any other ideal norm of thought.

We have seen how he seems to vacillate in his determination of
it. At one time, 'scientific' thought, mere passive mirroring of
outward nature, purely registrative cognition; at another time,
thought in the exclusive service of survival, would seem to be his

2. H. Spencer, *Principles of Psychology* (sic) , 1855. [B.W.]

ideal. Let us consider the latter ideal first, since it has the polyp's authority in its favor: "We must survive—that end must regulate all our thought." The poor man who said to Talleyrand, *"Il faut bien que je vive!"* expressed it very well. But criticise this ideal, or transcend it as Talleyrand did by his cool reply, *"Je n'en vois pas la nécessité,"* and it can say nothing more for itself. *A priori* it is a mere brute teleological affirmation on a par with all others. Vainly you should hope to prove it to a person bent on suicide, who has but the one longing—to escape, to cease. Vainly you would argue with a Buddhist or a German pessimist, for they feel the full imperious strength of the desire, but have an equally profound persuasion of its essential wrongness and mendacity. Vainly, too, would you talk to a Christian, or even to any believer in the simple creed that the deepest meaning of the world is moral. For they hold that mere conformity with the outward—worldly success and survival—is not the absolute and exclusive end. In the *failures* to 'adjust'—in the rubbish-heap, according to Spencer—lies, for them, the real key to the truth—the sole mission of life being to teach that the outward actual is not the whole of being.

And now—if, falling back on the scientific ideal, you say that to *know* is the one τέλος of intelligence—not only will the inimitable Turkish cadi in Layard's Nineveh praise God in your face that he seeks not that which he requires not, and ask, "Will much knowledge create thee a double belly?"—not only may I, if it please me, legitimately refuse to stir from my fool's paradise of theosophy and mysticism, in spite of all your calling (since, after all, your true knowledge and my pious feeling have alike nothing to back them save their seeming good to our respective personalities) —not only this, but to the average sense of mankind, whose ideal of mental nature is best expressed by the word 'richness,' your statistical and cognitive intelligence will seem insufferably narrow, dry, tedious, and unacceptable.

The truth appears to be that every individual man may, if it please him, set up his private categorical imperative of what rightness or excellence in thought shall consist in, and these different ideals, instead of entering upon the scene armed with a warrant—whether derived from the polyp or from a transcendental source—appear only as so many brute affirmations left to fight it out upon the chessboard among themselves. They are, at best, postulates, each of which must depend on the general consensus of experience as a whole to bear out its validity. The formula which proves to have the most massive destiny will be the true one. But this is a point which can only be solved *ambulando,* and not by any *a priori* definition. The attempt to forestall the decision is free to all to make, but all make it at their risk. Our respective hypotheses and postulates help to shape the course of thought, but the only thing which we all agree in assuming is, that thought will be coerced away from them if they are wrong. If Spencer to-day says, "Bow to the actual," whilst Swinburne spurns "compromise with the nature of things," I exclaim, *"Fiat justitia, pereat mundus,"* and Mill says, "To hell I will go, rather than 'adjust' myself to an evil God," what umpire can there be between us but the future? The idealists and the empiricists confront each other like Guelphs and Ghibellines, but each alike waits for adoption, as it were, by the course of events.

In other words, we are all fated to be *a priori* teleologists whether we will or not. Interests which we bring with us, and simply posit or take our stand upon, are the very flour out of which our mental dough is kneaded. The organism of thought, from the vague dawn of discomfort or ease in the polyp to the intellectual joy of Laplace among his formulas, is teleological through and through. Not a cognition occurs but feeling is there to comment on it, to stamp it as of greater or less worth. Spencer and Plato are *ejusdem farinæ.* To attempt to hoodwink teleology out of sight by saying nothing about it, is the vainest of procedures. Spencer merely takes sides with the τέλος he happens to prefer, whether it be that of physical well-being or that of cognitive registration. He represents a particular teleology. Well might teleology (had she a voice) exclaim with Emerson's Brahma:

> "If the red slayer think he slays,
>   Or if the slain think he is slain,
> They know not well the subtle ways
>   I keep, and pass and turn again.
>   .   .   .   .   .   .
> "They reckon ill who leave me out;
>   When me they fly, I am the wings;
> I am the doubter and the doubt." . . .

But now a scientific man, feeling something uncanny in this omnipresence of a teleological factor dictating *how* the mind shall correspond—an interest seemingly tributary to nothing non-mental—may ask us what we meant by saying sometime back that in one sense it is perfectly possible to express the existence of interests in non-mental terms. We meant simply this: That the reactions or outward consequences of the interests could be so expressed. The interest of survival which has hitherto been treated as an ideal *should-be,* presiding from the start and marking out the way in which an animal must react, is, from an outward and physical point of view, nothing more than an objective future implication of the reaction (if it occurs) as an actual fact. If the animal's brain acts fortuitously in the right way, he survives. His young do the same. The reference to survival in no way preceded or conditioned the intelligent act; but the fact of survival was merely bound up with it as an incidental consequence, and may, therefore, be called accidental, rather than instrumental, to the production of intelligence. It is the same with all other interests. They are pleasures and pains incidentally implied in the workings of the nervous mechanism, and, therefore, in their ultimate origin, non-mental; for the idiosyncrasies of our nervous centres are mere 'spontaneous variations,' like any of those which form the ultimate data for Darwin's theory. A brain which functions so as to insure survival may, therefore, be called intelligent in no other sense than a tooth, a limb, or a stomach, which should serve the same end—the sense, namely, of appropriate; as when we say 'that is an intelligent device,' meaning a device fitted to secure a certain end which we assume. If *nirvana* were the end, instead of survival, then it is true the means would be different, but in both cases alike the end would not precede the means, or even be coeval with them, but depend utterly upon them, and follow them in point of time. The fox's cunning and the hare's speed are thus alike creations of the non-mental. The τέλος they entail is no more an agent in one case than another, since in both alike it is a resultant. Spencer, then, seems justified in not admitting it to appear as an irreducible ultimate factor of Mind, any more than of Body.

This position is perfectly unassailable so long as one describes the phenomena in this manner from without. The τέλος in that case can only be hypothetically, not imperatively, stated: *if* such and such be the end, then such brain functions are the most intelligent, just as such and such digestive functions are the most appropriate. But such and such cannot be declared *as* the end, except by the commenting mind of an outside spectator. The organs themselves, in their working at any instant, cannot but be supposed indifferent as to what product they are destined fatally to bring forth; cannot be imagined whilst fatally producing one result to have at the same time a notion of a different result which should be their truer end, but which they are unable to secure.

Nothing can more strikingly show, it seems to me, the essential difference between the point of view of consciousness and that of outward existence. We can describe the latter only in teleological terms, hypothetically, or else by the addition of a supposed contemplating mind which measures what it sees going on by its private teleological standard, and judges it intelligent. But consciousness itself is not merely intelligent in this sense. It is *intelligent intelligence*. It seems both to supply the means and the standard by which they are measured. It not only *serves* a final purpose, but *brings* a final purpose—posits, declares it. This purpose is not a mere hypothesis—'*if* survival is to occur, then brain must so perform,' etc.—but an imperative decree: 'Survival *shall* occur, and, therefore, brain *must* so perform!' It seems hopelessly impossible to formulate anything of this sort in non-mental terms, and this is why I must still contend that the phenomena of subjective 'interest,' as soon as the animal consciously realizes the latter, appears upon the scene as an absolutely new factor, which we can only suppose to be latent thitherto in the physical environment by crediting the physical atoms, etc., each with a consciousness of its own, approving or condemning its motions.

This, then, must be our conclusion: That no law of the *cogitandum*, no normative receipt for excellence in thinking, can be authoritatively promulgated. The only formal canon that we can apply to mind which is unassailable is the barren truism that it must think rightly. We can express this in terms of correspondence by saying that thought must correspond with truth; but whether that truth be actual or ideal is left undecided.

We have seen that the invocation of the polyp to decide for us that it is actual (apart from the fact that he does not decide in that way) is based on a principle which refutes itself if consistently carried out. Spencer's formula has crumbled into utter worthlessness in our hands, and we have nothing to replace it by except our several individual hypotheses, convictions, and beliefs. Far from being vouched for by the past, these are verified only by the future. They are all of them, in some sense, laws of the ideal. They have to keep house together, and the weakest goes to the wall. The survivors constitute the right way of thinking. While the issue is still undecided, we can only call them our prepossessions. But, decided or not, 'go on' we each must for one set of interests or another. The question for each of us in the battle of life is, "Can we *come out* with it?" Some of these interests admit to-day of little dispute. Survival, physical well-being, and undistorted cognition of what is, will hold their ground. But it is truly strange to see writers like Messrs. Huxley and Clifford, who show themselves able to call most things in question, unable, when it comes to the interest of cognition, to touch it with their solvent doubt. They assume some mysterious imperative laid upon the mind, declaring that the infinite ascertainment of facts is its supreme duty, which he who evades is a blasphemer and child of shame. And yet these authors can hardly have failed to reflect, at some moment or other, that the disinterested love of information, and still more the love of consistency in thought (that true scientific *æstrus*), and the ideal fealty to Truth (with a capital T), are all so many particular forms of aesthetic interest, late in their evolution, arising in conjunction with a vast number of similar aesthetic interests, and bearing with them no *a priori* mark of being worthier than these. If we may doubt one, we may doubt all. How shall I say that knowing fact with Messrs. Huxley and Clifford is a better use to put my mind to than feeling good with Messrs. Moody and Sankey, unless by slowly and painfully finding out that in the long run it works best?

I, for my part, cannot escape the consideration, forced upon me at every turn, that the knower is not simply a mirror floating with no foot-hold anywhere, and passively reflecting an order that he comes upon and finds simply existing. The knower is an actor, and coefficient of the truth on one side, whilst on the other he registers the truth which he helps to create. Mental interests, hypotheses, postulates, so far as they are bases for human action—action which to a great extent transforms the world—help to *make* the truth which they declare. In other words, there belongs to mind, from its birth upward, a spontaneity, a vote. It is in the game, and not a mere looker-on; and its judgments of the *should-be*, its ideals, cannot be peeled off from the body of the *cogitandum* as if they were excrescences, or meant, at most, survival. We know so little about the ultimate nature of things, or of ourselves, that it would be sheer folly dogmatically to say that an ideal rational order may not be real. The only objective criterion of reality is coerciveness, in the long run, over thought. Objective facts, Spencer's outward relations, are real only because they coerce sensation. Any interest which should be coercive on the same massive scale would be *eodem jure* real. By its very essence, the reality of a thought is proportionate to the way it grasps us. Its intensity, its seriousness— its interest, in a word—taking these qualities, not at any given instant, but as shown by the total upshot of experience. If judgments of the *should-be* are fated to grasp us in this way, they are what 'correspond.' The ancients placed the conception of Fate at the bottom of things—deeper than the gods themselves. 'The fate of thought,' utterly barren and indeterminate as such a formula is, is the only unimpeachable regulative Law of Mind.

3.

The Sentiment of Rationality*

. . . When, for example, we think that we have rationally explained the connection of the facts A and B by classing both under their common attribute x, it is obvious that we have really explained only so much of these items as *is* x. To explain the connection of choke-damp and suffocation by the lack of oxygen is to leave untouched all the other peculiarities both of choke-damp and of suffocation,—such as convulsions and agony on the one hand, density and explosibility on the other. In a word, so far as A and B contain l, m, n, and o, p, q, respectively, in addition to x, they are not explained by x. Each additional particularity makes its distinct appeal. A single explanation of a fact only explains it from a single point of view. The entire fact is not accounted for until each and all of its characters have been classed with their likes elsewhere. To apply this now to the case of the universe, we see that the explanation of the world by molecular movements explains it only so far as it actually *is* such movements. To invoke the 'Unknowable' explains only so much as is unknowable, 'Thought' only so much as is thought, 'God' only so much as is God. *Which* thought? *Which* God?—are questions that have to be answered by bringing in again the residual data from which the general term was abstracted. All those data that cannot be analytically identified with the attribute invoked as universal principle, remain as independent kinds or natures, associated empirically with the said attribute but devoid of rational kinship with it.

Hence the unsatisfactoriness of all our speculations. On the one hand, so far as they retain any multiplicity in their terms, they fail

* *The Will to Believe and Other Essays in Popular Philosophy* (New York and London: Longmans, Green & Co., 1897). This essay as far as p. 30 is extracted from an article published in 1879 (*Mind*, 4, 317–346). The portion that follows was published in 1882 (*Princeton Review*, 2, 58–86).

to get us out of the empirical sand-heap world; on the other, so far as they eliminate multiplicity, the practical man despises their empty barrenness. The most they can say is that the elements of the world are such and such, and that each is identical with itself wherever found; but the question Where is it found? the practical man is left to answer by his own wit. Which, of all the essences, shall here and now be held the essence of this concrete thing, the fundamental philosophy never attempts to decide. We are thus led to the conclusion that the simple classification of things is, on the one hand, the best possible theoretic philosophy, but is, on the other, a most miserable and inadequate substitute for the fulness of the truth. It is a monstrous abridgment of life, which, like all abridgments is got by the absolute loss and casting out of real matter. This is why so few human beings truly care for philosophy. The particular determinations which she ignores are the real matter exciting needs, quite as potent and authoritative as hers. What does the moral enthusiast care for philosophical ethics? Why does the *Æsthetik* of every German philosopher appear to the artist an abomination of desolation?

> Grau, theurer Freund, ist alle Theorie
> Und grün des Lebens goldner Baum.

The entire man, who feels all needs by turns, will take nothing as an equivalent for life but the fulness of living itself. Since the essences of things are as a matter of fact disseminated through the whole extent of time and space, it is in their spread-outness and alternation that he will enjoy them. When weary of the concrete clash and dust and pettiness, he will refresh himself by a bath in the eternal springs, or fortify himself by a look at the immutable natures. But he will only be a visitor, not a dweller in the region; he will never carry the philosophic yoke upon his shoulders, and when tired of the gray monotony of her problems and insipid spaciousness of her results, will always escape gleefully into the teeming and dramatic richness of the concrete world.

So our study turns back here to its beginning. Every way of classifying a thing is but a way of handling it for some particular purpose. Conceptions, 'kinds,' are teleological instruments. No abstract concept can be a valid substitute for a concrete reality except with reference to a particular interest in the conceiver. The interest of theoretic rationality, the relief of identification, is but one of a thousand human purposes. When others rear their heads, it must pack up its little bundle and retire till its turn recurs. The exaggerated dignity and value that philosophers have claimed for their solutions is thus greatly reduced. The only virtue their theoretic conception need have is simplicity, and a simple conception is an equivalent for the world only so far as the world is simple—the world meanwhile, whatever simplicity it may harbor, being also a mightily complex affair. Enough simplicity remains, however, and enough urgency in our craving to reach it, to make the theoretic function one of the most invincible of human impulses. The quest of the fewest elements of things is an ideal that some will follow, as long as there are men to think at all.

But suppose the goal attained. Suppose that at last we have a system unified in the sense that has been explained. Our world can now be conceived simply, and our mind enjoys the relief. Our universal concept has made the concrete chaos rational. But now I ask, Can that which is the ground of rationality in all else be itself properly called rational? It would seem at first sight that it might. One is tempted at any rate to say that, since the craving for rationality is appeased by the identification of one thing with another, a datum which left nothing else outstanding might quench that craving definitively, or be rational *in se*. No otherness being left to annoy us, we should sit down at peace. . . .

But, unfortunately, this first answer will not hold. Our mind is so wedded to the process of seeing an *other* beside every item of its experience, that when the notion of an absolute datum is presented to it, it goes through its usual procedure and remains pointing at the void beyond, as if in that lay further matter for contemplation. In short, it spins for itself the further positive consideration of a nonentity enveloping the being of its datum; and as that leads nowhere, back recoils the thought toward its datum again. But there is no natural bridge between nonentity and this particular datum, and the thought stands oscillating to and fro, wondering "Why was there anything but nonentity; why just this universal datum and not another?" and finds no end, in wandering mazes lost. Indeed, . . . in reflecting men it is just when the attempt to fuse the manifold into a single totality has been most successful, when the conception of the universe as a unique fact is nearest its perfection, that the craving for further explanation, the ontological wonder-sickness, arises in its extremest form. As Schopenhauer says, "The uneasiness which keeps the never-resting clock of metaphysics in motion, is the consciousness that the non-existence of this world is just as possible as its existence."

The notion of nonentity may thus be called the parent of the philosophic craving in its subtilest and profoundest sense. Absolute existence is absolute mystery, for its relations with the nothing remain unmediated to our understanding. One philosopher only has pretended to throw a logical bridge over this chasm. Hegel, by trying to show that nonentity and concrete being are linked together by a series of identities of a synthetic kind, binds everything conceivable into a unity, with no outlying notion to disturb the free rotary circulation of the mind within its bounds. Since such unchecked movement gives the feeling of rationality, he must be held, if he has succeeded, to have eternally and absolutely quenched all rational demands.

But for those who deem Hegel's heroic effort to have failed, nought remains but to confess that when all things have been unified to the supreme degree, the notion of a possible, other than the actual, may still haunt our imagination and prey upon our system. The bottom of being is left logically opaque to us, as something which we simply come upon and find, and about which (if we wish to act) we should pause and wonder as little as possible. The philosopher's logical tranquillity is thus in essence no other than the boor's. They differ only as to the point at which each refuses to let further considerations upset the absoluteness of the data he assumes. The boor does so immediately, and is liable at any moment to the ravages of many kinds of doubt. The philosopher does not do so till unity has been reached, and is warranted against the inroads of those considerations, but only practically, not essentially, secure from the blighting breath of the ultimate Why? If he cannot exorcise this question, he must ignore or blink it, and, assuming the data of his system as something given, and the gift as ultimate, simply proceed to a life of contemplation or of action based on it. There is no doubt that this acting on an opaque necessity is accompanied by a certain pleasure. See the

reverence of Carlyle for brute fact: "There is an infinite significance in fact." "Necessity," says Dühring, and he means not rational but given necessity, "is the last and highest point that we
can reach. . . . It is not only the interest of ultimate and definitive knowledge, but also that of the feelings, to find a last repose
and an ideal equilibrium in an uttermost datum which can simply
not be other than it is."

Such is the attitude of ordinary men in their theism, God's fiat
being in physics and morals such an uttermost datum. Such also is
the attitude of all hard-minded analysts and *Verstandesmenschen.*
Lotze, Renouvier, and Hodgson promptly say that of experience as
a whole no account can be given, but neither seek to soften the
abruptness of the confession nor to reconcile us with our impotence.

But mediating attempts may be made by more mystical minds.
The peace of rationality may be sought through ecstasy when logic
fails. To religious persons of every shade of doctrine moments
come when the world, as it is, seems so divinely orderly, and the
acceptance of it by the heart so rapturously complete, that intellectual questions vanish; nay, the intellect itself is hushed to
sleep—as Wordsworth says, "thought is not; in enjoyment it
expires." Ontological emotion so fills the soul that ontological
speculation can no longer overlap it and put her girdle of inter-
rogation-marks round existence. Even the least religious of men
must have felt with Walt Whitman, when loafing on the grass on
some transparent summer morning, that "swiftly arose and spread
round him the peace and knowledge that pass all the argument of
the earth." At such moments of energetic living we feel as if there
were something diseased and contemptible, yea vile, in theoretic
grubbing and brooding. In the eye of healthy sense the philosopher is at best a learned fool.

Since the heart can thus wall out the ultimate irrationality
which the head ascertains, the erection of its procedure into a
systematized method would be a philosophic achievement of first-
rate importance. But as used by mystics hitherto it has lacked
universality, being available for few persons and at few times,
and even in these being apt to be followed by fits of reaction and
dryness; and if men should agree that the mystical method is a

subterfuge without logical pertinency, a plaster but no cure, and that the idea of nonentity can never be exorcised, empiricism will be the ultimate philosophy. Existence then will be a brute fact to which as a whole the emotion of ontologic wonder shall rightfully cleave, but remain eternally unsatisfied. Then wonderfulness or mysteriousness will be an essential attribute of the nature of things, and the exhibition and emphasizing of it will continue to be an ingredient in the philosophic industry of the race. Every generation will produce its Job, its Hamlet, its Faust, or its Sartor Resartus.

With this we seem to have considered the possibilities of purely theoretic rationality. But we saw at the outset that rationality meant only unimpeded mental function. Impediments that arise in the theoretic sphere might perhaps be avoided if the stream of mental action should leave that sphere betimes and pass into the practical. Let us therefore inquire what constitutes the feeling of rationality in its *practical* aspect. If thought is not to stand forever pointing at the universe in wonder, if its movement is to be diverted from the issueless channel of purely theoretic contemplation, let us ask what conception of the universe will awaken active impulses capable of effecting this diversion. A definition of the world which will give back to the mind the free motion which has been blocked in the purely contemplative path may so far make the world seem rational again.

Well, of two conceptions equally fit to satisfy the logical demand, that one which awakens the active impulses, or satisfies other æsthetic demands better than the other, will be accounted the more rational conception, and will deservedly prevail.

There is something improbable in the supposition that an analysis of the world may yield a number of formulæ, all consistent with the facts. In physical science different formulæ may explain the phenomena equally well—the one-fluid and the two-fluid theories of electricity, for example. Why may it not be so with the world? Why may there not be different points of view for surveying it, within each of which all data harmonize, and which the observer may therefore either choose between, or simply cumulate one upon another? A Beethoven string-quartet is truly, as some one has said, a scraping of horses' tails on cats' bowels, and may be exhaustively described in such terms; but the application of this description in no way precludes the simultaneous applicability of an entirely different description. Just so a thoroughgoing interpretation of the world in terms of mechanical sequence is compatible with its being interpreted teleologically, for the mechanism itself may be designed.

If, then, there were several systems excogitated, equally satisfying to our purely logical needs, they would still have to be passed in review, and approved or rejected by our æsthetic and practical nature. Can we define the tests of rationality which these parts of our nature would use?

Philosophers long ago observed the remarkable fact that mere familiarity with things is able to produce a feeling of their rationality. The empiricist school has been so much struck by this circumstance as to have laid it down that the feeling of rationality and the feeling of familiarity are one and the same thing, and that no other kind of rationality than this exists. The daily contemplation of phenomena juxtaposed in a certain order begets an acceptance of their connection, as absolute as the repose engendered by theoretic insight into their coherence. To explain a thing is to pass easily back to its antecedents; to know it is easily to foresee its consequents. Custom, which lets us do both, is thus the source of whatever rationality the thing may gain in our thought.

In the broad sense in which rationality was defined at the outset of this essay, it is perfectly apparent that custom must be one of its factors. We said that any perfectly fluent and easy thought was devoid of the sentiment of irrationality. Inasmuch then as custom acquaints us with all the relations of a thing, it teaches us to pass fluently from that thing to others, and *pro tanto* tinges it with the rational character.

Now, there is one particular relation of greater practical importance than all the rest—I mean the relation of a thing to its future consequences. So long as an object is unusual, our expectations are baffled; they are fully determined as soon as it becomes familiar. I therefore propose this as the first practical requisite which a philosophic conception must satisfy: *It must, in a general way at least, banish uncertainty from the future.* The permanent presence of the sense of futurity in the mind has been strangely ignored by most writers, but the fact is that our consciousness at a given moment is never free from the ingredient of expectancy. Every one knows how when a painful thing has to be undergone in the near future, the vague feeling that it is impending penetrates all our thought with uneasiness and subtly vitiates our mood even when it does not control our attention; it keeps us from being at rest, at home in the given present. The same is true when a great happiness awaits us. But when the future is neutral and perfectly certain, 'we do not mind it,' as we say, but give an undisturbed attention to the actual. Let now this haunting sense of futurity be thrown off its bearings or left without an object, and immediately uneasiness takes possession of the mind. But in every novel or unclassified experience this is just what occurs; we do not know what will come next; and novelty *per se* becomes a mental irritant, while custom *per se* is a mental sedative, merely because the one baffles while the other settles our expectations.

Every reader must feel the truth of this. What is meant by coming 'to feel at home' in a new place, or with new people? It is simply that, at first, when we take up our quarters in a new room, we do not know what draughts may blow in upon our back, what doors may open, what forms may enter, what interesting objects may be found in cupboards and corners. When after a few days we have learned the range of all these possibilities, the feeling of strangeness disappears. And so it does with people, when we have got past the point of expecting any essentially new manifestations from their character.

The utility of this emotional effect of expectation is perfectly obvious; 'natural selection,' in fact, was bound to bring it about sooner or later. It is of the utmost practical importance to an animal that he should have prevision of the qualities of the objects that surround him, and especially that he should not come to rest in presence of circumstances that might be fraught either with peril or advantage—go to sleep, for example, on the brink of precipices, in the dens of enemies, or view with indifference some new-appearing object that might, if chased, prove an important addition to the larder. Novelty *ought* to irritate him. All curiosity has thus a practical genesis. We need only look at the physiognomy of a dog or a horse when a new object comes into his view, his mingled fascination and fear, to see that the element of conscious insecurity or perplexed expectation lies at the root of his emotion. A dog's curiosity about the movements of his master or a strange object only extends as far as the point of deciding what is going to happen next. That settled, curiosity is quenched. The dog quoted by Darwin, whose behavior in presence of a newspaper moved by the wind seemed to testify to a sense 'of the supernatural,' was merely exhibiting the irritation of an uncertain future. A newspaper which could move spontaneously was in itself so unexpected that the poor brute could not tell what new wonders the next moment might bring forth.

To turn back now to philosophy. An ultimate datum, even though it be logically unrationalized, will, if its quality is such as to define expectancy, be peacefully accepted by the mind; while if it leave the least opportunity for ambiguity in the future, it will to that extent cause mental uneasiness if not distress. Now, in the ultimate explanations of the universe which the craving for rationality has elicited from the human mind, the demands of expectancy to be satisfied have always played a fundamental part. The term set up by philosophers as primordial has been one which banishes the incalculable. 'Substance,' for example, means, as Kant says, *das Beharrliche,* which will be as it has been, because its being is essential and eternal. And although we may not be able to prophesy in detail the future phenomena to which the substance shall give rise, we may set our minds at rest in a general way, when we have called the substance God, Perfection, Love, or Reason, by the reflection that whatever is in store for us can never at bottom be inconsistent with the character of this term; so that our attitude even toward the unexpected is in a general sense defined. Take again the notion of immortality, which for common people seems to be the touchstone of every philosophic or religious creed: what is this but a way of saying that the determination of expectancy is the essential factor of rationality? The wrath of science against miracles, of certain philosophers against the doctrine of free-will, has precisely the same root—dislike to admit any ultimate factor in things which may rout our prevision or upset the stability of our outlook.

Anti-substantialist writers strangely overlook this function in the doctrine of substance: "If there be such a *substratum*," says Mill, "suppose it at this instant miraculously annihilated, and let the sensations continue to occur in the same order, and how would the *substratum* be missed? By what signs should we be able to discover that its existence had terminated? Should we not have as much reason to believe that it still existed as we now have? And if we should not then be warranted in believing it, how can we be so now?" Truly enough, if we have already securely bagged our facts in a certain order, we can dispense with any further warrant for that order. But with regard to the facts yet to come the case is far different. It does not follow that if substance may be dropped from our conception of the irrecoverably past, it need be an equally empty complication to our notions of the future. Even if it were true that, for aught we know to the contrary, the substance might develop at any moment a wholly new set of attributes, the mere logical form of referring things to a substance would still (whether rightly or wrongly) remain accompanied by a feeling of rest and future confidence. In spite of the acutest nihilistic criticism, men will therefore always have a liking for any philosophy which explains things *per substantiam*.

A very natural reaction against the theosophizing conceit and hide-bound confidence in the upshot of things, which vulgarly optimistic minds display, has formed one factor of the scepticism of empiricists, who never cease to remind us of the reservoir of possibilities alien to our habitual experience which the cosmos may contain, and which, for any warrant we have to the contrary, may turn it inside out to-morrow. Agnostic substantialism like that of Mr. Spencer, whose Unknowable is not merely the unfathomable but the absolute-irrational, on which, if consistently represented in thought, it is of course impossible to count, performs the same function of rebuking a certain stagnancy and smugness in the manner in which the ordinary philistine feels his security. But considered as anything else than as reactions against an opposite excess, these philosophies of uncertainty cannot be acceptable; the general mind will fail to come to rest in their presence, and will seek for solutions of a more reassuring kind.

We may then, I think, with perfect confidence lay down as a first point gained in our inquiry, that a prime factor in the philosophic craving is the desire to have expectancy defined; and that no philosophy will definitively triumph which in an emphatic manner denies the possibility of gratifying this need.

We pass with this to the next great division of our topic. It is not sufficient for our satisfaction merely to know the future as determined, for it may be determined in either of many ways, agreeable or disagreeable. For a philosophy to succeed on a universal scale it must define the future *congruously with our spontaneous powers*. A philosophy may be unimpeachable in other respects, but either of two defects will be fatal to its universal acceptance. First, its ultimate principle must not be one that essentially baffles and disappoints our dearest desires and most cherished powers. A pessimistic principle like Schopenhauer's incurably vicious Will-substance, or Hartmann's wicked jack-of-all-trades the Unconscious, will perpetually call forth essays at other philosophies. Incompatibility of the future with their desires and active tendencies is, in fact, to most men a source of more fixed disquietude than uncertainty itself. Witness the attempts to overcome the 'problem of evil,' the 'mystery of pain.' There is no 'problem of good.'

But a second and worse defect in a philosophy than that of contradicting our active propensities is to give them no object whatever to press against. A philosophy whose principle is so incommensurate with our most intimate powers as to deny them all relevancy in universal affairs, as to annihilate their motives at one blow, will be even more unpopular than pessimism. Better face the enemy than the eternal Void! This is why materialism will always fail of universal adoption, however well it may fuse things into an atomistic unity, however clearly it may prophesy the future eternity. For materialism denies reality to the objects of almost all the impulses which we most cherish. The real *meaning* of the impulses, it says, is something which has no emotional interest for us whatever. Now, what is called 'extradition' is quite as characteristic of our emotions as of our senses: both point to an object as the cause of the present feeling. What an intensely objective reference lies in fear! In like manner an enraptured man and a dreary-feeling man are not simply aware of their subjective states; if they were, the force of their feelings would all evaporate. Both believe there is outward cause why they should feel as they do: either, "It is a glad world! how good life is!" or, "What a loathsome tedium is existence!" Any philosophy which annihilates the validity of the reference by explaining away its objects or translating them into terms of no emotional pertinency, leaves the mind with little to care or act for. This is the opposite condition from that of nightmare, but when acutely brought home to consciousness it produces a kindred horror. In nightmare we have motives to act, but no power; here we have powers, but no motives. A nameless *unheimlichkeit* comes over us at the thought of there being nothing eternal in our final purposes, in the objects of those loves and aspirations which are our deepest energies. The monstrously lopsided equation of the universe and its knower, which we postulate as the ideal of cognition, is perfectly paralleled by the no less lopsided equation of the universe and the *doer*. We demand in it a character for which our emotions and active propensities shall be a match. Small as we are, minute as is the point by which the cosmos impinges upon each one of us, each one desires to feel that his reaction at that point is congruous with the demands of the vast whole—that he balances the latter, so to speak, and is able to do what it expects of him.. But as his abilities to do lie wholly in the line of his natural propensities; as he enjoys reacting with such emotions as fortitude, hope, rapture, admiration, earnestness, and the like; and as he very unwillingly reacts with fear, disgust, despair, or doubt—a philosophy which should only legitimate emotions of the latter sort would be sure to leave the mind a prey to discontent and craving.

It is far too little recognized how entirely the intellect is built up of practical interests. The theory of evolution is beginning to do very good service by its reduction of all mentality to the type of reflex action. Cognition, in this view, is but a fleeting moment, a cross-section at a certain point, of what in its totality is a motor phenomenon. In the lower forms of life no one will pretend that cognition is anything more than a guide to appropriate action. The germinal question concerning things brought for the first time before consciousness is not the theoretic 'What is that?' but the practical 'Who goes there?' or rather, as Horwicz has admirably put it, 'What is to be done?'—'Was fang' ich an?' In all our discussions about the intelligence of lower animals, the only test we use is that of their *acting* as if for a purpose. Cognition, in short, is incomplete until discharged in act: and although it is true that the later mental development, which attains its maximum through the hypertrophied cerebrum of man, gives birth to a vast amount of theoretic activity over and above that which is immediately ministerial to practice, yet the earlier claim is only postponed, not effaced, and the active nature asserts its rights to the end.

When the cosmos in its totality is the object offered to consciousness, the relation is in no whit altered. React on it we must in some congenial way. It was a deep instinct in Schopenhauer which led him to reinforce his pessimistic argumentation by a running volley of invective against the practical man and his requirements. No hope for pessimism unless he is slain!

Helmholtz's immortal works on the eye and ear are to a great extent little more than a commentary on the law that practical utility wholly determines which parts of our sensations we shall be aware of, and which parts we shall ignore. We notice or discriminate an ingredient of sense only so far as we depend upon it to modify our actions. We *comprehend* a thing when we synthetize it by identity with another thing. But the other great department of our understanding, *acquaintance* (the two departments being recognized in all languages by the antithesis of such words as *wissen* and *kennen; scire* and *noscere,* etc.), what is that also but a synthesis—a synthesis of a passive perception with a certain tendency to reaction? We are acquainted with a thing as soon as we have learned how to behave toward it, or how to meet the behavior which we expect from it. Up to that point it is still 'strange' to us.

If there be anything at all in this view, it follows that however vaguely a philosopher may define the ultimate universal datum, he cannot be said to leave it unknown to us so long as he in the slightest degree pretends that our emotional or active attitude toward it should be of one sort rather than another. He who says, "life is real, life is earnest," however much he may speak of the fundamental mysteriousness of things, gives a distinct definition to that mysteriousness by ascribing to it the right to claim from us the particular mood called seriousness—which means the willingness to live with energy, though energy bring pain. The same is true of him who says that all is vanity. For indefinable as the predicate 'vanity' may be *in se,* it is clearly something that permits anæsthesia, mere escape from suffering, to be our rule of life. There can be no greater incongruity than for a disciple of Spencer to proclaim with one breath that the substance of things is unknowable, and with the next that the thought of it should inspire us with awe, reverence, and a willingness to add our co-operative push in the direction toward which its manifestations seem to be drifting. The unknowable may be unfathomed, but if it make such distinct demands upon our activity we surely are not ignorant of its essential quality. . . .

4.

The Will*

. . . Our volitional habits depend . . . first, on what the stock of
ideas is which we have; and, second, on the habitual coupling of
the several ideas with action or inaction respectively. How is it
when an alternative is presented to you for choice, and you are
uncertain what you ought to do? You first hesitate, and then you
deliberate. And in what does your deliberation consist? It consists
in trying to apperceive the case successively by a number of different ideas, which seem to fit it more or less, until at last you hit on
one which seems to fit it exactly. If that be an idea which is a
customary forerunner of action in you, which enters into one of
your maxims of positive behavior, your hesitation ceases, and you
act immediately. If, on the other hand, it be an idea which carries
inaction as its habitual result, if it ally itself with *prohibition,*
then you unhesitatingly refrain. The problem is, you see, to find
the right idea or conception for the case. This search for the right
conception may take days or weeks.

I spoke as if the action were easy when the conception once is
found. Often it is so, but it may be otherwise; and, when it is
otherwise, we find ourselves at the very centre of a moral situation,
into which I should now like you to look with me a little nearer.

The proper conception, the true head of classification, may be
hard to attain; or it may be one with which we have contracted no
settled habits of action. Or, again, the action to which it would
prompt may be dangerous and difficult; or else inaction may
appear deadly cold and negative when our impulsive feeling is
hot. In either of these latter cases it is hard to hold the right idea
steadily enough before the attention to let it exert its adequate
effects. Whether it be stimulative or inhibitive, it is *too reasonable*

* From *Talks to Teachers on Psychology and to Students on Some of Life's
Ideals* (New York: Henry Holt & Co., 1899) , chap. 15.

for us; and the more instinctive passional propensity then tends to extrude it from our consideration. We shy away from the thought of it. It twinkles and goes out the moment it appears in the margin of our consciousness; and we need a resolute effort of voluntary attention to drag it into the focus of the field, and to keep it there long enough for its associative and motor effects to be exerted. Every one knows only too well how the mind flinches from looking at considerations hostile to the reigning mood of feeling.

Once brought, however, in th's way to the centre of the field of consciousness, and held there, the reasonable idea will exert these effects inevitably; for the laws of connection between our consciousness and our nervous system provide for the action then taking place. Our moral effort, properly so called, terminates in our holding fast to the appropriate idea.

If, then, you are asked, *"In what does a moral act consist* when reduced to its simplest and most elementary form?" you can make only one reply. You can say that *it consists in the effort of attention by which we hold fast to an idea* which but for that effort of attention would be driven out of the mind by the other psychological tendencies that are there. *To think,* in short, is the secret of will, just as it is the secret of memory.

This comes out very clearly in the kind of excuse which we most frequently hear from persons who find themselves confronted by the sinfulness or harmfulness of some part of their behavior. "I never *thought,*" they say. "I never *thought* how mean the action was, I never *thought* of these abominable consequences." And what do we retort when they say this? We say: "Why *didn't* you think? What were you there for but to think?" And we read them a moral lecture on their irreflectiveness.

The hackneyed example of moral deliberation is the case of an habitual drunkard under temptation. He has made a resolve to reform, but he is now solicited again by the bottle. His moral triumph or failure literally consists in his finding the right *name* for the case. If he says that it is a case of not wasting good liquor already poured out, or a case of not being churlish and unsociable when in the midst of friends, or a case of learning something at last about a brand of whiskey which he never met before, or a case of celebrating a public holiday, or a case of stimulating himself to a more energetic resolve in favor of abstinence than any he has ever yet made, then he is lost. His choice of the wrong name seals his doom. But if, in spite of all the plausible good names with which his thirsty fancy so copiously furnishes him, he unwaveringly clings to the truer bad name, and apperceives the case as that of "being a drunkard, being a drunkard, being a drunkard," his feet are planted on the road to salvation. He saves himself by thinking rightly.

Thus are your pupils to be saved: first, by the stock of ideas with which you furnish them; second, by the amount of voluntary attention that they can exert in holding to the right ones, however unpalatable; and, third, by the several habits of acting definitely on these latter to which they have been successfully trained.

In all this the power of voluntarily attending is the point of the whole procedure. Just as a balance turns on its knife-edges, so on it our moral destiny turns. You remember that, when we were talking of the subject of attention, we discovered how much more intermittent and brief our acts of voluntary attention are than is commonly supposed. If they were all summed together, the time that they occupy would cover an almost incredibly small portion of our lives. But I also said, you will remember, that their brevity was not in proportion to their significance, and that I should return to the subject again. So I return to it now. It is not the mere size of a thing which constitutes its importance: it is its position in the organism to which it belongs. Our acts of voluntary attention, brief and fitful as they are, are nevertheless momentous and critical, determining us, as they do, to higher or lower destinies. The exercise of voluntary attention in the schoolroom must therefore be counted one of the most important points of training that take place there; and the first-rate teacher, by the keenness of the remoter interests which he is able to awaken, will provide abundant opportunities for its occurrence. I hope that you appreciate this now without any further explanation.

I have been accused of holding up before you, in the course of these talks, a mechanical and even a materialistic view of the mind. I have called it an organism and a machine. I have spoken of its reaction on the environment as the essential thing about it; and I have referred this, either openly or implicitly, to the construction of the nervous system. I have, in consequence, received notes from some of you, begging me to be more explicit on this point; and to let you know frankly whether I am a complete materialist, or not.

Now in these lectures I wish to be strictly practical and useful, and to keep free from all speculative complications. Nevertheless, I do not wish to leave any ambiguity about my own position; and I will therefore say, in order to avoid all misunderstanding, that in no sense do I count myself a materialist. I cannot see how such a thing as our consciousness can possibly be *produced* by a nervous machinery, though I can perfectly well see how, if 'ideas' do accompany the workings of the machinery, the *order* of the ideas might very well follow exactly the *order* of the machine's operations. Our habitual associations of ideas, trains of thought, and sequences of action, might thus be consequences of the succession of currents in our nervous systems. And the possible stock of ideas which a man's free spirit would have to choose from might depend exclusively on the native and acquired powers of his brain. If this were all, we might indeed adopt the fatalist conception which I sketched for you but a short while ago. Our ideas would be determined by brain currents, and these by purely mechanical laws.

But, after what we have just seen—namely, the part played by voluntary attention in volition—a belief in free will and purely spiritual causation is still open to us. The duration and amount of this attention *seem* within certain limits indeterminate. We *feel* as if we could make it really more or less, and as if our free action in this regard were a genuine critical point in nature—a point on which our destiny and that of others might hinge. The whole question of free will concentrates itself, then, at this same small point: "Is or is not the appearance of indetermination at this point an illusion?"

It is plain that such a question can be decided only by general analogies, and not by accurate observations. The free-willist believes the appearance to be a reality: the determinist believes that it is an illusion. I myself hold with the free-willists—not because I cannot conceive the fatalist theory clearly, or because I fail to understand its plausibility, but simply because, if free will *were* true, it would be absurd to have the belief in it fatally forced on our acceptance. Considering the inner fitness of things, one would rather think that the very first act of a will endowed with freedom should be to sustain the belief in the freedom itself. I accordingly believe freely in my freedom; I do so with the best of scientific consciences, knowing that the predetermination of the amount of my effort of attention can never receive objective proof, and hoping that, whether you follow my example in this respect or not, it will at least make you see that such psychological and psycho-physical theories as I hold do not necessarily force a man to become a fatalist or a materialist.

5.

From *The Principles of Psychology*

A.   THE STREAM OF THOUGHT*

We now begin our study of the mind from within. Most books start with sensations, as the simplest mental facts, and proceed synthetically, constructing each higher stage from those below it. But this is abandoning the empirical method of investigation. No one ever had a simple sensation by itself. Consciousness, from our natal day, is of a teeming multiplicity of objects and relations, and what we call simple sensations are results of discriminative attention, pushed often to a very high degree. It is astonishing what havoc is wrought in psychology by admitting at the outset apparently innocent suppositions, that nevertheless contain a flaw. The bad consequences develop themselves later on, and are irremediable, being woven through the whole texture of the work. The notion that sensations, being the simplest things, are the first things to take up in psychology is one of these suppositions. The only thing which psychology has a right to postulate at the outset is the fact of thinking itself, and that must first be taken up and analyzed. If sensations then prove to be amongst the elements of the thinking, we shall be no worse off as respects them than if we had taken them for granted at the start.

The first fact for us, then, as psychologists, is that thinking of some sort goes on. I use the word thinking, in accordance with what was [earlier] said, for every form of consciousness indiscriminately. If we could say in English 'it thinks,' as we say 'it rains' or 'it blows,' we should be stating the fact most simply and with the minimum of assumption. As we cannot, we must simply say that *thought goes on.*

---

* *The Principles of Psychology,* 2 vols. (New York: Henry Holt and Co., 1890), chap. 9. As the case with all selections from *The Principles,* portions of the text, and some footnotes of the remaining text, have been deleted. [B.W.]

FIVE CHARACTERS IN THOUGHT

How does it go on? We notice immediately five important characters in the process, of which it shall be the duty of the present
chapter to treat in a general way:

1. Every thought tends to be part of a personal consciousness.
2. Within each personal consciousness thought is always
changing.
3. Within each personal consciousness thought is sensibly continuous.
4. It always appears to deal with objects independent of itself.
5. It is interested in some parts of these objects to the exclusion
of others, and welcomes or rejects—*chooses* from among them, in a
word—all the while.

In considering these five points successively, we shall have to
plunge *in medias res* as regards our vocabulary, and use psychological terms which can only be adequately defined in later
chapters of the book. But every one knows what the terms mean in
a rough way; and it is only in a rough way that we are now to take
them. This chapter is like a painter's first charcoal sketch upon his
canvas, in which no niceties appear.

1. Thought Tends to Personal Form

When I say *every thought is part of a personal consciousness,*
'personal consciousness' is one of the terms in question. Its meaning we know so long as no one asks us to define it, but to give an
accurate account of it is the most difficult of philosophic tasks.
This task we must confront in the next chapter; here a preliminary word will suffice.

In this room—this lecture-room, say—there are a multitude of
thoughts, yours and mine, some of which cohere mutually, and
some not. They are as little each-for-itself and reciprocally independent as they are all-belonging-together. They are neither: no
one of them is separate, but each belongs with certain others and
with none beside. My thought belongs with my other thoughts,

and your thought with your other thoughts. Whether anywhere in the room there be a mere thought, which is nobody's thought, we have no means of ascertaining, for we have no experience of its like. The only states of consciousness that we naturally deal with are found in personal consciousnesses, minds, selves, concrete particular I's and you's.

Each of these minds keeps its own thoughts to itself. There is no giving or bartering between them. No thought even comes into direct *sight* of a thought in another personal consciousness than its own. Absolute insulation, irreducible pluralism, is the law. It seems as if the elementary psychic fact were not *thought* or *this thought* or *that thought,* but *my thought,* every thought being *owned.* Neither contemporaneity, nor proximity in space, nor similarity of quality and content are able to fuse thoughts together which are sundered by this barrier of belonging to different personal minds. The breaches between such thoughts are the most absolute breaches in nature. Every one will recognize this to be true, so long as the existence of *something* corresponding to the term 'personal mind' is all that is insisted on, without any particular view of its nature being implied. On these terms the personal self rather than the thought might be treated as the immediate datum in psychology. The universal conscious fact is not 'feelings and thoughts exist,' but 'I think' and 'I feel.' No psychology, at any rate, can question the *existence* of personal selves. The worst a psychology can do is so to interpret the nature of these selves as to rob them of their worth. A French writer, speaking of our ideas, says somewhere in a fit of anti-spiritualistic excitement that, misled by certain peculiarities which they display, we 'end by personifying' the procession which they make—such personification being regarded by him as a great philosophic blunder on our part. It could only be a blunder if the notion of personality meant something essentially different from anything to be found in the mental procession. But if that procession be itself the very 'original' of the notion of personality, to personify it cannot possibly be wrong. It is already personified. There are no marks of personality to be gathered *aliunde,* and then found lacking in the train of thought. It has them all already; so that to whatever farther analysis we may subject that form of personal selfhood under which thoughts appear, it is, and must remain, true that the thoughts which psychology studies do continually tend to appear as parts of personal selves.

I say 'tend to appear' rather than 'appear,' on account of . . . facts of subconscious personality, automatic writing, etc. . . . The buried feelings and thoughts proved now to exist in hysterical anæsthetics, in recipients of post-hypnotic suggestion, etc., themselves are parts of *secondary personal selves.* These selves are for the most part very stupid and contracted, and are cut off at ordinary times from communication with the regular and normal self of the individual; but still they form conscious unities, have continuous memories, speak, write, invent distinct names for themselves, or adopt names that are suggested; and, in short, are entirely worthy of that title of secondary personalities which is now commonly given them. According to M. Janet these secondary personalities are always abnormal, and result from the splitting of what ought to be a single complete self into two parts, of which one lurks in the background whilst the other appears on the surface as the only self the man or woman has. . . .

2. Thought Is in Constant Change

I do not mean necessarily that no one state of mind has any duration—even if true, that would be hard to establish. The change which I have more particularly in view is that which takes place in sensible intervals of time; and the result on which I wish to lay stress is this, that *no state once gone can recur and be identical with what it was before.* . . .

Does not the same piano-key, struck with the same force, make us hear in the same way? Does not the same grass give us the same feeling of green, the same sky the same feeling of blue, and do we not get the same olfactory sensation no matter how many times we put our nose to the same flask of cologne? It seems a piece of metaphysical sophistry to suggest that we do not; and yet a close attention to the matter shows that *there is no proof that the same bodily sensation is ever got by us twice.*

What is got twice is the same OBJECT. We hear the same *note* over and over again; we see the same *quality* of green, or smell the same objective perfume, or experience the same *species* of pain.

The realities, concrete and abstract, physical and ideal, whose permanent existence we believe in, seem to be constantly coming up again before our thought, and lead us, in our carelessness, to suppose that our 'ideas' of them are the same ideas. When we come, some time later, to the chapter on Perception, we shall see how inveterate is our habit of not attending to sensations as subjective facts, but of simply using them as stepping-stones to pass over to the recognition of the realities whose presence they reveal. The grass out of the window now looks to me of the same green in the sun as in the shade, and yet a painter would have to paint one part of it dark brown, another part bright yellow, to give its real sensational effect. We take no heed, as a rule, of the different way in which the same things look and sound and smell at different distances and under different circumstances. The sameness of the *things* is what we are concerned to ascertain; and any sensations that assure us of that will probably be considered in a rough way to be the same with each other. This is what makes off-hand testimony about the subjective identity of different sensations well-nigh worthless as a proof of the fact. The entire history of Sensation is a commentary on our inability to tell whether two sensations received apart are exactly alike. What appeals to our attention far more than the absolute quality or quantity of a given sensation is its *ratio* to whatever other sensations we may have at the same time. When everything is dark a somewhat less dark sensation makes us see an object white. Helmholtz calculates that the white marble painted in a picture representing an architectural view by moonlight is, when seen by daylight, from ten to twenty thousand times brighter than the real moonlit marble would be. . . .

Every thought we have of a given fact is, strictly speaking, unique, and only bears a resemblance of kind with our other thoughts of the same fact. When the identical fact recurs, we *must* think of it in a fresh manner, see it under a somewhat different angle, apprehend it in different relations from those in which it last appeared. And the thought by which we cognize it is the thought of it-in-those-relations, a thought suffused with the consciousness of all that dim context. Often we are ourselves struck at the strange differences in our successive views of the same thing.

We wonder how we ever could have opined as we did last month about a certain matter. We have outgrown the possibility of that state of mind, we know not how. From one year to another we see things in new lights. What was unreal has grown real, and what was exciting is insipid. The friends we used to care the world for are shrunken to shadows; the women, once so divine, the stars, the woods, and the waters, how now so dull and common; the young girls that brought an aura of infinity, at present hardly distinguishable existences; the pictures so empty; and as for the books, what *was* there to find so mysteriously significant in Goethe, or in John Mill so full of weight? Instead of all this, more zestful than ever is the work, the work; and fuller and deeper the import of common duties and of common goods.

But what here strikes us so forcibly on the flagrant scale exists on every scale, down to the imperceptible transition from one hour's outlook to that of the next. Experience is remoulding us every moment, and our mental reaction on every given thing is really a resultant of our experience of the whole world up to that date. The analogies of brain-physiology must again be appealed to to corroborate our view.

Our earlier chapters have taught us to believe that, whilst we think, our brain changes, and that, like the aurora borealis, its whole internal equilibrium shifts with every pulse of change. The precise nature of the shifting at a given moment is a product of many factors. The accidental state of local nutrition or blood-supply may be among them. But just as one of them certainly is the influence of outward objects on the sense-organs during the moment, so is another certainly the very special susceptibility in which the organ has been left at that moment by all it has gone through in the past. Every brain-state is partly determined by the nature of this entire past succession. Alter the latter in any part, and the brain-state must be somewhat different. Each present brain-state is a record in which the eye of Omniscience might read all the foregone history of its owner. . . .

I am sure that this concrete and total manner of regarding the mind's changes is the only true manner, difficult as it may be to carry it out in detail. If anything seems obscure about it, it will grow clearer as we advance. Meanwhile, if it be true, it is certainly also true that no two 'ideas' are ever exactly the same, which is the proposition we started to prove. The proposition is more important theoretically than it at first sight seems. For it makes it already impossible for us to follow obediently in the footprints of either the Lockian or the Herbartian school, schools which have had almost unlimited influence in Germany and among ourselves. No doubt it is often *convenient* to formulate the mental facts in an atomistic sort of way, and to treat the higher states of consciousness as if they were all built out of unchanging simple ideas. It is convenient often to treat curves as if they were composed of small straight lines, and electricity and nerve-force as if they were fluids. But in the one case as in the other we must never forget that we are talking symbolically, and that there is nothing in nature to answer to our words. *A permanently existing 'idea' or 'Vorstellung' which makes its appearance before the footlights of consciousness at periodical intervals, is as mythological an entity as the Jack of Spades.*

What makes it convenient to use the mythological formulas is the whole organization of speech, which, as was remarked a while ago, was not made by psychologists, but by men who were as a rule only interested in the facts their mental states revealed. They only spoke of their states as *ideas of this or of that thing.* What wonder, then, that the thought is most easily conceived under the law of the thing whose name it bears! If the thing is composed of parts, then we suppose that the thought of the thing must be composed of the thoughts of the parts. If one part of the thing has appeared in the same thing or in other things on former occasions, why then we must be having even now the very same 'idea' of that part which was there on those occasions. If the thing is simple, its thought is simple. If it is multitudinous, it must require a multitude of thoughts to think it. If a succession, only a succession of thoughts can know it. If permanent, its thought is permanent. And so on *ad libitum.* What after all is so natural as to assume that one object, called by one name, should be known by one affection of the mind? But, if language must thus influence us, the agglutinative languages, and even Greek and Latin with their declensions, would be the better guides. Names did not appear in them inalterable, but changed their shape to suit the context in which they lay. It must have been easier then than now to conceive of the same object as being thought of at different times in non-identical conscious states.

This, too, will grow clearer as we proceed. Meanwhile a necessary consequence of the belief in permanent self-identical psychic facts that absent themselves and recur periodically is the Humian doctrine that our thought is composed of separate independent parts and is not a sensibly continuous stream. That this doctrine entirely misrepresents the natural appearances is what I next shall try to show.

3. Within Each Personal Consciousness, Thought Is Sensibly Continuous

I can only define 'continuous' as that which is without breach, crack, or division. I have already said that the breach from one mind to another is perhaps the greatest breach in nature. The only breaches that can well be conceived to occur within the limits of a single mind would either be *interruptions, time*-gaps during which the consciousness went out altogether to come into existence again at a later moment; or they would be breaks in the *quality,* or content, of the thought, so abrupt that the segment that followed had no connection whatever with the one that went before. The proposition that within each personal consciousness thought feels continuous, means two things:

(1) That even where there is a time-gap the consciousness after it feels as if it belonged together with the consciousness before it, as another part of the same self;

(2) That the changes from one moment to another in the quality of the consciousness are never absolutely abrupt.

The case of the time-gaps, as the simplest, shall be taken first. And first of all, a word about time-gaps of which the consciousness may not be itself aware.

[In an earlier chapter] we saw that such time-gaps existed, and that they might be more numerous than is usually supposed. If the consciousness is not aware of them, it cannot feel them as interruptions. In the unconsciousness produced by nitrous oxide and other anæsthetics, in that of epilepsy and fainting, the broken edges of the sentient life may meet and merge over the gap, much as the feelings of space of the opposite margins of the 'blind spot' meet and merge over that objective interruption to the sensitiveness of the eye. Such consciousness as this, whatever it be for the onlooking psychologist, is for itself unbroken. It *feels* unbroken; a waking day of it is sensibly a unit as long as that day lasts, in the sense in which the hours themselves are units, as having all their parts next each other, with no intrusive alien substance between. To expect the consciousness to feel the interruptions of its objective continuity as gaps, would be like expecting the eye to feel a gap of silence because it does not hear, or the ear to feel a gap of darkness because it does not see. So much for the gaps that are unfelt.

With the felt gaps the case is different. On waking from sleep, we usually know that we have been unconscious, and we often have an accurate judgment of how long. The judgment here is certainly an inference from sensible signs, and its ease is due to long practice in the particular field. The result of it, however, is that the consciousness is, *for itself,* not what it was in the former case, but interrupted and continuous, in the mere time-sense of the words. But in the other sense of continuity, the sense of the parts being inwardly connected and belonging together because they are parts of a common whole, the consciousness remains sensibly continuous and one. What now is the common whole? The natural name for it is *myself, I,* or *me.*

When Paul and Peter wake up in the same bed, and recognize that they have been asleep, each one of them mentally reaches back and makes connection with but *one* of the two streams of thought which were broken by the sleeping hours. As the current of an electrode buried in the ground unerringly finds its way to its own similarly buried mate, across no matter how much intervening earth; so Peter's present instantly finds out Peter's past, and never by mistake knits itself on to that of Paul. Paul's thought in turn is as little liable to go astray. The past thought of Peter is appropriated by the present Peter alone. He may have a *knowledge,* and a correct one too, of what Paul's last drowsy states of mind were as he sank into sleep, but it is an entirely different sort of knowledge from that which he has of his own last states. He *remembers* his own states, whilst he only *conceives* Paul's. Remembrance is like direct feeling; its object is suffused with a warmth and intimacy to which no object of mere conception ever attains. This quality of warmth and intimacy and immediacy is what Peter's *present* thought also possesses for itself. So sure as this present is me, is mine, it says, so sure is anything else that comes with the same warmth and intimacy and immediacy, me and mine. What the qualities called warmth and intimacy may in themselves be will have to be matter for future consideration. But whatever past feelings appear with those qualities must be admitted to receive the greeting of the present mental state, to be owned by it, and accepted as belonging together with it in a common self. This community of self is what the time-gap cannot break in twain, and is why a present thought, although not ignorant of the time-gap, can still regard itself as continuous with certain chosen portions of the past.

Consciousness, then, does not appear to itself chopped up in bits. Such words as 'chain' or 'train' do not describe it fitly as it presents itself in the first instance. It is nothing jointed; it flows. A 'river' or a 'stream' are the metaphors by which it is most naturally described. *In talking of it hereafter, let us call it the stream of thought, of consciousness, or of subjective life.*

But now there appears, even within the limits of the same self, and between thoughts all of which alike have this same sense of belonging together, a kind of jointing and separateness among the parts, of which this statement seems to take no account. I refer to the breaks that are produced by sudden *contrasts in the quality* of the successive segments of the stream of thought. If the words 'chain' and 'train' had no natural fitness in them, how came such words to be used at all? Does not a loud explosion rend the consciousness upon which it abruptly breaks, in twain? Does not every sudden shock, appearance of a new object, or change in a sensation, create a real interruption, sensibly felt as such, which cuts the conscious stream across at the moment at which it appears? Do not such interruptions smite us every hour of our lives, and have we the right, in their presence, still to call our consciousness a continuous stream?

This objection is based partly on a confusion and partly on a superficial introspective view.

The confusion is between the thoughts themselves, taken as subjective facts, and the things of which they are aware. It is natural to make this confusion, but easy to avoid it when once put on one's guard. The things are discrete and discontinuous; they do pass before us in a train or chain, making often explosive appearances and rending each other in twain. But their comings and goings and contrasts no more break the flow of the thought that thinks them than they break the time and the space in which they lie. A silence may be broken by a thunder-clap, and we may be so stunned and confused for a moment by the shock as to give no instant account to ourselves of what has happened. But that very confusion is a mental state, and a state that passes us straight over from the silence to the sound. The transition between the thought of one object and the thought of another is no more a break in the *thought* than a joint in a bamboo is a break in the wood. It is a part of the *consciousness* as much as the joint is a part of the *bamboo*.

The superficial introspective view is the overlooking, even when the things are contrasted with each other most violently, of the large amount of affinity that may still remain between the thoughts by whose means they are cognized. Into the awareness of the thunder itself the awareness of the previous silence creeps and continues; for what we hear when the thunder crashes is not thunder *pure,* but thunder-breaking-upon-silence-and-contrasting-with-it.[1] Our feeling of the same objective thunder, coming in this way, is quite different from what it would be were the thunder a continuation of previous thunder. The thunder itself we believe to abolish and exclude the silence; but the *feeling* of the thunder is also a feeling of the silence as just gone; and it would be difficult to find in the actual concrete consciousness of man a feeling so limited to the present as not to have an inkling of anything that went before. Here, again, language works against our perception of the truth. We name our thoughts simply, each after its thing, as if each knew its own thing and nothing else. What each really knows is clearly the thing it is named for, with dimly perhaps a thousand other things. It ought to be named after all of them, but

1. Cf. Brentano; *Psychologie,* vol. i, pp. 219–20. Altogether this chapter of Brentano's on the Unity of Consciousness is as good as anything with which I am acquainted.

it never is. Some of them are always things known a moment ago more clearly; others are things to be known more clearly a moment hence. Out own bodily position, attitude, condition, is one of the things of which *some* awareness, however inattentive, invariably accompanies the knowledge of whatever else we know. We think; and as we think we feel our bodily selves as the seat of the thinking. If the thinking be *our* thinking, it must be suffused through all its parts with that peculiar warmth and intimacy that make it come as ours. Whether the warmth and intimacy be anything more than the feeling of the same old body always there, is a matter for the next chapter to decide. *Whatever* the content of the ego may be, it is habitually felt *with* everything else by us humans, and must form a *liaison* between all the things of which we become successively aware. . . .

[The] difference in the rate of change lies at the basis of a difference of subjective states of which we ought immediately to speak. When the rate is slow we are aware of the object of our thought in a comparatively restful and stable way. When rapid, we are aware of a passage, a relation, a transition *from* it, or *between* it and something else. As we take, in fact, a general view of the wonderful stream of our consciousness, what strikes us first is this different pace of its parts. Like a bird's life, it seems to be made of an alternation of flights and perchings. The rhythm of language expresses this, where every thought is expressed in a sentence, and every sentence closed by a period. The resting-places are usually occupied by sensorial imaginations of some sort, whose peculiarity is that they can be held before the mind for an indefinite time, and contemplated without changing; the places of flight are filled with thoughts of relations, static or dynamic, that for the most part obtain between the matters contemplated in the periods of comparative rest.

Let us call the resting-places the 'substantive parts,' and the places of flight the 'transitive parts,' of the stream of thought. It then appears that the main end of our thinking is at all times the attainment of some other substantive part than the one from which we have just been dislodged. And we may say that the main use of the transitive parts is to lead us from one substantive conclusion to another.

Now it is very difficult, introspectively, to see the transitive parts for what they really are. If they are but flights to a conclusion, stopping them to look at them before the conclusion is reached is really annihilating them. Whilst if we wait till the conclusion *be* reached, it so exceeds them in vigor and stability that it quite eclipses and swallows them up in its glare. Let anyone try to cut a thought across in the middle and get a look at its section, and he will see how difficult the introspective observation of the transitive tracts is. The rush of the thought is so headlong that it almost always brings us up at the conclusion before we can arrest it. Or if our purpose is nimble enough and we do arrest it, it ceases forthwith to be itself. As a snowflake crystal caught in the warm hand is no longer a crystal but a drop, so, instead of catching the feeling of relation moving to its term, we find we have caught some substantive thing, usually the last word we were pronouncing, statically taken, and with its function, tendency, and particular meaning in the sentence quite evaporated. The attempt at introspective analysis in these cases is in fact like seizing a spinning top to catch its motion, or trying to turn up the gas quickly enough to see how the darkness looks. And the challenge to *produce* these psychoses, which is sure to be thrown by doubting psychologists at anyone who contends for their existence, is as unfair as Zeno's treatment of the advocates of motion, when, asking them to point out in what place an arrow *is* when it moves, he argues the falsity of their thesis from their inability to make to so preposterous a question an immediate reply.

The results of this introspective difficulty are baleful. If to hold fast and observe the transitive parts of thought's stream be so hard, then the great blunder to which all schools are liable must be the failure to register them, and the undue emphasizing of the more substantive parts of the stream. Were we not ourselves a moment since in danger of ignoring any feeling transitive between the silence and the thunder, and of treating their boundary as a sort of break in the mind? Now such ignoring as this has historically worked in two ways. One set of thinkers have been led by it to *Sensationalism*. Unable to lay their hands on any coarse feelings corresponding to the innumerable relations and forms of connection between the facts of the world, finding no *named* subjective modifications mirroring such relations, they have for the most part denied that feelings of relation exist, and many of them, like Hume, have gone so far as to deny the reality of most relations *out of the mind* as well as in it. Substantive psychoses, sensations and their copies and derivatives, juxtaposed like dominoes in a game, but really separate, everything else verbal illusion—such is the upshot of this view. The *Intellectualists,* on the other hand, unable to give up the reality of relations *extra mentem,* but equally unable to point to any distinct substantive feelings in which they were known, have made the same admission that the feelings do not exist. But they have drawn an opposite conclusion. The relations must be known, they say, in something that is no feeling, no mental modification continuous and consubstantial with the subjective tissue out of which sensations and other substantive states are made. They are known, these relations, by something that lies on an entirely different plane, by an *actus purus* of Thought, Intellect, or Reason, all written with capitals and considered to mean something unutterably superior to any fact of sensibility whatever.

But from our point of view both Intellectualists and Sensationalists are wrong. If there be such things as feelings at all, *then so surely as relations between objects exist in rerum naturâ, so surely, and more surely, do feelings exist to which these relations are known.* There is not a conjunction or a preposition, and hardly an adverbial phrase, syntactic form, or inflection of voice, in human speech, that does not express some shading or other of relation which we at some moment actually feel to exist between the larger objects of our thought. If we speak objectively, it is the real relations that appear revealed; if we speak subjectively, it is the stream of consciousness that matches each of them by an inward coloring of its own. In either case the relations are numberless, and no existing language is capable of doing justice to all their shades.

We ought to say a feeling of *and,* a feeling of *if,* a feeling of *but,* and a feeling of *by,* quite as readily as we say a feeling of *blue* or a feeling of *cold.* Yet we do not: so inveterate has our habit become of recognizing the existence of the substantive parts alone, that language almost refuses to lend itself to any other use. The Empiricists have always dwelt on its influence in making us suppose that where we have a separate name, a separate thing must needs be there to correspond with it; and they have rightly denied the existence of the mob of abstract entities, principles, and forces, in whose favor no other evidence than this could be brought up. But they have said nothing of that obverse error, of which we said a word in Chapter VII, of supposing that where there is *no* name no entity can exist. All *dumb* or anonymous psychic states have, owing to this error, been coolly suppressed; or, if recognized at all, have been named after the substantive perception they led to, as thoughts 'about' this object or 'about' that, the stolid word *about* engulfing all their delicate idiosyncrasies in its monotonous sound. Thus the greater and greater accentuation and isolation of the substantive parts have continually gone on. . . .

FEELINGS OF TENDENCY

So much for the transitive states. But there are other unnamed states or qualities of states that are just as important and just as cognitive as they, and just as much unrecognized by the traditional sensationalist and intellectualist philosophies of mind. The first fails to find them at all, the second finds their *cognitive function,* but denies that anything in the way of *feeling* has a share in bringing it about. Examples will make clear what these inarticulate psychoses, due to waxing and waning excitements of the brain, are like.

Suppose three successive persons say to us: 'Wait!' 'Hark!' 'Look!' Our consciousness is thrown into three quite different attitudes of expectancy, although no definite object is before it in any one of the three cases. Leaving out different actual bodily attitudes, and leaving out the reverberating images of the three words, which are of course diverse, probably no one will deny the existence of a residual conscious affection, a sense of the direction from which an impression is about to come, although no positive impression is yet there. Meanwhile we have no names for the psychoses in question but the names hark, look, and wait.

Suppose we try to recall a forgotten name. The state of our consciousness is peculiar. There is a gap therein; but no mere gap. It is a gap that is intensely active. A sort of wraith of the name is in it, beckoning us in a given direction, making us at moments tingle with the sense of our closeness, and then letting us sink back without the longed-for term. If wrong names are proposed to us, this singularly definite gap acts immediately so as to negate them. They do not fit into its mould. And the gap of one word does not feel like the gap of another, all empty of content as both might seem necessary to be when described as gaps. When I vainly try to recall the name of Spalding, my consciousness is far removed from what it is when I vainly try to recall the name of Bowles. Here some ingenious persons will say: "How *can* the two consciousnesses be different when the terms which might make them different are not there? All that is there, so long as the effort to recall is vain, is the bare effort itself. How should that differ in the two cases? You are making it seem to differ by prematurely filling it out with the different names, although these, by the hypothesis, have not yet come. Stick to the two efforts as they are, without naming them after facts not yet existent, and you'll be quite unable to designate any point in which they differ." Designate, truly enough. We can only designate the difference by borrowing the names of objects not yet in the mind. Which is to say that our psychological vocabulary is wholly inadequate to name the differences that exist, even such strong differences as these. But namelessness is compatible with existence. There are innumerable consciousnesses of emptiness, no one of which taken in itself has a name, but all different from each other. The ordinary way is to assume that they are all emptinesses of consciousness, and so the same state. But the feeling of an absence is *toto cælo* other than the absence of a feeling. It is an intense feeling. The rhythm of a lost word may be there without a sound to clothe it; or the evanescent sense of something which is the initial vowel or consonant may mock us fitfully, without growing more distinct. Every one must know the tantalizing effect of the blank rhythm of some forgotten verse, restlessly dancing in one's mind, striving to be filled out with words.

Again, what is the strange difference between an experience tasted for the first time and the same experience recognized as familiar, as having been enjoyed before, though we cannot name it or say where or when? A tune, an odor, a flavor sometimes carry this inarticulate feeling of their familiarity so deep into our consciousness that we are fairly shaken by its mysterious emotional power. But strong and characteristic as this psychosis is—it probably is due to the submaximal excitement of wide-spreading associ-

ational brain-tracts—the only name we have for all its shadings is
'sense of familiarity.'

When we read such phrases as 'naught but,' 'either one or the
other,' '*a* is *b*, but,' 'although it is, nevertheless,' 'it is an excluded
middle, there is no *tertium quid*,' and a host of other verbal
skeletons of logical relation, is it true that there is nothing more in
our minds than the words themselves as they pass? What then is
the meaning of the words which we think we understand as we
read? What makes that meaning different in one phrase from what
it is in the other? 'Who?' 'When?' 'Where?' Is the difference of felt
meaning in these interrogatives nothing more than their difference
of sound? And is it not (just like the difference of sound itself)
known and understood in an affection of consciousness correlative
to it, though so impalpable to direct examination? Is not the same
true of such negatives as 'no,' 'never,' 'not yet'?

The truth is that large tracts of human speech are nothing but
signs of direction in thought, of which direction we nevertheless
have an acutely discriminative sense, though no definite sensorial
image plays any part in it whatsoever. Sensorial images are stable
psychic facts; we can hold them still and look at them as long as
we like. These bare images of logical movement, on the contrary,
are psychic transitions, always on the wing, so to speak, and not to
be glimpsed except in flight. Their function is to lead from one set
of images to another. As they pass, we feel both the waxing and
the waning images in a way altogether peculiar and a way quite
different from the way of their full presence. If we try to hold fast
the feeling of direction, the full presence comes and the feeling of
direction is lost. The blank verbal scheme of the logical movement
gives us the fleeting sense of the movement as we read it, quite as
well as does a rational sentence awakening definite imaginations
by its words.

What is that first instantaneous glimpse of some one's meaning
which we have, when in vulgar phrase we say we 'twig' it? Surely
an altogether specific affection of our mind. And has the reader
never asked himself what kind of a mental fact is his *intention of
saying a thing* before he has said it? It is an entirely definite
intention, distinct from all other intentions, an absolutely distinct
state of consciousness, therefore; and yet how much of it consists of
definite sensorial images, either of words or of things? Hardly

anything! Linger, and the words and things come into the mind; the anticipatory intention, the divination is there no more. But as the words that replace it arrive, it welcomes them successively and calls them right if they agree with it, it rejects them and calls them wrong if they do not. It has therefore a nature of its own of the most positive sort, and yet what can we say about it without using words that belong to the later mental facts that replace it? The intention *to-say-so-and-so* is the only name it can receive. One may admit that a good third of our psychic life consists in these rapid premonitory perspective views of schemes of thought not yet articulate. How comes it about that a man reading something aloud for the first time is able immediately to emphasize all his words aright, unless from the very first he have a sense of at least the form of the sentence yet to come, which sense is fused with his consciousness of the present word, and modifies its emphasis in his mind so as to make him give it the proper accent as he utters it? Emphasis of this kind is almost altogether a matter of grammatical construction. If we read 'no more' we expect presently to come upon a 'than'; if we read 'however' at the outset of a sentence it is a 'yet,' a 'still,' or a 'nevertheless,' that we expect. A noun in a certain position demands a verb in a certain mood and number, in another position it expects a relative pronoun. Adjectives call for nouns, verbs for adverbs, etc., etc. And this foreboding of the coming grammatical scheme combined with each successive uttered word is so practically accurate that a reader incapable of understanding four ideas of the book he is reading aloud, can nevertheless read it with the most delicately modulated expression of intelligence.

Some will interpret these facts by calling them all cases in which certain images, by laws of association, awaken others so very rapidly that we think afterwards we felt the very *tendencies* of the nascent images to arise, before they were actually there. For this school the only possible materials of consciousness are images of a perfectly definite nature. Tendencies exist, but they are facts for the outside psychologist rather than for the subject of the observation. The tendency is thus a *psychical* zero; only its *results* are felt.

Now what I contend for, and accumulate examples to show, is that 'tendencies' are not only descriptions from without, but that they are among the *objects* of the stream, which is thus aware of them from within, and must be described as in very large measure constituted of *feelings* of *tendency*, often so vague that we are unable to name them at all. It is, in short, the re-instatement of the vague to its proper place in our mental life which I am so anxious to press on the attention. Mr. Galton and Prof. Huxley have, as we shall see in Chapter XVIII, made one step in advance in exploding the ridiculous theory of Hume and Berkeley that we can have no images but of perfectly definite things. Another is made in the overthrow of the equally ridiculous notion that, whilst simple objective qualities are revealed to our knowledge in subjective feelings, relations are not. But these reforms are not half sweeping and radical enough. What must be admitted is that the definite images of traditional psychology form but the very smallest part of our minds as they actually live. The traditional psychology talks like one who should say a river consists of nothing but pailsful, spoonsful, quartpotsful, barrelsful, and other moulded forms of water. Even were the pails and the pots all actually standing in the stream, still between them the free water would continue to flow. It is just this free water of consciousness that psychologists resolutely overlook. Every definite image in the mind is steeped and dyed in the free water that flows round it. With it goes the sense of its relations, near and remote, the dying echo of whence it came to us, the dawning sense of whither it is to lead. The significance, the value, of the image is all in this halo of penumbra that surrounds and escorts it—or rather that is fused into one with it and has become bone of its bone and flesh of its flesh; leaving it, it is true, an image of the same *thing* it was before, but making it an image of that thing newly taken and freshly understood.

What is that shadowy scheme of the 'form' of an opera, play, or book, which remains in our mind and on which we pass judgment when the actual thing is done? What is our notion of a scientific or philosophical system? Great thinkers have vast premonitory glimpses of schemes of relation between terms, which hardly even as verbal images enter the mind, so rapid is the whole process.[2]

2. Mozart describes thus his manner of composing: First bits and crumbs of the piece come and gradually join together in his mind; then the soul getting warmed to the work, the thing grows more and more, "and I spread it out

We all of us have this permanent consciousness of whither our thought is going. It is a feeling like any other, a feeling of what thoughts are next to arise, before they have arisen. This field of view of consciousness varies very much in extent, depending largely on the degree of mental freshness or fatigue. When very fresh, our minds carry an immense horizon with them. The present image shoots its perspective far before it, irradiating in advance the regions in which lie the thoughts as yet unborn. Under ordinary conditions the halo of felt relations is much more circumscribed. And in states of extreme brain-fag the horizon is narrowed almost to the passing word—the associative machinery, however, providing for the next word turning up in orderly sequence, until at last the tired thinker is led to some kind of a conclusion. At certain moments he may find himself doubting whether his thoughts have not come to a full stop; but the vague sense of a *plus ultra* makes him ever struggle on towards a more definite expression of what it may be; whilst the slowness of his utterance shows how difficult, under such conditions, the labor of thinking must be.

The awareness that our *definite* thought has come to a stop is an entirely different thing from the awareness that our thought is definitively completed. The expression of the latter state of mind is the falling inflection which betokens that the sentence is ended, and silence. The expression of the former state is 'hemming and hawing,' or else such phrases as '*et cetera*,' or 'and so forth.' But notice that every part of the sentence to be left incomplete feels differently as it passes, by reason of the premonition we have that we shall be unable to end it. The 'and so forth' casts its shadow back, and is as integral a part of the object of the thought as the distinctest of images would be. . . .

There is a common class of mistakes which shows how brain-processes begin to be excited before the thoughts attached to them are *due*—due, that is, in substantive and vivid form. I mean those

broader and clearer, and at last it gets almost finished in my head, even when it is a long piece, so that I can see the whole of it at a single glance in my mind, as if it were a beautiful painting or a handsome human being; in which way I do not hear it in my imagination at all as a succession—the way it must come later—but all at once, as it were. It is a rare feast. All the inventing and making goes on in me as in a beautiful strong dream. But the best of all is the *hearing of it all at once*."

mistakes of speech or writing by which, in Dr. Carpenter's words, "we mispronounce or misspell a word, by introducing into it a letter or syllable of some other, whose turn is shortly to come; or, it may be, the whole of the anticipated word is substituted for the one which ought to have been expressed." In these cases one of two things must have happened: either some local accident of nutrition blocks the process that is *due*, so that other processes discharge that ought as yet to be but nascently aroused; or some opposite local accident *furthers* the *latter processes* and makes them explode before their time. In the chapter on Association of Ideas, numerous instances will come before us of the actual effect on consciousness of neuroses not yet maximally aroused.

It is just like the 'overtones' in music. Different instruments give the 'same note,' but each in a different voice, because each gives more than that note, namely, various upper harmonics of it which differ from one instrument to another. They are not separately heard by the ear; they blend with the fundamental note, and suffuse it, and alter it; and even so do the waxing and waning brain-processes at every moment blend with and suffuse and alter the psychic effect of the processes which are at their culminating point.

Let us use the words *psychic overtone, suffusion,* or *fringe,* to designate the influence of a faint brain-process upon our thought, as it makes it aware of relations and objects but dimly perceived.[3]

If we then consider the *cognitive function* of different states of mind, we may feel assured that the difference between those that

---

3. It is so hard to make one's self clear that I may advert to a misunderstanding of my views by the late Prof. Thos. Maguire of Dublin (*Lectures on Philosophy,* 1885). This author considers that by the 'fringe' I mean some sort of psychic material by which sensations in themselves separate are made to cohere together, and wittily says that I ought to "see that uniting sensations by their 'fringes' is more vague than to construct the universe out of oysters by platting their beards" (p. 211). But the fringe, as I use the word, means nothing like this; it is part of the *object cognized*—substantive *qualities* and *things* appearing to the mind in a *fringe of relations.* Some parts—the transitive parts—of our stream of thought cognize the relations rather than the things; but both the transitive and the substantive parts form one continuous stream, with no discrete 'sensations' in it such as Prof. Maguire supposes, and supposes me suppose, to be there.

are mere 'acquaintance,' and those that are 'knowledges-*about*' is reducible almost entirely to the absence or presence of psychic fringes or overtones. Knowledge *about* a thing is knowledge of its relations. Acquaintance with it is limitation to the bare impression which it makes. Of most of its relations we are only aware in the penumbral nascent way of a 'fringe' of unarticulated affinities about it. And, before passing to the next topic in order, I must say a little of this sense of affinity, as itself one of the most interesting features of the subjective stream.

In all our voluntary thinking there is some topic or subject about which all the members of the thought revolve. Half the time this topic is a problem, a gap we cannot yet fill with a definite picture, word, or phrase, but which, in the manner described some time back, influences us in an intensely active and determinate psychic way. Whatever may be the images and phrases that pass before us, we feel their relation to this aching gap. To fill it up is our thought's destiny. Some bring us nearer to that consummation. Some the gap negates as quite irrelevant. Each swims in a felt fringe of relations of which the aforesaid gap is the term. Or instead of a definite gap we may merely carry a mood of interest about with us. Then, however vague the mood, it will still act in the same way, throwing a mantle of felt affinity over such representations, entering the mind, as suit it, and tingeing with the feeling of tediousness or discord all those with which it has no concern.

Relation, then, to our topic or interest is constantly felt in the fringe, and particularly the relation of harmony and discord, of furtherance or hindrance of the topic. When the sense of furtherance is there, we are 'all right'; with the sense of hindrance we are dissatisfied and perplexed, and cast about us for other thoughts. Now *any* thought the quality of whose fringe lets us feel ourselves 'all right,' is an acceptable member of our thinking, whatever kind of thought it may otherwise be. Provided we only feel it to have a place in the scheme of relations in which the interesting topic also lies, that is quite sufficient to make of it a relevant and appropriate portion of our train of ideas.

For the important thing about a train of thought is its conclusion. That is the *meaning*, or, as we say, the topic of the thought.

That is what abides when all its other members have faded from memory. Usually this conclusion is a word or phrase or particular image, or practical attitude or resolve, whether rising to answer a problem or fill a pre-existing gap that worried us, or whether accidentally stumbled on in revery. In either case it stands out from the other segments of the stream by reason of the peculiar interest attaching to it. This interest *arrests* it, makes a sort of crisis of it when it comes, induces attention upon it and makes us treat it in a substantive way.

The parts of the stream that precede these substantive conclusions are but the means of the latter's attainment. And, provided the same conclusion be reached, the means may be as mutable as we like, for the 'meaning' of the stream of thought will be the same. What difference does it make what the means are? *"Qu'importe le flacon, pourvu qu'on ait l'ivresse?"* . . .

There are every year works published whose contents show them to be by real lunatics. To the reader, the book quoted from seems pure nonsense from beginning to end. It is impossible to divine, in such a case, just what sort of feeling of rational relation between the words may have appeared to the author's mind. The border line between objective sense and nonsense is hard to draw; that between subjective sense and nonsense, impossible. Subjectively, any collocation of words may make sense—even the wildest words in a dream—if one only does not doubt their belonging together. Take the obscurer passages in Hegel: it is a fair question whether the rationality included in them be anything more than the fact that the words all belong to a common vocabulary, and are strung together on a scheme of predication and relation—immediacy, self-relation, and what not—which has habitually recurred. Yet there seems no reason to doubt that the subjective feeling of the rationality of these sentences was strong in the writer as he penned them, or even that some readers by straining may have reproduced it in themselves.

To sum up, certain kinds of verbal associate, certain grammatical expectations fulfilled, stand for a good part of our impression that a sentence has a meaning and is dominated by the Unity of one Thought. Nonsense in grammatical form sounds half rational; sense with grammatical-sequence upset sounds nonsensical; e.g., "Elba the Napoleon English faith had banished broken to he Saint because Helena at." Finally, there is about each word the psychic 'overtone' of feeling that it brings us nearer to a forefelt conclusion. Suffuse all the words of a sentence, as they pass, with these three fringes or halos of relation, let the conclusion seem worth arriving at, and all will admit the sentence to be an expression of thoroughly continuous, unified, and rational thought.

Each word, in such a sentence, is felt, not only as a word, but as having a *meaning*. The 'meaning' of a word taken thus dynamically in a sentence may be quite different from its meaning when taken statically or without context. The dynamic meaning is usually reduced to the bare fringe we have described, of felt suitability or unfitness to the context and conclusion. The static meaning, when the word is concrete, as 'table,' 'Boston,' consists of sensory images awakened; when it is abstract, as 'criminal legislation,' 'fallacy,' the meaning consists of other words aroused, forming the so-called 'definition.'

Hegel's celebrated dictum that pure being is identical with pure nothing results from his taking the words statically, or without the fringe they wear in a context. Taken in isolation, they agree in the single point of awakening no sensorial images. But taken dynamically, or as significant—as *thought*—their fringes of relation, their affinities and repugnances, their function and meaning, are felt and understood to be absolutely opposed.

Such considerations as these remove all appearance of paradox from those cases of extremely deficient visual imagery of whose existence Mr. Galton has made us aware (see below).* An exceptionally intelligent friend informs me that he can frame no image whatever of the appearance of his breakfast-table. When asked how he then remembers it at all, he says he simply '*knows*' that it seated four people, and was covered with a white cloth on which were a butter-dish, a coffee-pot, radishes, and so forth. The mind-stuff of which this 'knowing' is made seems to be verbal images exclusively. But if the words 'coffee,' 'bacon,' 'muffins,' and 'eggs'

* II, 51–57. Not included [B.W.].

lead a man to speak to his cook, to pay his bills, and to take measures for the morrow's meal exactly as visual and gustatory memories would, why are they not, for all practical intents and purposes, as good a kind of material in which to think? In fact, we may suspect them to be for most purposes better than terms with a richer imaginative coloring. The scheme of relationship and the conclusion being the essential things in thinking, that kind of mind-stuff which is handiest will be the best for the purpose. Now words, uttered or unexpressed, are the handiest mental elements we have. Not only are they very *rapidly* revivable, but they are revivable as actual sensations more easily than any other items of our experience. Did they not possess some such advantage as this, it would hardly be the case that the older men are and the more effective as thinkers, the more, as a rule, they have lost their visualizing power and depend on words. This was ascertained by Mr. Galton to be the case with members of the Royal Society. The present writer observes it in his own person most distinctly.

On the other hand, a deaf and dumb man can weave his tactile and visual images into a system of thought quite as effective and rational as that of a word-user. *The question whether thought is possible without language* has been a favorite topic of discussion among philosophers. Some interesting reminiscences of his childhood by Mr. Ballard, a deaf-mute instructor in the National College at Washington, show it to be perfectly possible. . . .

Here we may pause. The reader sees by this time that it makes little or no difference in what sort of mind-stuff, in what quality of imagery, his thinking goes on. The only images *intrinsically* important are the halting-places, the substantive conclusions, provisional or final, of the thought. Throughout all the rest of the stream, the feelings of relation are everything, and the terms related almost naught. These feelings of relation, these psychic overtones, halos, suffusions, or fringes about the terms, may be the same in very different systems of imagery. A diagram may help to accentuate this indifference of the mental means where the end is the same. Let A be some experience from which a number of thinkers start. Let Z be the practical conclusion rationally inferrible from it. One gets to the conclusion by one line, another by another; one follows a course of English, another of German, verbal imagery. With one, visual images predominate; with another, tactile. Some trains are tinged with emotions, others not; some are very abridged, synthetic and rapid, others, hesitating and broken into many steps. But when the penultimate terms of all the trains, however differing *inter se,* finally shoot into the same conclusion, we say and rightly say, that all the thinkers have had substantially the same thought. It would probably astound each of them beyond measure to be let into his neighbor's mind and to find how different the scenery there was from that in his own. . . .

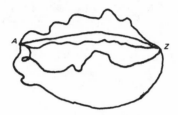

4. Human Thought Appears to Deal with Objects Independent of Itself; That Is, It Is Cognitive, or Possesses the Function of Knowing

For Absolute Idealism, the infinite Thought and its objects are one. The Objects are, through being thought; the eternal Mind is, through thinking them. Were a human thought alone in the world there would be no reason for any other assumption regarding it. Whatever it might have before it would be its vision, would be there, in *its* 'there,' or then, in *its* 'then'; and the question would never arise whether an extra-mental duplicate of it existed or not. The reason why we all believe that the objects of our thoughts have a duplicate existence outside, is that there are *many* human thoughts, each with the *same* objects, as we cannot help supposing. The judgment that *my* thought has the same object as *his* thought is what makes the psychologist call my thought cognitive of an outer reality. The judgment that my own past thought and my own present thought are of the same object is what makes *me* take the object out of either and project it by a sort of triangulation into an independent position, from which it may *appear* to both. *Sameness* in a multiplicity of objective appearances is thus the basis of our belief in realities outside of thought. In Chapter XII we shall have to take up the judgment of sameness again.

To show that the question of reality being extra-mental or not is not likely to arise in the absence of repeated experiences of the *same,* take the example of an altogether unprecedented experience, such as a new taste in the throat. Is it a subjective quality of feeling, or an objective quality felt? You do not even ask the question at this point. It is simply *that taste.* But if a doctor hears you describe it, and says: "Ha! Now you know what *heartburn* is," then it becomes a quality already existent *extra mentem tuam,* which you in turn have come upon and learned. The first spaces, times, things, qualities, experienced by the child probably appear, like the first heartburn, in this absolute way, as simple *beings,* neither in nor out of thought. But later, by having other thoughts than this present one, and making repeated judgments of sameness among their objects, he corroborates in himself the notion of realities, past and distant as well as present, which realities no one single thought either possesses or engenders, but which all may contemplate and know. This, as was stated in the last chapter, is the *psychological* point of view, the relatively uncritical non-idealistic point of view of all natural science, beyond which this book cannot go. A mind which has become conscious of its own cognitive function, plays what we have called 'the psychologist' upon itself. It not only knows the things that appear before it; it knows that it knows them. This stage of reflective condition is, more or less explicitly, our habitual adult state of mind.

It cannot, however, be regarded as primitive. The consciousness of objects must come first. We seem to lapse into this primordial condition when consciousness is reduced to a minimum by the inhalation of anæsthetics or during a faint. Many persons testify that at a certain stage of the anæsthetic process objects are still cognized whilst the thought of self is lost. . . .

Many philosophers, however, hold that the reflective consciousness of the self is essential to the cognitive function of thought. They hold that a thought, in order to know a thing at all, must expressly distinguish between the thing and its own self. This is a perfectly wanton assumption, and not the faintest shadow of reason exists for supposing it true. As well might I contend that I cannot dream without dreaming that I dream, swear without swearing that I swear, deny without denying that I deny, as maintain that I cannot know without knowing that I know. I may have either acquaintance-with, or knowledge-about, an object O without thinking about myself at all. It suffices for this that I think O, and that it exist. If, in addition to thinking O, I also think that I exist and that I know O, well and good; I then know one more thing, a fact about O, of which I previously was unmindful. That, however, does not prevent me from having already known it a good deal. O *per se,* or O *plus* P, are as good objects of knowledge as O *plus me* is. The philosophers in question simply substitute one particular object for all others, and call it *the* object *par excellence.* It is a case of the 'psychologist's fallacy.' *They* know the object to be one thing and the thought another; and they forthwith foist their own knowledge into that of the thought of which they pretend to give a true account. To conclude, then, *thought may, but need not, in knowing, discriminate between its object and itself.*

We have been using the word Object. *Something must now be said about the proper use of the term Object in Psychology.*

In popular parlance the word object is commonly taken without reference to the act of knowledge, and treated as synonymous with individual subject of existence. Thus if anyone ask what is the mind's object when you say 'Columbus discovered America in 1492,' most people will reply 'Columbus,' or 'America,' or, at most, 'the discovery of America.' They will name a substantive kernel or nucleus of the consciousness, and say the thought is 'about' that—as indeed it is—and they will call that your thought's 'object.' Really that is usually only the grammatical object, or more likely the grammatical subject, of your sentence. It is at most your 'fractional object'; or you may call it the 'topic' of your thought, or the 'subject of your discourse.' But the *Object* of your thought is really its entire content or deliverance, neither more nor less. It is a vicious use of speech to take out a substantive kernel from its content and call that its object; and it is an equally vicious use of speech to add a substantive kernel not articulately included in its content, and to call that its object. Yet either one of these two sins we commit, whenever we content ourselves with saying that a given thought is simply 'about' a certain topic, or that that topic is its 'object.' The object of my thought in the previous sentence, for example, is strictly speaking neither Columbus, nor America, nor its discovery. It is nothing short of the entire sentence, 'Columbus-discovered-America-in-1492.' And if we wish to speak of it substantively, we must make a substantive of it by writing it out thus with hyphens between all its words. Nothing but this can possibly name its delicate idiosyncrasy. And if we wish to *feel* that idiosyncrasy we must reproduce the thought as it was uttered, with every word fringed and the whole sentence bathed in that original halo of obscure relations, which, like an horizon, then spread about its meaning.

Our psychological duty is to cling as closely as possible to the actual constitution of the thought we are studying. We may err as much by excess as by defect. If the kernel or 'topic,' Columbus, is in one way less than the thought's object, so in another way it may be more. That is, when named by the psychologist, it may mean much more than actually is present to the thought of which he is reporter. Thus, for example, suppose you should go on to think: 'He was a daring genius!' An ordinary psychologist would not hesitate to say that the object of your thought was still 'Columbus.' True, your thought is *about* Columbus. It 'terminates' in Columbus, leads from and to the direct idea of Columbus. But for the moment it is not fully and immediately Columbus, it is only 'he,' or rather 'he-was-a-daring-genius'; which, though it may be an unimportant difference for conversational purposes, is, for introspective psychology, as great a difference as there can be.

The object of every thought, then, is neither more nor less than all that the thought thinks, exactly as the thought thinks it, however complicated the matter, and however symbolic the manner of the thinking may be. It is needless to say that memory can seldom accurately reproduce such an object, when once it has passed from before the mind. It either makes too little or too much of it. Its best plan is to repeat the verbal sentence, if there was one, in which the object was expressed. But for inarticulate thoughts there is not even this resource, and introspection must confess that the task exceeds her powers. The mass of our thinking vanishes forever, beyond hope of recovery, and psychology only gathers up a few of the crumbs that fall from the feast.

The next point to make clear is that, *however complex the object may be, the thought of it is one undivided state of consciousness.* . . .

The ordinary associationist-psychology supposes . . . that whenever an object of thought contains many elements, the thought itself must be made up of just as many ideas, one idea for each element, and all fused together in appearance, but really separate. The enemies of this psychology find (as we have already seen) little trouble in showing that such a bundle of separate ideas would never form one thought at all, and they contend that an Ego must be added to the bundle to give it unity, and bring the various ideas into relation with each other. We will not discuss the ego just yet, but it is obvious that if things are to be thought in relation, they must be thought together, and in one *something*, be that something ego, psychosis, state of consciousness, or whatever you please. If not thought with each other, things are not thought in relation at all. Now most believers in the ego make the same mistake as the associationists and sensationists whom they oppose. Both agree that the elements of the subjective stream are discrete and separate and constitute what Kant calls a 'manifold.' But while the associationists think that a 'manifold' can form a single knowledge, the egoists deny this, and say that the knowledge comes only when the manifold is subjected to the synthetizing activity of an ego. Both make an identical initial hypothesis; but the egoist, finding it won't express the facts, adds another hypothesis to correct it. Now I do not wish just yet to 'commit myself' about the existence or nonexistence of the ego, but I do contend that we need not invoke it for this particular reason—namely, because the manifold of ideas has to be reduced to unity. *There is no manifold of coexisting ideas;* the notion of such a thing is a chimera. *Whatever things are thought in relation are thought from the outset in a unity, in a single pulse of subjectivity, a single psychosis, feeling, or state of mind.*

The reason why this fact is so strangely garbled in the books seems to be what on an earlier page I called the psychologist's fallacy. We have the inveterate habit, whenever we try introspectively to describe one of our thoughts, of dropping the thought as it is in itself and talking of something else. We describe the things that appear to the thought, and we describe other thoughts *about* those things—as if these and the original thought were the same. If, for example, the thought be 'the pack of cards is on the table,' we say, "Well, isn't it a thought of the pack of cards? Isn't it of the cards as included in the pack? Isn't it of the table? And of the legs of the table as well? The table has legs—how can you think the table without virtually thinking its legs? Hasn't our thought then, all these parts—one part for the pack and another for the table? And within the pack-part a part for each card, as within the table-part a part for each leg? And isn't each of these parts an idea? And can our thought, then, be anything but an assemblage or pack of ideas, each answering to some element of what it knows?"

Now not one of these assumptions is true. The thought taken as an example is, in the first place, not of 'a pack of cards.' It is of 'the-pack-of-cards-is-on-the-table,' an entirely different subjective phenomenon, whose Object implies the pack, and every one of the cards in it, but whose conscious constitution bears very little resemblance to that of the thought of the pack *per se*. What a thought *is*, and what it may be developed into, or explained to stand for, and be equivalent to, are two things, not one.

An analysis of what passes through the mind as we utter the phrase *the pack of cards is on the table* will, I hope, make this clear, and may at the same time condense into a concrete example a good deal of what has gone before.

It takes time to utter the phrase. Let the horizontal line in [the figure below] represent time. Every part of it will then stand for a fraction, every point for an instant, of the time. Of course the thought has *time-parts*. The part 2–3 of it, though continuous with 1–2, is yet a different part from 1–2. Now I say of these time-parts that we cannot take any one of them so short that it will not after some fashion or other be a thought of the whole object 'the pack of cards is on the table.' They melt into each other like dissolving views, and no two of them feel the object just alike, but each feels the total object in a unitary undivided way. This is what I mean by denying that in the thought any parts can be found corresponding to the object's parts. Time-parts are not such parts.

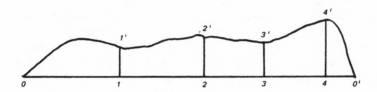

Now let the vertical dimensions of the figure stand for the objects or contents of the thoughts. A line vertical to any point of the horizontal as 1–1′, will then symbolize the object in the mind at the instant 1; a space above the horizontal, as 1–1′–2′–2, will symbolize all that passes through the mind during the time 1–2 whose line it covers. The entire diagram from 0 to 0′ represents a finite length of thought's stream.

Can we now define the psychic constitution of each vertical section of this segment? We can, though in a very rough way. Immediately after 0, even before we have opened our mouths to speak, the entire thought is present to our mind in the form of an intention to utter that sentence. This intention, though it has no simple name, and though it is a transitive state immediately displaced by the first word, is yet a perfectly determinate phase of thought, unlike anything else. Again, immediately before 0′, after the last word of the sentence is spoken, all will admit that we again think its entire content as we inwardly realize its completed deliverance. All vertical sections made through any other parts of the diagram will be respectively filled with other ways of feeling the sentence's meaning. Through 2, for example, the cards will be the part of the object most emphatically present to the mind; through 4, the table. The stream is made higher in the drawing at its end than at its beginning, because the final way of feeling the content is fuller and richer than the initial way. As Joubert says, "We only know just what we meant to say, after we have said it." And as M. Y. Egger remarks, "Before speaking, one barely knows what one intends to say, but afterwards one is filled with admiration and surprise at having said and thought it so well."

This latter author seems to me to have kept at much closer quarters with the facts than any other analyst of consciousness. But even he does not quite hit the mark, for, as I understand him, he thinks that each word as it occupies the mind *displaces* the rest of the thought's content. He distinguishes the 'idea' (what I have called the total *object* or meaning) from the consciousness of the words, calling the former a very feeble state, and contrasting it with the liveliness of the words, even when these are only silently rehearsed. "The feeling," he says, "of the words makes ten or twenty times more noise in our consciousness than the sense of the phrase, which for consciousness is a very slight matter." And having distinguished these two things, he goes on to separate them in time, saying that the idea may either precede or follow the words, but that it is a 'pure illusion' to suppose them simultaneous. Now I believe that in all cases where the words are *understood,* the total idea may be and usually is present not only before and after the phrase has been spoken, but also whilst each separate word is uttered. It is the overtone, halo, or fringe of the word, *as spoken in that sentence.* It is never absent; no word in an understood sentence comes to consciousness as a mere noise. We feel its meaning as it passes; and although our object differs from one moment to another as to its verbal kernel or nucleus, yet it is *similar* throughout the entire segment of the stream. The same object is known everywhere, now from the point of view, if we may so call it, of this word, now from the point of view of that. And in our feeling of each word there chimes an echo or foretaste of every other. The consciousness of the 'Idea' and that of the words are thus consubstantial. They are made of the same 'mind-stuff,' and form an unbroken stream. Annihilate a mind at any instant, cut its thought through whilst yet uncompleted, and examine the object present to the cross-section thus suddenly made; you will find, not the bald word in process of utterance, but that word suffused with the whole idea. The word may be so loud, as M. Egger would say, that we cannot *tell* just how its suffusion, as such, feels, or how it differs from the suffusion of the next word. But it does differ; and we may be sure that, could we see into the brain, we should find the same processes active through the entire sentence in different degrees, each one in turn becoming maximally excited and then yielding the momentary verbal 'kernel,' to the thought's content, at other times being only sub-excited, and then combining with the other sub-excited processes to give the overtone or fringe. . . .

The last peculiarity of consciousness to which attention is to be drawn in this first rough description of its stream is that

5. It Is Always Interested More in One Part of Its Object Than in Another, and Welcomes and Rejects, or Chooses, All the While It Thinks

The phenomena of selective attention and of deliberative will are of course patent examples of this choosing activity. But few of us are aware how incessantly it is at work in operations not ordinarily called by these names. Accentuation and Emphasis are present in every perception we have. We find it quite impossible to disperse our attention impartially over a number of impressions. A monotonous succession of sonorous strokes is broken up into rhythms, now of one sort, now of another, by the different accent which we place on different strokes. The simplest of these rhythms is the double one, tick-tóck, tick-tóck, tick-tóck. Dots dispersed on a surface are perceived in rows and groups. Lines separate into diverse figures. The ubiquity of the distinctions, *this* and *that, here* and *there, now* and *then,* in our minds is the result of our laying the same selective emphasis on parts of place and time.

But we do far more than emphasize things, and unite some, and keep others apart. We actually *ignore* most of the things before us. Let me briefly show how this goes on.

To begin at the bottom, what are our very senses themselves but organs of selection? Out of the infinite chaos of movements, of which physics teaches us that the outer world consists, each sense-organ picks out those which fall within certain limits of velocity. To these it responds, but ignores the rest as completely as if they did not exist. It thus accentuates particular movements in a manner for which objectively there seems no valid ground; for, as Lange says, there is no reason whatever to think that the gap in Nature between the highest sound-waves and the lowest heat-waves is an abrupt break like that of our sensations; or that the difference between violet and ultra-violet rays has anything like the objective importance subjectively represented by that between light and darkness. Out of what is in itself an undistinguishable, swarming *continuum,* devoid of distinction or emphasis, our senses make for us, by attending to this motion and ignoring that, a world full of contrasts, of sharp accents, of abrupt changes, of picturesque light and shade.

If the sensations we receive from a given organ have their causes thus picked out for us by the conformation of the organ's termination, Attention, on the other hand, out of all the sensations yielded, picks out certain ones as worthy of its notice and suppresses all the rest. Helmholtz's work on Optics is little more than a study of those visual sensations of which common men never become aware—blind spots, *muscæ volitantes,* after-images, irradiation, chromatic fringes, marginal changes of color, double images, astigmatism, movements of accommodation and convergence, retinal rivalry, and more besides. We do not even know without special training on which of our eyes an image falls. So habitually ignorant are most men of this that one may be blind for years of a single eye and never know the fact.

Helmholtz says that we notice only those sensations which are signs to us of *things.* But what are things? Nothing, as we shall abundantly see, but special groups of sensible qualities, which happen practically or æsthetically to interest us, to which we therefore give substantive names, and which we exalt to this exclusive status of independence and dignity. But in itself, apart from my interest, a particular dust-wreath on a windy day is just as much of an individual thing, and just as much or as little deserves an individual name, as my own body does.

And then, among the sensations we get from each separate thing, what happens? The mind selects again. It chooses certain of the sensations to represent the thing most *truly,* and considers the rest as its appearances, modified by the conditions of the moment. Thus my table-top is named *square,* after but one of an infinite number of retinal sensations which it yields, the rest of them being sensations of two acute and two obtuse angles; but I call the latter *perspective* views, and the four right angles the *true* form of the table, and erect the attribute squareness into the table's essence, for æsthetic reasons of my own. In like manner, the real form of the circle is deemed to be the sensation it gives when the line of vision is perpendicular to its centre—all its other sensations are signs of this sensation. The real sound of the cannon is the sensation it makes when the ear is close by. The real color of the brick is the sensation it gives when the eye looks squarely at it from a near point, out of the sunshine and yet not in the gloom; under other circumstances it gives us othèr color-sensations which are but signs of this—we then see it looks pinker or blacker than it really is. The reader knows no object which he does not represent to himself by preference as in some typical attitude, of some normal size, at some characteristic distance, of some standard tint, etc., etc. But all these essential characteristics, which together form for us the genuine objectivity of the thing and are contrasted with what we call the subjective sensation it may yield us at a given moment, are mere sensations like the latter. The mind chooses to suit itself, and decides what particular sensation shall be held more real and valid than all the rest.

Thus perception involves a twofold choice. Out of all present sensations, we notice mainly such as are significant of absent ones; and out of all the absent associates which these suggest, we again pick out a very few to stand for the objective reality *par excellence*. We could have no more exquisite example of selective industry.

That industry goes on to deal with the things thus given in perception. A man's empirical thought depends on the things he has experienced, but what these shall be is to a large extent determined by his habits of attention. A thing may be present to him a thousand times, but if he persistently fails to notice it, it cannot be said to enter into his experience. We are all seeing flies, moths, and beetles by the thousand, but to whom, save an entomologist, do they say anything distinct? On the other hand, a thing met only once in a lifetime may leave an indelible experience in the memory. Let four men make a tour in Europe. One will bring home only picturesque impressions—costumes and colors, parks and views and works of architecture, pictures and statues. To another all this will be non-existent; and distances and prices, populations and drainage-arrangements, door- and window-fastenings, and other useful statistics will take their place. A third will give a rich account of the theatres, restaurants, and public balls, and naught beside; whilst the fourth will perhaps have been so wrapped in his own subjective broodings as to tell little more than a few names of places through which he passed. Each has selected, out of the same mass of presented objects, those which suited his private interest and has made his experience thereby.

If, now, leaving the empirical combination of objects, we ask how the mind proceeds *rationally* to connect them, we find selection again to be omnipotent. In a future chapter we shall see that all Reasoning depends on the ability of the mind to break up the totality of the phenomenon reasoned about, into parts, and to pick out from among these the particular one which, in our given emergency, may lead to the proper conclusion. Another predicament will need another conclusion, and require another element to be picked out. The man of genius is he who will always stick in his bill at the right point, and bring it out with the right element—'reason' if the emergency be theoretical, 'means' if it be practical—transfixed upon it. I here confine myself to this brief statement, but it may suffice to show that Reasoning is but another form of the selective activity of the mind.

If now we pass to its æsthetic department, our law is still more obvious. The artist notoriously selects his items, rejecting all tones, colors, shapes, which do not harmonize with each other and with the main purpose of his work. That unity, harmony, 'convergence of characters,' as M. Taine calls it, which gives to works of art their superiority over works of nature, is wholly due to *elimination*. Any natural subject will do, if the artist has wit enough to pounce upon some one feature of it as characteristic, and suppress all merely accidental items which do not harmonize with this.

Ascending still higher, we reach the plane of Ethics, where choice reigns notoriously supreme. An act has no ethical quality whatever unless it be chosen out of several all equally possible. To sustain the arguments for the good course and keep them ever before us, to stifle our longing for more flowery ways, to keep the foot unflinchingly on the arduous path, these are characteristic ethical energies. But more than these; for these but deal with the means of compassing interests already felt by the man to be supreme. The ethical energy *par excellence* has to go farther and choose which *interest* out of several, equally coercive, shall become supreme. The issue here is of the utmost pregnancy, for it decides a man's entire career. When he debates, Shall I commit this crime? choose that profession? accept that office, or marry this fortune?— his choice really lies between one of several equally possible future Characters. What he shall *become* is fixed by the conduct of this moment. Schopenhauer, who enforces his determinism by the argument that with a given fixed character only one reaction is possible under given circumstances, forgets that, in these critical ethical moments, what consciously *seems* to be in question is the complexion of the character itself. The problem with the man is less what act he shall now choose to do, than what being he shall now resolve to become.

Looking back, then, over this review, we see that the mind is at every stage a theatre of simultaneous possibilities. Consciousness consists in the comparison of these with each other, the selection of some, and the suppression of the rest by the reinforcing and inhibiting agency of attention. The highest and most elaborated mental products are filtered from the data chosen by the faculty next beneath, out of the mass offered by the faculty below that, which mass in turn was sifted from a still larger amount of yet simpler material, and so on. The mind, in short, works on the data it receives very much as a sculptor works on his block of stone. In a sense the statue stood there from eternity. But there were a thousand different ones beside it, and the sculptor alone is to thank for having extricated this one from the rest. Just so the world of each of us, howsoever different our several views of it may be, all lay embedded in the primordial chaos of sensations, which gave the mere *matter* to the thought of all of us indifferently. We may, if we like, by our reasonings unwind things back to that black and jointless continuity of space and moving clouds of swarming atoms which science calls the only real world. But all the while the world we feel and live in will be that which our ancestors and we, by slowly cumulative strokes of choice, have extricated out of this, like sculptors, by simply rejecting certain portions of the given stuff. Other sculptors, other statues from the same stone! Other minds, other worlds from the same monotonous and inexpressive chaos! My world is but one in a million alike embedded, alike real to those who may abstract them. How different must be the worlds in the consciousness of ant, cuttle-fish, or crab!

But in my mind and your mind the rejected portions and the

selected portions of the original world-stuff are to a great extent
the same. The human race as a whole largely agrees as to what it
shall notice and name, and what not. And among the noticed
parts we select in much the same way for accentuation and preference or subordination and dislike. There is, however, one entirely
extraordinary case in which no two men ever are known to choose
alike. One great splitting of the whole universe into two halves is
made by each of us; and for each of us almost all of the interest
attaches to one of the halves; but we all draw the line of division
between them in a different place. When I say that we all call the
two halves by the same names, and that those names are 'me' and
'not-me' respectively, it will at once be seen what I mean. The
altogether unique kind of interest which each human mind feels
in those parts of creation which it can call *me* or *mine* may be a
moral riddle, but it is a fundamental psychological fact. No mind
can take the same interest in his neighbor's *me* as in his own. The
neighbor's *me* falls together with all the rest of things in one
foreign mass, against which his own *me* stands out in startling
relief. Even the trodden worm, as Lotze somewhere says, contrasts
his own suffering self with the whole remaining universe, though
he have no clear conception either of himself or of what the universe may be. He is for me a mere part of the world; for him it is I
who am the mere part. Each of us dichotomizes the Kosmos in a
different place. . . .

B.   THE CONSCIOUSNESS OF SELF*

Let us begin with the Self in its widest acceptation, and follow it
up to its most delicate and subtle form, advancing from the study
of the empirical, as the Germans call it, to that of the pure, Ego.

The Empirical Self or Me

The Empirical Self of each of us is all that he is tempted to call
by the name of *me*. But it is clear that between what a man calls
me and what he simply calls *mine* the line is difficult to draw. We
feel and act about certain things that are ours very much as we feel

* From *The Principles of Psychology*, chap. 10.

and act about ourselves. Our fame, our children, the work of our hands, may be as dear to us as our bodies are, and arouse the same feelings and the same acts of reprisal if attacked. And our bodies themselves, are they simply ours, or are they *us?* Certainly men have been ready to disown their very bodies and to regard them as mere vestures, or even as prisons of clay from which they should some day be glad to escape.

We see then that we are dealing with a fluctuating material. The same object being sometimes treated as a part of me, at other times as simply mine, and then again as if I had nothing to do with it at all. *In its widest possible sense,* however, *a man's Self is the sum total of all that he* CAN *call his,* not only his body and his psychic powers, but his clothes and his house, his wife and children, his ancestors and friends, his reputation and works, his lands and horses, and yacht and bank-account. All these things give him the same emotions. If they wax and prosper, he feels triumphant; if they dwindle and die away, he feels cast down—not necessarily in the same degree for each thing, but in much the same way for all. Understanding the Self in this widest sense, we may begin by dividing the history of it into three parts, relating respectively to—

1. Its constituents;
2. The feelings and emotions they arouse—*Self-feelings;*
3. The actions to which they prompt—*Self-seeking and Self-preservation.*

1. *The constituents of the Self* may be divided into two classes, those which make up respectively—

(a) The material Self;
(b) The social Self;
(c) The spiritual Self; and
(d) The pure Ego.

(a) The body is the innermost part of *the material Self* in each of us; and certain parts of the body seem more intimately ours than the rest. The clothes come next. The old saying that the human person is composed of three parts—soul, body and clothes

—is more than a joke. We so appropriate our clothes and identify ourselves with them that there are few of us who, if asked to choose between having a beautiful body clad in raiment perpetually shabby and unclean, and having an ugly and blemished form always spotlessly attired, would not hesitate a moment before making a decisive reply. Next, our immediate family is a part of ourselves. Our father and mother, our wife and babes, are bone of our bone and flesh of our flesh. When they die, a part of our very selves is gone. If they do anything wrong, it is our shame. If they are insulted, our anger flashes forth as readily as if we stood in their place. Our home comes next. Its scenes are part of our life; its aspects awaken the tenderest feelings of affection; and we do not easily forgive the stranger who, in visiting it, finds fault with its arrangements or treats it with contempt. All these different things are the objects of instinctive preferences coupled with the most important practical interests of life. We all have a blind impulse to watch over our body, to deck it with clothing of an ornamental sort, to cherish parents, wife and babes, and to find for ourselves a home of our own which we may live in and 'improve.'

An equally instinctive impulse drives us to collect property; and the collections thus made become, with different degrees of intimacy, parts of our empirical selves. The parts of our wealth most intimately ours are those which are saturated with our labor. There are few men who would not feel personally annihilated if a life-long construction of their hands or brains—say an entomological collection or an extensive work in manuscript—were suddenly swept away. The miser feels similarly towards his gold, and although it is true that a part of our depression at the loss of possessions is due to our feeling that we must now go without certain goods that we expected the possessions to bring in their train, yet in every case there remains, over and above this, a sense of the shrinkage of our personality, a partial conversion of ourselves to nothingness, which is a psychological phenomenon by itself. We are all at once assimilated to the tramps and poor devils whom we so despise, and at the same time removed farther than ever away from the happy sons of earth who lord it over land and sea and men in the full-blown lustihood that wealth and power can give, and before whom, stiffen ourselves as we will by appealing to anti-snobbish first principles, we cannot escape an emotion, open or sneaking, of respect and dread.

(*b*) *A man's Social Self* is the recognition which he gets from his mates. We are not only gregarious animals, liking to be in sight of our fellows, but we have an innate propensity to get ourselves noticed, and noticed favorably, by our kind. No more fiendish punishment could be devised, were such a thing physically possible, than that one should be turned loose in society and remain absolutely unnoticed by all the members thereof. If no one turned round when we entered, answered when we spoke, or minded what we did, but if every person we met 'cut us dead,' and acted as if we were non-existing things, a kind of rage and impotent despair would ere long well up in us, from which the cruelest bodily tortures would be a relief; for these would make us feel that, however bad might be our plight, we had not sunk to such a depth as to be unworthy of attention at all.

Properly speaking, *a man has as many social selves as there are individuals who recognize him* and carry an image of him in their mind. To wound any one of these his images is to wound him.[1] But as the individuals who carry the images fall naturally into classes, we may practically say that he has as many different social selves as there are distinct *groups* of persons about whose opinion he cares. He generally shows a different side of himself to each of these different groups. Many a youth who is demure enough before his parents and teachers, swears and swaggers like a pirate among his 'tough' young friends. We do not show ourselves to our children as to our club-companions, to our customers as to the laborers we employ, to our own masters and employers as to our intimate friends. From this there results what practically is a division of the man into several selves; and this may be a discordant splitting, as where one is afraid to let one set of his acquaintances know him as he is elsewhere; or it may be a perfectly harmonious division of labor, as where one tender to his children is stern to the soldiers or prisoners under his command.

The most peculiar social self which one is apt to have is in the

---

1. "Who filches from me my good name," etc.

mind of the person one is in love with. The good or bad fortunes of this self cause the most intense elation and dejection—unreasonable enough as measured by every other standard than that of the organic feeling of the individual. To his own consciousness he *is* not, so long as this particular social self fails to get recognition, and when it is recognized his contentment passes all bounds.

A man's *fame*, good or bad, and his *honor* or dishonor, are names for one of his social selves. The particular social self of a man called his honor is usually the result of one of those splittings of which we have spoken. It is his image in the eyes of his own 'set,' which exalts or condemns him as he conforms or not to certain requirements that may not be made of one in another walk of life. Thus a layman may abandon a city infected with cholera; but a priest or a doctor would think such an act incompatible with his honor. A soldier's honor requires him to fight or to die under circumstances where another man can apologize or run away with no stain upon his social self. A judge, a statesman are in like manner debarred by the honor of their cloth from entering into pecuniary relations perfectly honorable to persons in private life. Nothing is commoner than to hear people discriminate between their different selves of this sort: "As a man I pity you, but as an official I must show you no mercy; as a politician I regard him as an ally, but as a moralist I loathe him"; etc., etc. What may be called 'club-opinion' is one of the very strongest forces in life. The thief must not steal from other thieves; the gambler must pay his gambling-debts, though he pay no other debts in the world. The code of honor of fashionable society has throughout history been full of permissions as well as of vetoes, the only reason for following either of which is that so we best serve one of our social selves. You must not lie in general, but you may lie as much as you please if asked about your relations with a lady; you must accept a challenge from an equal, but if challenged by an inferior you may laugh him to scorn: these are examples of what is meant.

(c) *By the Spiritual Self,* so far as it belongs to the Empirical Me, I mean a man's inner or subjective being, his psychic faculties or dispositions, taken concretely; not the bare principle of personal Unity, or 'pure' Ego, which remains still to be discussed. These psychic dispositions are the most enduring and intimate part of the self, that which we most verily seem to be. We take a purer self-satisfaction when we think of our ability to argue and discriminate, of our moral sensibility and conscience, of our indomitable will, than when we survey any of our other possessions. Only when these are altered is a man said to be *alienatus a se*.

Now this spiritual self may be considered in various ways. We may divide it into faculties, as just instanced, isolating them one from another, and identifying ourselves with either in turn. This is an *abstract* way of dealing with consciousness, in which, as it actually presents itself, a plurality of such faculties are always to be simultaneously found; or we may insist on a concrete view, and then the spiritual self in us will be either the entire stream of our personal consciousness, or the present 'segment' or 'section' of that stream, according as we take a broader or a narrower view—both the stream and the section being concrete existences in time, and each being a unity after its own peculiar kind. But whether we take it abstractly or concretely, our considering the spiritual self at all is a reflective process, is the the result of our abandoning the outward-looking point of view, and of our having become able to think of subjectivity as such, *to think ourselves as thinkers*.

This attention to thought as such, and the identification of ourselves with it rather than with any of the objects which it reveals, is a momentous and in some respects a rather mysterious operation, of which we need here only say that as a matter of fact it exists; and that in everyone, at an early age, the distinction between thought as such, and what it is 'of' or 'about,' has become familiar to the mind. The deeper grounds for this discrimination may possibly be hard to find; but superficial grounds are plenty and near at hand. Almost anyone will tell us that thought is a different sort of existence from things, because many sorts of thought are of no things—e.g., pleasures, pains, and emotions; others are of non-existent things—errors and fictions; others again of existent things, but in a form that is symbolic and does not resemble them—abstract ideas and concepts; whilst in the thoughts that do resemble the things they are 'of' (percepts, sensations), we can feel, alongside of the thing known, the thought of it going on as an altogether separate act and operation in the mind.

Now this subjective life of ours, distinguished as such so clearly from the objects known by its means, may, as aforesaid, be taken by us in a concrete or in an abstract way. Of the concrete way I will say nothing just now, except that the actual 'section' of the stream will ere long, in our discussion of the nature of the principle of *unity* in consciousness, play a very important part. The abstract way claims our attention first. If the stream as a whole is identified with the Self far more than any outward thing, a *certain portion of the stream abstracted from the rest* is so identified in an altogether peculiar degree, and is felt by all men as a sort of innermost centre within the circle, of sanctuary within the citadel, constituted by the subjective life as a whole. Compared with this element of the stream, the other parts, even of the subjective life, seem transient external possessions, of which each in turn can be disowned, whilst that which disowns them remains. Now, *what is this self of all the other selves?*

Probably all men would describe it in much the same way up to a certain point. They would call it the *active* element in all consciousness; saying that whatever qualities a man's feelings may possess, or whatever content his thought may include, there is a spiritual something in him which seems to *go out* to meet these qualities and contents, whilst they seem to *come in* to be received by it. It is what welcomes or rejects. It presides over the perception of sensations, and by giving or withholding its assent it influences the movements they tend to arouse. It is the home of interest—not the pleasant or the painful, not even pleasure or pain, as such, but that within us to which pleasure and pain, the pleasant and the painful speak. It is the source of effort and attention, and the place from which appear to emanate the fiats of the will. A physiologist who should reflect upon it in his own person could hardly help, I should think, connecting it more or less vaguely with the process by which ideas or incoming sensations are 'reflected' or pass over into outward acts. Not necessarily that it should *be* this process or the mere feeling of this process, but that it should be in some close way *related* to this process; for it plays a part analogous to it in the psychic life, being a sort of junction at which sensory ideas terminate and from which motor ideas proceed, and forming a kind of link between the two. Being more incessantly there than any other single element of the mental life, the other elements end by seeming to accrete round it and to belong to it. It becomes opposed to them as the permanent is opposed to the changing and inconstant.

One may, I think, without fear of being upset by any future Galtonian circulars, believe that all men must single out from the rest of what they call themselves some central principle of which each would recognize the foregoing to be a fair general description—accurate enough, at any rate, to denote what is meant, and keep it unconfused with other things. The moment, however, they came to closer quarters with it, trying to define more accurately its precise nature, we should find opinions beginning to diverge. Some would say that it is a simple active substance, the soul, of which they are thus conscious; others, that it is nothing but a fiction, the imaginary being denoted by the pronoun I; and between these extremes of opinion all sorts of intermediaries would be found.

Later we must ourselves discuss them all, and sufficient to that day will be the evil thereof. *Now,* let us try to settle for ourselves as definitely as we can, just how this central nucleus of the Self may *feel,* no matter whether it be a spiritual substance or only a delusive word.

For this central part of the Self is *felt.* It may be all that Transcendentalists say it is, and all that Empiricists say it is into the bargain, but it is at any rate no *mere ens rationis,* cognized only in an intellectual way, and no *mere* summation of memories or *mere* sound of a word in our ears. It is something with which we also have direct sensible acquaintance, and which is as fully present at any moment of consciousness in which it *is* present, as in a whole lifetime of such moments. When, just now, it was called an abstraction, that did not mean that, like some general notion, it could not be presented in a particular experience. It only meant that in the stream of consciousness it never was found all alone. But when it is found, it is *felt;* just as the body is felt, the feeling of which is also an abstraction, because never is the body felt all alone, but always together with other things. *Now can we tell more precisely in what the feeling of this central active self consists*—not necessarily as yet what the active self *is,* as a being or principle, but what we *feel* when we become aware of its existence?

I think I can in my own case; and as what I say will be likely to meet with opposition if generalized (as indeed it may be in part inapplicable to other individuals), I had better continue in the first person, leaving my description to be accepted by those to whose introspection it may commend itself as true, and confessing my inability to meet the demands of others, if others there be.

First of all, I am aware of a constant play of furtherances and hindrances in my thinking, of checks and releases, tendencies which run with desire, and tendencies which run the other way. Among the matters I think of, some range themselves on the side of the thought's interests, whilst others play an unfriendly part thereto. The mutual inconsistencies and agreements, reinforcements and obstructions, which obtain amongst these objective matters reverberate backwards and produce what seem to be incessant reactions of my spontaneity upon them, welcoming or opposing, appropriating or disowning, striving with or against, saying yes or no. This palpitating inward life is, in me, that central nucleus which I just tried to describe in terms that all men might use.

But when I forsake such general descriptions and grapple with particulars, coming to the closest possible quarters with the facts, *it is difficult for me to detect in the activity any purely spiritual element at all. Whenever my introspective glance succeeds in turning around quickly enough to catch one of these manifestations of spontaneity in the act, all it can ever feel distinctly is some bodily process, for the most part taking place within the head.* Omitting for a moment what is obscure in these introspective results, let me try to state those particulars which to my own consciousness seem indubitable and distinct.

In the first place, the acts of attending, assenting, negating, making an effort, are felt as movements of something in the head. In many cases it it possible to describe these movements quite exactly. In attending to either an idea or a sensation belonging to a particular sense-sphere, the movement is the adjustment of the sense-organ, felt as it occurs. I cannot think in visual terms, for example, without feeling a fluctuating play of pressures, convergences, divergences, and accommodations in my eyeballs. The direction in which the object is conceived to lie determines the character of these movements, the feeling of which becomes, for my consciousness, identified with the manner in which I make myself ready to receive the visible thing. My brain appears to me as if all shot across with lines of direction, of which I have become conscious as my attention has shifted from one sense-organ to another, in passing to successive outer things, or in following trains of varying sense-ideas.

When I try to remember or reflect, the movements in question, instead of being directed towards the periphery, seem to come from the periphery inwards and feel like a sort of *withdrawal* from the outer world. As far as I can detect, these feelings are due to an actual rolling outwards and upwards of the eyeballs, such as I believe occurs in me in sleep, and is the exact opposite of their action in fixating a physical thing. In reasoning, I find that I am apt to have a kind of vaguely localized diagram in my mind, with the various fractional objects of the thought disposed at particular points thereof; and the oscillations of my attention from one of them to another are most distinctly felt as alternations of direction in movements occurring inside the head.

In consenting and negating, and in making a mental effort, the movements seem more complex, and I find them harder to describe. The opening and closing of the glottis play a great part in these operations, and, less distinctly, the movements of the soft palate, etc., shutting off the posterior nares from the mouth. My glottis is like a sensitive valve, intercepting my breath instantaneously at every mental hesitation or felt aversion to the objects of my thought, and as quickly opening, to let the air pass through my throat and nose, the moment the repugnance is overcome. The feeling of the movement of this air is, in me, one strong ingredient of the feeling of assent. The movements of the muscles of the brow and eyelids also respond very sensitively to every fluctuation in the agreeableness or disagreeableness of what comes before my mind.

In *effort* of any sort, contractions of the jaw-muscles and of those of respiration are added to those of the brow and glottis, and thus the feeling passes out of the head properly so called. It passes out of the head whenever the welcoming or rejecting of the object is *strongly* felt. Then a set of feelings pour in from many bodily parts, all 'expressive' of my emotion, and the head-feelings proper are swallowed up in this larger mass.

In a sense, then, it may be truly said that, in one person at least, *the 'Self of selves,' when carefully examined, is found to consist* mainly of the collection of these peculiar motions in the head or between the head and throat. I do not for a moment say that this is *all* it consists of, for I fully realize how desperately hard is introspection in this field. But I feel quite sure that these cephalic motions are the portions of my innermost activity of which I am *most distinctly aware.* If the dim portions which I cannot yet define should prove to be like unto these distinct portions in me, and I like other men, *it would follow that our entire feeling of spiritual activity, or what commonly passes by that name, is really a feeling of bodily activities whose exact nature is by most men overlooked.*

Now, without pledging ourselves in any way to adopt this hypothesis, let us dally with it for a while to see to what consequences it might lead if it were true.

In the first place, the nuclear part of the Self, intermediary between ideas and overt acts, would be a collection of activities physiologically in no essential way different from the overt acts themselves. If we divide all possible physiological acts into *adjustments* and *executions,* the nuclear self would be the adjustments collectively considered; and the less intimate, more shifting self, so far as it was active, would be the executions. But both adjustments and executions would obey the reflex type. Both would be the result of sensorial and ideational processes discharging either into each other within the brain, or into muscles and other parts outside. The peculiarity of the adjustments would be that they are minimal reflexes few in number, incessantly repeated, constant amid great fluctuations in the rest of the mind's content, and entirely unimportant and uninteresting except through their uses in furthering or inhibiting the presence of various things, and actions before consciousness. These characters would naturally keep us from introspectively paying much attention to them in detail, whilst they would at the same time make us aware of them as a coherent group of processes, strongly contrasted with all the other things consciousness contained—even with the other constituents of the 'Self,' material, social, or spiritual as the case might be. They are reactions, and they are *primary* reactions. Everything arouses them; for objects which have no other effects will for a moment contract the brow and make the glottis close. It is as if all that visited the mind had to stand an entrance-examination, and just show its face so as to be either approved or sent back. These primary reactions are like the opening or the closing of the door. In the midst of psychic change they are the permanent core of turnings-towards and turnings-from, of yieldings and arrests, which naturally seem central and interior in comparison with the foreign matters, *apropos* to which they occur, and hold a sort of arbitrating, decisive position, quite unlike that held by any of the other constituents of the Me. It would not be surprising, then, if we were to feel them as the birthplace of conclusions and the starting point of acts, or if they came to appear as what we called a while back the 'sanctuary within the citadel' of our personal life.

If they really were the innermost sanctuary, the *ultimate* one of all the selves whose being we can ever directly experience, it would follow that *all* that is experienced is, strictly considered, *objective;* that this Objective falls asunder into two contrasted parts, one realized as 'Self,' the other as 'not-Self'; and that over and above these parts there *is* nothing save the fact that they are known, the fact of the stream of thought being there as the indispensable subjective condition of their being experienced at all. But this *condition* of the experience is not one of the *things experienced* at the moment; this knowing is not immediately *known*. It is only known in subsequent reflection. Instead, then, of the stream of thought being one of *con*-sciousness, "thinking its own existence along with whatever else it thinks" (as Ferrier says), it might be better called a stream of *Sciousness* pure and simple, thinking objects of some of which it makes what it calls a 'Me,' and only aware of its 'pure' Self in an abstract, hypothetic or conceptual way. Each 'section' of the stream would then be a bit of sciousness or knowledge of this sort, including and contemplating its 'me' and its 'not-me' as objects which work out their drama together, but not yet including or contemplating its own subjective being. The sciousness in question would be the *Thinker,* and the existence of this thinker would be given to us rather as a logical postulate than as that direct inner perception of spiritual activity which we naturally believe ourselves to have. 'Matter,' as something behind physical phenomena, is a postulate of this sort. Between the postulated Matter and the postulated Thinker, the sheet of phenomena would then swing, some of them (the 'realities') pertaining more to the matter, others (the fictions, opinions, and errors) pertaining more to the Thinker. But *who* the Thinker would be, or how many distinct Thinkers we ought to suppose in the universe, would all be subjects for an ulterior metaphysical inquiry.

Speculations like this traverse common-sense; and not only do they traverse common-sense (which in philosophy is no insuperable objection) but they contradict the fundamental assumption of *every* philosophic school. Spiritualists, transcendentalists, and empiricists alike admit in us a continual direct perception of the thinking activity in the concrete. However they may otherwise disagree, they vie with each other in the cordiality of their recognition of our *thoughts* as the one sort of existent which skepticism cannot touch. I will therefore treat the last few pages as a parenthetical digression, and from now to the end of the volume revert to the path of common-sense again. I mean by this that I will continue to assume (as I have assumed all along, especially in the last chapter) a direct awareness of the process of our thinking as such, simply insisting on the fact that it is an even more inward and subtle phenomenon than most of us suppose. At the conclusion of the volume, however, I may permit myself to revert again to the doubts here provisionally mooted, and will indulge in some metaphysical reflections suggested by them. . . .

But what is this abstract numerical principle of identity, this 'Number One' within me, for which, according to proverbial philosophy, I am supposed to keep so constant a 'lookout'? Is it the inner nucleus of my spiritual self, that collection of obscurely felt 'adjustments,' *plus* perhaps that still more obscurely perceived subjectivity as such, of which we recently spoke? Or is it perhaps the concrete stream of my thought in its entirety, or some one section of the same? Or may it be the indivisible Soul-Substance, in which, according to the orthodox tradition, my faculties inhere? Or, finally, can it be the mere pronoun I? Surely it is none of these things, that self for which I feel such hot regard. Though all of them together were put within me, I should still be cold, and fail to exhibit anything worthy of the name of selfishness or of devotion to 'Number One.' To have a self that I can *care for,* nature must first present me with some *object* interesting enough to make me instinctively wish to appropriate it for its *own* sake, and out of it to manufacture one of those material, social, or spiritual selves, which we have already passed in review. We shall find that all the facts of rivalry and substitution that have so struck us, all the shiftings and expansions and contractions of the sphere of what shall be considered me and mine, are but results of the fact that certain *things* appeal to primitive and instinctive impulses of our nature, and that we follow their destinies with an excitement that owes nothing to a reflective source. These objects our consciousness treats as the primordial constituents of its Me. Whatever other objects, whether by association with the fate of these, or in any other way, come to be followed with the same sort of interest, form our remoter and more secondary self. *The words* ME, *then, and* SELF, *so far as they arouse feeling and connote emotional worth, are* OBJECTIVE *designations, meaning* ALL THE THINGS *which have the power to produce in a stream of consciousness excitement of a certain peculiar sort.* Let us try to justify this proposition in detail.

The most palpable selfishness of a man is his bodily selfishness; and his most palpable self is the body to which that selfishness relates. Now I say that he identifies himself with this body because he loves *it,* and that he does not love it because he finds it to be identified with himself. Reverting to natural history-psychology will help us to see the truth of this. In the chapter on Instincts we shall learn that every creature has a certain selective interest in certain portions of the world, and that this interest is as often connate as acquired. Our *interest in things* means the attention and emotion which the thought of them will excite, and the actions which their presence will evoke. Thus every species is particularly interested in its own prey or food, its own enemies, its own sexual mates, and its own young. These things fascinate by their intrinsic power to do so; they are cared for for their own sakes.

Well, it stands not in the least otherwise with our bodies. They too are percepts in our objective field—they are simply the most interesting percepts there. What happens to them excites in us emotions and tendencies to action more energetic and habitual than any which are excited by other portions of the 'field.' What my comrades call my bodily selfishness or self-love, is nothing but the sum of all the outer acts which this interest in my body spontaneously draws from me. My 'selfishness' is here but a descriptive name for grouping together the outward symptoms which I show. When I am led by self-love to keep my seat whilst ladies stand, or to grab something first and cut out my neighbor, what I really love is the comfortable seat, is the thing itself which I grab. I love them primarily, as the mother loves her babe, or a generous man an heroic deed. Wherever, as here, self-seeking is the outcome of simple instinctive propensity, it is but a name for certain reflex acts. Something rivets my attention fatally, and fatally provokes the 'selfish' response. Could an automaton be so skilfully constructed as to ape these acts, it would be called selfish as properly as I. It is true that I am no automaton, but a thinker. But my thoughts, like my acts, are here concerned only with the outward things. They need neither know nor care for any pure principle within. In fact the more utterly 'selfish' I am in this primitive way, the more blindly absorbed my thought will be in the objects and impulses of my lusts, and the more devoid of any inward-looking glance. A baby, whose consciousness of the pure Ego, of himself as a thinker, is not usually supposed developed, is, in this way, as some German has said, *'der vollendeteste Egoist.'* His corporeal person, and what ministers to its needs, are the only self he can possibly be said to love. His so-called self-love is but a name for his insensibility to all but this one set of things. It may be that he needs a pure principle of subjectivity, a soul or pure Ego (he certainly needs a stream of thought) to make him sensible at all to anything, to make him discriminate and love *überhaupt*—how that may be, we shall see ere long; but this pure Ego, which would then be the *condition* of his loving, need no more be the *object* of his love than it need be the object of his thought. If his interests lay altogether in other bodies than his own, if all his instincts were altruistic and all his acts suicidal, still he would need a principle of *consciousness* just as he does now. Such a principle cannot then be the principle of his bodily *selfishness* any more than it is the principle of any other tendency he may show.

So much for the bodily self-love. But my *social* self-love, my interest in the images other men have framed of me, is also an interest in a set of objects external to my thought. These thoughts in other men's minds are out of my mind and 'ejective' to me. They come and go, and grow and dwindle, and I am puffed up with pride, or blush with shame, at the result, just as at my success or failure in the pursuit of a material thing. So that here again, just as in the former case, the pure principle seems out of the game as an *object* of regard, and present only as the general form or condition under which the regard and the thinking go on in me at all.

But, it will immediately be objected, this is giving a mutilated account of the facts. Those images of me in the minds of other men are, it is true, things outside of me, whose changes I perceive just as I perceive any other outward change. But the pride and shame which I feel are not concerned merely with *those* changes. I feel as if something else had changed too, when I perceive my image in your mind to have changed for the worse, something in me to which that image belongs, and which a moment ago I felt inside of me, big and strong and lusty, but now weak, contracted, and collapsed. Is not this latter change the change I feel the shame about? Is not the condition of this thing inside of me the proper object of my egoistic concern, of my self-regard? And is it not, after all, my pure Ego, my bare numerical principle of distinction from other men, and no empirical part of me at all?

No, it is no such pure principle, it is simply my total empirical selfhood again, my historic Me, a collection of objective facts, to which the depreciated image in your mind 'belongs.' In what capacity is it that I claim and demand a respectful greeting from you instead of this expression of disdain? It is not as being a bare I that I claim it, it is as being an I who has always been treated with respect, who belongs to a certain family and 'set,' who has certain powers, possessions, and public functions, sensibilities, duties, and purposes, and merits and deserts. All this is what your disdain negates and contradicts; this is 'the thing inside of me' whose changed treatment I feel the shame about; this is what was lusty, and now, in consequence of your conduct, is collapsed; and this certainly is an empirical objective thing. Indeed, the thing that is felt modified and changed for the worse during my feeling of shame is often more concrete even than this—it is simply my bodily person, in which your conduct immediately and without any reflection at all on my part works those muscular, glandular, and vascular changes which together make up the 'expression' of shame. In this instinctive, reflex sort of shame, the body is just as much the entire vehicle of the self-feeling as, in the coarser cases which we first took up, it was the vehicle of the self-seeking. As, in simple 'hoggishness,' a succulent morsel gives rise, by the reflex mechanism, to behavior which the bystanders find 'greedy,' and consider to flow from a certain sort of 'self-regard'; so here your disdain gives rise, by a mechanism quite as reflex and immediate, to another sort of behavior, which the bystanders call 'shame-faced' and which they consider due to another kind of self-regard. But in both cases there may be no particular self *regarded* at all by the mind; and the name self-regard may be only a descriptive title imposed from without the reflex acts themselves, and the feelings that immediately result from their discharge.

After the bodily and social selves come the spiritual. But which of my spiritual selves do I really care for? My Soul-Substance? my 'transcendental Ego, or Thinker'? my pronoun I? my subjectivity as such? my nucleus of cephalic adjustments? or my more phe-nomenal and perishable powers, my loves and hates, willingnesses and sensibilities, and the like? Surely the latter. But they, rela-tively to the central principle, whatever it may be, are external and objective. They come and go, and it remains—"so shakes the magnet, and so stands the pole." It may indeed have to be there for them to be loved, but being there is not identical with being loved itself.

To sum up, then, *we see no reason to suppose that 'self-love' is primarily, or secondarily, or ever, love for one's mere principle of conscious identity.* It is always love for something which, as compared with that principle, is superficial, transient, liable to be taken up or dropped at will. . . .

Unless his consciousness were something more than cognitive, unless it experienced a partiality for certain of the objects, which, in succession, occupy its ken, it could not long maintain itself in existence; for, by an inscrutable necessity, each human mind's appearance on this earth is conditioned upon the integrity of the body with which it belongs, upon the treatment which that body gets from others, and upon the spiritual dispositions which use it as their tool, and lead it either towards longevity or to destruction. *Its own body, then, first of all, its friends next, and finally its spiritual dispositions,* MUST *be the supremely interesting* OBJECTS *for each human mind.* . . .

My own body and what ministers to its needs are thus the primitive object, instinctively determined, of my egoistic interests. Other objects may become interesting derivatively through association with any of these things, either as means or as habitual concomitants; *and so in a thousand ways the primitive sphere of the egoistic emotions may enlarge* and change its boundaries.

This sort of interest is really the *meaning of the word 'my.'* Whatever has it is *eo ipso* a part of me. My child, my friend dies, and where he goes I feel that part of myself now is and evermore shall be:

> For this losing is true-dying;
> This is lordly man's down-lying;
> This his slow but sure reclining,
> Star by star his world resigning.

The fact remains, however, that certain special sorts of thing tend primordially to possess this interest, and form the *natural* me. But all these things are *objects,* properly so called, to the subject which does the thinking. And this latter fact upsets at once the dictum of the old-fashioned sensationalist psychology, that altruistic passions and interests are contradictory to the nature of things, and that if they appear anywhere to exist, it must be as secondary products, resolvable at bottom into cases of selfishness, taught by experience a hypocritical disguise. If the zoological and evolutionary point of view is the true one, there is no reason why any object whatever *might* not arouse passion and interest as primitively and instinctively as any other, whether connected or not with the interests of the me. The phenomenon of passion is in origin and essence the same, whatever be the target upon which it is discharged; and what the target actually happens to be is solely a question of fact. I might conceivably be as much fascinated, and as primitively so, by the care of my neighbor's body as by the care of my own. The only check to such exuberant altruistic interests is natural selection, which would weed out such as were very harmful to the individual or to his tribe. Many such interests, however, remain unweeded out—the interest in the opposite sex, for example, which seems in mankind stronger than is called for by its utilitarian need; and alongside of them remain interests, like that in alcoholic intoxication, or in musical sounds, which, for aught we can see, are without any utility whatever. The sympathetic instincts and the egoistic ones are thus co-ordinate. They arise, so far as we can tell, on the same psychologic level. The only difference between them is, that the instincts called egoistic form much the larger mass. . . .

THE SENSE OF PERSONAL IDENTITY

In the last chapter it was stated in as radical a way as possible that the thoughts which we actually know to exist do not fly about loose, but seem each to belong to some one thinker and not to another. Each thought, out of a multitude of other thoughts of which it may think, is able to distinguish those which belong to its own Ego from those which do not. The former have a warmth and intimacy about them of which the latter are completely devoid, being merely conceived, in a cold and foreign fashion, and not appearing as blood-relatives, bringing their greetings to us from out of the past.

Now this consciousness of personal sameness may be treated either as a subjective phenomenon or as an objective deliverance, as a feeling, or as a truth. We may explain how one bit of thought can come to judge other bits to belong to the same Ego with itself; or we may criticise its judgment and decide how far it may tally with the nature of things.

As a mere subjective phenomenon the judgment presents no difficulty or mystery peculiar to itself. It belongs to the great class of judgments of sameness; and there is nothing more remarkable in making a judgment of sameness in the first person than in the second or the third. The intellectual operations seem essentially alike, whether I say 'I am the same,' or whether I say 'the pen is the same, as yesterday.' It is as easy to think this as to think the opposite and say 'neither I nor the pen is the same.'

This sort of *bringing of things together into the object of a single judgment* is of course essential to all thinking. The things are conjoined *in* the thought, whatever may be the relation in which they appear to the thought. The thinking them is *thinking* them together, even if only with the result of judging that they do not *belong* together. This sort of *subjective synthesis*, essential to knowledge as such (whenever it has a complex object), must not be confounded with *objective synthesis* or union instead of difference or disconnection, known among the things.[2] The subjective synthesis is involved in thought's mere existence. Even a really disconnected world could only be *known* to be such by having its parts temporarily united in the Object of some pulse of consciousness.[3]

The sense of personal identity is not, then, this mere synthetic form essential to all thought. It is the sense of a sameness perceived *by* thought and predicated of things *thought-about*. These things are a present self and a self of yesterday. The thought not only thinks them both, but thinks that they are identical. The psychologist, looking on and playing the critic, might prove the thought wrong, and show there was no real identity—there might have been no yesterday, or, at any rate, no self of yesterday; or, if there were, the sameness predicated might not obtain, or might be predicated on insufficient grounds. In either case the personal identity would not exist as a *fact;* but it would exist as a *feeling* all the same; the consciousness of it by the thought would be there, and the psychologist would still have to analyze that, and show where its illusoriness lay. Let us now be the psychologist and see whether it be right or wrong when it says, *I am the same self that I was yesterday.*

We may immediately call it right and intelligible so far as it posits a past time with past thoughts or selves contained therein—these were data which we assumed at the outset of the book. Right

2. "Also nur dadurch, dass ich ein Mannigfaltiges gegebener Vorstellungen in *einem Bewusstsein* verbinden kann, ist es möglich dass ich die *Identität des Bewusstseins* in diesen *Vorstellungen* selbst vorstelle, d. h. die analytische Einheit der Apperception ist nur unter der Voraussetzung irgend einer synthetischen möglich." In this passage (*Kritik der reinen Vernunft*, 2te Aufl. § 16) Kant calls by the names of analytic and synthetic apperception what we here mean by objective and subjective synthesis respectively. It were much to be desired that some one might invent a good pair of terms in which to record the distinction—those used in the text are certainly very bad, but Kant's seem to me still worse. 'Categorical unity' and 'transcendental synthesis' would also be good Kantian, but hardly good human, speech.

3. So that we might say, by a sort of bad pun, "only a connected world can be known as disconnected." I say bad pun, because the point of view shifts between the connectedness and the disconnectedness. The disconnectedness is of the realities known; the connectedness is of the knowledge of them; and reality and knowledge of it are, from the psychological point of view held fast to in these pages, two different facts.

also and intelligible so far as it thinks of a present self—that
present self we have just studied in its various forms. The only
question for us is as to what the consciousness may mean when it
calls the present self the *same* with one of the past selves which it
has in mind.

We spoke a moment since of warmth and intimacy. This leads
us to the answer sought. For, whatever the thought we are criticis-
ing may think about its present self, that self comes to its acquaintance, or is actually felt, with warmth and intimacy. Of course this
is the case with the *bodily* part of it; we feel the whole cubic mass
of our body all the while, it gives us an unceasing sense of personal
existence. Equally do we feel the inner 'nucleus of the spiritual
self,' either in the shape of yon faint physiological adjustments, or
(adopting the universal psychological belief), in that of the pure
activity of our thought taking place as such. Our remoter spiritual,
material, and social selves, so far as they are realized, come also
with a glow and a warmth; for the thought of them infallibly
brings some degree of organic emotion in the shape of quickened
heart-beats, oppressed breathing, or some other alteration, even
though it be a slight one, in the general bodily tone. The character of 'warmth,' then, in the present self, reduces itself to either of
two things—something in the feeling which we have of the
thought itself, as thinking, or else the feeling of the body's actual
existence at the moment—or finally to both. We cannot realize our
present self without simultaneously feeling one or other of these
two things. Any other fact which brings these two things with it
into consciousness will be thought with a warmth and an intimacy
like those which cling to the present self.

Any *distant* self which fulfils this condition will be thought with
such warmth and intimacy. But which distant selves *do* fulfil the
condition, when represented?

Obviously those, and only those, which fulfilled it when they
were alive. *Them* we shall imagine with the animal warmth upon
them, to them may possibly cling the aroma, the echo of the
thinking taken in the act. And by a natural consequence, we shall
assimilate them to each other and to the warm and intimate self
we now feel within us as we think, and separate them as a collection from whatever selves have not this mark, much as out of a
herd of cattle let loose for the winter on some wide western prairie

the owner picks out and sorts together when the time for the round-up comes in the spring, all the beasts on which he finds his own particular brand.

The various members of the collection thus set apart are felt to belong with each other whenever they are thought at all. The animal warmth, etc., is their herd-mark, the brand from which they can never more escape. It runs through them all like a thread through a chaplet and makes them into a whole, which we treat as a unit, no matter how much in other ways the parts may differ *inter se*. Add to this character the farther one that the distant selves appear to our thought as having for hours of time been *continuous* with each other, and the most recent ones of them continuous with the Self of the present moment, melting into it by slow degrees; and we get a still stronger bond of union. As we think we see an identical bodily thing when, in spite of changes of structure, it exists continuously before our eyes, or when, however interrupted its presence, its quality returns unchanged; so here we think we experience an identical *Self* when it appears to us in an analogous way. Continuity makes us unite what dissimilarity might otherwise separate; similarity makes us unite what discontinuity might hold apart. And thus it is, finally, that Peter, awakening in the same bed with Paul, and recalling what both had in mind before they went to sleep, reidentifies and appropriates the 'warm' ideas as his, and is never tempted to confuse them with those cold and pale-appearing ones which he ascribes to Paul. As well might he confound Paul's body, which he only sees, with his own body, which he sees but also feels. Each of us when he awakens says, Here's the same old self again, just as he says, Here's the same old bed, the same old room, the same old world.

The sense of our own personal identity, then, is exactly like any one of our other perceptions of sameness among phenomena. It is a conclusion grounded either on the resemblance in a fundamental respect, or on the continuity before the mind, of the phenomena compared.

And it must not be taken to mean more than these grounds warrant, or treated as a sort of metaphysical or absolute Unity in which all differences are overwhelmed. The past and present selves compared are the same just so far as they *are* the same, and no farther. A uniform feeling of 'warmth,' of bodily existence (or an equally uniform feeling of pure psychic energy?) pervades them all; and this is what gives them a *generic* unity, and makes them the same in *kind*. But this generic unity coexists with generic differences just as real as the unity. And if from the one point of view they are one self, from others they are as truly not one but many selves. And similarly of the attribute of continuity; it gives its own kind of unity to the self—that of mere connectedness, or unbrokenness, a perfectly definite phenomenal thing—but it gives not a jot or tittle more. And this unbrokenness in the stream of selves, like the unbrokenness in an exhibition of 'dissolving views,' in no wise implies any farther unity or contradicts any amount of plurality in other respects.

And accordingly we find that, where the resemblance and the continuity are no longer felt, the sense of personal identity goes too. We hear from our parents various anecdotes about our infant years, but we do not appropriate them as we do our own memories. Those breaches of decorum awaken no blush, those bright sayings no self-complacency. That child is a foreign creature with which our present self is no more identified in feeling than it is with some stranger's living child to-day. Why? Partly because great time-gaps break up all these early years—we cannot ascend to them by continuous memories; and partly because no representation of how the child *felt* comes up with the stories. We know what he said and did; but no sentiment of his little body, of his emotions, of his psychic strivings as they felt to him, comes up to contribute an element of warmth and intimacy to the narrative we hear, and the main bond of union with our present self thus disappears. It is the same with certain of our dimly-recollected experiences. We hardly know whether to appropriate them or to disown them as fancies, or things read or heard and not lived through. Their animal heat has evaporated; the feelings that accompanied them are so lacking in the recall, or so different from those we now enjoy, that no judgment of identity can be decisively cast.

Resemblance among the parts of a continuum of feelings (especially bodily feelings) experienced along with things widely different in all other regards, *thus constitutes the real and verifiable 'personal identity' which we feel.* . . .

But in leaving the matter here, and saying that this sum of passing things is all, these [Hume and Herbart and their successors] writers have neglected certain more subtle aspects of the Unity of Consciousness, to which we next must turn.

Our recent simile of the herd of cattle will help us. It will be remembered that the beasts were brought together into one herd because their owner found on each of them his brand. The 'owner' symbolizes here that 'section' of consciousness, or pulse of thought, which we have all along represented as the vehicle of the judgment of identity; and the 'brand' symbolizes the characters of warmth and continuity, by reason of which the judgment is made. There is found a *self*-brand, just as there is found a herd-brand. Each brand, so far, is the mark, or cause of our knowing, that certain things belong-together. But if the brand is the *ratio cognoscendi* of the belonging, the belonging in the case of the herd, is in turn the *ratio existendi* of the brand. No beast would be so branded unless he belonged to the owner of the herd. They are not his because they are branded; they are branded because they are his. So that it seems as if our description of the belonging-together of the various selves, as a belonging-together which is merely *represented,* in a later pulse of thought, had knocked the bottom out of the matter, and omitted the most characteristic one of all the features found in the herd—a feature which common-sense finds in the phenomenon of personal identity as well, and for our omission of which she will hold us to a strict account. For common-sense insists that the unity of all the selves is not a mere appearance of similarity or continuity, ascertained after the fact. She is sure that it involves a real belonging to a real Owner, to a pure spiritual entity of some kind. Relation to this entity is what makes the self's constituents stick together as they do for thought. The individual beasts do not stick together, for all that they wear the same brand. Each wanders with whatever accidental mates it finds. The herd's unity is only potential, its centre ideal, like the 'centre of gravity' in physics, until the herdsman or owner comes. He furnishes a real centre of accretion to which the beasts are driven and by which they are held. The beasts stick together by sticking severally to him. Just so, common-sense insists, there must be a real proprietor in the case of the selves, or else their actual accretion into a 'personal consciousness' would never have taken place. To the usual empiricist explanation of personal consciousness this is a formidable reproof, because all the individual thoughts and feelings which have succeeded each other 'up to date' are represented by ordinary Associationism as in some inscrutable way 'integrating' or gumming themselves together on their own account, and thus fusing into a stream. All the incomprehensibilities which in Chapter VI we saw to attach to the idea of things fusing without a *medium* apply to the empiricist description of personal identity.

But in our own account the medium is fully assigned, the herdsman is there, in the shape of something not among the things collected, but superior to them all, namely, the real, present onlooking, remembering, 'judging thought' or identifying 'section' of the stream. This is what collects—'owns' some of the past facts which it surveys, and disowns the rest—and so makes a unity that is actualized and anchored and does not merely float in the blue air of possibility. And the reality of such pulses of thought, with their function of knowing, it will be remembered that we did not seek to deduce or explain, but simply assumed them as the ultimate kind of fact that the psychologist must admit to exist.

But this assumption, though it yields much, still does not yield all that common-sense demands. The unity into which the Thought—as I shall for a time proceed to call, with a capital T, the present mental state—binds the individual past facts with each other and with itself, does not exist until the Thought is there. It is as if wild cattle were lassoed by a newly-created settler and then owned for the first time. But the essence of the matter to common-sense is that the past thoughts never were wild cattle, they were always owned. The Thought does not capture them, but as soon as it comes into existence it finds them already its own. How is this possible unless the Thought have a *substantial* identity with a former owner—not a mere continuity or a resemblance, as in our account, but a *real unity?* Common-sense in fact would drive us to admit what we may for the moment call an Arch-Ego, dominating the entire stream of thought and all the selves that may be represented in it, as the ever self-same and changeless principle implied in their union. The 'Soul' of Metaphysics and the 'Transcendental Ego' of the Kantian Philosophy, are, as we shall soon see, but attempts to satisfy this urgent demand of common-sense. But, for a time at least, we can still express without any such hypotheses that appearance of never-lapsing ownership for which common-sense contends.

For how would it be if the Thought, the present judging

Thought, instead of being in any way substantially or transcendentally identical with the former owner of the past self, merely inherited his 'title,' and thus stood as his legal representative now? It would then, if its birth coincided exactly with the death of another owner, *find* the past self already its own as soon as it found it at all, and the past self would thus never be wild, but always owned, by a title that never lapsed. We can imagine a long succession of herdsmen coming rapidly into possession of the same cattle by transmission of an original title by bequest. May not the 'title' of a collective self be passed from one Thought to another in some analogous way?

It is a patent fact of consciousness that a transmission like this actually occurs. Each pulse of cognitive consciousness, each Thought, dies away and is replaced by another. The other, among the things it knows, knows its own predecessor, and finding it 'warm,' in the way we have described, greets it, saying: "Thou art *mine,* and part of the same self with me." Each later Thought, knowing and including thus the Thoughts which went before, is the final receptacle—and appropriating them is the final owner—of all that they contain and own. Each Thought is thus born an owner, and dies owned, transmitting whatever it realized as its Self to its own later proprietor. As Kant says, it is as if elastic balls were to have not only motion but knowledge of it, and a first ball were to transmit both its motion and its consciousness to a second, which took both up into *its* consciousness and passed them to a third, until the last ball held all that the other balls had held, and realized it as its own. It is this trick which the nascent thought has of immediately taking up the expiring thought and 'adopting' it, which is the foundation of the appropriation of most of the remoter constituents of the self. Who owns the last self owns the self before the last, for what possesses the possessor possesses the possessed.

It is impossible to discover any *verifiable* features in personal identity, which this sketch does not contain, impossible to imagine how any transcendental non-phenomenal sort of an Arch-Ego, were he there, could shape matters to any other result, or be known in time by any other fruit, than just this production of a stream of consciousness each 'section' of which should know, and knowing, hug to itself and adopt, all those that went before—thus standing as the *representative* of the entire past stream; and which should similarly adopt the objects already adopted by any portion of this spiritual stream. Such standing-as-representative, and such adopting, are perfectly clear phenomenal relations. The Thought which, whilst it knows another Thought and the Object of that Other, appropriates the Other and the Object which the Other appropriated, is still a perfectly distinct phenomenon from that Other; it may hardly resemble it; it may be far removed from it in space and time.

The only point that is obscure is the *act of appropriation* itself. Already in enumerating the constituents of the self and their rivalry, I had to use the word appropriate. And the quick-witted reader probably noticed at the time, in hearing how one constituent was let drop and disowned and another one held fast to and espoused, that the phrase was meaningless unless the constituents were objects in the hands of something else. A thing cannot appropriate itself; it *is* itself; and still less can it disown itself. There must be an agent of the appropriating and disowning; but that agent we have already named. It is the Thought to whom the various 'constituents' are known. That Thought is a vehicle of choice as well as of cognition; and among the choices it makes are these appropriations, or repudiations, of its 'own.' But the Thought never is an object in its own hands, it never appropriates or disowns itself. It appropriates *to* itself, it is the actual focus of accretion, the hook from which the chain of past selves dangles, planted firmly in the Present, which alone passes for real, and thus keeping the chain from being a purely ideal thing. Anon the hook itself will drop into the past with all it carries, and then be treated as an object and appropriated by a new Thought in the new present which will serve as living hook in turn. The present moment of consciousness is thus, as Mr. Hodgson says, the darkest in the whole series. It may feel its own immediate existence—we have all along admitted the possibility of this, hard as it is by direct introspection to ascertain the fact—but nothing can be known *about* it till it be dead and gone. Its appropriations are therefore less to *itself* than to the most intimately felt *part of its present Object, the body, and the central adjustments,* which accompany the act of thinking, in the head. *These are the real nucleus of our personal identity,* and it is their actual existence, realized as a solid present fact, which makes us say 'as sure as

I exist, those past facts were part of myself.' They are the kernel to which the *represented* parts of the Self are assimilated, accreted, and knit on; and even were Thought entirely unconscious of itself in the act of thinking, these 'warm' parts of its present object would be a firm basis on which the consciousness of personal identity would rest.[4] Such consciousness, then, as a psychologic fact, can be fully described without supposing any other agent than a succession of perishing thoughts, endowed with the functions of appropriation and rejection, and of which some can know and appropriate or reject objects already known, appropriated, or rejected by the rest.

To illustrate by diagram, let A, B, and C stand for three successive thoughts, each with its object inside of it. If B's object be A, and C's object be B; then A, B, and C would stand for three pulses in a consciousness of personal identity. Each pulse would *be* something different from the others; but B would know and adopt A, and C would know and adopt A and B. Three successive states of the same brain, on which each experience in passing leaves its mark, might very well engender thoughts differing from each other in just such a way as this.

4. Some subtle reader will object that the Thought cannot call any part of its Object 'I' and knit other parts on to it, without first knitting that part on to *Itself;* and that it cannot knit it on to Itself without knowing Itself—so that our supposition that the Thought may conceivably have no immediate knowledge of Itself is thus overthrown. To which the reply is that we must take care not to be duped by words. The words *I* and *me* signify nothing mysterious and unexampled—they are at bottom only names of *emphasis;* and Thought is always emphasizing something. Within a tract of space which it cognizes, it contrasts a *here* with a *there;* within a tract of time a *now* with a *then;* of a pair of things it calls one *this,* the other *that.* I and *thou,* I and *it,* are distinctions exactly on a par with these—distinctions possible in an exclusively *objective* field of knowledge, the 'I' meaning for the Thought nothing but the bodily life which it momentarily feels. The sense of my bodily existence, however obscurely recognized as such, *may* then be the absolute original of my conscious selfhood, the fundamental perception that *I am.* All appropriations *may* be made *to* it, *by* a Thought not at the moment immediately cognized by itself. Whether these are not only logical possibilities but actual facts is something not yet dogmatically decided in the text.

The passing Thought then seems to be the Thinker; and though there *may* be another non-phenomenal Thinker behind that, so far we do not seem to need him to express the facts. . . .

C. CONCEPTION: THE SENSE OF SAMENESS*

In Chapter VIII . . . the distinction was drawn between two kinds of knowledge of things, bare acquaintance with them and knowledge about them. The possibility of two such knowledges depends on a fundamental psychical peculiarity which may be entitled *"the principle of constancy in the mind's meanings,"* and which may be thus expressed: *"The same matters can be thought of in successive portions of the mental stream, and some of these portions can know that they mean the same matters which the other portions meant."* One might put it otherwise by saying that *"the mind can always intend, and know when it intends, to think of the Same."*

This *sense of sameness* is the very keel and backbone of our thinking. We saw . . . how the consciousness of personal identity reposed on it, the present thought finding in its memories a warmth and intimacy which it recognizes as the same warmth and intimacy it now feels. This sense of identity of the knowing subject is held by some philosophers to be the only vehicle by which the world hangs together. It seems hardly necessary to say that a sense of identity of the known object would perform exactly the same unifying function, even if the sense of subjective identity were lost. And without the intention to think of the same outer things over and over again, and the sense that we were doing so, our sense of our own personal sameness would carry us but a little way towards making a universe of our experience. . . .

The function by which we thus identify a numerically distinct and permanent subject of discourse is called CONCEPTION; *and the thoughts which are its vehicles are called* concepts. But the word 'concept' is often used as if it stood for the object of discourse itself; and this looseness feeds such evasiveness in discussion that I

* From *The Principles of Psychology*, chap. 12.

shall avoid the use of the expression concept altogether, and speak of 'conceiving state of mind,' or something similar, instead. The word 'conception' is unambiguous. It properly denotes neither the mental state nor what the mental state signifies, but the relation between the two, namely, the *function* of the mental state in signifying just that particular thing. It is plain that one and the same mental state can be the vehicle of many conceptions, can mean a particular thing, and a great deal more besides. If it has such a multiple conceptual function, it may be called an act of compound conception.

We may conceive realities supposed to be extra-mental, as steam-engine; fictions, as mermaid; or mere *entia rationis*, like difference or nonentity. But whatever we do conceive, our conception is of that and nothing else—nothing else, that is, *instead* of that, though it may be of much else *in addition* to that. Each act of conception results from our attention singling out some one part of the mass of matter for thought which the world presents, and holding fast to it, without confusion.[1] Confusion occurs when we do not know whether a certain object proposed to us is the same with one of our meanings or not; so that the conceptual function

1. In later chapters we shall see that determinate relations exist between the various data thus fixed upon by the mind. These are called *a priori* or axiomatic relations. Simple inspection of the data enables us to perceive them; and one inspection is as effective as a million for engendering in us the conviction that between *those* data that relation must always hold. To change the relation we should have to make the data different. 'The guarantee for the uniformity and adequacy' of the data can only be the mind's own power to fix upon any objective content, and to mean that content as often as it likes. This right of the mind to 'construct' permanent ideal objects for itself out of the data of experience seems, singularly enough, to be a stumbling-block to many. Professor Robertson in his clear and instructive article "Axioms" in the Encyclopædia Britannica (9th edition) suggests that it may only be where *movements* enter into the constitution of the ideal object (as they do in geometrical figures) that we can "*make* the ultimate relations to be what for us they must be in all circumstances." He makes, it is true, a concession in favor of conceptions of number abstracted from "subjective occurrences succeeding each other in time" because these also are acts "of construction, dependent on the power we have of voluntarily determining the flow of subjective consciousness." "The content of passive sensation," on the other hand, "may indefinitely vary beyond any control of ours." What if it do vary, so long as we can continue to think of and mean the qualities it varied from? We can 'make' ideal objects for ourselves out of irrecoverable bits of passive experience quite as perfectly as out of easily repeatable active experiences. And when we have got our objects together and compared them, we do not *make*, but *find*, their relations.

requires, to be complete, that the thought should not only say 'I
mean this,' but also say 'I don't mean that.'[2]

Each conception thus eternally remains what it is, and never can
become another. The mind may change its states, and its meanings, at different times; may drop one conception and take up
another, but the dropped conception can in no intelligible sense
be said to *change into* its successor. The paper, a moment ago
white, I may now see to have been scorched black. But my conception 'white' does not change into my conception 'black.' On the
contrary, it stays alongside of the objective blackness, as a
different meaning in my mind, and by so doing lets me judge the
blackness as the paper's change. Unless it stayed, I should simply
say 'blackness' and know no more. Thus, amid the flux of opinions
and of physical things, the world of conceptions, or things intended to be thought about, stands stiff and immutable, like
Plato's Realm of Ideas.[3]

Some conceptions are of things, some of events, some of qualities. Any fact, be it thing, event, or quality, may be conceived
sufficiently for purposes of identification, if only it be singled out
and marked so as to separate it from other things. Simply calling it
'this' or 'that' will suffice. To speak in technical language, a
subject may be conceived by its *denotation*, with no *connotation*,
or a very minimum of connotation, attached. The essential point
is that it should be re-identified by us as that which the talk is
about; and no full representation of it is necessary for this, even
when it is a fully representable thing.

In this sense, creatures extremely low in the intellectual scale
may have conception. All that is required is that they should
recognize the same experience again. A polyp would be a conceptual thinker if a feeling of 'Hello! thingumbob again!' ever
flitted through its mind.

Most of the objects of our thought, however, are to some degree
represented as well as merely pointed out. Either they are things
and events perceived or imagined, or they are qualities appre-

2. Cf. Hodgson, *Time and Space*, § 46. Lotze, *Logic*, § 11.
3. "For though a man in a fever should from sugar have a bitter taste, which
at another time would produce a sweet one, yet the idea of bitter in that man's
mind would be as distinct as if he had tasted only gall." (Locke's *Essay*, bk. II.
chap. xi. § 3. Read the whole section!)

hended in a positive way. Even where we have no intuitive acquaintance with the nature of a thing, if we know any of the relations of it at all, anything *about* it, that is enough to individualize and distinguish it from all the other things which we might mean. Many of our topics of discourse are thus *problematical,* or defined by their relations only. We think of a thing *about* which certain facts must obtain, but we do not yet know how the thing will look when it is realized. Thus we conceive of a perpetual-motion machine. It is a *quæsitum* of a perfectly definite kind—we can always tell whether the actual machines offered us do or do not agree with what we mean by it. The natural possibility or impossibility of the thing does not touch the question of its conceivability in this problematic way. 'Round square,' 'black-white-thing,' are absolutely definite conceptions; it is a mere accident, as far as conception goes, that they happen to stand for things which nature never lets us sensibly perceive.[4] . . .

It is easy to lay bare the false assumption which underlies the whole discussion of the question [of abstract ideas] as hitherto carried on. That assumption is that ideas, in order to know, must be cast in the exact likeness of whatever things they know, and that the only things that can be known are those which ideas can resemble. The error has not been confined to nominalists. *Omnis cognitio fit per assimilationem cognoscentis et cogniti* has been the

4. Black round things, square white things, *per contra*, Nature gives us freely enough. But the combinations which she refuses to realize may exist as distinctly, in the shape of postulates, as those which she gives may exist in the shape of positive images, in our mind. As a matter of fact, she *may* realize a warm cold thing whenever two points of the skin, so near together as not to be locally distinguished, are touched, the one with a warm, the other with a cold, piece of metal. The warmth and the cold are then often felt as if in the same objective place. Under similar conditions two objects, one sharp and the other blunt, may feel like one sharp blunt thing. The same space may appear of two colors if, by optical artifice, one of the colors is made to appear as if seen *through* the other.—Whether any two attributes whatever shall be compatible or not, in the sense of appearing or not to occupy the same place and moment, depends simply on *de facto* peculiarities of natural bodies and of our sense-organs. *Logically,* any one combination of qualities is to the full as *conceivable* as any other, and has as distinct a meaning for thought. What necessitates this remark is the confusion deliberately kept up by certain authors . . . between the inconceivable and the not-distinctly-imaginable. How do we know *which* things we cannot imagine unless by first conceiving them, meaning *them* and not other things?

maxim, more or less explicitly assumed, of writers of every school. Practically it amounts to saying that an idea must *be* a duplicate edition of what it knows[5]—in other words, that it can only know itself—or, more shortly still, that knowledge in any strict sense of the word, as a self-transcendent function, is impossible.

Now our own blunt statements about the ultimateness of the cognitive relation, and the difference between the 'object' of the thought and its mere 'topic' or 'subject of discourse' are all at variance with any such theory; and we shall find more and more occasion, as we advance in this book, to deny its general truth. All that a state of mind need do, in order to take cognizance of a reality, intend it, or be 'about' it, is to lead to a remoter state of mind which either acts upon the reality or resembles it. The only class of thoughts which can with any show of plausibility be said to resemble their objects are sensations. The stuff of which all our other thoughts are composed is symbolic, and a thought attests its pertinency to a topic by simply *terminating,* sooner or later, in a sensation which resembles the latter.

But Mill and the rest believe that a thought must *be* what it means, and mean what it *is,* and that if it be a picture of an entire individual, it cannot mean any part of him to the exclusion of the rest. I say nothing here of the preposterously false descriptive psychology involved in the statement that the only things we can mentally picture are individuals completely determinate in all regards. . . . For even if it were true that our images were always of concrete individuals, it would not in the least follow that our meanings were of the same.

The sense of our meaning is an entirely peculiar element of the thought. It is one of those evanescent and 'transitive' facts of mind which introspection cannot turn round upon, and isolate and hold up for examination, as an entomologist passes round an insect on a pin. In the (somewhat clumsy) terminology I have used, it pertains to the 'fringe' of the subjective state, and is a 'feeling of tendency,' whose neural counterpart is undoubtedly a lot of dawning and dying processes too faint and complex to be traced. The geometer, with his one definite figure before him, knows perfectly

5. E.g.: "The knowledge of things must mean that the mind finds itself in them, or that, in some way, the difference between them and the mind is dissolved." (E. Caird, *Philosophy of Kant,* first edition, p. 553.)

that his thoughts apply to countless other figures as well, and that although he *sees* lines of a certain special bigness, direction, color, etc., he *means* not one of these details. When I use the word *man* in two different sentences, I may have both times exactly the same sound upon my lips and the same picture in my mental eye, but I may mean, and at the very moment of uttering the word and imagining the picture, know that I mean, two entirely different things. Thus when I say: "What a wonderful man Jones is!" I am perfectly aware that I mean by man to exclude Napoleon Bonaparte or Smith. But when I say: "What a wonderful thing Man is!" I am equally well aware that I mean to *in*clude not only Jones, but Napoleon and Smith as well. This added consciousness is an absolutely positive sort of feeling, transforming what would otherwise be mere noise or vision into something *understood;* and determining the sequel of my thinking, the later words and images, in a perfectly definite way. We saw in Chapter IX that the image *per se,* the nucleus, is *functionally* the least important part of the thought. *Our doctrine, therefore, of the 'fringe' leads to a perfectly satisfactory decision of the nominalistic and conceptualistic controversy,* so far as it touches psychology. *We must decide in favor of the conceptualists,* and affirm that the power to think things, qualities, relations, or whatever other elements there may be, isolated and abstracted from the total experience in which they appear, is the most indisputable function of our thought.

Universals

After abstractions, universals! The 'fringe,' which lets us believe in the one, lets us believe in the other too. An individual conception is of something restricted, in its application, to a single case. A universal or general conception is of an entire class, or of something belonging to an entire class, of things. The conception of an abstract quality is, taken by itself, neither universal nor particular.[6]

6. The traditional conceptualist doctrine is that an abstract must *eo ipso* be a universal. Even modern and independent authors like Prof. Dewey (*Psychology,* 207) obey the tradition: "The mind seizes upon some one aspect, . . . abstracts or prescinds it. This very seizure of some one element generalizes the one abstracted. . . . Attention, in drawing it forth, makes it a distinct content of consciousness, and thus universalizes it; it is considered no longer in its particular connection with the object, but on its own account; that is, as an idea, or what it signifies to the mind; and significance is always universal."

If I abstract *white* from the rest of the wintry landscape this morning, it is a perfectly definite conception, a self-identical quality which I may mean again; but, as I have not yet individualized it by expressly meaning to restrict it to this particular snow, nor thought at all of the possibility of other things to which it may be applicable, it is so far nothing but a 'that,' a 'floating adjective,' as Mr. Bradley calls it, or a topic broken out from the rest of the world. Properly it is, in this state, a singular—I have 'singled it out'; and when, later, I universalize or individualize its application, and my thought turns to mean either *this* white or *all possible* whites, I am in reality meaning two new things and forming two new conceptions.[7] Such an alteration of my meaning has nothing to do with any change in the image I may have in my mental eye, but solely with the vague consciousness that surrounds the image, of the sphere to which it is intended to apply. . . .

An idea neither is what it knows, nor knows what it is; nor will swarms of copies of the same 'idea,' recurring in stereotyped form, or 'by the irresistible laws of association formed into one idea,' ever be the same thing as a thought of '*all the possible members*' of a class. We must mean *that* by an altogether special bit of consciousness *ad hoc*. But it is easy to translate Berkeley's, Hume's, and Mill's notion of a swarm of ideas into cerebral terms, and so to make them stand for something real; and, in this sense, I think the doctrine of these authors less hollow than the opposite one which makes the vehicle of universal conceptions to be an *actus purus* of the soul. If each 'idea' stand for some special nascent nerve-process, then the aggregate of these nascent processes might have for its conscious correlate a psychic 'fringe,' which should be just that universal meaning, or intention that the name or mental picture employed should mean all the possible individuals of the class. Every peculiar complication of brain-processes must have some peculiar correlate in the soul. To one set of processes will correspond the thought of an indefinite taking of the extent of a word like *man;* to another set that of a particular taking; and to a third set that of a universal taking, of the extent of the same word. The thought corresponding to either set of processes is always itself a

---

7. C. F. Reid's *Intellectual Powers*, Essay v. chap. iii.—*Whiteness* is one thing, *the whiteness of this sheet of paper* another thing.

unique and singular event, whose dependence on its peculiar nerve-process I of course am far from professing to explain.** . . .

. . . Thus, my arm-chair is one of the things of which I have a conception; I knew it yesterday and recognized it when I looked at it. But if I think of it to-day as the same arm-chair which I looked

---

** James appends a lengthy passage from his article "On Some Omissions of Introspective Psychology," *Mind* (January, 1884), from which we take a portion [B.W.]: "The contrast is not, then, as the Platonists would have it, between certain subjective facts called images and sensations, and others called acts of relating intelligence; the former being blind perishing things, knowing not even their own existence as such, whilst the latter combine the poles in the mysterious synthesis of their cognitive sweep. The contrast is really between two *aspects*, in which all mental facts without exception may be taken; their structural aspect, as being subjective, and their functional aspect, as being cognitions. In the former aspect, the highest as well as the lowest is a feeling, a peculiarly tinged segment of the stream. This tingeing is its sensitive body, the *wie ihm zu Muthe ist*, the way it feels whilst passing. In the latter aspect, the lowest mental fact as well as the highest may grasp some bit of truth as its content, even though that truth were as relationless a matter as a bare unlocalized and undated quality of pain. From the cognitive point of view, all mental facts are intellections. From the subjective point of view all are feelings. Once admit that the passing and evanescent are as real parts of the stream as the distinct and comparatively abiding; once allow that fringes and halos, inarticulate perceptions, whereof the objects are as yet unnamed, mere nascencies of cognition, premonitions, awarenesses of direction, are thoughts *sui generis*, as much as articulate imaginings and propositions are; once restore, I say, the *vague* to its psychological rights, and the matter presents no further difficulty.

"And then we see that the current opposition of Feeling to Knowledge is quite a false issue. If every feeling is at the same time a bit of knowledge, we ought no longer to talk of mental states differing by having more or less of the cognitive quality; they only differ in knowing more or less, in having much fact or little fact for their object. The feeling of a broad scheme of relations is a feeling that knows much; the feeling of a simple quality is a feeling that knows little. But the knowing itself, whether of much or of little, has the same essence, and is as good knowing in the one case as in the other. Concept and image, thus discriminated through their objects, are consubstantial in their inward nature, as modes of feeling. The one, as particular, will no longer be held to be a relatively base sort of entity, to be taken as a matter of course, whilst the other, as universal, is celebrated as a sort of standing miracle, to be adored but not explained. Both concept and image, *qua* subjective, are singular and particular. Both are moments of the stream, which come in and in an instant are no more. The word universality has no meaning as applied to their psychic body or structure, which is always finite. It only has a meaning when applied to their use, import, or reference to the kind of object they may reveal. The representation, as such, of the universal object is as particular as that of an object about which we know so little that the interjection 'Ha!' is all it can evoke from us in the way of speech. Both should be weighed in the same scales, and have the same measure meted out to them, whether of worship or of contempt."

at yesterday, it is obvious that the very conception of it as the same is an additional complication to the thought, whose inward constitution must alter in consequence. In short, it is logically impossible that the same thing should be *known as the same* by two successive copies of the same thought. As a matter of fact, the thoughts by which we know that we mean the same thing are apt to be very different indeed from each other. We think the thing now in one context, now in another; now in a definite image, now in a symbol. Sometimes our sense of its identity pertains to the mere fringe, sometimes it involves the nucleus, of our thought. We never can break the thought asunder and tell just which one of its bits is the part that lets us know which subject is referred to; but nevertheless we always *do* know which of all possible subjects we have in mind. Introspective psychology must here throw up the sponge; the fluctuations of subjective life are too exquisite to be arrested by its coarse means. It must confine itself to bearing witness to the fact that all sorts of different subjective states do form the vehicle by which the same is known; and it must contradict the opposite view. . . .

The distinction between having and operating is as natural in the mental as in the material world. As our hands may hold a bit of wood and a knife, and yet do naught with either; so our mind may simply be aware of a thing's existence, and yet neither attend to it nor discriminate it, neither locate nor count nor compare nor like nor dislike nor deduce it, nor recognize it articulately as having been met with before. At the same time we know that, instead of staring at it in this entranced and senseless way, we may rally our activity in a moment, and locate, class, compare, count, and judge it. There is nothing involved in all this which we did not postulate at the very outset of our introspective work: realities, namely, *extra mentem,* thoughts, and possible relations of cognition between the two. The result of the thoughts' operating on the data given to sense is to transform the order in which experience *comes* into an entirely different order, that of the *conceived* world. There is no spot of light, for example, which I pick out and proceed to define as a pebble, which is not thereby torn from its mere time- and space-neighbors, and thought in conjunction with things physically parted from it by the width of nature. Compare the form in which facts appear in a text-book of physics, as logically subordinated laws, with that in which we naturally make their acquaintance. The conceptual scheme is a sort of sieve in which we try to gather up the world's contents. Most facts and relations fall through its meshes, being either too subtle or insignificant to be fixed in any conception. But whenever a physical reality is caught and identified as the same with something already conceived, it remains on the sieve, and all the predicates and relations of the conception with which it is identified become its predicates and relations too; it is subjected to the sieve's network, in other words. Thus comes to pass what Mr. Hodgson calls the translation of the perceptual into the conceptual order of the world.

In Chapter XXII we shall see how this translation always takes place for the sake of some subjective *interest,* and how the conception with which we handle a bit of sensible experience is really nothing but a teleological instrument. *This whole function of conceiving, of fixing, and holding fast to meanings, has no significance apart from the fact that the conceiver is a creature with partial purposes and private ends. . . .*

D.   THE PERCEPTION OF TIME*

. . . I shall deal with what is sometimes called internal perception, or the perception of *time,* and of events as occupying a date therein, especially when the date is a past one, in which case the perception in question goes by the name of *memory.* To remember a thing as past, it is necessary that the notion of 'past' should be one of our 'ideas.' We shall see in the chapter on Memory that many things come to be thought by us as past, not because of any intrinsic quality of their own, but rather because they are associated with other things which for us signify pastness. But how do these things get *their* pastness? What is the *original* of our experience of pastness, from whence we get the meaning of the term? It is this question which the reader is invited to consider in the

* From *The Principles of Psychology,* chap. 15. James notes, "This chapter is reprinted almost verbatim from the *Journal of Speculative Philosophy,* vol. xx. (1886), p. 374."

present chapter. We shall see that we have a constant feeling *sui generis* of pastness, to which every one of our experiences in turn falls a prey. To think a thing as past is to think it amongst the objects or in the direction of the objects which at the present moment appear affected by this quality. This is the original of our notion of past time, upon which memory and history build their systems. And in this chapter we shall consider this immediate sense of time alone.

If the constitution of consciousness were that of a string of bead-like sensations and images, all separate,

"we never could have any knowledge except that of the present instant. The moment each of our sensations ceased it would be gone for ever; and we should be as if we had never been. . . . We should be wholly incapable of acquiring experience. . . . Even if our ideas were associated in trains, but only as they are in imagination, we should still be without the capacity of acquiring knowledge. One idea, upon this supposition, would follow another. But that would be all. Each of our successive states of consciousness, the moment it ceased, would be gone forever. Each of those momentary states would be our whole being."[1]

We might, nevertheless, under these circumstances, *act* in a rational way, provided the mechanism which produced our trains of images produced them in a rational order. We should make appropriate speeches, though unaware of any word except the one just on our lips; we should decide upon the right policy without ever a glimpse of the total grounds of our choice. Our consciousness would be like a glow-worm spark, illuminating the point it immediately covered, but leaving all beyond in total darkness. Whether a very highly developed practical life be possible under such conditions as these is more than doubtful; it is, however, conceivable.

I make the fanciful hypothesis merely to set off our real nature by the contrast. Our feelings are not thus contracted, and our consciousness never shrinks to the dimensions of a glow-worm spark. *The knowledge of some other part of the stream, past or future, near or remote, is always mixed in with our knowledge of the present thing.*

A simple sensation, as we shall hereafter see, is an abstraction,

1. James Mill, *Analysis*, vol. i., p. 319 (J. S. Mill's Edition) .

and all our concrete states of mind are representations of objects with some amount of complexity. Part of the complexity is the echo of the objects just past, and, in a less degree, perhaps, the foretaste of those just to arrive. Objects fade out of consciousness slowly. If the present thought is of A B C D E F G, the next one will be of B C D E F G H, and the one after that of C D E F G H I—the lingerings of the past dropping successively away, and the incomings of the future making up the loss. These lingerings of old objects, these incomings of new, are the germs of memory and expectation, the retrospective and the prospective sense of time. They give that continuity to consciousness without which it could not be called a stream.

The Sensible Present Has Duration

Let any one try, I will not say to arrest, but to notice or attend to, the *present* moment of time. One of the most baffling experiences occurs. Where is it, this present? It has melted in our grasp, fled ere we could touch it, gone in the instant of becoming. As a poet, quoted by Mr. Hodgson, says,

"Le moment où je parle est déjà loin de moi,"

and it is only as entering into the living and moving organization of a much wider tract of time that the strict present is apprehended at all. It is, in fact, an altogether ideal abstraction, not only never realized in sense, but probably never even conceived of by those unaccustomed to philosophic meditation. Reflection leads us to the conclusion that it *must* exist, but that it *does* exist can never be a fact of our immediate experience. The only fact of our immediate experience is what Mr. E. R. Clay has well called 'the *specious* present.' . . .

In short, the practically cognized present is no knife-edge, but a saddle-back, with a certain breadth of its own on which we sit perched, and from which we look in two directions into time. The unit of composition of our perception of time is a *duration*, with a bow and a stern, as it were—a rearward- and a forward-looking end. It is only as parts of this *duration-block* that the relation of *succession* of one end to the other is perceived. We do not first feel one end and then feel the other after it, and from the perception of the succession infer an interval of time between, but we seem to feel the interval of time as a whole, with its two ends embedded in it. The experience is from the outset a synthetic datum, not a simple one; and to sensible perception its elements are inseparable, although attention looking back may easily decompose the experience, and distinguish its beginning from its end.

When we come to study the perception of Space, we shall find it quite analogous to time in this regard. Date in time corresponds to position in space; and although we now mentally construct large spaces by mentally imagining remoter and remoter positions, just as we now construct great durations by mentally prolonging a series of successive dates, yet the original experience of both space and time is always of something already given as a unit, inside of which attention afterward discriminates parts in relation to each other. Without the parts already given as *in* a time and *in* a space, subsequent discrimination of them could hardly do more than perceive them as *different* from each other; it would have no motive for calling the difference temporal order in this instance and spatial position in that.

And just as in certain experiences we may be conscious of an extensive space full of objects, without locating each of them distinctly therein; so, when many impressions follow in excessively rapid succession in time, although we may be distinctly aware that they occupy some duration, and are not simultaneous, we may be quite at a loss to tell which comes first and which last; or we may even invert their real order in our judgment. In complicated reaction-time experiments, where signals and motions, and clicks of the apparatus come in exceedingly rapid order, one is at first much perplexed in deciding what the order is, yet of the fact of its occupancy of time we are never in doubt. . . .

We Have No Sense for Empty Time

Although subdividing the time by beats of sensation aids our accurate knowledge of the amount of it that elapses, such subdivision does not seem at the first glance essential to our perception of its flow. Let one sit with closed eyes and, abstracting entirely from the outer world, attend exclusively to the passage of time, like one who wakes, as the poet says, "to hear time flowing in the middle of the night, and all things moving to a day of doom." There seems under such circumstances as these no variety in the material content of our thought, and what we notice appears, if anything, to be the pure series of durations budding, as it were, and growing beneath our indrawn gaze. Is this really so or not? The question is important, for, if the experience be what it roughly seems, we have a sort of special sense for pure time—a sense to which empty duration is an adequate stimulus; while if it be an illusion, it must be that our perception of time's flight, in the experiences quoted, is due to the *filling* of the time, and to our *memory* of a content which it had a moment previous, and which we feel to agree or disagree with its content now.

It takes but a small exertion of introspection to show that the latter alternative is the true one, and that *we can no more intuit a duration than we can intuit an extension, devoid of all sensible content.* Just as with closed eyes we perceive a dark visual field in which a curdling play of obscurest luminosity is always going on; so, be we never so abstracted from distinct outward impressions, we are always inwardly immersed in what Wundt has somewhere called the twilight of our general consciousness. Our heart-beats, our breathing, the pulses of our attention, fragments of words or sentences that pass through our imagination, are what people this dim habitat. Now, all these processes are rhythmical, and are apprehended by us, as they occur, in their totality; the breathing and pulses of attention, as coherent successions, each with its rise and fall; the heart-beats similarly, only relatively far more brief; the words not separately, but in connected groups. In short, empty our minds as we may, some form of *changing process* remains for us to feel, and cannot be expelled. And along with the sense of the process and its rhythm goes the sense of the length of time it lasts. Awareness of *change* is thus the condition on which our perception of time's flow depends; but there exists no reason to suppose that empty time's own changes are sufficient for the awareness of change to be aroused. The change must be of some concrete sort—an outward or inward sensible series, or a process of attention or volition.

And here again we have an analogy with space. The earliest form of distinct space-perception is undoubtedly that of a movement over some one of our sensitive surfaces, and this movement is originally given as a simple whole of feeling, and is only decomposed into its elements—successive positions successively occupied by the moving body—when our education in discrimination is much advanced. But a movement is a change, a process; so we see that in the time-world and the space-world alike the first known things are not elements, but combinations, not separate units, but wholes already formed. The condition of *being* of the wholes may be the elements; but the condition of our *knowing* the elements is our having already felt the wholes as wholes.

In the experience of watching empty time flow—'empty' to be taken hereafter in the relative sense just set forth—we tell it off in pulses. We say 'now! now! now!' or we count 'more! more! more!' as we feel it bud. This composition out of units of duration is called the law of time's *discrete flow*. The discreteness is, however, merely due to the fact that our successive acts of *recognition* or *apperception* of *what* it is are discrete. The sensation is as continuous as any sensation can be. All continuous sensations are *named* in beats. . . .

The Feeling of Past Time Is a Present Feeling

If asked why we perceive the light of the sun, or the sound of an explosion, we reply, "Because certain outer forces, ether-waves or air-waves, smite upon the brain, awakening therein changes, to which the conscious perceptions, light and sound, respond." But we hasten to add that neither light nor sound *copy* or *mirror* the ether- or air-waves; they represent them only symbolically. The *only* case, says Helmholtz, in which such copying occurs, and in which

"our perceptions can truly correspond with outer reality, is that of the *time-succession* of phenomena. Simultaneity, succession, and the regular return of simultaneity or succession, can obtain as well in sensations as in outer events. Events, like our perceptions of them, take place in time, so that the time-relations of the latter can furnish a true copy of those of the former. The sensation of the thunder follows the sensation of the lightning just as the sonorous convulsing of the air by the electric discharge reaches the observer's place later than that of the luminiferous ether."[2]

2. *Physiol. Optik*, p. 445.

One experiences an almost instinctive impulse, in pursuing such reflections as these, to follow them to a sort of crude speculative conclusion, and to think that he has at last got the mystery of cognition where, to use a vulgar phrase, 'the wool is short.' What more natural, we say, than that the sequences and durations of things *should* become known? The succession of the outer forces stamps itself as a like succession upon the brain. The brain's successive changes are copied exactly by correspondingly successive pulses of the mental stream. The mental stream, feeling itself, must feel the time-relations of its own states. But as these are copies of the outward time-relations, so must it know them too. That is to say, these latter time-relations arouse their own cognition; or, in other words, the mere existence of time in those changes out of the mind which affect the mind is a sufficient cause why time is perceived by the mind.

This philosophy is unfortunately too crude. Even though we *were* to conceive the outer successions as forces stamping their image on the brain, and the brain's successions as forces stamping their image on the mind,[3] still, between the mind's own changes *being* successive, and *knowing their own succession,* lies as broad a chasm as between the object and subject of any case of cognition in the world. *A succession of feelings, in and of itself, is not a feeling of succession. And since, to our successive feelings, a feeling of their own succession is added, that must be treated as an additional fact requiring its own special elucidation,* which this talk about outer time-relations stamping copies of themselves within, leaves all untouched.

I have shown, at the outset of the article, that what is past, to be known as past, must be known *with* what is present, and *during* the 'present' spot of time. . . .

If we represent the actual time-stream of our thinking by an horizontal line, the thought *of* the stream or of any segment of its length, past, present, or to come, might be figured in a perpendicular raised upon the horizontal at a certain point. The length of this perpendicular stands for a certain object or content, which in

---

3. Succession, time *per se, is* no force. Our talk about its devouring tooth, etc., is all elliptical. Its *contents* are what devour. The law of inertia is incompatible with time's being assumed as an efficient cause of anything.

this case is the time thought of, and all of which is thought of together at the actual moment of the stream upon which the perpendicular is raised. . . .

There is thus a sort of *perspective projection* of past objects upon present consciousness, similar to that of wide landscapes upon a camera-screen.

And since we saw a while ago that our maximum distinct *intuition* of duration hardly covers more than a dozen seconds (while our maximum vague intuition is probably not more than that of a minute or so), we must suppose that *this amount of duration is pictured fairly steadily in each passing instant of consciousness* by virtue of some fairly constant feature in the brain-process to which the consciousness is tied. *This feature of the brain-process, whatever it be, must be the cause of our perceiving the fact of time at all.*[4] The duration thus steadily perceived is hardly more than the 'specious present,' as it was called a few pages back. Its *content* is in a constant flux, events dawning into its forward end as fast as they fade out of its rearward one, and each of them changing its time-coefficient from 'not yet,' or 'not quite yet,' to 'just gone' or 'gone,' as it passes by. Meanwhile, the specious present, the intuited duration, stands permanent, like the rainbow on the waterfall, with its own quality unchanged by the events that stream through it. Each of these, as it slips out, retains the power of being reproduced; and when reproduced, is reproduced with the duration and neighbors which it originally had. Please observe, however, that the reproduction of an event, *after* it has once completely dropped out of the rearward end of the specious present, is an entirely different psychic fact from its direct perception in the specious present as a thing immediately past. A creature might be entirely devoid of *reproductive* memory, and yet have the time-sense; but the latter would be limited, in his case, to the few seconds immediately passing by. Time older than that he would never recall. I assume reproduction in the text, because I am speaking of human beings who notoriously possess it. Thus memory gets strewn with *dated* things—dated in the sense of being before or after each other. The date of a thing is a mere relation of

4. The cause of the perceiving, not the object perceived!

before or *after* the present thing or some past or future thing. Some things we date simply by mentally tossing them into the past or future *direction*. So in space we think of England as simply to the eastward, of Charleston as lying south. But, again, we may date an event exactly, by fitting it between two terms of a past or future series explicitly conceived, just as we may accurately think of England or Charleston being just so many miles away.

The things and events thus vaguely or exactly dated become thenceforward those signs and symbols of longer time-spaces, of which we previously spoke. According as we think of a multitude of them, or of few, so we imagine the time they represent to be long or short. But *the original paragon and prototype of all conceived times is the specious present, the short duration of which we are immediately and incessantly sensible.* . . .

E. Sensation*

We often hear the opinion expressed that all our sensations at first appear to us as subjective or internal, and are afterwards and by a special act on our part 'extradited' or 'projected' so as to appear located in an outer world. . . .

It seems to me that there is not a vestige of evidence for this view. It hangs together with the opinion that our sensations are originally devoid of all spatial content, an opinion which I confess that I am wholly at a loss to understand. As I look at my bookshelf opposite I cannot frame to myself an idea, however imaginary, of any feeling which I could ever possibly have got from it except the feeling of the same big extended sort of outward fact which I now perceive. So far is it from being true that our first way of feeling things is the feeling of them as subjective or mental, that the exact opposite seems rather to be the truth. Our earliest, most instinctive, least developed kind of consciousness is the objective kind; and only as reflection becomes developed do we become aware of an inner world at all. Then indeed we enrich it more and more, even to the point of becoming idealists, with the spoils of the outer world which at first was the only world we knew. But subjective

* From *The Principles of Psychology*, chap. 17.

consciousness, aware of itself as subjective, does not at first exist. Even an attack of pain is surely felt at first objectively as something in space which prompts to motor reaction, and to the very end it is located, not in the mind, but in some bodily part. . . .

Another confusion, much more common than the denial of all objective character to sensations, is the assumption that they are all originally located *inside the body* and are projected outward by a secondary act. This secondary judgment is always false, according to M. Taine, so far as the place of the sensation itself goes. But it happens to *hit* a real object which is at the point towards which the sensation is projected; so we may call its result, according to this author, a *veridical hallucination*. The word Sensation, to begin with, is constantly, in psychological literature, used as if it meant one and the same thing with the *physical impression* either in the terminal organs or in the centres, which is its antecedent condition, and this notwithstanding that by sensation we mean a mental, not a physical, fact. But those who expressly mean by it a mental fact still leave to it a physical *place,* still think of it as objectively inhabiting the very neural tracts which occasion its appearance when they are excited; and then (going a step farther) they think that it must *place itself* where *they* place it, or be subjectively sensible of that place as its habitat in the first instance, and afterwards have to be *moved* so as to appear elsewhere.

All this seems highly confused and unintelligible. Consciousness, as we saw in an earlier chapter . . . cannot properly be said to *inhabit* any place. It has dynamic relations with the brain, and cognitive relations with everything and anything. From the one point of view *we* may say that a sensation is in the same place with the brain (if we like), just as from the other point of view we may say that it is in the same place with whatever quality it may be cognizing. But the supposition that a sensation primitively *feels either itself or its object to be in the same place with the brain* is absolutely groundless, and neither *a priori* probability nor facts from experience can be adduced to show that such a deliverance forms any part of the original cognitive function of our sensibility.

Where, then, do we feel the objects of our original sensations to be?

Certainly a child newly born in Boston, who gets a sensation from the candle-flame which lights the bedroom, or from his diaper-pin, does not feel either of these objects to be situated in longitude 72° W. and latitude 41° N. He does not feel them to be in the third story of the house. He does not even feel them in any distinct manner to be to the right or the left of any of the other sensations which he may be getting from other objects in the room at the same time. He does not, in short, know anything *about* their space-relations to anything else in the world. The flame fills its own place, the pain fills its own place; but as yet these places are neither identified with, nor discriminated from, any other places. That comes later. For the places thus first sensibly known are elements of the child's space-world which remain with him all his life; and by memory and later experience he learns a vast number of things *about* those places which at first he did not know. But to the end of time certain places of the world remain defined for him as the places *where those sensations were;* and his only possible answer to the question *where anything is* will be to say 'there,' and to name some sensation or other like those first ones, which shall identify the spot. Space *means* but the aggregate of all our possible sensations. There is no duplicate space known *aliunde* or created by an 'epoch-making achievement' into which our sensations, originally spaceless, are dropped. They *bring* space and all its places to our intellect, and do not derive it thence.

By his body, then, the child later means simply *that place where* the pain from the pin, and a lot of other sensations like it, were or are felt. It is no more true to say that he locates that pain in his body, than to say that he locates his body in that pain. Both are true: that pain is part of what he *means by the word 'body.'* Just so by the outer world the child means nothing more than *that place where* the candle-flame and a lot of other sensations like it are felt. He no more locates the candle in the outer world than he locates the outer world in the candle. Once again, he does both; for the candle is part of what he *means* by 'outer world.' . . .

F.   THE PERCEPTION OF SPACE*

Every single visual sensation or 'field of view' is limited. To get a new field of view for our object the old one must disappear. But

* From *The Principles of Psychology,* chap. 20.

the disappearance may be only partial. Let the first field of view be A B C. If we carry our attention to the limit C, it ceases to be the limit, and becomes the centre of the field, and beyond it appear fresh parts where there were none before: A B C changes, in short, to C D E. But although the parts A B are lost to sight, yet their image abides in the memory; and if we think of our first object A B C as having existed or as still existing at all, we must think of it as it was originally presented, namely, as spread out from C in one direction just as C D E is spread out in another. A B and D E can never coalesce in one place (as they could were they objects of different senses) because they can never be perceived at once: we must lose one to see the other. So (the letters standing now for 'things') we get to conceive of the successive fields of things after the analogy of the several things which we perceive in a single field. They must be out- and along-side of each other, and we conceive that their juxtaposed spaces must make a larger space. A B C + C D E must, in short, be imagined to exist in the form of A B C D E or not imagined at all.

We can usually recover anything lost from sight by moving our attention and our eyes back in its direction; and through these constant changes every field of seen things comes at last to be thought of as always having a fringe of *other things possible to be seen* spreading in all directions round about it. Meanwhile the movements concomitantly with which the various fields alternate are also felt and remembered; and gradually (through association) this and that movement come in our thought to suggest this or that extent of fresh objects introduced. Gradually, too, since the objects vary indefinitely in kind, we abstract from their several natures and think separately of their mere extents, of which extents the various movements remain as the only constant introducers and associates. More and more, therefore, do we think of movement and seen extent as mutually involving each other, until at last (with Bain and J. S. Mill) we may get to regard them as synonymous, and say, "What is the *meaning of the word extent*, unless it be possible movement?" We forget in this conclusion that (whatever intrinsic extensiveness the movements may appear endowed with) that seen spreadoutness which is the pattern of the abstract extensiveness which we imagine came to us originally from the retinal sensation.

The muscular sensations of the eyeball *signify* this sort of visible spreadoutness, just as this visible spreadoutness may come in later experience to *signify* the 'real' bulks, distances, lengths and breadths known to touch and locomotion. To the very end, however, in us seeing men, the quality, the nature, the *sort of thing we mean* by extensiveness, would seem to be the sort of feeling which our retinal stimulations bring.

In one deprived of sight the principles by which the notion of real space is constructed are the same. Skin-feelings take in him the place of retinal-feelings in giving the quality of lateral spreadoutness, as our attention passes from one extent of them to another, awakened by an object sliding along. Usually the moving object is our hand; and feelings of movement in our joints invariably accompany the feelings in the skin. But the feeling of the skin is what the blind man *means* by his skin; so the size of the skin-feelings stands as the absolute or real size, and the size of the joint-feelings becomes a sign of these. Suppose, for example, a blind baby with (to make the description shorter) a blister on his toe, exploring his leg with his finger-tip and feeling a pain shoot up sharply the instant the blister is touched. The experiment gives him four different kinds of sensation—two of them protracted, two sudden. The first pair are the movement-feeling in the joints of the upper limb, and the movement-feeling on the skin of the leg and foot. These, attended to together, have their extents identified as one objective space—the hand moves through the same space in which the leg lies. The second pair of objects are the pain in the blister, and the peculiar feeling the blister gives to the finger. Their spaces also fuse; and as each marks the end of a peculiar movement-series (arm moved, leg stroked), the movement-spaces are *emphatically* identified with each other at *that* end. Were there other small blisters distributed down the leg, there would be a number of these emphatic points; the movement-spaces would be identified, not only as totals, but point for point.

Just so with spaces beyond the body's limits. Continuing the joint-feeling beyond the toe, the baby hits another object, which he can still think of when he brings his hand back to its blister again. That object at the end of that joint-feeling means a new place for him, and the more such objects multiply in his experience the wider does the space of his conception grow. If, wandering through the woods to-day by a new path, I find myself suddenly in a glade which affects my senses exactly as did another I reached last week at the end of a different walk, I believe the two identical affections to present the same persisting glade, and infer that I have attained it by two differing roads. The spaces walked over grow congruent by their extremities; though apart from the common sensation which those extremities give me, I should be under no necessity of connecting one walk with another at all. The case in no whit differs when shorter movements are concerned. If, moving first one arm and then another, the blind child gets the same kind of sensation upon the hand, and gets it again as often as he repeats either process, he judges that he has touched the same object by both motions, and concludes that the motions terminate in a common place. From place to place marked in this way he moves, and adding the places moved through, one to another, he builds up his notion of the extent of the outer world. The seeing man's process is identical; only his units, which may be successive bird's-eye views, are much larger than in the case of the blind.

G.   THE PERCEPTION OF REALITY*

Belief

Everyone knows the difference between imagining a thing and believing in its existence, between supposing a proposition and acquiescing in its truth. In the case of acquiescence or belief, the object is not only apprehended by the mind, but is held to have reality. Belief is thus the mental state or function of cognizing reality. As used in the following pages, 'Belief' will mean every degree of assurance, including the highest possible certainty and conviction.

There are, as we know, two ways of studying every psychic state.

* From *The Principles of Psychology*, chap. 21.

First, the way of analysis: What does it consist in? What is its inner nature? Of what sort of mind-stuff is it composed? Second, the way of history: What are its conditions of production, and its connection with other facts?

Into the first way we cannot go very far. *In its inner nature, belief, or the sense of reality, is a sort of feeling more allied to the emotions than to anything else.* Mr. Bagehot distinctly calls it the 'emotion' of conviction. I just now spoke of it as acquiescence. It resembles more than anything what in the psychology of volition we know as consent. Consent is recognized by all to be a manifestation of our active nature. . . .

Prof. Brentano, in an admirable chapter of his *Psychologie,* expresses this by saying that conception and belief (which he names *judgment*) are two different fundamental psychic phenomena. What I myself have called (above, p. 71) the 'object' of thought may be comparatively simple, like "Ha! what a pain," or "It-thunders"; or it may be complex, like "Columbus-discovered-America-in-1492," or "There-exists-an-all-wise-Creator-of-the-world." In either case, however, the mere thought of the object may exist as something quite distinct from the belief in its reality. The belief, as Brentano says, presupposes the mere thought. . . .

Admitting, then, that this attitude is a state of consciousness *sui generis,* about which nothing more can be said in the way of internal analysis, let us proceed to the second way of studying the subject of belief: *Under what circumstances do we think things real?* We shall soon see how much matter this gives us to discuss.

The Various Orders of Reality

Suppose a new-born mind, entirely blank and waiting for experience to begin. Suppose that it begins in the form of a visual impression (whether faint or vivid is immaterial) of a lighted candle against a dark background, and nothing else, so that whilst this image lasts it constitutes the entire universe known to the mind in question. Suppose, moreover (to simplify the hypothesis), that the candle is only imaginary, and that no 'original' of it is recognized by us psychologists outside. Will this hallucinatory candle be believed in, will it have a real existence for the mind?

What possible sense (for that mind) would a suspicion have that the candle was not real? What would doubt or disbelief of it imply? When *we*, the onlooking psychologists, say the candle is unreal, we mean something quite definite, viz., that there is a world known to *us* which *is* real, and to which we perceive that the candle does not belong; it belongs exclusively to that individual mind, has no *status* anywhere else, etc. It exists, to be sure, in a fashion, for it forms the content of that mind's hallucination; but the hallucination itself, though unquestionably it is a sort of existing fact, has no knowledge of *other* facts; and since those *other* facts are the realities *par excellence* for us, and the only things we believe in, the candle is simply outside of our reality and belief altogether.

By the hypothesis, however, the *mind which sees the candle* can spin no such considerations as these about it, for of other facts, actual or possible, it has no inkling whatever. That candle is its all, its absolute. Its entire faculty of attention is absorbed by it. It *is*, it is *that*; it is *there*; no other possible candle, or quality of this candle, no other possible place, or possible object in the place, no alternative, in short, suggests itself as even conceivable; so how can the mind help believing the candle real? The supposition that it might possibly not do so is, under the supposed conditions, unintelligible.

This is what Spinoza long ago announced:

"Let us conceive a boy," he said, "imagining to himself a horse, and taking note of nothing else. As this imagination involves the existence of the horse, *and the boy has no perception which annuls its existence,* he will necessarily contemplate the horse as present, nor will he be able to doubt of its existence, however little certain of it he may be. I deny that a man in so far as he imagines [*percipit*] affirms nothing. For what is it to imagine a winged horse but to affirm that the horse [that horse, namely] has wings? For if the mind had nothing before it but the winged horse it would contemplate the same as present, would have no cause to doubt of its existence, nor any power of dissenting from its existence, unless the imagination of the winged horse were joined to an idea which contradicted [*tollit*] its existence." (*Ethics*, II. 49, Scholium.)

The sense that anything we think of is unreal can only come, then, when that thing is contradicted by some other thing of which we think. *Any object which remains uncontradicted is* ipso facto *believed and posited as absolute reality.*

Now, how comes it that one thing thought of can be contradicted by another? It cannot unless it begins the quarrel by saying something inadmissable about that other. Take the mind with the candle, or the boy with the horse. If either of them say, 'That candle or that horse, even when I don't see it, exists in *the outer world,*' he pushes into 'the outer world' an object which may be incompatible with everything which he otherwise knows of that world. If so, he must take his choice of which to hold by, the present perceptions or the other knowledge of the world. If he holds to the other knowledge, the present perceptions are contradicted, *so far as their relation to that world goes.* Candle and horse, whatever they may be, are not existents in outward space. They are existents, of course; they are mental objects; mental objects have existence as mental objects. But they are situated in their own spaces, the space in which they severally appear, and neither of those spaces is the space in which the realities called 'the outer world' exist.

Take again the horse with wings. If I merely dream of a horse with wings, my horse interferes with nothing else and has not to be contradicted. That horse, its wings, and its place are all equally real. That horse exists no otherwise than as winged, and is moreover really there, for that place exists no otherwise than as the place of that horse, and claims as yet no connection with the other places of the world. But if with this horse I make an inroad into the *world otherwise known,* and say, for example, 'That is my old mare Maggie, having grown a pair of wings where she stands in her stall,' the whole case is altered; for now the horse and place are identified with a horse and place otherwise known, and *what* is known of the latter objects is incompatible with what is perceived with the former. 'Maggie in her stall with wings! Never!' The wings are unreal, then, visionary. I have dreamed a lie about Maggie in her stall.

The reader will recognize in these two cases the two sorts of judgment called in the logic-books existential and attributive respectively. 'The candle exists as an outer reality' is an existential, 'My Maggie has got a pair of wings' is an attributive, proposition;[1] and it follows from what was first said that *all propositions, whether attributive or existential, are believed through the very fact of being conceived, unless they clash with other propositions believed at the same time, by affirming that their terms are the same with the terms of these other propositions.* A dream-candle has existence, true enough; but not the same existence (existence for itself, namely, or *extra mentem meam*) which the candles of waking perception have. A dream-horse has wings; but then neither horse nor wings are the same with any horses or wings known to memory. That we can at any moment think of the same thing which at any former moment we thought of is the ultimate law of our intellectual constitution. But when we now think of it incompatibly with our other ways of thinking it, then we must choose which way to stand by, for we cannot continue to think in two contradictory ways at once. *The whole distinction of real and unreal, the whole psychology of belief, disbelief, and doubt, is thus grounded on two mental facts—first, that we are liable to think differently of the same; and second, that when we have done so, we can choose which way of thinking to adhere to and which to disregard.*

The subjects adhered to become real subjects, the attributes adhered to real attributes, the existence adhered to real existence; whilst the subjects disregarded become imaginary subjects, the attributes disregarded erroneous attributes, and the existence disregarded an existence in no man's land, in the limbo 'where foot-

---

1. In both existential and attributive judgments a synthesis is represented. The syllable *ex* in the word Existence, *da* in the word *Dasein*, express it. 'The candle exists' is equivalent to 'The candle is *over there.*' And the 'over there' means real space, space related to other reals. The proposition amounts to saying: 'The candle is in the same space with other reals.' It affirms of the candle a very concrete predicate—namely, this relation to other particular concrete things. *Their* real existence, as we shall later see, resolves itself into their peculiar relation to *ourselves.* Existence is thus no substantive quality when we predicate it of any object; it is a relation, ultimately terminating in ourselves, and at the moment when it terminates, becoming a *practical* relation. But of this more anon. I only wish now to indicate the superficial nature of the distinction between the existential and the attributive proposition.

less fancies dwell.' The real things are, in M. Taine's terminology, the *reductives* of the things judged unreal.

The Many Worlds

Habitually and practically we do not *count* these disregarded things as existents at all. For them *væ victis* is the law in the popular philosophy; they are not even treated as appearances; they are treated as if they were mere waste, equivalent to nothing at all. To the genuinely philosophic mind, however, they still have existence, though not the same existence, as the real things. *As* objects of fancy, *as* errors, *as* occupants of dreamland, etc., they are in their way as indefeasible parts of life, as undeniable features of the Universe, as the realities are in their way. The total world of which the philosophers must take account is thus composed of the realities *plus* the fancies and illusions.

Two sub-universes, at least, connected by relations which philosophy tries to ascertain! Really there are more than two sub-universes of which we take account, some of us of this one, and others of that. For there are various categories both of illusion and of reality, and alongside of the world of absolute error (i.e., error confined to single individuals) but still within the world of absolute reality (i.e., reality believed by the complete philosopher) there is the world of collective error, there are the worlds of abstract reality, of relative or practical reality, of ideal relations, and there is the supernatural world. The popular mind conceives of all these sub-worlds more or less disconnectedly; and when dealing with one of them, forgets for the time being its relations to the rest. The complete philosopher is he who seeks not only to assign to every given object of his thought its right place in one or other of these sub-worlds, but he also seeks to determine the relation of each sub-world to the others in the total world which *is*.

The most important sub-universes commonly discriminated from each other and recognized by most of us as existing, each with its own special and separate style of existence, are the following:

(1) The world of sense, or of physical 'things' as we instinctively apprehend them, with such qualities as heat, color, and sound,

and such 'forces' as life, chemical affinity, gravity, electricity, all existing as such within or on the surface of the things.

(2) The world of science, or of physical things as the learned conceive them, with secondary qualities and 'forces' (in the popular sense) excluded, and nothing real but solids and fluids and their 'laws' (i.e., customs) of motion.[2]

(3) The world of ideal relations, or abstract truths believed or believable by all, and expressed in logical, mathematical, metaphysical, ethical, or æsthetic propositions.

(4) The world of 'idols of the tribe,' illusions or prejudices common to the race. All educated people recognize these as forming one sub-universe. The motion of the sky round the earth, for example, belongs to this world. That motion is not a recognized item of any of the other worlds; but as an 'idol of the tribe' it really exists. For certain philosophers 'matter' exists only as an idol of the tribe. For science, the 'secondary qualities' of matter are but 'idols of the tribe.'

(5) The various supernatural worlds, the Christian heaven and hell, the world of the Hindoo mythology, the world of Swedenborg's *visa et audita,* etc. Each of these is a consistent system, with definite relations among its own parts. Neptune's trident, e.g., has no status of reality whatever in the Christian heaven; but within the classic Olympus certain definite things are true of it, whether one believe in the the reality of the classic mythology as a whole or not. The various worlds of deliberate fable may be ranked with these worlds of faith—the world of the *Iliad,* that of *King Lear,* of the *Pickwick Papers,* etc.[3]

---

2. I define the scientific universe here in the radical mechanical way. Practically, it is oftener thought of in a mongrel way and resembles in more points the popular physical world.

3. It thus comes about that we can say such things as that Ivanhoe did not *really* marry Rebecca, as Thackeray *falsely* makes him do. The real Ivanhoe-world is the one which Scott wrote down for us. *In that world* Ivanhoe does *not* marry Rebecca. The objects within that world are knit together by perfectly definite relations, which can be affirmed or denied. Whilst absorbed in the novel, we turn our backs on all other worlds, and, for the time, the Ivanhoe-world remains our absolute reality. When we wake from the spell, however, we find a still more real world, which reduces Ivanhoe, and all things connected with him, to the fictive status, and relegates them to one of the sub-universes grouped under No. 5.

(6) The various worlds of individual opinion, as numerous as men are.

(7) The worlds of sheer madness and vagary, also indefinitely numerous.

Every object we think of gets at last referred to one world or another of this or of some similar list. It settles into our belief as a common-sense object, a scientific object, an abstract object, a mythological object, an object of some one's mistaken conception, or a madman's object; and it reaches this state sometimes immediately, but often only after being hustled and bandied about amongst other objects until it finds some which will tolerate its presence and stand in relations to it which nothing contradicts. The molecules and ether-waves of the scientific world, for example, simply kick the object's warmth and color out, they refuse to have any relations with them. But the world of 'idols of the tribe' stands ready to take them in. Just so the world of classic myth takes up the winged horse; the world of individual hallucination, the vision of the candle; the world of abstract truth, the proposition that justice is kingly, though no actual king be just. The various worlds themselves, however, appear (as aforesaid) to most men's minds in no very definitely conceived relation to each other, and our attention, when it turns to one, is apt to drop the others for the time being out of its account. Propositions concerning the different worlds are made from 'different points of view'; and in this more or less chaotic state the consciousness of most thinkers remains to the end. Each world *whilst it is attended to* is real after its own fashion; only the reality lapses with the attention.

The World of 'Practical Realities'

Each thinker, however, has dominant habits of attention; and these *practically elect from among the various worlds some one to be for him the world of ultimate realities.* From this world's objects he does not appeal. Whatever positively contradicts them must get into another world or die. The horse, e.g., may have wings to its heart's content, so long as it does not pretend to be the real world's horse—*that* horse is absolutely wingless. For most men, as we shall immediately see, the 'things of sense' hold this prerogative position, and are the absolutely real world's nucleus. Other things, to be sure, may be real for this man or for that— things of science, abstract moral relations, things of the Christian theology, or what not. But even for the special man, these things are usually real with a less real reality than that of the things of sense. They are taken less seriously; and the very utmost that can be said for anyone's belief in them is that it is as strong as his 'belief in his own senses.'

In all this the everlasting partiality of our nature shows itself, our inveterate propensity to choice. For, in the strict and ultimate sense of the word existence, everything which can be thought of at all exists as *some* sort of object, whether mythical object, individual thinker's object, or object in outer space and for intelligence at large. Errors, fictions, tribal beliefs, are parts of the whole great Universe which God has made, and He must have meant all these things to be in it, each in its respective place. But for us finite creatures, " 'tis to consider too curiously to consider so." The mere fact of appearing as an object at all is not enough to constitute reality. That may be metaphysical reality, reality for God; but what we need is practical reality, reality for ourselves; and, to have that, an object must not only appear, but it must appear both *interesting* and *important*. The worlds whose objects are neither interesting nor important we treat simply negatively, we brand them as *un*real.

In the relative sense, then, the sense in which we contrast reality with simple *un*reality, and in which one thing is said to have *more* reality than another, and to be more believed, *reality means simply relation to our emotional and active life.* This is the only sense which the word ever has in the mouths of practical men. *In this sense, whatever excites and stimulates our interest is real;* whenever an object so appeals to us that we turn to it, accept it, fill our mind with it, or practically take account of it, so far it is real for us, and we believe it. Whenever, on the contrary, we ignore it, fail to consider it or act upon it, despise it, reject it, forget it, so far it is unreal for us and disbelieved. Hume's account of the matter was then essentially correct, when he said that belief in anything was simply the having the idea of it in a lively and active manner. . . .

The object of belief, then, reality or real existence, is something quite different from all the other predicates which a subject may possess. Those are properties intellectually or sensibly intuited. When we add any one of them to the subject, we increase the intrinsic content of the latter, we enrich its picture in our mind. But adding reality does not enrich the picture in any such inward way; it leaves it inwardly as it finds it, and only fixes it and stamps it in to *us*.

"The real," as Kant says, "contains no more than the possible. A hundred real dollars do not contain a penny more than a hundred possible dollars. . . . By whatever, and by however many, predicates I may think a thing, nothing is added to it if I add that the thing exists. . . . Whatever, therefore, our concept of an object may contain, we must always step outside of it in order to attribute to it existence."

The 'stepping outside' of it is the establishment either of immediate practical relations between it and ourselves, or of relations between it and other objects with which we have immediate practical relations. Relations of this sort, which are as yet not transcended or superseded by others, are *ipso facto* real relations, and confer reality upon their objective term. *The* fons et origo *of all reality, whether from the absolute or the practical point of view, is thus subjective, is ourselves.* As bare logical thinkers, without emotional reaction, we give reality to whatever objects we think of, for they are really phenomena, or objects of our passing thought, if nothing more. But, *as thinkers with emotional reaction, we give what seems to us a still higher degree of reality to whatever things we select and emphasize and turn to* WITH A WILL. These are our *living* realities; and not only these, but all the other things which are intimately connected with these. Reality, starting from our Ego, thus sheds itself from point to point—first, upon all objects which have an immediate sting of interest for our Ego in them, and next, upon the objects most continuously related with these. It only fails when the connecting thread is lost. A whole system may be real, if it only hang to our Ego by one immediately *stinging* term. But what contradicts any such stinging term, even though it be another stinging term itself, is either not believed, or only believed after settlement of the dispute.

We reach thus the important conclusion that *our own reality, that sense of our own life which we at every moment possess, is the ultimate of ultimates for our belief.* 'As sure as I exist!'—this is our uttermost warrant for the being of all other things. As Descartes made the indubitable reality of the *cogito* go bail for the reality of all that the *cogito* involved, so we all of us, feeling our own present reality with absolutely coercive force, ascribe an all but equal degree of reality, first to whatever things we lay hold on with a sense of personal need, and second, to whatever farther things continuously belong with these. "Mein Jetzt und Hier," as Prof. Lipps says, "ist der letzte Angelpunkt für alle Wirklichkeit, also alle Erkenntniss."

The world of living realities as contrasted with unrealities is thus anchored in the Ego, considered as an active and emotional term.[4] That is the hook from which the rest dangles, the absolute support. And as from a painted hook it has been said, that one can only hang a painted chain, so conversely, from a real hook only a real chain can properly be hung. *Whatever things have intimate and continuous connection with my life are things of whose reality I cannot doubt.* Whatever things fail to establish this connection are things which are practically no better for me than if they existed not at all.

In certain forms of melancholic perversion of the sensibilities and reactive powers, nothing touches us intimately, rouses us, or wakens natural feeling. The consequence is the complaint so often heard from melancholic patients, that nothing is believed in by them as it used to be, and that all sense of reality is fled from life. They are sheathed in india-rubber; nothing penetrates to the quick or draws blood, as it were. According to Griesinger, "I see, I hear!" such patients say, "but the objects do not reach me, it is as if there were a wall between me and the outer world!" . . .

---

4. I use the notion of the Ego here, as common-sense uses it. Nothing is pre-judged as to the results (or absence of results) of ulterior attempts to analyze the notion.

The Paramount Reality of Sensations

But now we are met by questions of detail. What does this stirring, this exciting power, this interest, consist in, which some objects have? which *are* those 'intimate relations' with our life which give reality? And what things stand in these relations immediately, and what others are so closely connected with the former that (in Hume's language) we 'carry our disposition' also on to them?

In a simple and direct way these questions cannot be answered at all. The whole history of human thought is but an unfinished attempt to answer them. For what have men been trying to find out, since men were men, but just those things: "Where do our true interests lie—which relations shall we call the intimate and real ones—which things shall we call living realities and which not?" A few psychological points can, however, be made clear.

Any relation to our mind at all, in the absence of a stronger relation, suffices to make an object real. The barest appeal to our attention is enough for that. Revert to the beginning of the chapter, and take the candle entering the vacant mind. The mind was waiting for just some such object to make its spring upon. It makes its spring and the candle is believed. But when the candle appears at the same time with other objects, it must run the gauntlet of their rivalry, and then it becomes a question which of the various candidates for attention shall compel belief. As a rule we believe as much as we can. We would believe everything if we only could. When objects are represented by us quite unsystematically they conflict but little with each other, and the number of them which in this chaotic manner we can believe is limitless. The primitive savage's mind is a jungle in which hallucinations, dreams, superstitions, conceptions, and sensible objects all flourish alongside of each other, unregulated except by the attention turning in this way or in that. The child's mind is the same. It is only as objects become permanent and their relations fixed that discrepancies and contradictions are felt and must be settled in some stable way. As a rule, the success with which a contradicted object maintains itself in our belief is proportional to several qualities which it must possess. Of these the one which would be put first by most people, because it characterizes objects of sensation, is its—

(1) Coerciveness over attention, or the mere power to possess consciousness: then follow—

(2) Liveliness, or sensible pungency, especially in the way of exciting pleasure or pain;

(3) Stimulating effect upon the will, i.e., capacity to arouse active impulses, the more instinctive the better;

(4) Emotional interest, as object of love, dread, admiration, desire, etc.;

(5) Congruity with certain favorite forms of contemplation— unity, simplicity, permanence, and the like;

(6) Independence of other causes, and its own causal importance.

These characters run into each other. Coerciveness is the result of liveliness or emotional interest. What is lively and interesting stimulates *eo ipso* the will; congruity holds of active impulses as well as of contemplative forms; causal independence and importance suit a certain contemplative demand, etc. I will therefore abandon all attempt at a formal treatment, and simply proceed to make remarks in the most convenient order of exposition.

As a whole, sensations are more lively and are judged more real than conceptions; things met with every hour more real than things seen once; attributes perceived when awake, more real than attributes perceived in a dream. But, owing to the *diverse relations contracted by the various objects with each other,* the simple rule that the lively and permanent is the real is often enough disguised. A conceived thing may be deemed more real than a certain sensible thing, if it only be intimately related to other sensible things more vivid, permanent, or interesting than the first one. Conceived molecular vibrations, e.g., are by the physicist judged more real than felt warmth, because so intimately related to all those other facts of motion in the world which he has made his special study. Similarly, a rare thing may be deemed more real than a permanent thing if it be more widely related to other permanent things. All the occasional crucial observations of science are examples of this. A rare experience, too, is likely to be judged more real than a permanent one, if it be more interesting and exciting. Such is the sight of Saturn through a telescope; such are the occasional insights and illuminations which upset our habitual ways of thought.

But no mere floating conception, no mere disconnected rarity, ever displaces vivid things or permanent things from our belief. A conception, to prevail, must *terminate* in the world of orderly sensible experience. A rare phenomenon, to displace frequent ones, must belong with others more frequent still. The history of science is strewn with wrecks and ruins of theory—essences and principles, fluids and forces—once fondly clung to, but found to hang together with no facts of sense. And exceptional phenomena solicit our belief in vain until such time as we chance to conceive them as of kinds already admitted to exist. What science means by 'verification' is no more than this, that no object of conception shall be believed which sooner or later has not some permanent and vivid object of sensation for its *term*. . . .

Sensible objects are thus either our realities or the tests of our realities. Conceived objects must show sensible effects or else be disbelieved. And the effects, even though reduced to relative unreality when their causes come to view (as heat, which molecular vibrations make unreal), are yet the things on which our knowledge of the causes rests. Strange mutual dependence this, in which the appearance needs the reality in order to exist, but the reality needs the appearance in order to be known! . . .

H. On 'Essence'*

. . . Men are so ingrainedly partial that, for common-sense and scholasticism (which is only common-sense grown articulate), the notion that there is no one quality genuinely, absolutely, and exclusively essential to anything is almost unthinkable. "A thing's essence makes it *what* it is. Without an exclusive essence it would be nothing in particular, would be quite nameless, we could not say it was this rather than that. What you write on, for example— why talk of its being combustible, rectangular, and the like, when

* From *The Principles of Psychology*, chap. 22.

you know that these are mere accidents, and that what it really is, and was made to be, is just *paper* and nothing else?" The reader is pretty sure to make some such comment as this. But he is himself merely insisting on an aspect of the thing which suits his own petty purpose, that of *naming* the thing; or else on an aspect which suits the manufacturer's purpose, that of *producing an article for which there is a vulgar demand.* Meanwhile the reality overflows these purposes at every pore. Our usual purpose with it, our commonest title for it, and the properties which this title suggests, have in reality nothing sacramental. They characterize *us* more than they characterize the thing. But we are so stuck in our prejudices, so petrified intellectually, that to our vulgarest names, with their suggestions, we ascribe an eternal and exclusive worth. The thing must be, essentially, what the vulgarest name connotes; what less usual names connote, it can be only in an 'accidental' and relatively unreal sense.[1]

Locke undermined the fallacy. But none of his successors, so far as I know, have radically escaped it, or seen that *the only meaning of essence is teleological, and that classification and conception are purely teleological weapons of the mind.* The essence of a thing is that one of its properties which is so *important for my interests* that in comparison with it I may neglect the rest. Amongst those other things which have this important property I class it, after this property I name it, as a thing endowed with this property I conceive it; and whilst so classing, naming, and conceiving it, all other truth about it becomes to me as naught.[2] The properties which are important vary from man to man and from hour to

1. Readers brought up on *Popular Science* may think that the molecular structure of things is their real essence in an absolute sense, and that water is H–O–H more deeply and truly than it is a solvent of sugar or a slaker of thirst. Not a whit! It is *all* of these things with equal reality and the only reason why *for the chemist* it is H–O–H primarily, and only secondarily the other things, is that *for his purpose of deduction and compendious definition,* the H–O–H aspect of it is the more useful one to bear in mind.

2. "We find that we take for granted irresistibly that each kind [of thing] has some character which distinguishes it from other classes. . . . What is the foundation of this postulate? What is the ground of this assumption that there must exist a definition which we have never seen, and which perhaps no one has seen in a satisfactory form? . . . I reply that our conviction that there must needs be characteristic marks by which things can be defined in words is founded upon the assumption of *the necessary possibility of reasoning.*" (W. Whewell: *Hist. of Scientific Ideas*, bk. VIII. chap. I, § 9.)

hour.[3] Hence divers appellations and conceptions for the same thing. But many objects of daily use—as paper, ink, butter, horse-car—have properties of such constant unwavering importance, and have such stereotyped names, that we end by believing that to conceive them in those ways is to conceive them in the only true way. Those are no truer ways of conceiving them than any others; they are only more important ways, more frequently serviceable ways.[4] . . .

3. I may quote a passage from an article entitled "The Sentiment of Rationality," published in vol. IV of Mind, 1879: "What is a *conception?* It is a *teleological instrument.* It is a partial aspect of a thing which *for our purpose* we regard as its essential aspect, as the representative of the entire thing. In comparison with this aspect, whatever other properties and qualities the thing may have are unimportant accidents which we may without blame ignore. But the essence, the ground of conception, varies with the end we have in view. A substance like oil has as many different essences as it has uses to different individuals. One man conceives it as a combustible, another as a lubricator, another as a food; the chemist thinks of it as a hydrocarbon; the furniture-maker as a darkener of wood; the speculator as a commodity whose market-price to-day is this and to-morrow that. The soap-boiler, the physicist, the clothes-scourer severally ascribe to it other essences in relation to their needs. Ueberweg's doctrine that the essential quality of a thing is the quality of most *worth* is strictly true; but Ueberweg has failed to note that the worth is wholly relative to the temporary interests of the conceiver. And, even, when his interest is distinctly defined in his own mind, the discrimination of the quality in the object which has the closest connection with it is a thing which no rules can teach. The only *a priori* advice that can be given to a man embarking on life with a certain purpose is the somewhat barren counsel: Be sure that in the circumstances that meet you, you attend to the *right* ones for your purpose. To pick out the right ones is the measure of the man. 'Millions,' says Hartmann, 'stare at the phenomenon before a *genialer Kopf* pounces on the concept.' The genius is simply he to whom, when he opens his eyes upon the world, the 'right' characters are the prominent ones. The fool is he who, with the same purposes as the genius, infallibly gets his attention tangled amid the accidents."

4. Only if one of our purposes were itself truer than another, could one of our conceptions become the truer conception. To be a truer purpose, however, our purpose must conform more to some absolute standard of purpose in things to which our purposes ought to conform. This shows that the whole doctrine of essential characters is intimately bound up with a teleological view of the world. Materialism becomes self-contradictory when it denies teleology, and yet in the same breath calls atoms, etc., the *essential* facts. The world contains consciousness as well as atoms—and the one must be written down as just as essential as the other, in the absence of any declared purpose regarding them on the creator's part, or in the absence of any creator. As far as we ourselves go, the atoms are worth more for purposes of deduction, the consciousness for purposes of inspiration. We may fairly write the Universe in either way, thus: ATOMS-producing-consciousness; or CONSCIOUSNESS-produced-by-atoms. Atoms alone, or consciousness alone, are precisely equal mutilations of the

I. NECESSARY TRUTHS AND THE
EFFECTS OF EXPERIENCE*

The Genesis of the Pure Sciences

. . . THE PURE SCIENCES EXPRESS RESULTS OF COMPARISON *exclusively; comparison is not a conceivable effect of the order in which outer impressions are experienced—it is one of the house-born portions of our mental structure; therefore the pure sciences form a body of propositions with whose genesis experience has nothing to do.*

First, consider the nature of comparison. *The relations of resemblance and difference among things have nothing to do with the time- and space-order in which we may experience the latter.* Suppose a hundred beings created by God and gifted with the faculties of memory and comparison. Suppose that upon each of them the same lot of sensations are imprinted, but in different orders. Let some of them have no single sensation more than once. Let some have this one and others that one repeated. Let every conceivable permutation prevail. And then let the magic-lantern show die out, and keep the creatures in a void eternity, with naught but their memories to muse upon. Inevitably in their long leisure they will begin to play with the items of their experience and rearrange them, make classificatory series of them, place gray between white and black, orange between red and yellow, and trace all other degrees of resemblance and difference. And this new construction will be absolutely identical in all the hundred creatures, the diversity of the sequence of the original experiences

truth. If, without believing in a God, I still continue to talk of what the world 'essentially is,' I am just as much entitled to define it as a place in which my nose itches, or as a place where at a certain corner I can get a mess of oysters for twenty cents, as to call it an evolving nebula differentiating and integrating itself. It is hard to say which of the three abstractions is the more rotten or miserable substitute for the world's concrete fulness. To conceive it merely as 'God's work' would be a similar mutilation of it, so long as we said not what God, or what kind of work. The only real truth about the world, apart from particular purposes, is the *total* truth.

* From *The Principles of Psychology*, chap. 28.

having no effect as regards this rearrangement. Any and every form of sequence will give the same result, because· the result expresses the relation between the *inward natures* of the sensations; and to that the question of their outward succession is quite irrelevant. Black will differ from white just as much in a world in which they always come close together as in one in which they always come far apart; just as much in one in which they appear rarely as in one in which they appear all the time.

But the advocate of 'persistent outer relations' may still return to the charge: These *are* what make us so sure that white and black differ, he may say; for in a world where sometimes black resembled white and sometimes differed from it, we could never be so sure. It is because in this world black and white have *always* differed that the sense of their differences has become a necessary form of thought. The pair of colors on the one hand and the sense of difference on the other, inseparably experienced, not only by ourselves but by our ancestors, have become inseparably connected in the mind. Not through any essential structure of the mind, which made difference the only possible feeling which they could arouse; no, but because they simply *did* differ so often that at last they begat in us an impotency to imagine them doing anything else, and made us accept such a fabulous account as that just presented, of creatures to whom a single experience would suffice to make us feel the necessariness of this relation.

I know not whether Mr. Spencer would subscribe to this or not—nor do I care, for there are mysteries which press more for solution than the meaning of this vague writer's words. But to me such an explanation of our difference-judgment is absolutely unintelligible. We now find black and white different, the explanation says, *because we have always so found them.* But why should we always have so found them? Why should difference have popped into our heads so invariably with the thought of them? There must have been either a subjective or an objective reason. The subjective reason can only be that our minds were so constructed that a sense of difference was the only sort of conscious transition possible between black and white; the objective reason can only be that difference was always there, with these colors, outside the mind as an objective fact. The subjective reason

explains outer frequency by inward structure, not inward structure by outer frequency; and so surrenders the experience-theory.
The objective reason simply says that if an outer difference is there
the mind must needs know it—which is no explanation at all, but
a mere appeal to the fact that somehow the mind does know what
is there.

The only clear thing to do is to give up the sham of a pretended
explanation, and to fall back on the fact that the sense of
difference *has* arisen, in some natural manner doubtless, but in a
manner which we do not understand. It was by the back-stairs
way, at all events; and, from the very first, happened to be the
only mode of reaction by which consciousness could feel the transition from one term to another of what (in *consequence* of this
very reaction) we now call a contrasted pair.

In noticing the differences and resemblances of things, and their
degrees, the mind feels its own activity, and has given the name of
comparison thereto. It need not compare its materials, but if once
roused to do so, it can compare them with but one result, and this
a fixed consequence of the nature of the materials themselves.
Difference and resemblance are thus relations between ideal objects, or conceptions as such. To learn whether black and white
differ, I need not consult the world of experience at all; the mere
ideas suffice. *What I mean* by black differs from *what I mean* by
white, whether such colors exist *extra mentem meam* or not. If
they ever do so exist, they *will* differ. White things may blacken,
but the black of them will differ from the white of them, so long as
I mean anything definite by these three words.[1]

*I shall now in what follows call all propositions which express
time- and space-relations empirical propositions; and I shall give*

1. "Though a man in a fever should from sugar have a bitter taste which
at another time would produce a sweet one, yet the idea of bitter in that
man's mind would be as clear and distinct from the idea of sweet as if he had
tasted only gall. Nor does it make any more confusion between the two ideas
of sweet and bitter that the same sort of body produces at one time one and
at another time another idea by the taste, than it makes a confusion in two
ideas of white and sweet, or white and round, that the same piece of sugar
produces them both in the mind at the same time." Locke's *Essay*, bk. ii. ch.
xi. § 3.

the name of rational propositions to all propositions which express the results of a comparison. The latter denomination is in a sense arbitrary, for resemblance and difference are not usually held to be the only rational relations between things. I will next proceed to show, however, how many other rational relations commonly supposed distinct can be resolved into these, so that my definition of rational propositions will end, I trust, by proving less arbitrary than it now appears to be.

Series of Even Difference and Mediate Comparison

In Chapter XII we saw that the mind can at successive moments *mean the same,* and that it gradually comes into possession of a stock of permanent and fixed meanings, ideal objects, or conceptions, some of which are universal qualities, like the black and white of our example, and some, individual things. We now see that not only are the objects permanent mental possessions, but the results of their comparison are permanent too. The objects and their differences together form an immutable system. *The same objects, compared in the same way, always give the same results;* if the result be not the same, then the objects are not those originally meant.

This last principle, which we may call the *axiom of constant result,* holds good throughout all our mental operations, not only when we compare, but when we add, divide, class, or infer a given matter in any conceivable way. Its most general expression would be *"the Same operated on in the same way gives the Same."* In mathematics it takes the form of "equals added to, or subtracted from, equals give equals," and the like. We shall meet with it again.

The next thing which we observe is that *the operation of comparing may be repeated on its own results;* in other words, that we can think of the various resemblances and differences which we find and compare them with each other, making differences and resemblances of a higher order. *The mind thus becomes aware of sets of similar differences, and forms series of terms with the same kind and amount of difference between them, terms which, as they succeed each other, maintain a constant direction of serial increase.* This sense of constant direction in a series of operations we saw in Chapter XIII to be a cardinal mental fact. "A differs from B differs from C differs from D, etc.," makes a *series* only when the differences are in the same direction. In any such difference-series all terms differ in just the same way from their predecessors. The numbers 1, 2, 3, 4, 5, . . . the notes of the chromatic scale in music, are familiar examples. As soon as the mind grasps such a series as a whole, it perceives that *two terms taken far apart differ more than two terms taken near together,* and that any one term differs more from a remote than from a near successor, and this no matter what the terms may be, or what the sort of difference may be, provided it is always the same sort.

This PRINCIPLE OF MEDIATE COMPARISON might be briefly (though obscurely) expressed by the formula *"more than the more is more than the less"*—the words *more* and *less* standing simply for degrees of increase along a constant direction of differences. Such a formula would cover all possible cases, as, earlier than early is earlier than late, worse than bad is worse than good, east of east is east of west; etc., etc., *ad libitum.*[2] Symbolically, we might write it as $a < b < c < d$ . . . and say that any number of intermediaries may be expunged without obliging us to alter anything in what remains written.

The principle of mediate comparison is only one form of a law which holds in many series of homogeneously related terms, the law that *skipping intermediary terms leaves relations the same.* THIS AXIOM OF SKIPPED INTERMEDIARIES or of TRANSFERRED RELATIONS occurs, as we soon shall see, in logic as the fundamental principle of inference, in arithmetic as the fundamental property of the number-series, in geometry as that of the straight line, the plane and the parallel. *It seems to be on the whole the broadest and deepest law of man's thought.*

In certain lists of terms the result of comparison may be to find no-difference, or equality in place of difference. Here also intermediaries may be skipped, and mediate comparison be carried on with the general result expressed by the *axiom of mediate equality,* "equals of equals are equal," which is the great principle of the mathematical sciences. This too as a result of the mind's mere acuteness, and in utter independence of the order in which

2. Cf. Bradley, *Logic,* p. 226.

experiences come associated together. Symbolically, again: $a = b = c = d \ldots$, with the same consequence as regards expunging terms which we saw before.

Classificatory Series

Thus we have a rather intricate system of necessary and immutable *ideal truths of comparison,* a system applicable to terms *experienced* in any order of sequence or frequency, or even to terms never experienced or to be experienced, such as the mind's imaginary constructions would be. These truths of comparison result in *Classifications.* It is, for some unknown reason, a great æsthetic delight for the mind to break the order of experience and class its materials in serial orders, proceeding from step to step of difference, and to contemplate untiringly the crossings and inosculations of the series among themselves. The first steps in most of the sciences are purely classificatory. Where facts fall easily into rich and intricate series (as plants and animals and chemical compounds do), the mere sight of the series fill the mind with a satisfaction *sui generis;* and a world whose *real* materials naturally lend themselves to serial classification is *pro tanto* a more rational world, a world with which the mind will feel more intimate, than with a world in which they do not. By the pre-evolutionary naturalists, whose generation has hardly passed away, classifications were supposed to be ultimate insights into God's mind, filling us with adoration of his ways. The fact that Nature lets us make them was a proof of the presence of his Thought in her bosom. So far as the facts of experience can *not* be serially classified, therefore, so far experience fails to be rational in *one* of the ways, at least, which we crave.

The Logic-Series

Closely akin to the function of comparison is that of *judging, predicating, or subsuming.* In fact, these elementary intellectual functions run into each other so, that it is often only a question of practical convenience whether we shall call a given mental operation by the name of one or of the other. Comparisons result in groups of like things; and presently (through discrimination and abstraction) in conceptions of the *respects* in which the likenesses

obtain. The groups are *genera* or *classes,* the respects are *characters* or *attributes.* The attributes again may be compared, forming
genera of higher orders, and their characters singled out; so that
we have a new sort of series, *that of predication, or of kind
including kind.* Thus horses are quadrupeds, quadrupeds animals,
animals machines, machines liable to wear out, etc. In such a series
as this the several couplings of terms may have been made out
originally at widely different times and under different circumstances. But memory may bring them together afterwards; and
whenever it does so, our faculty of apprehending serial increase
makes us conscious of them as a single system of successive terms
united by the same relation.[3]

Now whenever we become thus conscious, we may become aware
of an additional relation which is of the highest intellectual
importance, inasmuch as upon it the whole structure of logic is
reared. *The principle of mediate predication or subsumption* is
only the axiom of skipped intermediaries applied to a series of
successive predications. It expresses the fact that any earlier term
in the series stands to any later term in the same relation in which
it stands to any intermediate term; in other words, that *whatever
has an attribute has all the attributes of that attribute;* or more
briefly still, that *whatever is of a kind is of that kind's kind.* A
little explanation of this statement will bring out all that it
involves.

We learned in the chapter on Reasoning what our great motive
is for abstracting attributes and predicating them. It is that our
varying practical purposes require us to lay hold of different
angles of the reality at different times. But for these we should be
satisfied to 'see it whole,' and always alike. The purpose, however,
makes one aspect essential; so, to avoid dispersion of the attention,
we treat the reality as if for the time being it were nothing but
that aspect, and we let its supernumerary determinations go. In
short, we substitute the aspect for the whole real thing. *For our
purpose* the aspect *can* be substituted for the whole, and the two

3. This apprehension of them as forming a single system is what Mr. Bradley
means by the act of *construction* which underlies all reasoning. The awareness, which then supervenes, of the additional relation of which I speak in
the next paragraph of my text, is what this author calls the act of *inspection.*
Cf. *Principles of Logic,* bk. II. pt. I. chap. III.

treated as the same; and the word *is* (which couples the whole with its aspect or attribute in the categoric judgment) expresses (among other things) the identifying operation performed. The predication-series a is b, b is c, c is d, . . . closely resembles for certain practical purposes the equation-series $a = b$, $b = c$, $c = d$, etc.

But what is our purpose in predicating? Ultimately, it may be anything we please; but proximately and immediately, it is always the gratification of a certain curiosity as to whether the object in hand is or is not *of a kind* connected with that ultimate purpose. Usually the connection is not obvious, and we only find that the object S is of a kind connected with P, after first finding that it is of a kind M, which itself is connected with P. Thus, to fix our ideas by an example, we have a curiosity (our ultimate purpose being conquest over nature) as to how Sirius may move. It is not obvious whether Sirius is a kind of thing which moves in the line of sight or not. When, however, we find it to be a kind of thing in whose spectrum the hydrogen-line is shifted, and when we reflect that *that* kind of thing is a kind of thing which moves in the line of sight; we conclude that Sirius does so move. Whatever Sirius's attribute is, Sirius is; its adjective's adjective can supersede its own adjective in our thinking, and this with no loss to our knowledge, *so long as we stick to the definite purpose in view.*

Now please note that this elimination of intermediary kinds and transfer of *is*'s along the line, results from our insight into the very meaning of the word *is,* and into the constitution of any series of terms connected by that relation. It has naught to do with what any particular thing is or is not; but, *whatever* any given thing may be, we see that it also is whatever *that* is, indefinitely. To grasp in one view a succession of *is*'s is to apprehend this relation between the terms which they connect; just as to grasp a list of successive equals is to apprehend their *mutual* equality throughout. The principle of mediate subsumption thus expresses relations of ideal objects as such. It can be discovered by a mind left at leisure with any set of meanings (however originally obtained), of which some are predicable of others. The moment we string them in a serial line, that moment we see that we can drop intermediaries, use remote terms just like near ones, and put a genus in the place of a species. This shows that *the principle of mediate sub-*

sumption has nothing to do with the particular order of our experiences, or with the outer coexistences and sequences of terms. Were it a mere outgrowth of habit and association, we should be forced to regard it as having no universal validity; for every hour of the day we meet things which we consider to be of this kind or of that, but later learn that they have none of the kind's properties, that they *do not* belong to the kind's kind. Instead, however, of correcting the principle by these cases, we correct the cases by the principle. We say that if the thing we named an M has not M's properties, then we were either mistaken in calling it an M, or mistaken about M's properties; or else that it is no longer M, but has changed. But we never say that it is an M without M's properties; for by conceiving a thing as of the kind M I mean that it *shall* have M's properties, be of M's kind, even though I should never be able to find in the real world anything which is an M. The principle emanates from my perception of what a lot of successive is's *mean.* This perception can no more be confirmed by one set, or weakened by another set, of outer facts, than the perception that black is not white can be confirmed by the fact that snow never blackens, or weakened by the fact that photographer's paper blackens as soon as you lay it in the sun.

The abstract scheme of successive predications, extended indefinitely, with all the possibilities of substitution which it involves, is thus an immutable system of truth which flows from the very structure and form of our thinking. *If* any real terms ever do fit into such a scheme, they will obey its laws; *whether* they do is a question as to nature's facts, the answer to which can only be empirically ascertained. *Formal logic* is the name of the Science which traces in skeleton form all the remote relations of terms connected by successive *is*'s with each other, and enumerates their possibilities of mutual substitution. To our principle of mediate subsumption she has given various formulations, of which the best is perhaps this broad expression, that *the same can be substituted for the same in any mental operation.*[4]

4. Realities fall under this only so far as they prove to *be* the same. So far as they cannot be substituted for each other, for the purpose in hand, so far they are not the same; though for other purposes and in other respects they might be substituted, and then be treated as the same. Apart from purpose, of course, no realities ever are absolutely and exactly the same.

The ordinary logical series contains but three terms—"Socrates, man, mortal." But we also have 'Sorites'—Socrates, man, animal, machine, run down, mortal, etc.—and it violates psychology to represent these as syllogisms with terms suppressed. The ground of there being any logic at all is our power to grasp any series as a whole, and the more terms it holds the better. This synthetic consciousness of an uniform direction of advance through a multiplicity of terms is, apparently, what the brutes and lower men cannot accomplish, and what gives to us our extraordinary power of ratiocinative thought. The mind which can grasp a string of *is*'s as a whole—the objects linked by them may be ideal or real, physical, mental, or symbolic, indifferently—can also apply to it the principle of skipped intermediaries. *The logic-list is thus in its origin and essential nature just like those graded classificatory lists which we erewhile described.* The 'rational proposition' which lies at the basis of all reasoning, the *dictum de omni et nullo* in all the various forms in which it may be expressed, the fundamental law of thought, is thus *only the result of the function of comparison* in a mind which has come by some lucky variation to apprehend a series of more than two terms at once. So far, then, *both Systematic Classification and Logic are seen to be incidental results of the mere capacity for discerning difference and likeness,* which capacity is a thing with which the *order of experience,* properly so styled, has absolutely nothing to do.

But how comes it (it may next be asked) when systematic classifications have so little ultimate theoretic importance—for the conceiving of things according to their mere degrees of resemblance always yields to other modes of conceiving when these can be obtained—that the logical relations among things should form such a mighty engine for dealing with the facts of life?

Chapter XXII already gave the reason. . . . This world *might* be a world in which all things differed, and in which what properties there were were ultimate and had no farther predicates. In such a world there would be as many kinds as there were separate things. We could never subsume a new thing under an old kind; or if we could, no consequences would follow. Or, again, this might be a world in which innumerable things were of a kind, but in which no concrete thing remained of the same kind long, but all objects were in a flux. Here again, though we could subsume and infer, our logic would be of no practical use to us, for the subjects of our propositions would have changed whilst we were talking. In such worlds, logical relations would obtain, and be known (doubtless) as they are now, but they would form a merely theoretic scheme and be of no use for the conduct of life. But our world is no such world. It is a very peculiar world, and plays right into logic's hands. *Some* of the things, at least, which it contains are of the same kind as other things; *some* of them remain always of the kind of which they once were; and some of the properties of them cohere indissolubly and are always found together. *Which* things these latter things are we learn by experience in the strict sense of the word, and the results of the experience are embodied in 'empirical propositions.' Whenever such a thing is met with by us now, our sagacity notes it to be of a certain kind; our learning immediately recalls that kind's kind, and then *that* kind's kind, and so on; so that a moment's thinking may make us aware that the thing is of a kind so remote that we could never have directly perceived the connection. The flight to this last kind *over the heads of the intermediaries* is the essential feature of the intellectual operation here. Evidently it is a pure outcome of our sense for apprehending serial increase; and, unlike the several propositions themselves which make up the series (and which may all be empirical), it has nothing to do with the time- and space-order in which the things have been experienced. . . .

. . . There is thus no denying the fact that *the mind is filled with necessary and eternal relations which it finds between certain of its ideal conceptions, and which form a determinate system, independent of the order of frequency in which experience may have associated the conception's originals in time and space.*

Shall we continue to call these sciences 'intuitive,' 'innate,' or 'a priori' bodies of truth, or not?* Personally I should like to do so.

---

* Some readers may expect me to plunge into the old debate as to whether the *a priori* truths are 'analytic' or 'synthetic.' It seems to me that the distinction is one of Kant's most unhappy legacies, for the reason that it is impossible to make it sharp. No one will say that such analytic judgments as "equidistant lines can nowhere meet" are *pure* tautologies. The predicate is a somewhat new way of conceiving as well as of naming the subject. There is *something* 'ampliative' in our greatest truisms, our state of mind is richer after than before we have uttered them. This being the case, the question "at what point

But I hesitate to use the terms on account of the odium which controversial history has made the whole of their connotation for many worthy persons. The most politic way not to alienate these readers is to flourish the name of the immortal Locke. For in truth I have done nothing more in the previous pages than to make a little more explicit the teachings of Locke's fourth book . . .

. . . None of these eternal verities has anything to say about facts, about what is or is not in the world. Logic does not say whether Socrates, men, mortals or immortals *exist:* arithmetic does not tell us where her 7's, 5's, and 12's are to be *found;* geometry affirms not that circles and rectangles are *real.* All that these sciences make us sure of is, that *if* these things are anywhere to be found, the eternal verities will obtain of them. . . .

. . . Take those aspects of phenomena which interest you as a human being most, and class the phenomena as perfect and imperfect, as ends and means to ends, as high and low, beautiful and ugly, positive and negative, harmonious and discordant, fit and unfit, natural and unnatural, etc., and barren are all your results. In the ideal world the kind 'precious' has characteristic properties. What is precious should be preserved; unworthy things should be sacrificed for its sake; exceptions made on its account; its preciousness is a reason for other things' actions, and the like. But none of these things need happen to your 'precious' object in the real world. Call the things of nature as much as you like by sentimental, moral, and aesthetic names, no natural consequences follow from the naming. They may be of the kinds you allege, but they are not of *'the kind's kind.'* . . .

. . . The sentimental facts and relations are butchered at a blow.

---

does the new state of mind cease to be *implicit* in the old?" is too vague to be answered. The only sharp way of defining synthetic propositions would be to say that they express a relation between *two data* at least. But it is hard to find any proposition which cannot be construed as doing this. Even verbal definitions do it . . . All philosophic interest vanishes from the question, the moment one ceases to ascribe to *any a priori* truths (whether analytic or synthetic) that "legislative character for all possible experience" which Kant believed in. We ourselves have denied such legislative character, and contended that it was for experience itself to prove whether its data can or cannot be assimilated to those ideal terms between which *a priori* relations obtain. The analytic-synthetic debate is thus for us devoid of all significance. On the whole, the best recent treatment of the question known to me is in one of A. Spir's works, his Denken und Wirklichkeit, I think, but I cannot now find the page.

But the rationality yielded is so superbly complete in *form* that to many minds this atones for the loss, and reconciles the thinker to the notion of a purposeless universe, in which all the things and qualities men love, *dulcissima mundi nomina,* are but illusions of our fancy attached to accidental clouds of dust which will be dissipated by the eternal cosmic weather as carelessly as they were formed.

The popular notion that 'Science' is forced on the mind *ab extra,* and that our interests have nothing to do with its constructions, is utterly absurd. The craving to believe that the things of the world belong to kinds which are related by inward rationality together, is the parent of Science as well as of sentimental philosophy; and the original investigator always preserves a healthy sense of how plastic the materials are in his hands. . . .

But alongside of these ideal relations between terms which the world verifies, there are other ideal relations not as yet so verified. I refer to those propositions (no longer expressing mere results of comparison) which are formulated in such metaphysical and aesthetic axioms as "The Principle of things is one;" "The quantity of existence is unchanged;" "Nature is simple and invariable;" "Nature acts by the shortest ways;" *"Ex nihilo nihil fit;"* "Nothing can be evolved which was not involved;" "Whatever is in the effect must be in the cause;" "A thing can only work where it is;" "A thing can only affect another of its own kind;" *"Cessante causa, cessat et effectus;"* "Nature makes no leaps;" "Things belong to discrete and permanent kinds;" "Nothing is or happens without a reason;" "The world is throughout rationally intelligible;" etc., etc., etc. Such principles as these, which might be multiplied to satiety,* are properly to be called *postulates of rationality,* not propositions of fact. If nature *did* obey them, she *would* be *pro tanto* more intelligible; and we seek meanwhile so to conceive her phenomena as to show that she does obey them. To a certain extent we succeed. For example, instead of the 'quantity of existence' so vaguely postulated as unchanged, Nature allows us to suppose that curious sum of distances and velocities which for want of a better term we call 'energy.' For the effect being 'contained in the

---

* Perhaps the most influential of all these postulates is that the nature of the world must be such that sweeping statements may be made about it.

cause,' nature lets us substitute 'the effect *is* the cause,' so soon as she lets us conceive both effect and cause as the same molecules, in two successive positions.—But all around these incipient successes (as all around the molecular world, so soon as we add to it as its 'effects' those illusory 'things' of common-sense which we had to butcher for its sake) , there still spreads a vast field of irrationalized fact whose items simply *are* together, and from one to another of which we can pass by no ideally 'rational' way.

It is not that these more metaphysical postulates of rationality are absolutely barren—though barren enough they were when used, as the scholastics used them, as immediate propositions of fact. They have a fertility as ideals, and keep us uneasy and striving always to recast the world of sense until its lines become more congruent with theirs. Take for example the principle that 'nothing can happen without a cause.' We have no definite idea of what we mean by cause, or of what causality consists in. But the principle expresses a demand for *some* deeper sort of inward connection between phenomena than their merely habitual time-sequence seems to us to be. The word 'cause' is, in short, an altar to an unknown god; an empty pedestal still marking the place of a hoped-for statue. *Any* really inward belonging-together of the sequent terms, if discovered, would be accepted as what the word cause was meant to stand for. So we seek, and seek; and in the molecular systems we find a sort of inward belonging in the notion of identity of matter with change of collocation. Perhaps by still seeking we may find other sorts of inward belonging, even between the molecules and those 'secondary qualities,' etc., which they produce upon our minds. . . .

6.

From *Essays in Radical Empiricism*

A.   Does 'Consciousness' Exist?*

'Thoughts' and 'things' are names for two sorts of objects, which common-sense will always find contrasted and will always practically oppose to each other. Philosophy, reflecting on the contrast, has varied in the past in her explanations of it, and may be expected to vary in the future. At first, 'spirit and matter,' 'soul and body,' stood for a pair of equipollent substances quite on a par in weight and interest. But one day Kant undermined the soul and brought in the transcendental ego, and ever since then the bipolar relation has been very much off its balance. The transcendental ego seems nowadays in rationalist quarters to stand for everything, in empiricist quarters for almost nothing. In the hands of such writers as Schuppe, Rehmke, Natorp, Münsterberg—at any rate in his earlier writings—Schubert-Soldern and others, the spiritual principle attenuates itself to a thoroughly ghostly condition, being only a name for the fact that the 'content' of experience *is known*. It loses personal form and activity—these passing over to the content—and becomes a bare *Bewusstheit* or *Bewusstsein überhaupt,* of which in its own right absolutely nothing can be said.

I believe that 'consciousness,' when once it has evaporated to this estate of pure diaphaneity, is on the point of disappearing altogether. It is the name of a nonentity, and has no right to a place among first principles. Those who still cling to it are clinging to a mere echo, the faint rumor left behind by the disappearing 'soul' upon the air of philosophy. During the past year, I have read a number of articles whose authors seemed just on the point of abandoning the notion of consciousness, and substituting for it

* Reprinted from the *Journal of Philosophy, Psychology and Scientific Methods,* vol. I, no. 18 (1904). This and the next six selections first collected in book form as *Essays in Radical Empiricism* (New York & London: Longmans. Green & Co., 1912). Some footnotes have been deleted. Notes marked 'Ed.' signify the previous editor, R. B. Perry.

that of an absolute experience not due to two factors. But they were not quite radical enough, not quite daring enough in their negations. For twenty years past I have mistrusted 'consciousness' as an entity; for seven or eight years past I have suggested its non-existence to my students, and tried to give them its pragmatic equivalent in realities of experience. It seems to me that the hour is ripe for it to be openly and universally discarded.

To deny plumply that 'consciousness' exists seems so absurd on the face of it—for undeniably 'thoughts' do exist—that I fear some readers will follow me no farther. Let me then immediately explain that I mean only to deny that the word stands for an entity, but to insist most emphatically that it does stand for a function. There is, I mean, no aboriginal stuff or quality of being, contrasted with that of which material objects are made, out of which our thoughts of them are made; but there is a function in experience which thoughts perform, and for the performance of which this quality of being is invoked. That function is *knowing*. 'Consciousness' is supposed necessary to explain the fact that things not only are, but get reported, are known. Whoever blots out the notion of consciousness from his list of first principles must still provide in some way for that function's being carried on.

I

My thesis is that if we start with the supposition that there is only one primal stuff or material in the world, a stuff of which everything is composed, and if we call that stuff 'pure experience,' then knowing can easily be explained as a particular sort of relation towards one another into which portions of pure experience may enter. The relation itself is a part of pure experience; one of its 'terms' becomes the subject or bearer of the knowledge, the knower,[1] the other becomes the object known. This will need much explanation before it can be understood. The best way to get it understood is to contrast it with the alternative view; and for that we may take the recentest alternative, that in which the evaporation of the definite soul-substance has proceeded as far as it can go without being yet complete. If neo-Kantism has expelled

1. In my *Psychology* I have tried to show that we need no knower other than the 'passing thought.' [See above, pp. 82 ff.—B.W.]

earlier forms of dualism, we shall have expelled all forms if we are able to expel neo-Kantism in its turn.

For the thinkers I call neo-Kantian, the word consciousness to-day does no more than signalize the fact that experience is indefeasibly dualistic in structure. It means that not subject, not object, but object-plus-subject is the minimum that can actually be. The subject-object distinction meanwhile is entirely different from that between mind and matter, from that between body and soul. Souls were detachable, had separate destinies; things could happen to them. To consciousness as such nothing can happen, for, timeless itself, it is only a witness of happenings in time, in which it plays no part. It is, in a word, but the logical correlative of 'content' in an Experience of which the peculiarity is that *fact comes to light* in it, that *awareness of content* takes place. Consciousness as such is entirely impersonal—'self' and its activities belong to the content. To say that I am self-conscious, or conscious of putting forth volition, means only that certain contents, for which 'self' and 'effort of will' are the names, are not without witness as they occur.

Thus, for these belated drinkers at the Kantian spring, we should have to admit consciousness as an 'epistemological' necessity, even if we had no direct evidence of its being there.

But in addition to this, we are supposed by almost every one to have an immediate consciousness of consciousness itself. When the world of outer fact ceases to be materially present, and we merely recall it in memory, or fancy it, the consciousness is believed to stand out and to be felt as a kind of impalpable inner flowing, which, once known in this sort of experience, may equally be detected in presentations of the outer world. "The moment we try to fix our attention upon consciousness and to see *what,* distinctly, it is," says a recent writer, "it seems to vanish. It seems as if we had before us a mere emptiness. When we try to introspect the sensation of blue, all we can see is the blue; the other element is as if it were diaphanous. Yet it *can* be distinguished, if we look attentively enough, and know that there is something to look for."[2] "Consciousness" (*Bewusstheit*), says another philosopher, "is inexplicable and hardly describable, yet all conscious experi-

2. G. E. Moore: *Mind,* vol. XII, N. S. [1903], p. 450.

ences have this in common that what we call their content has this peculiar reference to a centre for which 'self' is the name, in virtue of which reference alone the content is subjectively given, or appears. . . . While in this way consciousness, or reference to a self, is the only thing which distinguishes a conscious content from any sort of being that might be there with no one conscious of it, yet this only ground of the distinction defies all closer explanations. The existence of consciousness, although it is the fundamental fact of psychology, can indeed be laid down as certain, can be brought out by analysis, but can neither be defined nor deduced from anything but itself."[3]

'Can be brought out by analysis,' this author says. This supposes that the consciousness is one element, moment, factor—call it what you like—of an experience of essentially dualistic inner constitution, from which, if you abstract the content, the consciousness will remain revealed to its own eye. Experience, at this rate, would be much like a paint of which the world pictures were made. Paint has a dual constitution, involving, as it does, a menstruum[4] (oil, size or what not) and a mass of content in the form of pigment suspended therein. We can get the pure menstruum by letting the pigment settle, and the pure pigment by pouring off the size or oil. We operate here by physical subtraction; and the usual view is, that by mental subtraction we can separate the two factors of experience in an analogous way—not isolating them entirely, but distinguishing them enough to know that they are two.

II

Now my contention is exactly the reverse of this. *Experience, I believe, has no such inner duplicity; and the separation of it into consciousness and content comes, not by way of subtraction, but by way of addition*—the addition, to a given concrete piece of it, of other sets of experiences, in connection with which severally its use or function may be of two different kinds. The paint will also serve here as an illustration. In a pot in a paint-shop, along with

3. Paul Natorp: *Einleitung in die Psychologie*, 1888, pp. 14, 112.
4. "Figuratively speaking, consciousness may be said to be the one universal solvent, or menstruum, in which the different concrete kinds of psychic acts and facts are contained, whether in concealed or in obvious form." G. T. Ladd: *Psychology, Descriptive and Explanatory*, 1894, p. 30.

other paints, it serves in its entirety as so much saleable matter. Spread on a canvas, with other paints around it, it represents, on the contrary, a feature in a picture and performs a spiritual function. Just so, I maintain, does a given undivided portion of experience, taken in one context of associates, play the part of a knower, of a state of mind, of 'consciousness'; while in a different context the same undivided bit of experience plays the part of a thing known, of an objective 'content.' In a word, in one group it figures as a thought, in another group as a thing. And, since it can figure in both groups simultaneously, we have every right to speak of it as subjective and objective both at once. The dualism connoted by such double-barrelled terms as 'experience,' 'phenomenon,' 'datum,' '*Vorfindung*'—terms which, in philosophy at any rate, tend more and more to replace the single-barrelled terms of 'thought' and 'thing'—that dualism, I say, is still preserved in this account, but reinterpreted, so that, instead of being mysterious and elusive, it becomes verifiable and concrete. It is an affair of relations, it falls outside, not inside, the single experience considered, and can always be particularized and defined.

The entering wedge for this more concrete way of understanding the dualism was fashioned by Locke when he made the word 'idea' stand indifferently for thing and thought, and by Berkeley when he said that what common sense means by realities is exactly what the philosopher means by ideas. Neither Locke nor Berkeley thought his truth out into perfect clearness, but it seems to me that the conception I am defending does little more than consistently carry out the 'pragmatic' method which they were the first to use.

If the reader will take his own experiences, he will see what I mean. Let him begin with a perceptual experience, the 'presentation,' so called, of a physical object, his actual field of vision, the room he sits in, with the book he is reading as its centre; and let him for the present treat this complex object in the common-sense way as being 'really' what it seems to be, namely, a collection of physical things cut out from an environing world of other physical things with which these physical things have actual or potential relations. Now at the same time it is just *those self-same things* which his mind, as we say, perceives; and the whole philosophy of perception from Democritus's time downwards has been just one long wrangle over the paradox that what is evidently one reality should be in two places at once, both in outer space and in a person's mind. 'Representative' theories of perception avoid the logical paradox, but on the other hand they violate the reader's sense of life, which knows no intervening mental image but seems to see the room and the book immediately just as they physically exist.

The puzzle of how the one identical room can be in two places is at bottom just the puzzle of how one identical point can be on two lines. It can, if it be situated at their intersection; and similarly, if the 'pure experience' of the room were a place of intersection of two processes, which connected it with different groups of associates respectively, it could be counted twice over, as belonging to either group, and spoken of loosely as existing in two places, although it would remain all the time a numerically single thing.

Well, the experience is a member of diverse processes that can be followed away from it along entirely different lines. The one self-identical thing has so many relations to the rest of experience that you can take it in disparate systems of association, and treat it as belonging with opposite contexts. In one of these contexts it is your 'field of consciousness'; in another it is 'the room in which you sit,' and it enters both contexts in its wholeness, giving no pretext for being said to attach itself to consciousness by one of its parts or aspects, and to outer reality by another. What are the two processes, now, into which the room-experience simultaneously enters in this way?

One of them is the reader's personal biography, the other is the history of the house of which the room is part. The presentation, the experience, the *that* in short (for until we have decided *what* it is it must be a mere *that*) is the last term of a train of sensations, emotions, decisions, movements, classifications, expectations, etc., ending in the present, and the first term of a series of similar 'inner' operations extending into the future, on the reader's part. On the other hand, the very same *that* is the *terminus ad quem* of a lot of previous physical operations, carpentering, papering, furnishing, warming, etc., and the *terminus a quo* of a lot of future ones, in which it will be concerned when undergoing the destiny of a physical room. The physical and the mental operations form curiously incompatible groups. As a room, the experience has occupied that spot and had that environment for thirty years. As your field of consciousness it may never have existed until now. As a room, attention will go on to discover endless new details in it. As your mental state merely, few new ones will emerge under attention's eye. As a room, it will take an earthquake, or a gang of men, and in any case a certain amount of time, to destroy it. As your subjective state, the closing of your eyes, or any instantaneous play of your fancy will suffice. In the real world, fire will consume it. In your mind, you can let fire play over it without effect. As an outer object, you must pay so much a month to inhabit it. As an inner content, you may occupy it for any length of time rent-free. If, in short, you follow it in the mental direction, taking it along with events of personal biography solely, all sorts of things are true of it which are false, and false of it which are true if you treat it as a real thing experienced, follow it in the physical direction, and relate it to associates in the outer world.

III

So far, all seems plain sailing, but my thesis will probably grow less plausible to the reader when I pass from percepts to concepts, or from the case of things presented to that of things remote. I believe, nevertheless, that here also the same law holds good. If we take conceptual manifolds, or memories, or fancies, they also are in their first intention mere bits of pure experience, and, as such, are single *thats* which act in one context as objects, and in another context figure as mental states. By taking them in their first intention, I mean ignoring their relation to possible perceptual experiences with which they may be connected, which they may lead to and terminate in, and which then they may be supposed to 'represent.' Taking them in this way first, we confine the problem to a world merely 'thought of' and not directly felt or seen. This world, just like the world of percepts, comes to us at first as a chaos of experiences, but lines of order soon get traced. We find that any bit of it which we may cut out as an example is connected with distinct groups of associates, just as our perceptual experiences are, that these associates link themselves with it by different relations, and that one forms the inner history of a person, while the other acts as an impersonal 'objective' world, either spatial and temporal, or else merely logical or mathematical, or otherwise 'ideal.'

The first obstacle on the part of the reader to seeing that these non-perceptual experiences have objectivity as well as subjectivity will probably be due to the intrusion into his mind of *percepts,* that third group of associates with which the non-perceptual experiences have relations, and which, as a whole, they 'represent,' standing to them as thoughts to things. This important function of the non-perceptual experiences complicates the question and confuses it; for, so used are we to treat percepts as the sole genuine realities that, unless we keep them out of the discussion, we tend altogether to overlook the objectivity that lies in non-perceptual experiences by themselves. We treat them, 'knowing' percepts as they do, as through and through subjective, and say that they are wholly constituted of the stuff called consciousness, using this term now for a kind of entity, after the fashion which I am seeking to refute.

Abstracting, then, from percepts altogether, what I maintain is, that any single non-perceptual experience tends to get counted twice over, just as a perceptual experience does, figuring in one context as an object or field of objects, in another as a state of mind: and all this without the least internal self-diremption on its own part into consciousness and content. It is all consciousness in one taking; and, in the other, all content.

I find this objectivity of non-perceptual experiences, this complete parallelism in point of reality between the presently felt and the remotely thought, so well set forth in a page of Münsterberg's *Grundzüge,* that I will quote it as it stands.

"I may only think of my objects," says Professor Münsterberg; "yet, in my living thought they stand before me exactly as perceived objects would do, no matter how different the two ways of apprehending them may be in their genesis. The book here lying on the table before me, and the book in the next room of which I think and which I mean to get, are both in the same sense given realities for me, realities which I acknowledge and of which I take account. If you agree that the perceptual object is not an idea within me, but that percept and thing, as indistinguishably one, are really experienced *there, outside,* you ought not to believe that the merely thought-of object is hid away inside of the thinking subject. The object of which I think, and of those existence I take cognizance without letting it now work upon my senses, occupies its definite place in the outer world as much as does the object which I directly see.

"What is true of the here and the there, is also true of the now and the then. I know of the thing which is present and perceived, but I know also of the thing which yesterday was but is no more, and which I only remember. Both can determine my present conduct, both are parts of the reality of which I keep account. It is true that of much of the past I am uncertain, just as I am uncertain of much of what is present if it be but dimly perceived. But the interval of time does not in principle alter my relation to the object, does not transform it from an object known into a mental state. . . . The things in the room here which I survey, and those in my distant home of which I think, the things of this minute and those of my long-vanished boyhood, influence and decide me alike, with a reality which my experience of them directly feels. They both make up my real world, they make it directly, they do not have first to be introduced to me and mediated by ideas which now and here arise within me. . . . This not-me character of my recollections and expectations does not imply that the external objects of which I am aware in those experiences should necessarily be there also for others. The objects of dreamers and hallucinated persons are wholly without general validity. But even were they centaurs and golden mountains, they still would be 'off there,' in fairy land, and not 'inside' of ourselves."[5]

This certainly is the immediate, primary, naïf or practical way of taking our thought-of world. Were there no perceptual world to serve as its 'reductive,' in Taine's sense, by being 'stronger' and more genuinely 'outer' (so that the whole merely thought-of world seems weak and inner in comparison), our world of thought would be the only world, and would enjoy complete reality in our belief. This actually happens in our dreams, and in our day-dreams so long as percepts do not interrupt them.

And yet, just as the seen room (to go back to our late example)

5. Münsterberg: *Grundzüge der Psychologie,* vol. i, p. 48.

is *also* a field of consciousness, so the conceived or recollected room is *also* a state of mind; and the doubling-up of the experience has in both cases similar grounds.

The room thought-of, namely, has many thought-couplings with many thought-of things. Some of these couplings are inconstant, others are stable. In the reader's personal history the room occupies a single date—he saw it only once perhaps, a year ago. Of the house's history, on the other hand, it forms a permanent ingredient. Some couplings have the curious stubbornness, to borrow Royce's term, of fact; others show the fluidity of fancy—we let them come and go as we please. Grouped with the rest of its house, with the name of its town, of its owner, builder, value, decorative plan, the room maintains a definite foothold, to which, if we try to loosen it, it tends to return, and to reassert itself with force. With these associates, in a word, it coheres, while to other houses, other towns, other owners, etc., it shows no tendency to cohere at all. The two collections, first of its cohesive, and, second, of its loose associates, inevitably come to be contrasted. We call the first collection the system of external realities, in the midst of which the room, as 'real,' exists; the other we call the stream of our internal thinking, in which, as a 'mental image,' it for a moment floats.[6] The room thus again gets counted twice over. It plays two different rôles, being *Gedanke* and *Gedachtes,* the thought-of-an-object, and the object-thought-of, both in one; and all this without paradox or mystery, just as the same material thing may be both low and high, or small and great, or bad and good, because of its relations to opposite parts of an environing world.

As 'subjective' we say that the experience represents; as 'objective' it is represented. What represents, and what is represented, is here numerically the same; but we must remember that no dualism of being represented and representing resides in the experience *per se.* In its pure state, or when isolated, there is no self-splitting of it into consciousness and what the consciousness is 'of.' Its subjectivity and objectivity are functional attributes solely,

6. For simplicity's sake I confine my exposition to 'external' reality. But there is also the system of ideal reality in which the room plays its part. Relations of comparison, of classification, serial order, value, also are stubborn, assign a definite place to the room, unlike the incoherence of its places in the mere rhapsody of our successive thoughts.

realized only when the experience is 'taken,' *i.e.,* talked of, twice, considered along with its two differing contexts respectively, by a new retrospective experience, of which that whole past complication now forms the fresh content.

The instant field of the present is at all times what I call the 'pure' experience. It is only virtually or potentially either object or subject as yet. For the time being, it is plain, unqualified actuality, or existence, a simple *that*. In this *naïf* immediacy it is of course *valid;* it is *there,* we *act* upon it; and the doubling of it in retrospection into a state of mind and a reality intended thereby, is just one of the acts. The 'state of mind,' first treated explicitly as such in retrospection, will stand corrected or confirmed, and the retrospective experience in its turn will get a similar treatment; but the immediate experience in its passing is always 'truth,'[7] practical truth, *something to act on,* at its own movement. If the world were then and there to go out like a candle, it would remain truth absolute and objective, for it would be 'the last word,' would have no critic, and no one would ever oppose the thought in it to the reality intended.[8]

I think I may now claim to have made my thesis clear. Consciousness connotes a kind of external relation, and does not denote a special stuff or way of being. *The peculiarity of our experiences, that they not only are, but are known, which their 'conscious' quality is invoked to explain, is better explained by their relations—these relations themselves being experiences—to one another.*

IV

Were I now to go on to treat of the knowing of perceptual by conceptual experiences, it would again prove to be an affair of

7. Note the ambiguity of this term, which is taken sometimes objectively and sometimes subjectively.

8. In the *Psychological Review* for July [1904], Dr. R. B. Perry has published a view of Consciousness which comes nearer to mine than any other with which I am acquainted. At present, Dr. Perry thinks, every field of experience is so much 'fact.' It becomes 'opinion' or 'thought' only in retrospection, when a fresh experience, thinking the same object, alters and corrects it. But the corrective experience becomes itself in turn corrected, and thus experience as a whole is a process in which what is objective originally forever turns subjective, turns into our apprehension of the object. I strongly recommend Dr. Perry's admirable article to my readers.

external relations. One experience would be the knower, the other the reality known; and I could perfectly well define, without the notion of 'consciousness,' what the knowing actually and practically amounts to—leading-towards, namely, and terminating-in percepts, through a series of transitional experiences which the world supplies. But I will not treat of this, space being insufficient.** I will rather consider a few objections that are sure to be urged against the entire theory as it stands.

V

First of all, this will be asked: "If experience has not 'conscious' existence, if it be not partly made of 'consciousness,' of what then is it made? Matter we know, and thought we know, and conscious content we know, but neutral and simple 'pure experience' is something we know not at all. Say *what* it consists of—for it must consist of something—or be willing to give it up!"

To this challenge the reply is easy. Although for fluency's sake I myself spoke early in this article of a stuff of pure experience, I have now to say that there is no *general* stuff of which experience at large is made. There are as many stuffs as there are 'natures' in the things experienced. If you ask what any one bit of pure experience is made of, the answer is always the same: "It is made of *that*, of just what appears, of space, of intensity, of flatness, brownness, heaviness, or what not." Shadworth Hodgson's analysis here leaves nothing to be desired. Experience is only a collective name for all these sensible natures, and save for time and space (and, if you like, for 'being') there appears no universal element of which all things are made.

VI

The next objection is more formidable, in fact it sounds quite crushing when one hears it first.

"If it be the self-same piece of pure experience, taken twice over, that serves now as thought and now as thing"—so the objection runs—"how comes it that its attributes should differ so fundamentally in the two takings. As thing, the experience is extended; as thought, it occupies no space or place. As thing, it is red, hard,

** See below, e.g., "A World of Pure Experience."

heavy; but who ever heard of a red, hard or heavy thought? Yet even now you said that an experience is made of just what appears, and what appears is just such adjectives. How can the one experience in its thing-function be made of them, consist of them, carry them as its own attributes, while in its thought-function it disowns them and attributes them elsewhere. There is a self-contradiction here from which the radical dualism of thought and thing is the only truth that can save us. Only if the thought is one kind of being can the adjectives exist in it 'intentionally' (to use the scholastic term) ; only if the thing is another kind, can they exist in it constitutively and energetically. No simple subject can take the same adjectives and at one time be qualified by it, and at another time be merely 'of' it, as of something only meant or known."

The solution insisted on by this objector, like many other common-sense solutions, grows the less satisfactory the more one turns it in one's mind. To begin with, *are* thought and thing as heterogeneous as is commonly said?

No one denies that they have some categories in common. Their relations to time are identical. Both, moreover, may have parts (for psychologists in general treat thoughts as having them) ; and both may be complex or simple. Both are of kinds, can be compared, added and subtracted and arranged in serial orders. All sorts of adjectives qualify our thoughts which appear incompatible with consciousness, being as such a bare diaphaneity. For instance, they are natural and easy, or laborious. They are beautiful, happy, intense, interesting, wise, idiotic, focal, marginal, insipid, confused, vague, precise, rational, casual, general, particular, and many things besides. Moreover, the chapters on 'Perception' in the psychology-books are full of facts that make for the essential homogeneity of thought with thing. How, if 'subject' and 'object' were separated 'by the whole diameter of being,' and had no attributes in common, could it be so hard to tell, in a presented and recognized material object, what part comes in through the sense-organs and what part comes 'out of one's own head'? Sensations and apperceptive ideas fuse here so intimately that you can no more tell where one begins and the other ends, than you can tell, in those cunning circular panoramas that have lately been exhibited, where the real foreground and the painted canvas join together.[9]

Descartes for the first time defined thought as the absolutely unextended, and later philosophers have accepted the description as correct. But what possible meaning has it to say that, when we think of a foot-rule or a square yard, extension is not attributable to our thought? Of every extended object the *adequate* mental picture must have all the extension of the object itself. The difference between objective and subjective extension is one of relation to a context solely. In the mind the various extents maintain no necessarily stubborn order relatively to each other, while in the physical world they bound each other stably, and, added together, made the great enveloping Unit which we believe in and call real Space. As 'outer,' they carry themselves adversely, so to speak, to one another, exclude one another and maintain their distances; while, as 'inner,' their order is loose, and they form a *durcheinander* in which unity is lost.[10] But to argue from this that inner experience is absolutely inextensive seems to me little short of absurd. The two worlds differ, not by the presence or absence of extension, but by the relations of the extensions which in both worlds exist.

Does not this case of extension now put us on the track of truth in the case of other qualities? It does; and I am surprised that the facts should not have been noticed long ago. Why, for example, do we call a fire hot, and water wet, and yet refuse to say that our mental state, when it is 'of' these objects, is either wet or hot? 'Intentionally,' at any rate, and when the mental state is a vivid image, hotness and wetness are in it just as much as they are in the physical experience. The reason is this, that, as the general chaos of all our experiences gets sifted, we find that there are some fires that will always burn sticks and always warm our bodies, and that

9. Spencer's proof of his 'Transfigured Realism' (his doctrine that there is an absolutely non-mental reality) comes to mind as a splendid instance of the impossibility of establishing radical heterogeneity between thought and thing. All his painfully accumulated points of difference run gradually into their opposites, and are full of exceptions. [Cf. Spencer: *Principles of Psychology*, part VII, ch. XIX.]

10. I speak here of the complete inner life in which the mind plays freely with its materials. Of course the mind's free play is restricted when it seeks to copy real things in real space.

there are some waters that will always put our fires; while there are other fires and waters that will not act at all. The general group of experiences that *act,* that do not only possess their natures intrinsically, but wear them adjectively and energetically, turning them against one another, comes inevitably to be contrasted with the group whose members, having identically the same natures, fail to manifest them in the 'energetic' way.[11] I make for myself now an experience of blazing fire; I place it near my body; but it does not warm me in the least. I lay a stick upon it, and the stick either burns or remains green, as I please. I call up water, and pour it on the fire, and absolutely no difference ensues. I account for all such facts by calling this whole train of experiences unreal, a mental train. Mental fire is what won't burn real sticks; mental water is what won't necessarily (though of course it may) put out even a mental fire. Mental knives may be sharp, but they won't cut real wood. Mental triangles are pointed, but their points won't wound. With 'real' objects, on the contrary, consequences always accrue; and thus the real experiences get sifted from the mental ones, the things from our thoughts of them, fanciful or true, and precipitated together as the stable part of the whole experience-chaos, under the name of the physical world. Of this our perceptual experiences are the nucleus, they being the originally *strong* experiences. We add a lot of conceptual experiences to them, making these strong also in imagination, and building out the remoter parts of the physical world by their means; and around this core of reality the world of laxly connected fancies and mere rhapsodical objects floats like a bank of clouds. In the clouds, all sorts of rules are violated which in the core are kept. Extensions there can be indefinitely located; motion there obeys no Newton's laws.

VII

There is a peculiar class of experiences to which, whether we take them as subjective or as objective, we *assign* their several natures as attributes, because in both contexts they affect their associates actively, though in neither quite as 'strongly' or as

11. [But there are also "mental activity trains," in which thoughts do "work on each other." Cf. below, p. 217, note, ED.]

sharply as things affect one another by their physical energies. I refer here to *appreciations,* which form an ambiguous sphere of being, belonging with emotion on the one hand, and having objective 'value' on the other, yet seeming not quite inner nor quite outer, as if a diremption had begun but had not made itself complete.

Experiences of painful objects, for example, are usually also painful experiences; perceptions of loveliness, of ugliness, tend to pass muster as lovely or as ugly perceptions; intuitions of the morally lofty are lofty intuitions. Sometimes the adjective wanders as if uncertain where to fix itself. Shall we speak of seductive visions or of visions of seductive things? Of wicked desires or of desires for wickedness? Of healthy thoughts or of thoughts of healthy objects? Of good impulses, or of impulses towards the good? Of feelings of anger, or of angry feelings? Both in the mind and in the thing, these natures modify their context, exclude certain associates and determine others, have their mates and incompatibles. Yet not as stubbornly as in the case of physical qualities, for beauty and ugliness, love and hatred, pleasant and painful can, in certain complex experiences, coexist.

If one were to make an evolutionary construction of how a lot of originally chaotic pure experiences became gradually differentiated into an orderly inner and outer world, the whole theory would turn upon one's success in explaining how or why the quality of an experience, once active, could become less so, and, from being an energetic attribute in some cases, elsewhere lapse into the status of an inert or merely internal 'nature.' This would be the 'evolution' of the psychical from the bosom of the physical, in which the æsthetic, moral and otherwise emotional experiences would represent a halfway stage.

VIII

But a last cry of *non possumus* will probably go up from many readers. "All very pretty as a piece of ingenuity," they will say, "but our consciousness itself intuitively contradicts you. We, for our part, *know* that we are conscious. We *feel* our thought, flowing as a life within us, in absolute contrast with the objects which it so unremittingly escorts. We can not be faithless to this immediate intuition. The dualism is a fundamental *datum:* Let no man join what God has put assunder."

My reply to this is my last word, and I greatly grieve that to many it will sound materialistic. I can not help that, however, for I, too, have my intuitions and I must obey them. Let the case be what it may in others, I am as confident as I am of anything that, in myself, the stream of thinking (which I recognize emphatically as a phenomenon) is only a careless name for what, when scrutinized, reveals itself to consist chiefly of the stream of my breathing. The 'I think' which Kant said must be able to accompany all my objects, is the 'I breathe' which actually does accompany them. There are other internal facts besides breathing (intracephalic muscular adjustments, etc., of which I have said a word in my larger *Psychology*), and these increase the assets of 'consciousness,' so far as the latter is subject to immediate perception,[12] but breath, which was ever the original of 'spirit,' breath moving outwards, between the glottis and the nostrils, is, I am persuaded, the essence out of which philosophers have constructed the entity known to them as consciousness. *That entity is fictitious, while thoughts in the concrete are fully real. But thoughts in the concrete are made of the same stuff as things are.*

I wish I might believe myself to have made that plausible in this article. In another article I shall try to make the general notion of a world composed of pure experiences still more clear.

B.   A World of Pure Experience*

. . . To be radical, an empiricism must neither admit into its constructions any element that is not directly experienced, nor exclude from them any element that is directly experienced. For such a philosophy, *the relations that connect experiences must themselves be experienced relations, and any kind of relation experienced must be accounted as 'real' as anything else in the system.* Elements may indeed be redistributed, the original placing of things getting corrected, but a real place must be found for

12. See above, pp. 82 ff.—B.W.

* First published in the *Journal of Philosophy, Psychology and Scientific Methods,* vol. I, no. 20 (1904) ; portions of text and some footnotes have been deleted. [B.W.]

every kind of thing experienced, whether term or relation, in the final philosophic arrangement.

Now, ordinary empiricism, in spite of the fact that conjunctive and disjunctive relations present themselves as being fully co-ordinate parts of experience, has always shown a tendency to do away with the connections of things, and to insist most on the disjunctions. Berkeley's nominalism, Hume's statement that what-ever things we distinguish are as 'loose and separate' as if they had 'no manner of connection,' James Mill's denial that similars have anything 'really' in common, the resolution of the causal tie into habitual sequence, John Mill's account of both physical things and selves as composed of discontinuous possibilities, and the general pulverization of all Experience by association and the mind-dust theory, are examples of what I mean.

The natural result of such a world-picture has been the efforts of rationalism to correct its incoherencies by the addition of transex-periential agents of unification, substances, intellectual categories and powers, or Selves; whereas, if empiricism had only been radical and taken everything that comes without disfavor, con-junction as well as separation, each at its face value, the results would have called for no such artificial correction. *Radical em-piricism,* as I understand it, *does full justice to conjunctive rela-tions,* without, however, treating them as rationalism always tends to treat them, as being true in some supernal way, as if the unity of things and their variety belonged to different orders of truth and vitality altogether.

II. Conjunctive Relations

Relations are of different degrees of intimacy. Merely to be 'with' one another in a universe of discourse is the most external relation that terms can have, and seems to involve nothing what-ever as to farther consequences. Simultaneity and time-interval come next, and then space-adjacency and distance. After them, similarity and difference, carrying the possibility of many infer-ences. Then relations of activity, tying terms into series involving change, tendency, resistance, and the causal order generally. Fi-nally, the relation experienced between terms that form states of mind, and are immediately conscious of continuing each other.

The organization of the Self as a system of memories, purposes, strivings, fulfilments or disappointments, is incidental to this most intimate of all relations, the terms of which seem in many cases actually to compenetrate and suffuse each other's being.[1]

Philosophy has always turned on grammatical particles. With, near, next, like, from, towards, against, because, for, through, my—these words designate types of conjunctive relation arranged in a roughly ascending order of intimacy and inclusiveness. *A priori*, we can imagine a universe of withness but no nextness; or one of nextness but no likeness, or of likeness with no activity, or of activity with no purpose, or of purpose with no ego. These would be universes, each with its own grade of unity. The universe of human experience is, by one or another of its parts, of each and all these grades. Whether or not it possibly enjoys some still more absolute grade of union does not appear upon the surface.

Taken as it does appear, our universe is to a large extent chaotic. No one single type of connection runs through all the experiences that compose it. If we take space-relations, they fail to connect minds into any regular system. Causes and purposes obtain only among special series of facts. The self-relation seems extremely limited and does not link two different selves together. *Prima facie*, if you should liken the universe of absolute idealism to an aquarium, a crystal globe in which goldfish are swimming, you would have to compare the empiricist universe to something more like one of those dried human heads with which the Dyaks of Borneo deck their lodges. The skull forms a solid nucleus; but innumerable feathers, leaves, strings, beads, and loose appendices of every description float and dangle from it, and, save that they terminate in it, seem to have nothing to do with one another. Even so my experiences and yours float and dangle, terminating, it is true, in a nucleus of common perception, but for the most part out of sight and irrelevant and unimaginable to one another. This imperfect intimacy, this bare relation of *withness* between some parts of the sum total of experience and other parts, is the fact that ordinary empiricism over-emphasizes against rationalism, the latter always tending to ignore it unduly. Radical empiricism, on the contrary, is fair to both the unity and the disconnection. It

1. [See "The Experience of Activity," below. ED.]

finds no reason for treating either as illusory. It allots to each its definite sphere of description, and agrees that there appear to be actual forces at work which tend, as time goes on, to make the unity greater.

The conjunctive relation that has given most trouble to philosophy is *the co-conscious transition,* so to call it, by which one experience passes into another when both belong to the same self. About the facts there is no question. My experiences and your experiences are 'with' each other in various external ways, but mine pass into mine, and yours pass into yours in a way in which yours and mine never pass into one another. Within each of our personal histories, subject, object, interest and purpose *are continuous or may be continuous.* Personal histories are processes of change in time, and *the change itself is one of the things immediately experienced.* 'Change' in this case means continuous as opposed to discontinuous transition. But continuous transition is one sort of a conjunctive relation; and to be a radical empiricist means to hold fast to this conjunctive relation of all others, for this is the strategic point, the position through which, if a hole be made, all the corruptions of dialectics and all the metaphysical fictions pour into our philosophy. The holding fast to this relation means taking it at its face value, neither less nor more; and to take it at its face value means first of all to take it just as we feel it, and not to confuse ourselves with abstract talk *about* it, involving words that drive us to invent secondary conceptions in order to neutralize their suggestions and to make our actual experience again seem rationally possible.

What I do feel simply when a later moment of my experience succeeds an earlier one is that though they are two moments, the transition from the one to the other is *continuous.* Continuity here is a definite sort of experience; just as definite as is the *discontinuity-experience* which I find it impossible to avoid when I seek to make the transition from an experience of my own to one of yours. In this latter case I have to get on and off again, to pass from a thing lived to another thing only conceived, and the break is positively experienced and noted. Though the functions exerted by my experience and by yours may be the same (*e.g.,* the same objects known and the same purposes followed), yet the sameness has in this case to be ascertained expressly (and often with difficulty and uncertainty) after the break has been felt; whereas in passing from one of my own moments to another the sameness of object and interest is unbroken, and both the earlier and the later experience are of things directly lived.

There is no other *nature*, no other whatness than this absence of break and this sense of continuity in that most intimate of all conjunctive relations, the passing of one experience into another when they belong to the same self. And this whatness is real empirical 'content,' just as the whatness of separation and discontinuity is real content in the contrasted case. Practically to experience one's personal continuum in this living way is to know the originals of the ideas of continuity and of sameness, to know what the words stand for concretely, to own all that they can ever mean. But all experiences have their conditions; and over-subtle intellects, thinking about the facts here, and asking how they are possible, have ended by substituting a lot of static objects of conception for the direct perceptual experiences. "Sameness," they have said, "must be a stark numerical identity; it can't run on from next to next. Continuity can't mean mere absence of gap; for if you say two things are in immediate contact, *at* the contact how can they be two? If, on the other hand, you put a relation of transition between them, that itself is a third thing, and needs to be related or hitched to its terms. An infinite series is involved," and so on. The result is that from difficulty to difficulty, the plain conjunctive experience has been discredited by both schools, the empiricists leaving things permanently disjoined, and the rationalists remedying the looseness by their Absolutes or Substances, or whatever other fictitious agencies of union they may have employed. From all which artificiality we can be saved by a couple of simple reflections: first, that conjunctions and separations are, at all events, co-ordinate phenomena which, if we take experiences at their face value, must be accounted equally real; and second, that if we insist on treating things as really separate when they are given as continuously joined, invoking, when union is required, transcendental principles to overcome the separateness we have assumed, then we ought to stand ready to perform the converse act. We ought to invoke higher principles of *dis*union, also, to make our merely experienced *dis*junctions more truly real. Failing thus, we ought to let the originally given continuities stand on their own bottom. We have no right to be lopsided or to blow capriciously hot and cold.

III. The Cognitive Relation

The first great pitfall from which such a radical standing by experience will save us is an artificial conception of the *relations between knower and known*. Throughout the history of philosophy the subject and its object have been treated as absolutely discontinuous entities; and thereupon the presence of the latter to the former, or the 'apprehension' by the former of the latter, has assumed a paradoxical character which all sorts of theories had to be invented to overcome. Representative theories put a mental 'representation,' 'image,' or 'content' into the gap, as a sort of intermediary. Common-sense theories left the gap untouched, declaring our mind able to clear it by a self-transcending leap. Transcendentalist theories left it impossible to traverse by finite knowers, and brought an Absolute in to perform the saltatory act. All the while, in the very bosom of the finite experience, every conjunction required to make the relation intelligible is given in full. Either the knower and the known are:

(1) the self-same piece of experience taken twice over in different contexts; or they are

(2) two pieces of *actual* experience belonging to the same subject, with definite tracts of conjunctive transitional experience between them; or

(3) the known is a *possible* experience either of that subject or another, to which the said conjunctive transitions *would* lead, if sufficiently prolonged.

To discuss all the ways in which one experience may function as the knower of another, would be incompatible with the limits of this essay.[2] I have just treated of type 1, the kind of knowledge

2. For brevity's sake I altogether omit mention of the type constituted by knowledge of the truth of general propositions. This type has been thoroughly and, so far as I can see, satisfactorily, elucidated in Dewey's *Studies in Logical Theory*. Such propositions are reducible to the *S-is-P* form; and the 'terminus' that verifies and fulfils is the *SP* in combination. Of course percepts may be involved in the mediating experiences, or in the satisfactoriness of the *P* in its new position.

called perception. This is the type of case in which the mind enjoys direct 'acquaintance' with a present object. In the other types the mind has 'knowledge-about' an object not immediately there. Of type 2, the simplest sort of conceptual knowledge, I have given some account in two [earlier] articles.[3] Type 3 can always formally and hypothetically be reduced to type 2, so that a brief description of that type will put the present reader sufficiently at my point of view, and make him see what the actual meanings of the mysterious cognitive relation may be.

Suppose me to be sitting here in my library at Cambridge, at ten minutes' walk from 'Memorial Hall,' and to be thinking truly of the latter object. My mind may have before it only the name, or it may have a clear image, or it may have a very dim image of the Hall, but such intrinsic differences in the image make no difference in its cognitive function. Certain *extrinsic* phenomena, special experiences of conjunction, are what impart to the image, be it what it may, its knowing office.

For instance, if you ask me what hall I mean by my image, and I can tell you nothing; or if I fail to point or lead you towards the Harvard Delta; or if, being led by you, I am uncertain whether the Hall I see be what I had in mind or not; you would rightly deny that I had 'meant' that particular Hall at all, even though my mental image might to some degree have resembled it. The resemblance would count in that case as coincidental merely, for all sorts of things of a kind resemble one another in this world without being held for that reason to take cognizance of one another.

On the other hand, if I can lead you to the Hall, and tell you of its history and present uses; if in its presence I feel my idea, however imperfect it may have been, to have led hither and to be now *terminated;* if the associates of the image and of the felt Hall run parallel, so that each term of the one context corresponds serially, as I walk, with an answering term of the others; why then my soul was prophetic, and my idea must be, and by common consent would be, called cognizant of reality. That percept was

3. ["On the Function of Cognition," *Mind*, vol. x, 1885, and "The Knowing of Things Together," *Psychological Review*, vol. ii, 1895. These articles are reprinted, the former in full, the latter in part, in *The Meaning of Truth*, pp. 1–50. Ed.] . . .

what I *meant,* for into it my idea has passed by conjunctive experiences of sameness and fulfilled intention. Nowhere is there jar, but every later moment continues and corroborates an earlier one.

In this continuing and corroborating, taken in no transcendental sense, but denoting definitely felt transitions, *lies all that the knowing of a percept by an idea can possibly contain or signify.* Wherever such transitions are felt, the first experience *knows* the last one. Where they do not, or where even as possibles they can not, intervene, there can be no pretence of knowing. In this latter case the extremes will be connected, if connected at all, by inferior relations—bare likeness or succession, or by 'withness' alone. Knowledge of sensible realities thus comes to life inside the tissue of experience. It is *made;* and made by relations that unroll themselves in time. Whenever certain intermediaries are given, such that, as they develop towards their terminus, there is experience from point to point of one direction followed, and finally of one process fulfilled, the result is that *their starting-point thereby becomes a knower and their terminus an object meant or known.* That is all that knowing (in the simple case considered) can be known-as, that is the whole of its nature, put into experiential terms. Whenever such is the sequence of our experiences we may freely say that we had the terminal object 'in mind' from the outset, even although *at* the outset nothing was there in us but a flat piece of substantive experience like any other, with no self-transcendency about it, and no mystery save the mystery of coming into existence and of being gradually followed by other pieces of substantive experience, with conjunctively transitional experiences between. That is what we *mean* here by the object's being 'in mind.' Of any deeper more real way of being in mind we have no positive conception, and we have no right to discredit our actual experience by talking of such a way at all.

I know that many a reader will rebel at this. "Mere intermediaries," he will say, "even though they be feelings of continuously growing fulfilment, only *separate* the knower from the known, whereas what we have in knowledge is a kind of immediate touch of the one by the other, an 'apprehension' in the etymological sense of the word, a leaping of the chasm as by lightning, an act by which two terms are smitten into one, over the head of their distinctness. All these dead intermediaries of yours are out of each other, and outside of their termini still."

But do not such dialectic difficulties remind us of the dog dropping his bone and snapping at its image in the water? If we knew any more real kind of union *aliunde,* we might be entitled to brand all our empirical unions as a sham. But unions by continuous transition are the only ones we know of, whether in this matter of a knowledge-about that terminates in an acquaintance, whether in personal identity, in logical predication through the copula 'is,' or elsewhere. If anywhere there were more absolute unions realized, they could only reveal themselves to us by just such conjunctive results. These are what the unions are *worth,* these are all that *we can ever practically mean* by union, by continuity. Is it not time to repeat what Lotze said of substances, that to *act like* one is to *be* one? Should we not say here that to be experienced as continuous is to be really continuous, in a world where experience and reality come to the same thing? In a picture gallery a painted hook will serve to hang a painted chain by, a painted cable will hold a painted ship. In a world where both the terms and their distinctions are affairs of experience, conjunctions that are experienced must be at least as real as anything else. They will be 'absolutely' real conjunctions, if we have no transphenomenal Absolute ready, to derealize the whole experienced world by, at a stroke. If, on the other hand, we had such an Absolute, not one of our opponents' theories of knowledge could remain standing any better than ours could; for the distinctions as well as the conjunctions of experience would impartially fall its prey. The whole question of how 'one' thing can know 'another' would cease to be a real one at all in a world where otherness itself was an illusion.

So much for the essentials of the cognitive relation, where the knowledge is conceptual in type, or forms knowledge 'about' an object. It consists in intermediary experiences (possible, if not actual) of continuously developing progress, and, finally, of fulfilment, when the sensible percept, which is the object, is reached. The percept here not only *verifies* the concept, proves its function of knowing that percept to be true, but the percept's existence as the terminus of the chain of intermediaries *creates* the function.

Whatever terminates that chain was, because it now proves itself to be, what the concept 'had in mind.'

The towering importance for human life of this kind of knowing lies in the fact that an experience that knows another can figure as its *representative,* not in any quasi-miraculous 'epistemological' sense, but in the definite practical sense of being its *substitute* in various operations, sometimes physical and sometimes mental, which lead us to its associates and results. By experimenting on our ideas of reality, we may save ourselves the trouble of experimenting on the real experiences which they severally mean. The ideas form related systems, corresponding point for point to the systems which the realities form; and by letting an ideal term call up its associates systematically, we may be led to a terminus which the corresponding real term would have led to in case we had operated on the real world. And this brings us to the general question of substitution.

IV. Substitution

In Taine's brilliant book on 'Intelligence,' substitution was for the first time named as a cardinal logical function, though of course the facts had always been familiar enough. What, exactly, in a system of experiences, does the 'substitution' of one of them for another mean?

According to my view, experience as a whole is a process in time, whereby innumerable particular terms lapse and are superseded by others that follow upon them by transitions which, whether disjunctive or conjunctive in content, are themselves experiences, and must in general be accounted at least as real as the terms which they relate. What the nature of the event called 'superseding' signifies, depends altogether on the kind of transition that obtains. Some experiences simply abolish their predecessors without continuing them in any way. Others are felt to increase or to enlarge their meaning, to carry out their purpose, or to bring us nearer to their goal. They 'represent' them, and may fulfil their function better than they fulfilled it themselves. But to 'fulfil a function' in a world of pure experience can be conceived and defined in only one possible way. In such a world transitions and arrivals (or terminations) are the only events that happen, though they happen by so many sorts of path. The only function that one experience can perform is to lead into another experience; and the only fulfilment we can speak of is the reaching of a certain experienced end. When one experience leads to (or can lead to) the same end as another, they agree in function. But the whole system of experiences as they are immediately given presents itself as a quasi-chaos through which one can pass out of an initial term in many directions and yet end in the same terminus, moving from next to next by a great many possible paths.

Either one of these paths might be a functional substitute for another, and to follow one rather than another might on occasion be an advantageous thing to do. As a matter of fact, and in a general way, the paths that run through conceptual experiences, that is, through 'thoughts' or 'ideas' that 'know' the things in which they terminate, are highly advantageous paths to follow. Not only do they yield inconceivably rapid transitions; but, owing to the 'universal' character[4] which they frequently possess, and to their capacity for association with one another in great systems, they outstrip the tardy consecutions of the things themselves, and sweep us on towards our ultimate termini in a far more labor-saving way than the following of trains of sensible perception ever could. Wonderful are the new cuts and the short-circuits which the thought-paths make. Most thought-paths, it is true, are substitutes for nothing actual; they end outside the real world altogether, in wayward fancies, utopias, fictions or mistakes. But where they do re-enter reality and terminate therein, we substitute them always; and with these substitutes we pass the greater number of our hours.

This is why I called our experiences, taken all together, a quasi-chaos. There is vastly more discontinuity in the sum total of experiences than we commonly suppose. The objective nucleus of every man's experience, his own body, is, it is true, a continuous percept; and equally continuous as a percept (though we may be inattentive to it) is the material environment of that body, changing by gradual transition when the body moves. But the distant

---

4. Of which all that need be said in this essay is that it also can be conceived as functional, and defined in terms of transitions, or of the possibility of such.

parts of the physical world are at all times absent from us, and form conceptual objects merely, into the perceptual reality of which our life inserts itself at points discrete and relatively rare. Round their several objective nuclei, partly shared and common and partly discrete, of the real physical world, innumerable thinkers, pursuing their several lines of physically true cogitation, trace paths that intersect one another only at discontinuous perceptual points, and the rest of the time are quite incongruent; and around all the nuclei of shared 'reality,' as around the Dyak's head of my late metaphor, floats the vast cloud of experiences that are wholly subjective, that are non-substitutional, that find not even an eventual ending for themselves in the perceptual world—the mere day-dreams and joys and sufferings and wishes of the individual minds. These exist *with* one another, indeed, and with the objective nuclei, but out of them it is probable that to all eternity no interrelated system of any kind will ever be made.

This notion of the purely substitutional or conceptual physical world brings us to the most critical of all the steps in the development of a philosophy of pure experience. The paradox of self-transcendency in knowledge comes back upon us here, but I think that our notions of pure experience and of substitution, and our radically empirical view of conjunctive transitions, are *Denkmittel* that will carry us safely through the pass.

V. What Objective Reference Is

Whosoever feels his experience to be something substitutional even while he has it, may be said to have an experience that reaches beyond itself. From inside of its own entity it says 'more,' and postulates reality existing elsewhere. For the transcendentalist, who holds knowing to consist in a *salto mortale* across an 'epistemological chasm,' such an idea presents no difficulty; but it seems at first sight as if it might be inconsistent with an empiricism like our own. Have we not explained that conceptual knowledge is made such wholly by the existence of things that fall outside of the knowing experience itself—by intermediary experiences and by a terminus that fulfils? Can the knowledge be there before these elements that constitute its being have come? And, if knowledge be not there, how can objective reference occur?

The key to this difficulty lies in the distinction between knowing as verified and completed, and the same knowing as in transit and on its way. To recur to the Memorial Hall example lately used, it is only when our idea of the Hall has actually terminated in the percept that we know 'for certain' that from the beginning it was truly cognitive of *that*. Until established by the end of the process, its quality of knowing that, or indeed of knowing anything, could still be doubted; and yet the knowing really was there, as the result now shows. We were *virtual* knowers of the Hall long before we were certified to have been its actual knowers, by the percept's retroactive validating power. Just so we are 'mortal' all the time, by reason of the virtuality of the inevitable event which will make us so when it shall have come.

Now the immensely greater part of all our knowing never gets beyond this virtual stage. It never is completed or nailed down. I speak not merely of our ideas of imperceptibles like ether-waves or dissociated 'ions,' or of 'ejects' like the contents of our neighbors' minds; I speak also of ideas which we might verify if we would take the trouble, but which we hold for true although unterminated perceptually, because nothing says 'no' to us, and there is no contradicting truth in sight. *To continue thinking unchallenged is, ninety-nine times out of a hundred, our practical substitute for knowing in the completed sense.* As each experience runs by cognitive transition into the next one, and we nowhere feel a collision with what we elsewhere count as truth or fact, we commit ourselves to the current as if the port were sure. We live, as it were, upon the front edge of an advancing wave-crest, and our sense of a determinate direction in falling forward is all we cover of the future of our path. It is as if a differential quotient should be conscious and treat itself as an adequate substitute for a traced-out curve. Our experience, *inter alia,* is of variations of rate and of direction, and lives in these transitions more than in the journey's end. The experiences of tendency are sufficient to act upon—what more could we have *done* at those moments even if the later verification comes complete?

This is what, as a radical empiricist, I say to the charge that the objective reference which is so flagrant a character of our experiences involves a chasm and a mortal leap. A positively conjunctive transition involves neither chasm nor leap. Being the very original of what we mean by continuity, it makes a continuum wherever it appears. I know full well that such brief words as these will leave the hardened transcendentalist unshaken. Conjunctive experiences *separate* their terms, he will still say: they are third things interposed, that have themselves to be conjoined by new links, and to invoke them makes our trouble infinitely worse. To 'feel' our motion forward is impossible. Motion implies terminus; and how can terminus be felt before we have arrived? The barest start and sally forwards, the barest tendency to leave the instant, involves the chasm and the leap. Conjunctive transitions are the most superficial of appearances, illusions of our sensibility which philosophical reflection pulverizes at a touch. Conception is our only trustworthy instrument, conception and the Absolute working hand in hand. Conception disintegrates experience utterly, but its disjunctions are easily overcome again when the Absolute takes up the task.

Such transcendentalists I must leave, provisionally at least, in full possession of their creed. I have no space for polemics in this article, so I shall simply formulate the empiricist doctrine as my hypothesis, leaving it to work or not work as it may.

Objective reference, I say then, is an incident of the fact that so much of our experience comes as an insufficient and consists of process and transition. Our fields of experience have no more definite boundaries than have our fields of view. Both are fringed forever by a *more* that continuously develops, and that continuously supersedes them as life proceeds. The relations, generally speaking, are as real here as the terms are, and the only complaint of the transcendentalist's with which I could at all sympathize would be his charge that, by first making knowledge to consist in external relations as I have done, and by then confessing that nine-tenths of the time these are not actually but only virtually there, I have knocked the solid bottom out of the whole business, and palmed off a substitute of knowledge for the genuine thing. Only the admission, such a critic might say, that our ideas are self-transcendent and 'true' already, in advance of the experiences that are to terminate them, can bring solidity back to knowledge in a world like this, in which transitions and terminations are only by exception fulfilled.

This seems to me an excellent place for applying the pragmatic method. When a dispute arises, that method consists in auguring what practical consequences would be different if one side rather than the other were true. If no difference can be thought of, the dispute is a quarrel over words. What then would the self-transcendency affirmed to exist in advance of all experiential mediation or termination, be *known as?* What would it practically result in for *us,* were it true?

It could only result in our orientation, in the turning of our expectations and practical tendencies into the right path; and the right path here, so long as we and the object are not yet face to face (or can never get face to face, as in the case of ejects), would be the path that led us into the object's nearest neighborhood. Where direct acquaintance is lacking, 'knowledge about' is the next best thing, and an acquaintance with what actually lies about the object, and is most closely related to it, puts such knowledge within our grasp. Ether-waves and your anger, for example, are things in which my thoughts will never *perceptually* terminate, but my concepts of them lead me to their very brink, to the chromatic fringes and to the hurtful words and deeds which are their really next effects.

Even if our ideas did in themselves carry the postulated self-transcendency, it would still remain true that their putting us into possession of such effects *would be the sold cash-value of the self-transcendency for us.* And this cash-value, it is needless to say, is *verbatim et litteratim* what our empiricist account pays in. On pragmatist principles therefore, a dispute over self-transcendency is a pure logomachy. Call our concepts of ejective things self-transcendent or the reverse, it makes no difference, so long as we don't differ about the nature of that exalted virtue's fruits—fruits for us, of course, humanistic fruits. If an Absolute were proved to exist for other reasons, it might well appear that *his* knowledge is terminated in innumerable cases where ours is still incomplete. That, however, would be a fact indifferent to our knowledge. The latter would grow neither worse not better, whether we acknowledged such an Absolute or left him out.

So the notion of a knowledge still *in transitu* and on its way joins hands here with that notion of a 'pure experience' which I tried to explain in my [essay] entitled "Does 'Consciousness' Exist?" The instant field of the present is always experience in its 'pure' state, plain unqualified actuality, a simple *that,* as yet undifferentiated into thing and thought, and only virtually classifiable as objective fact or as some one's opinion about fact. This is as true when the field is conceptual as when it is perceptual. 'Memorial Hall' is 'there' in my idea as much as when I stand before it. I proceed to act on its account in either case. Only in the later experience that supersedes the present one is this *naïf* immediacy retrospectively split into two parts, a 'consciousness' and its 'content,' and the content corrected or confirmed. While still pure, or present, any experience—mine, for example, of what I write about in these very lines—passes for 'truth.' The morrow may reduce it to 'opinion.' The transcendentalist in all his particular knowledges is as liable to this reduction as I am: his Absolute does not save him. Why, then, need he quarrel with an account of knowing that merely leaves it liable to this inevitable condition? Why insist that knowing is a static relation out of time when it practically seems so much a function of our active life? For a thing to be valid, says Lotze, is the same as to make itself valid. When the whole universe seems only to be making itself valid and to be still incomplete (else why its ceaseless changing?), why, of all things, should knowing be exempt? Why should it not be making itself valid like everything else? That some parts of it may be already valid or verified beyond dispute, the empirical philosopher, of course, like any one else, may always hope.

VI. *The Conterminousness of Different Minds*

With transition and prospect thus enthroned in pure experience, it is impossible to subscribe to the idealism of the English school. Radical empiricism has, in fact, more affinities with natural realism than with the views of Berkeley or of Mill, and this can be easily shown.

For the Berkeleyan school, ideas (the verbal equivalent of what I term experiences) are discontinuous. The content of each is wholly immanent, and there are no transitions with which they are consubstantial and through which their beings may unite. Your Memorial Hall and mine, even when both are percepts, are wholly out of connection with each other. Our lives are a congeries of solipsisms, out of which in strict logic only a God could compose a universe even of discourse. No dynamic currents run between my objects and your objects. Never can our minds meet in the *same*.

The incredibility of such a philosophy is flagrant. It is 'cold, strained, and unnatural' in a supreme degree; and it may be doubted whether even Berkeley himself, who took it so religiously, really believed, when walking through the streets of London, that his spirit and the spirits of his fellow wayfarers had absolutely different towns in view.

To me the decisive reason in favor of our minds meeting in *some* common objects at least is that, unless I make that supposition, I have no motive for assuming that your mind exists at all. Why do I postulate your mind? Because I see your body acting in a certain way. Its gestures, facial movements, words and conduct generally, are 'expressive,' so I deem it actuated as my own is, by an inner life like mine. This argument from analogy is my *reason*, whether an instinctive belief runs before it or not. But what is 'your body' here but a percept in *my* field? It is only as animating *that* object, *my* object, that I have any occasion to think of you at all. If the body that you actuate be not the very body that I see there, but some duplicate body of your own with which that has nothing to do, we belong to different universes, you and I, and for me to speak of you is folly. Myriads of such universes even now may coexist, irrelevant to one another; my concern is solely with the universe with which my own life is connected.

In that perceptual part of *my* universe which I call *your* body, your mind and my mind meet and may be called conterminous. Your mind actuates that body and mine sees it; my thoughts pass into it as into their harmonious cognitive fulfilment; your emotions and volitions pass into it as causes into their effects.

But that percept hangs together with all our other physical percepts. They are of one stuff with it; and if it be our common possession, they must be so likewise. For instance, your hand lays hold of one end of a rope and my hand lays hold of the other end. We pull against each other. Can our two hands be mutual objects in this experience, and the rope not be mutual also? What is true of the rope is true of any other percept. Your objects are over and over again the same as mine. If I ask you *where* some object of yours is, our old Memorial Hall, for example, you point to *my*

Memorial Hall with *your* hand which *I* see. If you alter an object in your world, put out a candle, for example, when I am present, *my* candle *ipso facto* goes out. It is only as altering my objects that I guess you to exist. If your objects do not coalesce with my objects, if they be not identically where mine are, they must be proved to be positively somewhere else. But no other location can be assigned for them, so their place must be what it seems to be, the same.

Practically, then, our minds meet in a world of objects which they share in common, which would still be there, if one or several of the minds were destroyed. I can see no formal objection to this supposition's being literally true. On the principles which I am defending, a 'mind' or 'personal consciousness' is the name for a series of experiences run together by certain definite transitions, and an objective reality is a series of similar experiences knit by different transitions. If one and the same experience can figure twice, once in a mental and once in a physical context (as I have tried, in my article on 'Consciousness,' to show that it can), one does not see why it might not figure thrice, or four times, or any number of times, by running into as many different mental contexts, just as the same point, lying at their intersection, can be continued into many different lines. Abolishing any number of contexts would not destroy the experience itself or its other contexts, any more than abolishing some of the point's linear continuations would destroy the others, or destroy the point itself.

I well know the subtle dialectic which insists that a term taken in another relation must needs be an intrinsically different term. The crux is always the old Greek one, that the same man can't be tall in relation to one neighbor, and short in relation to another, for that would make him tall and short at once. In this essay I can not stop to refute this dialectic, so I pass on, leaving my flank for the time exposed. But if my reader will only allow that the same 'now' both ends his past and begins his future; or that, when he buys an acre of land from his neighbor, it is the same acre that successively figures in the two estates; or that when I pay him a dollar, the same dollar goes into his pocket that came out of mine; he will also in consistency have to allow that the same object may conceivably play a part in, as being related to the rest of, any number of otherwise entirely different minds. This is enough for my present point: the common-sense notion of minds sharing the same object offers no special logical or epistemological difficulties of its own; it stands or falls with the general possibility of things being in conjunctive relation with other things at all.

In principle, then, let natural realism pass for possible. Your mind and mine *may* terminate in the same percept, not merely against it, as if it were a third external thing, but by inserting themselves into it and coalescing with it, for such is the sort of conjunctive union that appears to be experienced when a perceptual terminus 'fulfils.' Even so, two hawsers may embrace the same pile, and yet neither one of them touch any other part except that pile, of what the other hawser is attached to.

It is therefore not a formal question, but a question of empirical fact solely, whether, when you and I are said to know the 'same' Memorial Hall, our minds do terminate at or in a numerically identical percept. Obviously, as a plain matter of fact, they do *not*. Apart from color-blindness and such possibilities, we see the Hall in different perspectives. You may be on one side of it and I on another. The percept of each of us, as he sees the surface of the Hall, is moreover only his provisional terminus. The next thing beyond my percept is not your mind, but more percepts of my own into which my first percept develops, the interior of the Hall, for instance, or the inner structure of its bricks and mortar. If our minds were in a literal sense *con*terminous, neither could get beyond the percept which they had in common, it would be an ultimate barrier between them—unless indeed they flowed over it and became 'co-conscious' over a still larger part of their content, which (thought-transference apart) is not supposed to be the case. In point of fact the ultimate common barrier can always be pushed, by both minds, farther than any actual percepts of either, until at last it resolves itself into the mere notion of imperceptibles like atoms or ether, so that, where we do terminate in percepts, our knowledge is only speciously completed, being, in theoretical strictness, only a virtual knowledge of those remoter objects which conception carries out.

Is natural realism, permissible in logic, refuted then by empirical fact? Do our minds have no object in common after all?

Yes, they certainly have *Space* in common. On pragmatic principles we are obliged to predicate sameness wherever we can predicate no assignable point of difference. If two named things have every quality and function indiscernible, and are at the same time in the same place, they must be written down as numerically one thing under two different names. But there is no test discoverable, so far as I know, by which it can be shown that the place occupied by your percept of Memorial Hall differs from the place occupied by mine. The percepts themselves may be shown to differ; but if each of us be asked to point out where his percept is, we point to an identical spot. All the relations, whether geometrical or causal, of the Hall originate or terminate in that spot wherein our hands meet, and where each of us begins to work if he wishes to make the Hall change before the other's eyes. Just so it is with our bodies. That body of yours which you actuate and feel from within must be in the same spot as the body of yours which I see or touch from without. 'There' for me means where I place my finger. If you do not feel my finger's contact to be 'there' in *my* sense, when I place it on your body, where then do you feel it? Your inner actuations of your body meet my finger *there:* it is *there* that you resist its push, or shrink back, or sweep the finger aside with your hand. Whatever farther knowledge either of us may acquire of the real constitution of the body which we thus feel, you from within and I from without, it is in that same place that the newly conceived or perceived constituents have to be located, and it is *through* that space that your and my mental intercourse with each other has always to be carried on, by the mediation of impressions which I convey thither, and of the reactions thence which those impressions may provoke from you.

In general terms, then, whatever differing contents our minds may eventually fill a place with, the place itself is a numerically identical content of the two minds, a piece of common property in which, through which, and over which they join. The receptacle of certain of our experiences being thus common, the experiences themselves might some day become common also. If that day ever did come, our thoughts would terminate in a complete empirical identity, there would be an end, so far as *those* experiences went, to our discussions about truth. No points of difference appearing, they would have to count as the same. . . .

C. THE THING AND ITS RELATIONS*

. . . 'Pure experience' is the name which I gave to the immediate flux of life which furnishes the material to our later reflection with its conceptual categories. Only new-born babes, or men in semi-coma from sleep, drugs, illnesses, or blows, may be assumed to have an experience pure in the literal sense of a *that* which is not yet any definite *what*, tho' ready to be all sorts of whats; full both of oneness and of manyness, but in respects that don't appear; changing throughout, yet so confusedly that its phases interpenetrate and no points, either of distinction or of identity, can be caught. Pure experience in this state is but another name for feeling or sensation. But the flux of it no sooner comes than it tends to fill itself with emphases, and these salient parts become identified and fixed and abstracted; so that experience now flows as if shot through with adjectives and nouns and prepositions and conjunctions. Its purity is only a relative term, meaning the proportional amount of unverbalized sensation which it still embodies.

Far back as we go, the flux, both as a whole and in its parts, is that of things conjunct and separated. The great continua of time, space, and the self envelop everything, betwixt them, and flow together without interfering. The things that they envelop come as separate in some ways and as continuous in others. Some sensations coalesce with some ideas, and others are irreconcilable. Qualities compenetrate one space, or exclude each other from it. They cling together persistently in groups that move as units, or else they separate. Their changes are abrupt or discontinuous; and their kinds resemble or differ; and, as they do so, they fall into either even or irregular series.

In all this the continuities and the discontinuities are absolutely co-ordinate matters of immediate feeling. The conjunctions are as primordial elements of 'fact' as are the distinctions and disjunctions. In the same act by which I feel that this passing minute is a

---

* First published in the *Journal of Philosophy, Psychology and Scientific Methods*, vol. II, no. 2 (1905). Large sections have been deleted. [B.W.]

new pulse of my life, I feel that the old life continues into it, and the feeling of continuance in no wise jars upon the simultaneous feeling of a novelty. They, too, compenetrate harmoniously. Prepositions, copulas, and conjunctions, 'is,' 'isn't,' 'then,' 'before,' 'in,' 'on,' 'beside,' 'between,' 'next,' 'like,' 'unlike,' 'as,' 'but,' flower out of the stream of pure experience, the stream of concretes or the sensational stream, as naturally as nouns and adjectives do, and they melt into it again as fluidly when we apply them to a new portion of the stream. . . .

D. How Two Minds Can Know One Thing*

. . . While physical things, namely, are supposed to be permanent and to have their 'states,' a fact of consciousness exists but once and *is* a state. Its *esse* is *sentiri;* it is only so far as it is felt; and it is unambiguously and unequivocally exactly *what* is felt. The hypothesis under consideration would, however, oblige it to be felt equivocally, felt now as part of my mind and again at the same time *not* as a part of my mind, but of yours (for my mind is *not* yours), and this would seem impossible without doubling it into two distinct things, or, in other words, without reverting to the ordinary dualistic philosophy of insulated minds each knowing its object representatively as a third thing—and that would be to give up the pure-experience scheme altogether.

Can we see, then, any way in which a unit of pure experience might enter into and figure in two diverse streams of consciousness without turning itself into the two units which, on our hypothesis, it must not be?

II

There is a way; and the first step towards it is to see more precisely how the unit enters into either one of the streams of consciousness alone. Just what, from being 'pure,' does its becoming 'conscious' *once* mean?

* First published in the *Journal of Philosophy, Psychology and Scientific Methods,* vol. II, no. 7 (1905). First four pages have been deleted. [B.W.]

It means, first, that new experiences have supervened; and, second, that they have borne a certain assignable relation to the unit supposed. Continue, if you please, to speak of the pure unit as 'the pen.' So far as the pen's successors do but repeat the pen or, being different from it, are 'energetically'** related to it, it and they will form a group of stably existing physical things. So far, however, as its successors differ from it in another well-determined way, the pen will figure in their context, not as a physical, but as a mental fact. It will become a passing 'percept,' *my* percept of that pen. What now is that decisive well-determined way?

In the chapter on "The Self," in my *Principles of Psychology,* I explained the continuous identity of each personal consciousness as a name for the practical fact that new experiences come which look back on the old ones, find them 'warm,' and greet and appropriate them as 'mine.' These operations mean, when analyzed empirically, several tolerably definite things, viz.:

1. That the new experience has past time for its 'content,' and in that time a pen that 'was';

2. That 'warmth' was also about the pen, in the sense of a group of feelings ('interest' aroused, 'attention' turned, 'eyes' employed, etc.) that were closely connected with it and that now recur and evermore recur with unbroken vividness, though from the pen of now, which may be only an image, all such vividness may have gone;

3. That these feelings are the nucleus of 'me';

4. That whatever once was associated with them was, at least for that one moment, 'mine'—my implement if associated with hand-feelings, my 'percept' only, if only eye-feelings and attention-feelings were involved.

The pen, realized in this retrospective way as my percept, thus figures as a fact of 'conscious' life. But it does so only so far as 'appropriation' has occurred; and appropriation is *part of the content of a later experience* wholly additional to the originally 'pure' pen. *That* pen, virtually both objective and subjective, is at

** See selection above, "Does 'Consciousness' Exist?" [B.W.]

its own moment actually and intrinsically neither. It has to be looked back upon and *used,* in order to be classed in either distinctive way. But its use, so called, is in the hands of the other experience, while *it* stands, throughout the operation, passive and unchanged.

If this pass muster as an intelligible account of how an experience originally pure can enter into one consciousness, the next question is as to how it might conceivably enter into two.

III

Obviously no new kind of condition would have to be supplied. All that we should have to postulate would be a second subsequent experience, collateral and contemporary with the first subsequent one, in which a similar act of appropriation should occur. The two acts would interfere neither with one another nor with the originally pure pen. It would sleep undisturbed in its own past, no matter how many such successors went through their several appropriative acts. Each would know it as 'my' percept, each would class it as a 'conscious' fact.

Nor need their so classing it interfere in the least with their classing it at the same time as a physical pen. Since the classing in both cases depends upon the taking of it in one group or another of associates, if the superseding experience were of wide enough 'span' it could think the pen in both groups simultaneously, and yet distinguish the two groups. It would then see the whole situation conformably to what we call 'the representative theory of cognition,' and that is what we all spontaneously do. As a man philosophizing 'popularly,' I believe that what I see myself writing with is double—I think it in its relations to physical nature, and also in its relations to my personal life; I see that it is in my mind, but that it also is a physical pen.

The paradox of the same experience figuring in two consciousnesses seems thus no paradox at all. To be 'conscious' means not simply to be, but to be reported, known, to have awareness of one's being added to that being; and this is just what happens when the appropriative experience supervenes. The pen-experience in its original immediacy is not aware of itself, it simply *is,* and the second experience is required for what we call awareness of it to occur.[1] The difficulty of understanding what happens here is, therefore, not a logical difficulty: there is no contradiction involved. It is an ontological difficulty rather. Experiences come on an enormous scale, and if we take them all together, they come in a chaos of incommensurable relations that we can not straighten out. We have to abstract different groups of them, and handle these separately if we are to talk of them at all. But how the experiences ever *get themselves made,* or *why* their characters and relations are just such as appear, we can not begin to understand. Granting, however, that, by hook or crook, they *can* get themselves made, and can appear in the successions that I have so schematically described, then we have to confess that even although (as I began by quoting from the adversary) 'a feeling only is as it is felt,' there is still nothing absurd in the notion of its being felt in two different ways at once, as yours, namely, and as mine. It is, indeed, 'mine' only as it is felt as mine, and 'yours' only as it is felt as yours. But it is felt as neither *by itself,* but only when 'owned' by our two several remembering experiences, just as one undivided estate is owned by several heirs.

IV

One word, now, before I close, about the corollaries of the views set forth. Since the acquisition of conscious quality on the part of an experience depends upon a context coming to it, it follows that the sum total of all experiences, having no context, can not strictly be called conscious at all. It is a *that,* an Absolute, a 'pure' experience on an enormous scale, undifferentiated and undifferentiable into thought and thing. This the post-Kantian idealists have always practically acknowledged by calling their doctrine an *Identitätsphilosophie.* The question of the *Beseelung* of the All of

1. Shadworth Hodgson has laid great stress on the fact that the minimum of consciousness demands two subfeelings, of which the second retrospects the first. (Cf. the section "Analysis of Minima" in his *Philosophy of Reflection,* vol. I, p. 248; also the chapter entitled "The Moment of Experience" in his *Metaphysic of Experience,* vol. I, p. 34.) "We live forward, but we understand backward" is a phrase of Kierkegaard's which Höffding quotes. [H. Höffding: "A Philosophical Confession," *Journal of Philosophy, Psychology and Scientific Methods,* vol. II, 1905, p. 86.]

things ought not, then, even to be asked. No more ought the question of its *truth* to be asked, for truth is a relation inside of the sum total, obtaining between thoughts and something else, and thoughts, as we have seen, can only be contextual things. In these respects the pure experiences of our philosophy are, in themselves considered, so many little absolutes, the philosophy of pure experience being only a more comminuted *Identitätsphilosophie*.

Meanwhile, a pure experience can be postulated with any amount whatever of span or field. If it exert the retrospective and appropriative function on any other piece of experience, the latter thereby enters into its own conscious stream. And in this operation time intervals make no essential difference. After sleeping, my retrospection is as perfect as it is between two successive waking moments of my time. Accordingly if, millions of years later, a similarly retrospective experience should anyhow come to birth, my present thought would form a genuine portion of its long-span conscious life. 'Form a portion,' I say, but not in the sense that the two things could be entitatively or substantively one—they cannot, for they are numerically discrete facts—but only in the sense that the *functions* of my present thought, its knowledge, its purpose, its content and 'consciousness,' in short, being inherited, would be continued practically unchanged. Speculations like Fechner's, of an Earth-soul, of wider spans of consciousness enveloping narrower ones throughout the cosmos, are, therefore, philosophically quite in order, provided they distinguish the functional from the entitative point of view, and do not treat the minor consciousness under discussion as a kind of standing material of which the wider ones *consist*.[2]

E. The Place of Affectional Facts in a World of Pure Experience*

. . . First of all, then, it is a mistake to say, with the objectors whom I began by citing, that anger, love and fear are affections

---

2. [Cf. *A Pluralistic Universe*, Lect. iv, "Concerning Fechner," and Lect. v, "The Compounding of Consciousness." Ed.]

* First published in the *Journal of Philosophy, Psychology and Scientific Methods*, vol. ii, no. 11 (1905). Portions have been deleted. [B.W.]

purely of the mind. That, to a great extent at any rate, they are simultaneously affections of the body is proved by the whole literature of the James-Lange theory of emotion.[1] All our pains, moreover, are local, and we are always free to speak of them in objective as well as in subjective terms. We can say that we are aware of a painful place, filling a certain bigness in our organism, or we can say that we are inwardly in a 'state' of pain. All our adjectives of worth are similarly ambiguous—I instanced some of the ambiguities [in the first essay]. Is the preciousness of a diamond a quality of the gem? or is it a feeling in our mind? Practically we treat it as both or as either, according to the temporary direction of our thought. "Beauty," says Professor Santayana, "is pleasure objectified"; and in Sections 10 and 11 of his work, *The Sense of Beauty,* he treats in a masterly way of this equivocal realm. The various pleasures we receive from an object may count as 'feelings' when we take them singly, but when they combine in a total richness, we call the result the 'beauty' of the object, and treat it as an outer attribute which our mind perceives. We discover beauty just as we discover the physical properties of things. Training is needed to make us expert in either line. Single sensations also may be ambiguous. Shall we say an 'agreeable degree of heat,' or an 'agreeable feeling' occasioned by the degree of heat? Either will do; and language would lose most of its esthetic and rhetorical value were we forbidden to project words primarily connoting our affections upon the objects by which the affections are aroused. The man is really hateful; the action really mean; the situation really tragic—all in themselves and quite apart from our opinion. We even go so far as to talk of a weary road, a giddy height, a jocund morning or a sullen sky; and the term 'indefinite,' while usually applied only to our apprehensions, functions as a fundamental physical qualification of things in Spencer's 'law of evolution,' and doubtless passes with most readers for all right.

Psychologists, studying our perceptions of movement, have unearthed experiences in which movement is felt in general but not ascribed correctly to the body that really moves. Thus in optical vertigo, caused by unconscious movements of our eyes, both we

---

1. [Cf. *The Principles of Psychology,* vol. II, ch. XXV; and "The Physical Basis of Emotion," *The Psychological Review,* vol. I, 1894, p. 516. ED.]

and the external universe appear to be in a whirl. When clouds float by the moon, it is as if both clouds and moon and we ourselves shared in the motion. In the extraordinary case of amnesia of the Rev. Mr. Hanna, published by Sidis and Goodhart in their important work on *Multiple Personality,* we read that when the patient first recovered consciousness and "noticed an attendant walk across the room, he identified the movement with that of his own. He did not yet discriminate between his own movements and those outside himself." Such experiences point to a primitive stage of perception in which discriminations afterwards needful have not yet been made. A piece of experience of a determinate sort is there, but there at first as a 'pure' fact. Motion originally simply *is;* only later is it confined to this thing or to that. Something like this is true of every experience, however complex, at the moment of its actual presence. Let the reader arrest himself in the act of reading this article now. *Now* this is a pure experience, a phenomenon, or datum, a mere *that* or content of fact. *'Reading'* simply *is, is there;* and whether there for some one's consciousness, or there for physical nature, is a question not yet put. At the moment, it is there for neither; later we shall probably judge it to have been there for both.

With the affectional experiences which we are considering, the relatively 'pure' condition lasts. In practical life no urgent need has yet arisen for deciding whether to treat them as rigorously mental or as rigorously physical facts. So they remain equivocal; and, as the world goes, their equivocality is one of their great conveniences. . . .

. . . Take a mass of carrion, for example, and the 'disgustingness' which for us is part of the experience. The sun caresses it, and the zephyr woos it as if it were a bed of roses. So the disgustingness fails to *operate* within the realm of suns and breezes—it does not function as a physical quality. But the carrion 'turns our stomach' by what seems a direct operation—it *does* function physically, therefore, in that limited part of physics. We can treat it as physical or as non-physical according as we take it in the narrower or in the wider context, and conversely, of course, we must treat it as non-mental or as mental.

Our body itself is the palmary instance of the ambiguous. Sometimes I treat my body purely as a part of outer nature. Sometimes, again, I think of it as 'mine,' I sort it with the 'me,' and then certain local changes and determinations in it pass for spiritual happenings. Its breathing is my 'thinking,' its sensorial adjustments are my 'attention,' its kinesthetic alterations are my 'efforts,' its visceral perturbations are my 'emotions.' The obstinate controversies that have arisen over such statements as these (which sound so paradoxical, and which can yet be made so seriously) prove how hard it is to decide by bare introspection what it is in experiences that shall make them either spiritual or material. It surely can be nothing intrinsic in the individual experience. It is their way of behaving towards each other, their system of relations, their function; and all these things vary with the context in which we find it opportune to consider them. . . .

F.   THE EXPERIENCE OF ACTIVITY*

. . . The principle of pure experience is . . . a methodical postulate. Nothing shall be admitted as fact, it says, except what can be experienced at some definite time by some experient; and for every feature of fact ever so experienced, a definite place must be found somewhere in the final system of reality. In other words: Everything real must be experienceable somewhere, and every kind of thing experienced must somewhere be real.

Armed with these rules of method let us see what face the problems of activity present to us.

By the principle of pure experience, either the word 'activity' must have no meaning at all, or else the original type and model of what it means must lie in some concrete kind of experience that can be definitely pointed out. Whatever ulterior judgments we may eventually come to make regarding activity, *that sort* of thing will be what the judgments are about. The first step to take, then, is to ask where in the stream of experience we seem to find what we speak of as activity. What we are to think of the activity thus found will be a later question.

* First published in *The Psychological Review*, vol. XII, no. 1 (1905). Portions of text have been deleted, as have all footnotes, except the lengthy and crucial ones which appear below. [B.W.]

Now it is obvious that we are tempted to affirm activity wherever we find anything *going on*. Taken in the broadest sense, any apprehension of something *doing*, is an experience of activity. Were our world describable only by the words 'nothing happening,' 'nothing changing,' 'nothing doing,' we should unquestionably call it an 'inactive' world. Bare activity then, as we may call it, means the bare fact of event or change. 'Change taking place' is a unique content of experience, one of those 'conjunctive' objects which radical empiricism seeks so earnestly to rehabilitate and preserve. The sense of activity is thus in the broadest and vaguest way synonymous with the sense of 'life.' We should feel our own subjective life at least, even in noticing and proclaiming an otherwise inactive world. Our own reaction on its monotony would be the one thing experienced there in the form of something coming to pass.

This seems to be what certain writers have in mind when they insist that for an experient to be at all is to be active. It seems to justify, or at any rate to explain, Mr. Ward's expression that we *are* only as we are active, for we *are* only as experients; and it rules out Mr. Bradley's contention that "there is no original experience of anything like activity." What we ought to say about activities thus elementary, whose they are, what they effect, or whether indeed they effect anything at all—these are later questions, to be answered only when the field of experience is enlarged.

Bare activity would thus be predicable, though there were no definite direction, no actor, and no aim. Mere restless zigzag movement, or a wild *Ideenflucht*, or *Rhapsodie der Wahrnehmungen*, as Kant would say, would constitute an active as distinguished from an inactive world.

But in this actual world of ours, as it is given, a part at least of the activity comes with definite direction; it comes with desire and sense of goal; it comes complicated with resistances which it overcomes or succumbs to, and with the efforts which the feeling of resistance so often provokes; and it is in complex experiences like these that the notions of distinct agents, and of passivity as opposed to activity arise. Here also the notion of causal efficacy comes to birth. Perhaps the most elaborate work ever done in descriptive psychology has been the analysis by various recent writers of the more complex activity-situations. In their descriptions, exquisitely subtle some of them, the activity appears as the *gestaltqualität* or the *fundirte inhalt* (or as whatever else you may please to call the conjunctive form) which the content falls into when we experience it in the ways which the describers set forth. Those factors in those relations are what we mean by activity-situations; and to the possible enumeration and accumulation of their circumstances and ingredients there would seem to be no natural bound. Every hour of human life could contribute to the picture gallery; and this is the only fault that one can find with such descriptive industry—where is it going to stop? Ought we to listen forever to verbal pictures of what we have already in concrete form in our own breasts? They never take us off the superficial plane. We knew the facts already—less spread out and separated, to be sure—but we knew them still. We always felt our own activity, for example, as 'the expansion of an idea with which our Self is identified, against an obstacle'; and the following out of such a definition through a multitude of cases elaborates the obvious so as to be little more than an exercise in synonymic speech.

All the descriptions have to trace familiar outlines, and to use familiar terms. The activity is, for example, attributed either to a physical or to a mental agent, and is either aimless or directed. If directed it shows tendency. The tendency may or may not be resisted. If not, we call the activity immanent, as when a body moves in empty space by its momentum, or our thoughts wander at their own sweet will. If resistance is met, *its* agent complicates the situation. If now, in spite of resistance, the original tendency continues, effort makes its appearance, and along with effort, strain or squeeze. Will, in the narrower sense of the word, then comes upon the scene, whenever, along with the tendency, the strain and squeeze are sustained. But the resistance may be great enough to check the tendency, or even to reverse its path. In that case, we (if 'we' were the original agents or subjects of the tendency) are overpowered. The phenomenon turns into one of tension simply, or of necessity succumbed-to, according as the opposing power is only equal, or is superior to ourselves.

Whosoever describes an experience in such terms as these describes an experience *of* activity. If the word have any meaning, it must denote what there is found. *There* is complete activity in its original and first intention. What it is 'known-as' is what there appears. The experiencer of such a situation possesses all that the idea contains. He feels the tendency, the obstacle, the will, the strain, the triumph, or the passive giving up, just as he feels the time, the space, the swiftness or intensity, the movement, the weight and color, the pain and pleasure, the complexity, or whatever remaining characters the situation may involve. He goes through all that ever can be imagined where activity is supposed. If we suppose activities to go on outside of our experience, it is in forms like these that we must suppose them, or else give them some other name; for the word 'activity' has no imaginable content whatever save these experiences of process, obstruction, striving, strain, or release, ultimate *qualia* as they are of the life given us to be known.

Were this the end of the matter, one might think that whenever we had successfully lived through an activity-situation we should have to be permitted, without provoking contradiction, to say that we had been really active, that we had met real resistance and had really prevailed. Lotze somewhere says that to be an entity all that is necessary is to *gelten* as an entity, to operate, or be felt, experienced, recognized, or in any way realized, as such. In our activity-experiences the activity assuredly fulfils Lotze's demand. It makes itself *gelten*. It is witnessed at its work. No matter what activities there may really be in this extraordinary universe of ours, it is impossible for us to conceive of any one of them being either lived through or authentically known otherwise than in this dramatic shape of something sustaining a felt purpose against felt obstacles and overcoming or being overcome. What 'sustaining' means here is clear to anyone who has lived through the experience, but to no one else; just as 'loud,' 'red,' 'sweet,' mean something only to beings with ears, eyes, and tongues. The *percipi* in these originals of experience is the *esse;* the curtain is the picture. If there is anything hiding in the background, it ought not to be called activity, but should get itself another name.

This seems so obviously true that one might well experience astonishment at finding so many of the ablest writers on the subject flatly denying that the activity we live through in these situations is real. Merely to feel active is not to be active, in their sight.

The agents that appear in the experience are not real agents, the resistances do not really resist, the effects that appear are not really effects at all.[1] It is evident from this that mere descriptive analysis

1. *Verborum gratiâ:* "The feeling of activity is not able, *quâ* feeling, to tell us anything about activity" (Loveday: *Mind*, N. S., vol. x, [1901], p. 463) ; "A sensation or feeling or sense *of* activity . . . is not, looked at in another way, an experience *of* activity at all. It is a mere sensation shut up within which you could by no reflection get the idea of activity. . . . Whether this experience is or is not later on a character essential to our perception and our idea of activity, it, as it comes first, is not in itself an experience of activity at all. It, as it comes first, is only so for extraneous reasons and only so for an outside observer" (Bradley, *Appearance and Reality*, second edition, p. 605) ; "In dem Tätigkeitsgefühle liegt an sich nicht der geringste Beweis für das Vorhandensein einer psychischen Tätigkeit" (Münsterberg: *Grundzüge der Psychologie*) . I could multiply similar quotations and would have introduced some of them into my text to make it more concrete, save that the mingling of different points of view in most of these author's discussions (not in Münsterberg's) make it impossible to disentangle exactly what they mean. I am sure in any case, to be accused of misrepresenting them totally, even in this note, by omission of the context, so the less I name names and the more I stick to abstract characterization of a merely possible style of opinion, the safer it will be. And apropos of misunderstandings, I may add to this note a complaint on my own account. Professor Stout, in the excellent chapter on "Mental Activity," in vol. I of his *Analytic Psychology*, takes me to task for identifying spiritual activity with certain muscular feelings and gives quotations to bear him out. They are from certain paragraphs on 'the Self,' in which my attempt was to show what the central nucleus of the activities that we call 'ours' is. [*Principles of Psychology*, vol. I, pp. 299–305.] I found it in certain intracephalic movements which we habitually oppose, as 'subjective,' to the activities of the transcorporeal world. I sought to show that there is no direct evidence that we feel the activity of an inner spiritual agent as such (I should now say the activity of 'consciousness' as such, see [the first essay] "Does 'Consciousness' Exist?") . There are, in fact, three distinguishable 'activities' in the field of discussion: the elementary activity involved in the mere *that* of experience, in the fact that *something* is going on, and the farther specification of this *something* into two *whats*, an activity felt as 'ours,' and an activity ascribed to objects. Stout, as I apprehend him, identifies 'our' activity with that of the total experience-process, and when I circumscribe it as a part thereof, accuses me of treating it as a sort of external appendage to itself (Stout: *op. cit.*, vol. I, pp. 162–163) , as if I 'separated the activity from the process which is active.' But all the processes in question are active, and their activity is inseparable from their being. My book raised only the question of *which* activity deserved the name of 'ours.' So far as we are 'persons,' and contrasted and opposed to an 'environment,' movements in our body figure as our activities; and I am unable to find any other activities that are ours in this strictly personal sense. There is a wider sense in which the whole 'choir of heaven and furniture of the earth,' and their activities, are ours, for they are our 'objects.' But 'we' is here only another name for the total process of experience, another name for all that is, in fact; and I was dealing with the personal and individualized self exclusively in the passages with which Professor Stout finds fault.

of any one of our activity-experiences is not the whole story, that there is something still to tell *about* them that has led such able writers to conceive of a *Simon-pure* activity, of an activity *an sich,* that does, and doesn't merely appear to us to do, and compared with whose real doing all this phenomenal activity is but a specious sham.

The metaphysical question opens here; and I think that the state of mind of one possessed by it is often something like this: "It is all very well," we may imagine him saying, "to talk about certain experience-series taking on the form of feelings of activity, just as they might take on musical or geometric forms. Suppose that they do so; suppose we feel a will to stand a strain. Does our feeling do more than *record* the fact that the strain is sustained? The *real* activity, meanwhile, is the *doing* of the fact; and what is the doing made of before the record is made? What in the will *enables* it to act thus? And these trains of experience themselves, in which activities appear, what makes them *go* at all? Does the activity in one bit of experience bring the next bit into being? As an empiricist you cannot say so, for you have just declared activity to be only a kind of synthetic object, or conjunctive relation experienced between bits of experience already made. But what

---

The individualized self, which I believe to be the only thing properly called self, is a part of the content of the world experienced. The world experienced (otherwise called the 'field of consciousness') comes at all times with our body as its centre, centre of vision, centre of action, centre of interest. Where the body is is 'here'; when the body acts is 'now'; what the body touches is 'this'; all other things are 'there' and 'then' and 'that.' These words of emphasized position imply a systematization of things with reference to a focus of action and interest which lies in the body; and the systematization is now so instinctive (was it ever not so?) that no developed or active experience exists for us at all except in that ordered form. So far as 'thoughts' and 'feelings' can be active, their activity terminates in the activity of the body, and only through first arousing its activities can they begin to change those of the rest of the world. [Cf. also *A Pluralistic Universe,* p. 344, note 8. Ed.] The body is the storm centre, the origin of co-ordinates, the constant place of stress in all that experience-train. Everything circles round it, and is felt from its point of view. The word 'I,' then, is primarily a noun of position, just like 'this' and 'here.' Activities attached to 'this' position have prerogative emphasis, and, if activities have feelings, must be felt in a peculiar way. The word 'my' designates the kind of emphasis. I see no inconsistency whatever in defending, on the one hand, 'my' activities as unique and opposed to those of outer nature, and, on the other hand, in affirming, after introspection, that they consist in movements in the head. The 'my' of them is the emphasis, the feeling of perspective-interest in which they are dyed.

made them at all? What propels experience *überhaupt* into being? *There* is the activity that *operates;* the activity *felt* is only its superficial sign."

To the metaphysical question, popped upon us in this way, I must pay serious attention ere I end my remarks; but, before doing so, let me show that without leaving the immediate reticulations of experience, or asking what makes activity itself act, we still find the distinction between less real and more real activities forced upon us, and are driven to much soul-searching on the purely phenomenal plane.

We must not forget, namely, in talking of the ultimate character of our activity-experiences, that each of them is but a portion of a wider world, one link in the vast chain of processes of experience out of which history is made. Each partial process, to him who lives through it, defines itself by its origin and its goal; but to an observer with a wider mind-span who should live outside of it, that goal would appear but as a provisional halting-place, and the subjectively felt activity would be seen to continue into objective activities that led far beyond. We thus acquire a habit, in discussing activity-experiences, of defining them by their relation to something more. If an experience be one of narrow span, it will be mistaken as to what activity it is and whose. You think that *you* are acting while you are only obeying someone's push. You think you are doing *this,* but you are doing something of which you do not dream. For instance, you think you are but drinking this glass; but you are really creating the liver-cirrhosis that will end your days. You think you are just driving this bargain, but, as Stevenson says somewhere, you are laying down a link in the policy of mankind.

Generally speaking, the onlooker, with his wider field of vision, regards the *ultimate outcome* of an activity as what it is more really doing; and *the most previous agent* ascertainable, being the first source of action, he regards as the most real agent in the field. The others but transmit that agent's impulse; on him we put responsibility; we name him when one asks us 'Who's to blame?'

But the most previous agents ascertainable, instead of being of longer span, are often of much shorter span than the activity in view. Brain-cells are our best example. My brain-cells are believed to excite each other from next to next (by contiguous transmission of katabolic alteration, let us say) and to have been doing so long before this present stretch of lecturing-activity on my part began. If any one cell-group stops its activity, the lecturing will cease or show disorder of form. *Cessante causa, cessat et effectus*—does not this look as if the short-span brain activities were the more real activities, and the lecturing activities on my part only their effects? Moreover, as Hume so clearly pointed out, in my mental activity-situation the words physically to be uttered are represented as the activity's immediate goal. These words, however, cannot be uttered without intermediate physical processes in the bulb and vagi nerves, which processes nevertheless fail to figure in the mental activity-series at all. That series, therefore, since it leaves out vitally real steps of action, cannot represent the real activities. It is something purely subjective; the *facts* of activity are elsewhere. They are something far more interstitial, so to speak, than what my feelings record.

The *real* facts of activity that have in point of fact been systematically pleaded for by philosophers have, so far as my information goes, been of three principal types.

The first type takes a consciousness of wider time-span than ours to be the vehicle of the more real activity. Its will is the agent, and its purpose is the action done.

The second type assumes that 'ideas' struggling with one another are the agents, and that the prevalence of one set of them is the action.

The third type believes that nerve cells are the agents, and that resultant motor discharges are the acts achieved.

Now if we must de-realize our immediately felt activity-situations for the benefit of either of these types of substitute, we ought to know what the substitution practically involves. *What practical difference ought it to make if,* instead of saying naïvely that 'I' am active now in delivering this address, I say that a *wider thinker is active,* or that *certain ideas are active,* or that *certain nerve-cells are active,* in producing the result?

This would be the pragmatic meaning of the three hypotheses. Let us take them in succession in seeking a reply.

If we assume a wider thinker, it is evident that his purposes envelop mine. I am really lecturing *for* him; and although I cannot surely know to what end, yet if I take him religiously, I can trust it to be a good end, and willingly connive. I can be happy in thinking that my activity transmits his impulse, and that his ends prolong my own. So long as I take him religiously, in short, he does not de-realize my activities. He tends rather to corroborate the reality of them, so long as I believe both them and him to be good.

When now we turn to ideas, the case is different, inasmuch as ideas are supposed by the association psychology to influence each other only from next to next. The 'span' of an idea or pair of ideas, is assumed to be much smaller instead of being larger than that of my total conscious field. The same results may get worked out in both cases, for this address is being given anyhow. But the ideas supposed to 'really' work it out had no prevision of the whole of it; and if I was lecturing for an absolute thinker in the former case, so, by similar reasoning, are my ideas now lecturing for me, that is, accomplishing unwittingly a result which I approve and adopt. But, when this passing lecture is over, there is nothing in the bare notion that ideas have been its agents that would seem to guarantee that my present purposes in lecturing will be pro-longed. *I* may have ulterior developments in view; but there is no certainty that my ideas as such will wish to, or be able to, work them out.

The like is true if nerve-cells be the agents. The activity of a nerve-cell must be conceived of as a tendency of exceedingly short reach, an 'impulse' barely spanning the way to the next cell—for surely that amount of actual 'process' must be 'experienced' by the cells if what happens between them is to deserve the name of activity at all. But here again the gross resultant, as *I* perceive it, is indifferent to the agents, and neither wished or willed or foreseen. Their being agents now congruous with my will gives me no guarantee that like results will recur again from their activity. In point of fact, all sorts of other results do occur. My mistakes, impotencies, perversions, mental obstructions, and frustrations generally, are also results of the activity of cells. Although these are letting me lecture now, on other occasions they make me do things that I would willingly not do.

The question *Whose is the real activity?* is thus tantamount to the question *What will be the actual results?* Its interest is dra-matic; how will things work out? If the agents are of one sort, one way; if of another sort, they may work out very differently. The pragmatic meaning of the various alternatives, in short, is great. It makes no merely verbal difference which opinion we take up.

You see it is the old dispute come back! Materialism and teleology; elementary short-span actions summing themselves 'blindly,' or far foreseen ideals coming with effort into act.

Naïvely we believe, and humanly and dramatically we like to believe, that activities both of wider and of narrower span are at work in life together, that both are real, and that the long-span tendencies yoke the others in their service, encouraging them in the right direction, and damping them when they tend in other ways. But how to represent clearly the *modus operandi* of such steering of small tendencies by large ones is a problem which metaphysical thinkers will have to ruminate upon for many years to come. Even if such control should eventually grow clearly picturable, the question how far it is successfully exerted in this actual world can be answered only by investigating the details of fact. No philosophic knowledge of the general nature and con-stitution of tendencies, or of the relation of larger to smaller ones, can help us to predict which of all the various competing ten-dencies that interest us in this universe are likeliest to prevail. We know as an empirical fact that far-seeing tendencies often carry out their purpose, but we know also that they are often defeated by the failure of some contemptibly small process on which success depends. A little thrombus in a statesman's meningeal artery will throw an empire out of gear. I can therefore not even hint at any solution of the pragmatic issue. I have only wished to show you that that issue is what gives the real interest to all inquiries into what kinds of activity may be real. Are the forces that really act in the world more foreseeing or more blind? As between 'our' activi-ties as 'we' experience them, and those of our ideas, or of our brain-cells, the issue is well-defined.

I said a while back that I should return to the 'metaphysical' question before ending; so, with a few words about that, I will now close my remarks.

In whatever form we hear this question propounded, I think that it always arises from two things, a belief that *causality* must be exerted in activity, and a wonder as to how causality is made. If we take an activity-situation at its face-value, it seems as if we caught *in flagrante delicto* the very power that makes facts come and be. I now am eagerly striving, for example, to get this truth which I seem half to perceive, into words which shall make it show more clearly. If the words come, it will seem as if the striving itself had drawn or pulled them into actuality out from the state of merely possible being in which they were. How is this feat performed? How does the pulling *pull?* How do I get my hold on words not yet existent, and when they come by what means have I *made* them come? Really it is the problem of creation; for in the end the question is: How do I make them *be?* Real activities are those that really make things be, without which the things are not, and with which they are there. Activity, so far as we merely feel it, on the other hand, is only an impression of ours, it may be maintained; and an impression is, for all this way of thinking, only a shadow of another fact.

Arrived at this point, I can do little more than indicate the principles on which, as it seems to me, a radically empirical philosophy is obliged to rely in handling such a dispute.

If there *be* real creative activities in being, radical empiricism must say, somewhere they must be immediately lived. Somewhere the *that* of efficacious causing and the *what* of it must be experienced in one, just as the what and the that of 'cold' are experienced in one whenever a man has the sensation of cold here and now. It boots not to say that our sensations are fallible. They are indeed; but to see the thermometer contradict us when we say 'it is cold' does not abolish cold as a specific nature from the universe. Cold is in the arctic circle if not here. Even so, to feel that our train is moving when the train beside our window moves, to see the moon through a telescope come twice as near, or to see two pictures as one solid when we look through a stereoscope at them, leaves motion, nearness, and solidity still in being—if not here, yet each in its proper seat elsewhere. And wherever the seat of real causality *is*, as ultimately known 'for true' (in nerve-processes, if you will, that cause our feelings of activity as well as the movements which these seem to prompt), a philosophy of pure experience can consider the real causation as no other *nature* of thing than that which even in our most erroneous experiences appears to be at work. Exactly what appears there is what we *mean* by working, though we may later come to learn that working was not exactly *there*. Sustaining, persevering, striving, paying with effort as we go, hanging on, and finally achieving our intention—this *is* action, this *is* effectuation in the only shape in which, by a pure experience-philosophy, the whereabouts of it anywhere can be discussed. Here is creation in its first intention, here is causality at work.[2] To treat this offhand as the bare illusory surface of a world whose real causality is an unimaginable ontological principle hidden in the cubic deeps, is, for the more empirical way of thinking, only animism in another shape. You explain your given fact by your 'principle,' but the principle itself, when you look clearly at it, turns out to be nothing but a previous little spiritual copy of the fact. Away from that one and only kind of fact, your mind, considering causality, can never get.[3]

2. Let me not be told that this contradicts [the first essay] "Does 'Consciousness' Exist?" in which it was said that while 'thoughts' and 'things' have the same natures, the natures work 'energetically' on each other in the things (fire burns, water wets, etc.) but not in the thoughts. Mental activity-trains are composed of thoughts, yet their members do work on each other; they check, sustain, and introduce. They do so when the activity is merely associational as well as when effort is there. But, and this is my reply, they do so by other parts of their nature than those that energize physically. One thought in every developed activity-series is a desire or thought of purpose, and all the other thoughts acquire a feeling tone from their relation of harmony or oppugnancy to this. The interplay of these secondary tones (among which 'interest,' 'difficulty,' and 'effort' figure) runs the drama in the mental series. In what we term the physical drama, these qualities play absolutely no part. The subject needs careful working out; but I can see no inconsistency.

3. I have found myself more than once accused in print of being the assertor of a metaphysical principle of activity. Since literary misunderstandings retard the settlement of problems, I should like to say that such an interpretation of the pages I have published on Effort and on Will is absolutely foreign to what I meant to express. [*Principles of Psychology*, vol. ii, ch. xxvi.] I owe all my doctrines on this subject to Renouvier; and Renouvier, as I understand him, is (or at any rate then was) an out-and-out phenomenist, a denier of 'forces' in the most strenuous sense. [Cf. Ch. Renouvier: *Esquisse d'une Classification Systématique des Doctrines Philosophiques* (1885), vol. ii, pp. 390–392; *Essais de Critique Générale* (1859), vol. ii, §§ ix, xiii. For an acknowledgment of the author's general indebtedness to Renouvier, cf. *Some Problems of Philosophy*, p. 165, note. Ed.] Single clauses in my writing, or sentences read out of their connection, may possibly have been compatible with a transphenomenal principle of energy; but I defy anyone to show a single sentence which, taken with its context, should be naturally held to advocate that view. The misinterpretation probably arose at first from my defending (after Renouvier) the indeterminism of our efforts. 'Free will' was supposed by my critics to involve a supernatural agent. As a matter of plain history, the only 'free will' I have ever thought of defending is the character of novelty in fresh activity-situations. If an activity-process is the form of a whole 'field of consciousness,' and if each field of consciousness is not only in its totality unique (as is now commonly admitted) but has its elements unique (since in that situation they

I conclude, then, that real effectual causation as an ultimate nature, as a 'category,' if you like, of reality, is *just what we feel it to be,* just that kind of conjunction which our own activity-series reveal. We have the whole butt and being of it in our hands; and the healthy thing for philosophy is to leave off grubbing underground for what effects effectuation, or what makes action act, and to try to solve the concrete questions of where effectuation in this world is located, of which things are the true causal agents there, and of what the more remote effects consist.

From this point of view, the greater sublimity traditionally attributed to the metaphysical inquiry, the grubbing inquiry, entirely disappears. If we could know what causation really and transcendentally is in itself, the only *use* of the knowledge would be to help us to recognize an actual cause when we had one, and so to track the future course of operations more intelligently out. The mere abstract inquiry into causation's hidden nature is not more sublime than any other inquiry equally abstract. Causation inhabits no more sublime level than anything else. It lives, apparently, in the dirt of the world as well as in the absolute, or in man's unconquerable mind. The worth and interest of the world consists not in its elements, be these elements things, or be they the conjunctions of things; it exists rather in the dramatic outcome in the whole process, and in the meaning of the successive stages which the elements work out. . . .

G.   Is Radical Empiricism Solipsistic?*

If all the criticisms which the humanistic *Weltanschauung* is receiving were as *sachgemäss* as Mr. Bode's,[1] the truth of the matter

are all dyed in the total), then novelty is perpetually entering the world and what happens there is not pure *repetition,* as the dogma of the literal uniformity of nature requires. Activity-situations come, in short, each with an original touch. A 'principle' of free will, if there were one, would doubtless manifest itself in such phenomena, but I never saw, nor do I now see, what the principle could do except rehearse the phenomenon beforehand, or why it ever should be invoked.

* Reprinted from the *Journal of Philosophy, Psychology and Scientific Methods,* vol. II, no. 9 (1905).

1. [B. H. Bode: "'Pure Experience' and the External World," *Journal of Philosophy, Psychology and Scientific Methods,* vol. II (1905), p. 128.]

would more rapidly clear up. Not only is it excellently well written, but it brings its own point of view out clearly, and admits of a perfectly straight reply.

The argument (unless I fail to catch it) can be expressed as follows:

If a series of experiences be supposed, no one of which is endowed immediately with the self-transcendent function of reference to a reality beyond itself, no motive will occur within the series for supposing anything beyond it to exist. It will remain subjective, and contentedly subjective, both as a whole and in its several parts.

Radical empiricism, trying, as it does, to account for objective knowledge by means of such a series, egregiously fails. It can not explain how the notion of a physical order, as distinguished from a subjectively biographical order, of experiences, ever arose.

It pretends to explain the notion of a physical order, but does so by playing fast and loose with the concept of objective reference. On the one hand, it denies that such reference implies self-transcendency on the part of any one experience; on the other hand, it claims that experiences *point*. But, critically considered, there can be no pointing unless self-transcendency be also allowed. The conjunctive function of pointing, as I have assumed it, is, according to my critic, vitiated by the fallacy of attaching a bilateral relation to a term *a quo*, as if it could stick out substantively and maintain itself in existence in advance of the term *ad quem* which is equally required for it to be a concretely experienced fact. If the relation be made concrete, the term *ad quem* is involved, which would mean (if I succeed in apprehending Mr. Bode rightly) that this latter term, although not empirically there, is yet *noetically* there, in advance—in other words it would mean that any experience that 'points' must already have transcended itself, in the ordinary 'epistemological' sense of the word transcend.

Something like this, if I understand Mr. Bode's text, is the upshot of his state of mind. It is a reasonable-sounding state of mind, but it is exactly the state of mind which radical empiricism, by its doctrine of the reality of conjunctive relations, seeks to dispel. I very much fear—so difficult does mutual understanding seem in these exalted regions—that my able critic has failed to understand that doctrine as it is meant to be understood. I suspect that he performs on all these conjunctive relations (of which the aforesaid 'pointing' is only one) the usual rationalistic act of substitution—he takes them not as they are given in their first intention, as parts constitutive of experience's living flow, but only as they appear in retrospect, each fixed as a determinate object of conception, static, therefore, and contained within itself.

Against this rationalistic tendency to treat experience as chopped up into discontinuous static objects, radical empiricism protests. It insists on taking conjunctions at their 'face-value,' just as they come. Consider, for example, such conjunctions as 'and,' 'with,' 'near,' *'plus,'* 'towards.' While we live in such conjunctions our state is one of *transition* in the most literal sense. We are expectant of a 'more' to come, and before the more *has* come, the transition, nevertheless, is directed *towards* it. I fail otherwise to see how, if one kind of more comes, there should be satisfaction and feeling of fulfilment; but disappointment if the more comes in another shape. One more will continue, another more will arrest or deflect the direction, in which our experience is moving even now. We can not, it is true, *name* our different living 'ands' or 'withs' except by naming the different terms towards which they are moving us, but we *live* their specifications and differences before those terms explicitly arrive. Thus, though the various 'ands' are all bilateral relations, each requiring a term *ad quem* to define it when viewed in retrospect and articulately conceived, yet in its living moment any one of them may be treated as if it 'stuck out' from its term *a quo* and pointed in a special direction, much as a compass-needle (to use Mr. Bode's excellent simile) points at the pole, even though it stirs not from its box.

In Professor Höffding's massive little article in *The Journal of Philosophy, Psychology and Scientific Methods,* he quotes a saying of Kierkegaard's to the effect that we live forwards, but we understand backwards. Understanding backwards is, it must be confessed, a very frequent weakness of philosophers, both of the rationalistic and of the ordinary empiricist type. Radical empiricism alone insists on understanding forwards also, and refuses to substitute static concepts of the understanding for transitions in our moving life. A logic similar to that which my critic seems to employ here should, it seems to me, forbid him to say that our present is, while present, directed towards our future, or that any physical movement can have direction until its goal is actually reached.

At this point does it not seem as if the quarrel about self-transcendency in knowledge might drop? Is it not a purely verbal dispute? Call it self-transcendency or call it pointing, whichever you like—it makes no difference so long as real transitions towards real goals are admitted as things given *in* experience, and among experience's most indefeasible parts. Radical empiricism, unable to close its eyes to the transitions caught *in actu,* accounts for the self-transcendency or the pointing (whichever you may call it) as a process that occurs within experience, as an empirically mediated thing of which a perfectly definite description can be given. 'Epistemology,' on the other hand, denies this; and pretends that the self-transcendency is unmediated or, if mediated, then mediated in a super-empirical world. To justify this pretension, epistemology has first to transform all our conjunctions into static objects, and this, I submit, is an absolutely arbitrary act. But in spite of Mr. Bode's maltreatment of conjunctions, as I understand them—and as I understand him—I believe that at bottom we are fighting for nothing different, but are both defending the same continuities of experience in different forms of words.

There are other criticisms in the article in question, but, as this seems the most vital one, I will for the present, at any rate, leave them untouched.

7.

From *The Varieties of Religious Experience*

A. CIRCUMSCRIPTION OF THE TOPIC*

Most books on the philosophy of religion try to begin with a precise definition of what its essence consists of. Some of these would-be definitions may possibly come before us in later portions of this course, and I shall not be pedantic enough to enumerate any of them to you now. Meanwhile the very fact that they are so many and so different from one another is enough to prove that the word 'religion' cannot stand for any single principle or essence, but is rather a collective name. The theorizing mind tends always to the over-simplification of its materials. This is the root of all that absolutism and one-sided dogmatism by which both philosophy and religion have been infested. Let us not fall immediately into a one-sided view of our subject, but let us rather admit freely at the outset that we may very likely find no one essence, but many characters which may alternately be equally important in religion. If we should inquire for the essence of 'government,' for example, one man might tell us it was authority, another submission, another police, another an army, another an assembly, another a system of laws; yet all the while it would be true that no concrete government can exist without all these things, one of which is more important at one moment and others at another. The man who knows governments most completely is he who troubles himself least about a definition which shall give their essence. Enjoying an intimate acquaintance with all their particularities in turn, he would naturally regard an abstract conception in which these were unified as a thing more misleading than enlightening. And why may not religion be a conception equally complex?[1]

* From *The Varieties of Religious Experience: A Study in Human Nature* (New York & London: Longmans, Green & Co., 1902). Originally the Gifford Lectures, 1901–02. Lecture II. Some footnotes and portions of text have been deleted. [B.W.]

1. I can do no better here than refer my readers to the extended and admirable remarks on the futility of all these definitions of religion, in an article

Consider also the 'religious sentiment' which we see referred to in so many books, as if it were a single sort of mental entity.

In the psychologies and in the philosophies of religion, we find the authors attempting to specify just what entity it is. One man allies it to the feeling of dependence; one makes it a derivative from fear; others connect it with the sexual life; others still identify it with the feeling of the infinite, and so on. Such different ways of conceiving it ought of themselves to arouse doubt as to whether it possibly can be one specific thing; and the moment we are willing to treat the term 'religious sentiment' as a collective name for the many sentiments which religious objects may arouse in alternation, we see that it probably contains nothing whatever of a psychologically specific nature. There is religious fear, religious love, religious awe, religious joy, and so forth. But religious love is only man's natural emotion of love directed to a religious object; religious fear is only the ordinary fear of commerce, so to speak, the common quaking of the human breast, in so far as the notion of divine retribution may arouse it; religious awe is the same organic thrill which we feel in a forest at twilight, or in a mountain gorge; only this time it comes over us at the thought of our supernatural relations; and similarly of all the various sentiments which may be called into play in the lives of religious persons. As concrete states of mind, made up of a feeling *plus* a specific sort of object, religious emotions of course are psychic entities distinguishable from other concrete emotions; but there is no ground for assuming a simple abstract 'religious emotion' to exist as a distinct elementary mental affection by itself, present in every religious experience without exception.

As there thus seems to be no one elementary religious emotion, but only a common storehouse of emotions upon which religious objects may draw, so there might conceivably also prove to be no one specific and essential kind of religious object, and no one specific and essential kind of religious act.

The field of religion being as wide as this, it is manifestly impossible that I should pretend to cover it. My lectures must be limited to a fraction of the subject. And, although it would indeed be foolish to set up an abstract definition of religion's essence, and

by Professor Leuba, published in the *Monist* for January, 1901, after my own text was written.

then proceed to defend that definition against all comers, yet this
need not prevent me from taking my own narrow view of what
religion shall consist in *for the purpose of these lectures,* or, out of
the many meanings of the word, from choosing the one meaning
in which I wish to interest you particularly, and proclaiming
arbitrarily that when I say 'religion' I mean *that.* This, in fact, is
what I must do, and I will now preliminarily seek to mark out the
field I choose.

One way to mark it out easily is to say what aspects of the
subject we leave out. At the outset we are struck by one great
partition which divides the religious field. On the one side of it
lies institutional, on the other personal religion. As M. P. Sabatier
says, one branch of religion keeps the divinity, another keeps man
most in view. Worship and sacrifice, procedures for working on the
dispositions of the deity, theology and ceremony and ecclesiastical
organization, are the essentials of religion in the institutional
branch. Were we to limit our view to it, we should have to define
religion as an external art, the art of winning the favor of the
gods. In the more personal branch of religion it is on the contrary
the inner dispositions of man himself which form the centre of
interest, his conscience, his deserts, his helplessness, his incompleteness. And although the favor of the God, as forfeited or
gained, is still an essential feature of the story, the theology plays a
vital part therein, yet the acts to which this sort of religion
prompts are personal not ritual acts, the individual transacts the
business by himself alone, and the ecclesiastical organization, with
its priests and sacraments and other go-betweens, sinks to an altogether secondary place. The relation goes direct from heart to
heart, from soul to soul, between man and his maker.

Now in these lectures I propose to ignore the institutional
branch entirely, to say nothing of the ecclesiastical organization, to
consider as little as possible the systematic theology and the ideas
about the gods themselves, and to confine myself as far as I can to
personal religion pure and simple. To some of you personal religion, thus nakedly considered, will no doubt seem too incomplete a thing to wear the general name. "It is a part of religion,"
you will say, "but only its unorganized rudiment; if we are to
name it by itself, we had better call it man's conscience or morality

than his religion. The name 'religion' should be reserved for the fully organized system of feeling, thought, and institution, for the Church, in short, of which this personal religion, so called, is but a fractional element."

But if you say this, it will only show the more plainly how much the question of definition tends to become a dispute about names. Rather than prolong such a dispute, I am willing to accept almost any name for the personal religion of which I propose to treat. Call it conscience or morality, if you yourselves prefer, and not religion—under either name it will be equally worthy of our study. As for myself, I think it will prove to contain some elements which morality pure and simple does not contain, and these elements I shall soon seek to point out; so I will myself continue to apply the word 'religion' to it; and in the last lecture of all, I will bring in the theologies and the ecclesiasticisms, and say something of its relation to them.

In one sense at least the personal religion will prove itself more fundamental than either theology or ecclesiasticism. Churches, when once established, live at second-hand upon tradition; but the *founders* of every church owed their power originally to the fact of their direct personal communion with the divine. Not only the superhuman founders, the Christ, the Buddha, Mahomet, but all the originators of Christian sects have been in this case; so personal religion should still seem the primordial thing, even to those who continue to esteem it incomplete.

There are, it is true, other things in religion chronologically more primordial than personal devoutness in the moral sense. Fetishism and magic seem to have preceded inward piety historically—at least our records of inward piety do not reach back so far. And if fetishism and magic be regarded as stages of religion, one may say that personal religion in the inward sense and the genuinely spiritual ecclesiasticisms which it founds are phenomena of secondary or even tertiary order. But, quite apart from the fact that many anthropologists—for instance, Jevons and Frazer—expressly oppose 'religion' and 'magic' to each other, it is certain that the whole system of thought which leads to magic, fetishism, and the lower superstitions may just as well be called primitive science as called primitive religion. The question thus becomes a verbal one again; and our knowledge of all these early stages of thought and feeling is in any case so conjectural and imperfect that farther discussion would not be worth while.

Religion, therefore, as I now ask you arbitrarily to take it, shall mean for us *the feelings, acts, and experiences of individual men in their solitude, so far as they apprehend themselves to stand in relation to whatever they may consider the divine.* Since the relation may be either moral, physical, or ritual, it is evident that out of religion in the sense in which we take it, theologies, philosophies, and ecclesiastical organizations may secondarily grow. In these lectures, however, as I have already said, the immediate personal experiences will amply fill our time, and we shall hardly consider theology or ecclesiasticism at all. . . .

. . . Religion, whatever it is, is a man's total reaction upon life, so why not say that any total reaction upon life is a religion? Total reactions are different from casual reactions, and total attitudes are different from usual or professional attitudes. To get at them you must go behind the foreground of existence and reach down to that curious sense of the whole residual cosmos as an everlasting presence, intimate or alien, terrible or amusing, lovable or odious, which in some degree every one possesses. This sense of the world's presence, appealing as it does to our peculiar individual temperament, makes us either strenuous or careless, devout or blasphemous, gloomy or exultant, about life at large; and our reaction, involuntary and inarticulate and often half unconscious as it is, is the completest of all our answers to the question, "What is the character of this universe in which we dwell?" It expresses our individual sense of it in the most definite way. Why then not call these reactions our religion, no matter what specific character they may have? Non-religious as some of these reactions may be, in one sense of the word 'religious,' they yet belong to *the general sphere of the religious life,* and so should generically be classed as religious reactions. "He believes in No-God, and he worships him," said a colleague of mine of a student who was manifesting a fine atheistic ardor; and the more fervent opponents of Christian doctrine have often enough shown a temper which, psychologically considered, is indistinguishable from religious zeal.

But so very broad a use of the word 'religion' would be inconvenient, however defensible it might remain on logical grounds.

There are trifling, sneering attitudes even towards the whole of life; and in some men these attitudes are final and systematic. . . .

There must be something solemn, serious, and tender about any attitude which we denominate religious. If glad, it must not grin or snicker; if sad, it must not scream or curse. It is precisely as being *solemn* experiences that I wish to interest you in religious experiences. So I propose—arbitrarily again, if you please—to narrow our definition once more by saying that the word 'divine,' as employed therein, shall mean for us not merely the primal and enveloping and real, for that meaning if taken without restriction might well prove too broad. The divine shall mean for us only such a primal reality as the individual feels impelled to respond to solemnly and gravely, and neither by a curse nor a jest.

But solemnity, and gravity, and all such emotional attributes, admit of various shades; and, do what we will with our defining, the truth must at last be confronted that we are dealing with a field of experience where there is not a single conception that can be sharply drawn. The pretension, under such conditions, to be rigorously 'scientific' or 'exact' in our terms would only stamp us as lacking in understanding of our task. Things are more or less divine, states of mind are more or less religious, reactions are more or less total, but the boundaries are always misty, and it is everywhere a question of amount and degree. Nevertheless, at their extreme of development, there can never be any question as to what experiences are religious. The divinity of the object and the solemnity of the reaction are too well marked for doubt. Hesitation as to whether a state of mind is 'religious,' or 'irreligious,' or 'moral,' or 'philosophical,' is only likely to arise when the state of mind is weakly characterized, but in that case it will be hardly worthy of our study at all. . . .

. . . The Christian spurns the pinched and mumping sick-room attitude, and the lives of saints are full of a kind of callousness to diseased conditions of body which probably no other human records show. But whereas the merely moralistic spurning takes an effort of volition, the Christian spurning is the result of the excitement of a higher kind of emotion, in the presence of which no exertion of volition is required. The moralist must hold his breath and keep his muscles tense; and so long as this athletic attitude is possible all goes well—morality suffices. But the athletic attitude tends ever to break down, and it inevitably does break down even in the most stalwart when the organism begins to decay, or when morbid fears invade the mind. To suggest personal will and effort to one all sicklied o'er with the sense of irremediable impotence is to suggest the most impossible of things. What he craves is to be consoled in his very powerlessness, to feel that the spirit of the universe recognizes and secures him, all decaying and failing as he is. Well, we are all such helpless failures in the last resort. The sanest and best of us are of one clay with lunatics and prison inmates, and death finally runs the robustest of us down. And whenever we feel this, such a sense of the vanity and provisionality of our voluntary career comes over us that all our morality appears but as a plaster hiding a sore it can never cure, and all our well-doing as the hollowest substitute for that well-*being* that our lives ought to be grounded in, but, alas! are not.

And here religion comes to our rescue and takes our fate into her hands. There is a state of mind, known to religious men, but to no others, in which the will to assert ourselves and hold our own has been displaced by a willingness to close our mouths and be as nothing in the floods and water-spouts of God. In this state of mind, what we most dreaded has become the habitation of our safety, and the hour of our moral death has turned into our spiritual birthday. The time for tension in our soul is over, and that of happy relaxation, of calm deep breathing, of an eternal present, with no discordant future to be anxious about, has arrived. Fear is not held in abeyance as it is by mere morality, it is positively expunged and washed away.

We shall see abundant examples of this happy state of mind in later lectures of this course. We shall see how infinitely passionate a thing religion at its highest flights can be. Like love, like wrath, like hope, ambition, jealousy, like every other instinctive eagerness and impulse, it adds to life an enchantment which is not rationally or logically deducible from anything else. This enchantment, coming as a gift where it does come—a gift of our organism, the physiologists will tell us, a gift of God's grace, the theologians say—is either there or not there for us, and there are persons who can no more become possessed by it than they can fall in love with a given woman by mere word of command. Religious feeling is thus an absolute addition to the Subject's range of life. It gives him a new sphere of power. When the outward battle is 'lost, and the outer world disowns him, it redeems and vivifies an interior world which otherwise would be an empty waste.

If religion is to mean anything definite for us, it seems to me that we ought to take it as meaning this added dimension of emotion, this enthusiastic temper of espousal, in regions where morality strictly so called can at best but bow its head and acquiesce. It ought to mean nothing short of this new reach of freedom for us, with the struggle over, the keynote of the universe sounding in our ears, and everlasting possession spread before our eyes.[2]

This sort of happiness in the absolute and everlasting is what we find nowhere but in religion. It is parted off from all mere animal happiness, all mere enjoyment of the present, by that element of solemnity of which I have already made so much account. Solemnity is a hard thing to define abstractly, but certain of its marks are patent enough. A solemn state of mind is never crude or simple—it seems to contain a certain measure of its own opposite in solution. A solemn joy preserves a sort of bitter in its sweetness; a solemn sorrow is one to which we intimately consent. But there are writers who, realizing that happiness of a supreme sort is the prerogative of religion, forget this complication, and call all happiness, as such, religious. Mr. Havelock Ellis, for example, identifies religion with the entire field of the soul's liberation from oppressive moods.

"The simplest functions of physiological life," he writes, "may be its ministers. Every one who is at all acquainted with the Persian mystics knows how wine may be regarded as an instrument of religion. Indeed, in all countries and in all ages, some form of physical enlargement—singing, dancing, drinking, sexual excitement—has been intimately associated with worship. Even the momentary expansion of the soul in laughter is, to however slight an extent, a religious exercise. . . . Whenever an

2. Once more, there are plenty of men, constitutionally sombre men, in whose religious life this rapturousness is lacking. They are religious in the wider sense; yet in this acutest of all senses they are not so, and it is religion in the acutest sense that I wish, without disputing about words, to study first, so as to get at its typical *differentia*.

impulse from the world strikes against the organism, and the resultant is not discomfort or pain, not even the muscular contraction of strenuous manhood, but a joyous expansion or aspiration of the whole soul—there is religion. It is the infinite for which we hunger, and we ride gladly on every little wave that promises to bear us towards it."

But such a straight identification of religion with any and every form of happiness leaves the essential peculiarity of religious happiness out. The more commonplace happinesses which we get are 'reliefs,' occasioned by our momentary escapes from evils either experienced or threatened. But in its most characteristic embodiments, religious happiness is no mere feeling of escape. It cares no longer to escape. It consents to the evil outwardly as a form of sacrifice—inwardly it knows it to be permanently overcome. If you ask *how* religion thus falls on the thorns and faces death, and in the very act annuls annihilation, I cannot explain the matter, for it is religion's secret, and to understand it you must yourself have been a religious man of the extremer type. In our future examples, even of the simplest and healthiest-minded type of religious consciousness, we shall find this complex sacrificial constitution, in which a higher happiness holds a lower unhappiness in check. In the Louvre there is a picture, by Guido Reni, of St. Michael with his foot on Satan's neck. The richness of the picture is in large part due to the fiend's figure being there. The richness of its allegorical meaning also is due to his being there—that is, the world is all the richer for having a devil in it, *so long as we keep our foot upon his neck*. In the religious consciousness, that is just the position in which the fiend, the negative or tragic principle, is found; and for that very reason the religious consciousness is so rich from the emotional point of view. We shall see how in certain men and women it takes on a monstrously ascetic form. There are saints who have literally fed on the negative principle, on humiliation and privation, and the thought of suffering and death—their souls growing in happiness just in proportion as their outward state grew more intolerable. No other emotion than religious emotion can bring a man to this peculiar pass. And it is for that reason that when we ask our question about the value of religion for human life, I think we ought to look for the answer among these violenter examples rather than among those of a more moderate hue.

Having the phenomenon of our study in its acutest possible form to start with, we can shade down as much as we please later. And if in these cases, repulsive as they are to our ordinary worldly way of judging, we find ourselves compelled to acknowledge religion's value and treat it with respect, it will have proved in some way its value for life at large. By subtracting and toning down extravagances we may thereupon proceed to trace the boundaries of its legitimate sway.

To be sure, it makes our task difficult to have to deal so much with eccentricities and extremes. "How *can* religion on the whole be the most important of all human functions," you may ask, "if every several manifestation of it in turn have to be corrected and sobered down and pruned away?" Such a thesis seems a paradox impossible to sustain reasonably—yet I believe that something like it will have to be our final contention. That personal attitude which the individual finds himself impelled to take up towards what he apprehends to be the divine—and you will remember that this was our definition—will prove to be both a helpless and a sacrificial attitude. That is, we shall have to confess to at least some amount of dependence on sheer mercy, and to practice some amount of renunciation, great or small, to save our souls alive. The constitution of the world we live in requires it:

> "Entbehren sollst du! sollst entbehren!
> Das ist der ewige Gesang
> Der jedem an die Ohren klingt,
> Den, unser ganzes Leben lang
> Uns heiser jede Stunde singt."

For when all is said and done, we are in the end absolutely dependent on the universe; and into sacrifices and surrenders of some sort, deliberately looked at and accepted, we are drawn and pressed as into our only permanent positions of repose. Now in those states of mind which fall short of religion, the surrender is submitted to as an imposition of necessity, and the sacrifice is undergone at the very best without complaint. In the religious life, on the contrary, surrender and sacrifice are positively espoused: even unnecessary givings-up are added in order that the happiness may increase. *Religion thus makes easy and felicitous what in any case is necessary;* and if it be the only agency that can accomplish this result, its vital importance as a human faculty stands vindicated beyond dispute. It becomes an essential organ of our life, performing a function which no other portion of our nature can so successfully fulfill. From the merely biological point of view, so to call it, this is a conclusion to which, so far as I can now see, we shall inevitably be led, and led moreover by following the purely empirical method of demonstration which I sketched to you in the first lecture. Of the farther office of religion as a metaphysical revelation I will say nothing now.

But to foreshadow the terminus of one's investigations is one thing, and to arrive there safely is another. In the next lecture, abandoning the extreme generalities which have engrossed us hitherto, I propose that we begin our actual journey by addressing ourselves directly to the concrete facts.

B.   The Sick Soul*

. . . The worst kind of melancholy is that which takes the form of panic fear. Here is an excellent example, for permission to print which I have to thank the sufferer. The original is in French, and though the subject was evidently in a bad nervous condition at the time of which he writes, his case has otherwise the merit of extreme simplicity.** I translate freely.

Whilst in this state of philosophic pessimism and general depression of spirits about my prospects, I went one evening into a dressing-room in the twilight to procure some article that was there; when suddenly there fell upon me without any warning, just as if it came out of the darkness, a horrible fear of my own existence. Simultaneously there arose in my mind the image of an epileptic patient whom I had seen in the asylum, a black-haired youth with greenish skin, entirely idiotic, who used to sit all day on one of the benches, or rather shelves against the wall, with his knees drawn up against his chin, and the coarse gray undershirt, which was his only garment, drawn over them inclosing his entire figure. He sat there like a sort of sculptured Egyptian cat or Peruvian mummy, moving nothing but his black eyes and looking absolutely non-human. This image and my fear entered into a species of

* From Lectures VI and VII of *The Varieties of Religious Experience.*
** James is presenting a masked report of his own experience in 1870, following the earning of an M.D. from Harvard. [B.W.]

combination with each other. *That shape am I,* I felt, potentially. Nothing that I possess can defend me against that fate, if the hour for it should strike for me as it struck for him. There was such a horror of him, and such a perception of my own merely momentary discrepancy from him, that it was as if something hitherto solid within my breast gave way entirely, and I became a mass of quivering fear. After this the universe was changed for me altogether. I awoke morning after morning with a horrible dread at the pit of my stomach, and with a sense of the insecurity of life that I never knew before, and that I have never felt since.[1] It was like a revelation; and although the immediate feelings passed away, the experience has made me sympathetic with the morbid feelings of others ever since. It gradually faded, but for months I was unable to go out into the dark alone.

In general I dreaded to be left alone. I remember wondering how other people could live, how I myself had ever lived, so unconscious of that pit of insecurity beneath the surface of life. My mother in particular, a very cheerful person, seemed to me a perfect paradox in her unconsciousness of danger, which you may well believe I was very careful not to disturb by revelations of my own state of mind. I have always thought that this experience of melancholia of mine had a religious bearing.

On asking this correspondent to explain more fully what he meant by these last words, the answer he wrote was this:

I mean that the fear was so invasive and powerful that if I had not clung to scripture-texts like "The eternal God is my refuge," etc., "Come unto me, all ye that labor and are heavy-laden," etc., "I am the resurrection and the life," etc., I think I should have grown really insane.[2]

There is no need of more examples. The cases we have looked at are enough. One of them gives us the vanity of mortal things; another the sense of sin; and the remaining one describes the fear

1. Compare Bunyan: "There was I struck into a very great trembling, insomuch that at some times I could, for days together, feel my very body, as well as my mind, to shake and totter under the sense of the dreadful judgment of God, that should fall on those that have sinned that most fearful and unpardonable sin. I felt also such clogging and heat at my stomach, by reason of this my terror, that I was, especially at some times, as if my breast-bone would have split asunder. . . . Thus did I wind, and twine, and shrink, under the burden that was upon me; which burden also did so oppress me that I could neither stand, nor go, nor lie, either at rest or quiet."
2. For another case of fear equally sudden, see Henry James: *Society the Redeemed Form of Man,* Boston, 1879, pp. 43 ff. (A crisis experience of James's father. [B.W.])

of the universe—and in one or other of these three ways it always is that man's original optimism and self-satisfaction get leveled with the dust.

In none of these cases was there any intellectual insanity or delusion about matters of fact; but were we disposed to open the chapter of really insane melancholia, with its hallucinations and delusions, it would be a worse story still—desperation absolute and complete, the whole universe coagulating about the sufferer into a material of overwhelming horror, surrounding him without opening or end. Not the conception or intellectual perception of evil, but the grisly blood-freezing heart-palsying sensation of it close upon one, and no other conception or sensation able to live for a moment in its presence. How irrelevantly remote seem all our usual refined optimisms and intellectual and moral consolations in presence of a need of help like this! Here is the real core of the religious problem: Help! help! No prophet can claim to bring a final message unless he says things that will have a sound of reality in the ears of victims such as these. But the deliverance must come in as strong a form as the complaint, if it is to take effect; and that seems a reason why the coarser religious, revivalistic, orgiastic, with blood and miracles and supernatural operations, may possibly never be displaced. Some constitutions need them too much.

Arrived at this point, we can see how great an antagonism may naturally arise between the healthy-minded way of viewing life and the way that takes all this experience of evil as something essential. To this latter way, the morbid-minded way, as we might call it, healthy-mindedness pure and simple seems unspeakably blind and shallow. To the healthy-minded way, on the other hand, the way of the sick soul seems unmanly and diseased. With their grubbing in rat-holes instead of living in the light; with their manufacture of fears, and preoccupation with every unwholesome kind of misery, there is something almost obscene about these children of wrath and cravers of a second birth. If religious intolerance and hanging and burning could again become the order of the day, there is little doubt that, however it may have been in the past, the healthy-minded would at present show themselves the less indulgent party of the two.

In our own attitude, not yet abandoned, of impartial on-lookers, what are we to say of this quarrel? It seems to me that we are bound to say that morbid-mindedness ranges over the wider scale of experience, and that its survey is the one that overlaps. The method of averting one's attention from evil, and living simply in the light of good is splendid as long as it will work. It will work with many persons; it will work far more generally than most of us are ready to suppose; and within the sphere of its successful operation there is nothing to be said against it as a religious solution. But it breaks down impotently as soon as melancholy comes; and even though one be quite free from melancholy one's self, there is no doubt that healthy-mindedness is inadequate as a philosophical doctrine, because the evil facts which it refuses positively to account for are a genuine portion of reality; and they may after all be the best key to life's significance, and possibly the only openers of our eyes to the deepest levels of truth.

The normal process of life contains moments as bad as any of those which insane melancholy is filled with, moments in which radical evil gets its innings and takes its solid turn. The lunatic's visions of horror are all drawn from the material of daily fact. Our civilization is founded on the shambles, and every individual existence goes out in a lonely spasm of helpless agony. If you protest, my friend, wait till you arrive there yourself! To believe in the carnivorous reptiles of geologic time, is hard for our imagination—they seem too much like mere museum specimens. Yet there is no tooth in any one of those museum-skulls that did not daily through long years of the foretime hold fast to the body struggling in despair of some fated living victim. Forms of horror just as dreadful to their victims, if on a smaller spatial scale, fill the world about us to-day. Here on our very hearths and in our gardens the infernal cat plays with the panting mouse, or holds the hot bird fluttering in her jaws. Crocodiles and rattlesnakes and pythons are at this moment vessels of life as real as we are; their loathsome existence fills every minute of every day that drags its length along; and whenever they or other wild beasts clutch their living prey, the deadly horror which an agitated melancholiac feels is the literally right reaction on the situation.

It may indeed be that no religious reconciliation with the absolute totality of things is possible. Some evils, indeed, are ministerial to higher forms of good; but it may be that there are forms of evil so extreme as to enter into no good system whatsoever, and that, in respect of such evil, dumb submission or neglect to notice is the only practical resource. This question must confront us on a later day. But provisionally, and as a mere matter of program and method, since the evil facts are as genuine parts of nature as the good ones, the philosophic presumption whould be that they have some rational significance, and that systematic healthy-mindedness, failing as it does to accord to sorrow, pain, and death any positive and active attention whatever, is formally less complete than systems that try at least to include these elements in their scope.

The completest religions would therefore seem to be those in which the pessimistic elements are best developed. Buddhism, of course, and Christianity are the best known to us of these. They are essentially religions of deliverance: the man must die to an unreal life before he can be born into the real life. In my next lecture, I will try to discuss some of the psychological conditions of this second birth. Fortunately from now onward we shall have to deal with more cheerful subjects than those which we have recently been dwelling on.

C.   THE DIVIDED SELF AND THE PROCESS
OF ITS UNIFICATION*

The last lecture was a painful one, dealing as it did with evil as a pervasive element of the world we live in. At the close of it we were brought into full view of the contrast between the two ways of looking at life which are characteristic respectively of what we called the healthy-minded, who need to be born only once, and of the sick souls, who must be twice-born in order to be happy. The result is two different conceptions of the universe of our experience. In the religion of the once-born the world is a sort of rectilinear or one-storied affair, whose accounts are kept in one denomination, whose parts have just the values which naturally they appear to have, and of which a simple algebraic sum of pluses and minuses

---

* From Lecture VIII of *The Varieties of Religious Experience.*

will give the total worth. Happiness and religious peace consist in living on the plus side of the account. In the religion of the twice-born, on the other hand, the world is a double-storied· mystery. Peace cannot be reached by the simple addition of pluses and elimination of minuses from life. Natural good is not simply insufficient in amount and transient, there lurks a falsity in its very being. Cancelled as it all is by death if not by earlier enemies, it gives no final balance, and can never be the thing intended for our lasting worship. It keeps us from our real good, rather; and renunciation and despair of it are our first step in the direction of the truth. There are two lives, the natural and the spiritual, and we must lose the one before we can participate in the other.

In their extreme forms, of pure naturalism and pure salvationism, the two types are violently contrasted; though here as in most other current classifications, the radical extremes are somewhat ideal abstractions, and the concrete human beings whom we oftenest meet are intermediate varieties and mixtures. Practically, however, you all recognize the difference: you understand, for example, the disdain of the Methodist convert for the mere sky-blue healthy-minded moralist; and you likewise enter into the aversion of the latter to what seems to him the diseased subjectivism of the Methodist, dying to live, as he calls it, and making of paradox and the inversion of natural appearances the essence of God's truth.

The psychological basis of the twice-born character seems to be a certain discordancy or heterogeneity in the native temperament of the subject, an incompletely unified moral and intellectual constitution.

"Homo duplex, homo duplex!" writes Alphonse Daudet. "The first time that I perceived that I was two was at the death of my brother Henri, when my father cried out so dramatically, 'He is dead, he is dead!' While my first self wept, my second self thought, 'How truly given was that cry, how fine it would be at the theatre.' I was then fourteen years old.

"This horrible duality has often given me matter for reflection. Oh, this terrible second me, always seated whilst the other is on foot, acting, living, suffering, bestirring itself. This second me that I have never been able to intoxicate, to make shed tears, or put to sleep. And how it sees into things, and how it mocks!"[1]

1. *Notes sur la Vie*, p. 1.

Recent works on the psychology of character have had much to say upon this point. Some persons are born with an inner constitution which is harmonious and well balanced from the outset. Their impulses are consistent with one another, their will follows without trouble the guidance of their intellect, their passions are not excessive, and their lives are little haunted by regrets. Others are oppositely constituted. . . . Wrong living, impotent aspirations; "What I would, that do I not; but what I hate, that do I," as St. Paul says; self-loathing, self-despair; an unintelligible and intolerable burden to which one is mysteriously the heir. . . .

D.   Conversion*

. . . To begin with, there are two things in the mind of the candidate for conversion: first, the present incompleteness or wrongness, the 'sin' which he is eager to escape from; and, second, the positive ideal which he longs to compass. Now with most of us the sense of our present wrongness is a far more distinct piece of our consciousness than is the imagination of any positive ideal we can aim at. In a majority of cases, indeed, the 'sin' almost exclusively engrosses the attention, so that conversion is *"a process of struggling away from sin rather than of striving towards righteousness."*[1] A man's conscious wit and will, so far as they strain towards the ideal, are aiming at something only dimly and inaccurately imagined. Yet all the while the forces of more organic ripening within him are going on towards their own prefigured result, and his conscious strainings are letting loose subconscious allies behind the scenes, which in their way work towards rearrangement; and the rearrangement towards which all these deeper forces tend is pretty surely definite, and definitely different from what he consciously conceives and determines. It may consequently be actually interfered with (*jammed,* as it were like the lost word when we seek too energetically to recall it), by his voluntary efforts slanting from the true direction.

Starbuck seems to put his finger on the root of the matter when he says that to exercise the personal will is still to live in the

---

* From Lecture IX of *The Varieties of Religious Experience.*
1. E. D. Starbuck, *The Psychology of Religion*, p. 64.

region where the imperfect self is the thing most emphasized. Where, on the contrary, the subconscious forces take the lead, it is more probably the better self *in posse* which directs the operation. Instead of being clumsily and vaguely aimed at from without, it is then itself the organizing centre. What then must the person do? "He must relax," says Dr. Starbuck—"that is, he must fall back on the larger Power that makes for righteousness, which has been welling up in his own being, and let it finish in its own way the work it has begun. . . . The act of yielding, in this point of view, is giving one's self over to the new life, making it the centre of a new personality, and living, from within, the truth of it which had before been viewed objectively."[2]

"Man's extremity is God's opportunity" is the theological way of putting this fact of the need of self-surrender; whilst the physiological way of stating it would be, "Let one do all in one's power, and one's nervous system will do the rest." Both statements acknowledge the same fact.[3]

To state it in terms of our own symbolism: When the new centre of personal energy has been subconsciously incubated so long as to be just ready to open into flower, 'hands off' is the only word for us, it must burst forth unaided!

We have used the vague and abstract language of psychology. But since, in any terms, the crisis described is the throwing of our conscious selves upon the mercy of powers which, whatever they may be, are more ideal than we are actually, and make for our redemption, you see why self-surrender has been and always must be regarded as the vital turning-point of the religious life, so far as the religious life is spiritual and no affair of outer works and ritual and sacraments. One may say that the whole development of Christianity in inwardness has consisted in little more than the greater and greater emphasis attached to this crisis of self-surrender. From Catholicism to Lutheranism, and then to Calvinism; from that to Wesleyanism; and from this, outside of technical Christianity altogether, to pure 'liberalism' or transcendental idealism, whether or not of the mind-cure type, taking in the mediæval mystics, the quietists, the pietists, and quakers by the way, we can trace the stages of progress towards the idea of an

2. *Ibid.*, p. 115.
3. *Ibid.*, p. 113.

immediate spiritual help, experienced by the individual in his forlornness and standing in no essential need of doctrinal apparatus or propitiatory machinery.

Psychology and religion are thus in perfect harmony up to this point, since both admit that there are forces seemingly outside of the conscious individual that bring redemption to his life. Nevertheless psychology, defining these forces as 'subconscious,' and speaking of their effects as due to 'incubation,' or 'cerebration,' implies that they do not transcend the individual's personality; and herein she diverges from Christian theology, which insists that they are direct supernatural operations of the Deity. I propose to you that we do not yet consider this divergence final, but leave the question for a while in abeyance—continued inquiry may enable us to get rid of some of the apparent discord.

Revert, then, for a moment more to the psychology of self-surrender.

When you find a man living on the ragged edge of his consciousness, pent in to his sin and want and incompleteness, and consequently inconsolable, and then simply tell him that all is well with him, that he must stop his worry, break with his discontent, and give up his anxiety, you seem to him to come with pure absurdities. The only positive consciousness he has tells him that all is *not* well, and the better way you offer sounds simply as if you proposed to him to assert cold-blooded falsehoods. 'The will to believe' cannot be stretched as far as that. We can make ourselves more faithful to a belief of which we have the rudiments, but we cannot create a belief out of whole cloth when our perception actively assures us of its opposite. The better mind proposed to us comes in that case in the form of a pure negation of the only mind we have, and we cannot actively will a pure negation.

There are only two ways in which it is possible to get rid of anger, worry, fear, despair, or other undesirable affections. One is that an opposite affection should over-poweringly break over us, and the other is by getting so exhausted with the struggle that we have to stop—so we drop down, give up, and *don't care* any longer. Our emotional brain-centres strike work, and we lapse into a temporary apathy. Now there is documentary proof that this state of temporary exhaustion not infrequently forms part of the conversion crisis. So long as the egoistic worry of the sick soul guards the door, the expansive confidence of the soul of faith gains no presence. But let the former faint away, even but for a moment, and the latter can profit by the opportunity, and, having once acquired possession, may retain it. Carlyle's Teufelsdröckh passes from the everlasting No to the everlasting Yes through a 'Centre of Indifference.' . . .

E. Mysticism*

Over and over again in these lectures I have raised points and left them open and unfinished until we should have come to the subject of Mysticism. Some of you, I fear, may have smiles as you noted my reiterated postponements. But now the hour has come when mysticism must be faced in good earnest, and those broken threads wound up together. One may say truly, I think, that personal religious experience has its root and centre in mystical states of consciousness; so for us, who in these lectures are treating personal experience as the exclusive subject of our study, such states of consciousness ought to form the vital chapter from which the other chapters get their light. Whether my treatment of mystical states will shed more light or darkness, I do not know, for my own constitution shuts me out from their enjoyment almost entirely, and I can speak of them only at second hand. But though forced to look upon the subject so externally, I will be as objective and receptive as I can; and I think I shall at least succeed in convincing you of the reality of the states in question, and of the paramount importance of their function.

First of all, then, I ask, What does the expression 'mystical states of consciousness' mean? How do we part off mystical states from other states?

The words 'mysticism' and 'mystical' are often used as terms of mere reproach, to throw at any opinion which we regard as vague and vast and sentimental, and without a base in either facts or logic. For some writers a 'mystic' is any person who believes in thought-transference, or spirit-return. Employed in this way the word has little value: there are too many less ambiguous syn-

---

* From Lectures XVI and XVII of *The Varieties of Religious Experience*.

onyms. So, to keep it useful by restricting it, I will do what I did in the case of the word 'religion,' and simply propose to you four marks which, when an experience has them, may justify us in calling it mystical for the purpose of the present lectures. In this way we shall save verbal disputation, and the recriminations that generally go therewith.

1. *Ineffability.*—The handiest of the marks by which I classify a state of mind as mystical is negative. The subject of it immediately says that it defies expression, that no adequate report of its contents can be given in words. It follows from this that its quality must be directly experienced; it cannot be imparted or transferred to others. In this peculiarity mystical states are more like states of feeling than like states of intellect. No one can make clear to another who has never had a certain feeling, in what the quality or worth of it consists. One must have musical ears to know the value of a symphony; one must have been in love one's self to understand a lover's state of mind. Lacking the heart or ear, we cannot interpret the musician or the lover justly, and are even likely to consider him weak-minded or absurd. The mystic finds that most of us accord to his experiences an equally incompetent treatment.

2. *Noetic quality.*—Although so similar to states of feeling, mystical states seem to those who experience them to be also states of knowledge. They are states of insight into depths of truth unplumbed by the discursive intellect. They are illuminations, revelations, full of significance and importance, all inarticulate though they remain; and as a rule they carry with them a curious sense of authority for after-time.

These two characters will entitle any state to be called mystical, in the sense in which I use the word. Two other qualities are less sharply marked, but are usually found. These are:

3. *Transiency.*—Mystical states cannot be sustained for long. Except in rare instances, half an hour, or at most an hour or two, seems to be the limit beyond which they fade into the light of common day. Often, when faded, their quality can but imperfectly

be reproduced in memory; but when they recur it is recognized; and from one recurrence to another it is susceptible of continuous development in what is felt as inner richness and importance.

4. *Passivity.*—Although the oncoming of mystical states may be facilitated by preliminary voluntary operations, as by fixing the attention, or going through certain bodily performances, or in other ways which manuals of mysticism prescribe; yet when the characteristic sort of consciousness once has set in, the mystic feels as if his own will were in abeyance, and indeed sometimes as if he were grasped and held by a superior power. This latter peculiarity connects mystical states with certain definite phenomena of secondary or alternative personality, such as prophetic speech, automatic writing, or the mediumistic trance. When these latter conditions are well pronounced, however, there may be no recollection whatever of the phenomenon, and it may have no significance for the subject's usual inner life, to which, as it were, it makes a mere interruption. Mystical states, strictly so called, are never merely interruptive. Some memory of their content always remains, and a profound sense of their importance. They modify the inner life of the subject between the times of their recurrence. Sharp divisions in this region are, however, difficult to make, and we find all sorts of gradations and mixtures.

These four characteristics are sufficient to mark out a group of states of consciousness peculiar enough to deserve a special name and to call for careful study. Let it then be called the mystical group.

Our next step should be to gain acquaintance with some typical examples. Professional mystics at the height of their development have often elaborately organized experiences and a philosophy based thereupon. But you remember what I said in my first lecture: phenomena are best understood when placed within their series, studied in their germ and in their over-ripe decay, and compared with their exaggerated and degenerated kindred. The range of mystical experience is very wide, much too wide for us to cover in the time at our disposal. Yet the method of serial study is so essential for interpretation that if we really wish to reach conclusions we must use it. I will begin, therefore, with phenomena which claim no special religious significance, and end with those of which the religious pretensions are extreme.

The simplest rudiment of mystical experience would seem to be that deepened sense of the significance of a maxim or formula which occasionally sweeps over one. "I've heard that said all my life," we exclaim, "but I never realized its full meaning until now." "When a fellow-monk," said Luther, "one day repeated the words of the Creed: 'I believe in the forgiveness of sins,' I saw the Scripture in an entirely new light; and straightway I felt as if I were born anew. It was as if I had found the door of paradise thrown wide open."[1] This sense of deeper significance is not confined to rational propositions. Single words,[2] and conjunctions of words, effects of light on land and sea, odors and musical sounds, all bring it when the mind is tuned aright. Most of us can remember the strangely moving power of passages in certain poems read when we were young, irrational doorways as they were through which the mystery of fact, the wildness and the pang of life, stole into our hearts and thrilled them. The words have now perhaps become mere polished surfaces for us; but lyric poetry and music are alive and significant only in proportion as they fetch these vague vistas of a life continuous with our own, beckoning and inviting, yet ever eluding our pursuit. We are alive or dead to the eternal inner message of the arts according as we have kept or lost this mystical susceptibility.

A more pronounced step forward on the mystical ladder is found in an extremely frequent phenomenon, that sudden feeling, namely, which sometimes sweeps over us, of having 'been here before,' as if at some indefinite past time, in just this place, with just these people, we were already saying just these things. As Tennyson writes:

> Moreover, something is or seems,
> That touches me with mystic gleams,
> Like glimpses of forgotten dreams—

1. Newman's *Securus judicat orbis terrarum* is another instance.
2. 'Mesopotamia' is the stock comic instance. . . . Of John Foster it is said that "single words (as *chalcedony*), or the names of ancient heroes, had a mighty fascination over him. 'At any time the word *hermit* was enough to transport him.' The words *woods* and *forests* would produce the most powerful emotion." Foster's Life, by Ryland, New York, 1846, p. 3.

> Of something felt, like something here;
> Of something done, I know not where;
> Such as no language may declare.[3]

Sir James Crichton-Browne has given the technical name of 'dreamy states' to these sudden invasions of vaguely reminiscent consciousness. They bring a sense of mystery and of the metaphysical duality of things, and the feeling of an enlargement of perception which seems imminent but which never completes itself. In Dr. Crichton-Browne's opinion they connect themselves with the perplexed and scared disturbances of self-consciousness which occasionally precede epileptic attacks. I think that this learned alienist takes a rather absurdly alarmist view of an intrinsically insignificant phenomenon. He follows it along the downward ladder, to insanity; our path pursues the upward ladder chiefly. The divergence shows how important it is to neglect no part of a phenomenon's connections, for we make it appear admirable or dreadful according to the context by which we set it off.

Somewhat deeper plunges into mystical consciousness are met with in yet other dreamy states. Such feelings as these which Charles Kingsley describes are surely far from being uncommon, especially in youth:

> When I walk the fields, I am oppressed now and then with an innate feeling that everything I see has a meaning, if I could but understand it. And this feeling of being surrounded with truths which I cannot grasp amounts to indescribable awe sometimes. . . . Have you not felt that your real soul was imperceptible to your mental vision, except in a few hallowed moments?[4]

Nitrous oxide and ether, especially nitrous oxide, when sufficiently diluted with air, stimulate the mystical consciousness in an extraordinary degree. Depth beyond depth of truth seems revealed to the inhaler. This truth fades out, however, or escapes, at the moment of coming to; and if any words remain over in which it seemed to clothe itself, they prove to be the veriest nonsense. Nevertheless, the sense of a profound meaning having been there

---

3. "The Two Voices."
4. *Charles Kingsley's Life*, i, 55, quoted by Inge: *Christian Mysticism*, London, 1899, p. 341.

persists; and I know more than one person who is persuaded that in the nitrous oxide trance we have a genuine metaphysical revelation.

Some years ago I myself made some observations on this aspect of nitrous oxide intoxication, and reported them in print.* One conclusion was forced upon my mind at that time, and my impression of its truth has ever since remained unshaken. It is that our normal waking consciousness, rational consciousness as we call it, is but one special type of consciousness, whilst all about it, parted from it by the filmiest of screens, there lie potential forms of consciousness entirely different. We may go through life without suspecting their existence; but apply the requisite stimulus, and at a touch they are there in all their completeness, definite types of mentality which probably somewhere have their field of application and adaptation. No account of the universe in its totality can be final which leaves these other forms of consciousness quite disregarded. How to regard them is the question—for they are so discontinuous with ordinary consciousness. Yet they may determine attitudes though they cannot furnish formulas, and open a region though they fail to give a map. At any rate, they forbid a premature closing of our accounts with reality. Looking back on my own experiences, they all converge towards a kind of insight to which I cannot help ascribing some metaphysical significance. The keynote of it is invariably a reconciliation. It is as if the opposites of the world, whose contradictoriness and conflict make all our difficulties and troubles, were melted into unity. Not only do they, as contrasted species, belong to one and the same genus, but *one of the species, the nobler and better one, is itself the genus, and so soaks up and absorbs its opposite into itself.* This is a dark saying, I know, when thus expressed in terms of common logic, but I cannot wholly escape from its authority. I feel as if it must mean something, something like what the hegelian philosphy means, if one could only lay hold of it more clearly. Those who have ears to hear, let them hear; to me the living sense of its reality only comes in the artificial mystic state of mind. . . .

In mystical literature such self-contradictory phrases as 'dazzling obscurity,' 'whispering silence,' 'teeming desert,' are continually

* An addendum to "On Some Hegelisms," *The Will to Believe*, 294 ff. [B.W.]

met with. They prove that not conceptual speech, but music rather, is the element through which we are best spoken to by mystical truth. Many mystical scriptures are indeed little more than musical compositions. . . .

. . . Music gives us ontological messages which non-musical criticism is unable to contradict, though it may laugh at our foolishness in minding them. There is a verge of the mind which these things haunt; and whispers therefrom mingle with the operations of our understanding, even as the waters of the infinite ocean send their waves to break among the pebbles that lie upon our shores. . . .

My next task is to inquire whether we can invoke it as authoritative. Does it furnish any *warrant for the truth* of the twice-bornness and supernaturality and pantheism which it favors? I must give my answer to this question as concisely as I can.

In brief my answer is this—and I will divide it into three parts:

(1) Mystical states, when well developed, usually are, and have the right to be, absolutely authoritative over the individuals to whom they come.

(2) No authority emanates from them which should make it a duty for those who stand outside of them to accept their revelations uncritically.

(3) They break down the authority of the non-mystical or rationalistic consciousness, based upon the understanding and the senses alone. They show it to be only one kind of consciousness. They open out the possibility of other orders of truth, in which, so far as anything in us vitally responds to them, we may freely continue to have faith.

I will take up these points one by one.

1.

As a matter of psychological fact, mystical states of a well-pronounced and emphatic sort *are* usually authoritative over those who have them. They have been 'there,' and know. It is vain for rationalism to grumble about this. If the mystical truth that comes

to a man proves to be a force that he can live by, what mandate
have we of the majority to order him to live in another way? We
can throw him into prison or a madhouse, but we cannot change
his mind—we commonly attach it only the more stubbornly to its
beliefs. It mocks our utmost efforts, as a matter of fact, and in
point of logic it absolutely escapes our jurisdiction. Our own more
'rational' beliefs are based on evidence exactly similar in nature to
that which mystics quote for theirs. Our senses, namely, have assured us of certain states of fact; but mystical experiences are as
direct perceptions of fact for those who have them as any sensations ever were for us. The records show that even though the five
senses be in abeyance in them, they are absolutely sensational in
their epistemological quality, if I may be pardoned the barbarous
expression—that is, they are face to face presentations of what
seems immediately to exist.

The mystic is, in short, *invulnerable,* and must be left, whether
we relish it or not, in undisturbed enjoyment of his creed. Faith,
says Tolstoy, is that by which men live. And faith-state and mystic-
state are practically convertible terms.

2.

But I now proceed to add that mystics have no right to claim
that we ought to accept the deliverance of their peculiar experiences, if we are ourselves outsiders and feel no private call thereto.
The utmost they can ever ask of us in this life is to admit that they
establish a presumption. They form a consensus and have an un-
equivocal outcome; and it would be odd, mystics might say, if such
a unanimous type of experience should prove to be altogether
wrong. At bottom, however, this would only be an appeal to numbers, like the appeal of rationalism the other way; and the appeal
to numbers has no logical force. If we acknowledge it, it is for
'suggestive,' not for logical reasons: we follow the majority because
to do so suits our life.

But even this presumption from the unanimity of mystics is far
from being strong. In characterizing mystic states as pantheistic,
optimistic, etc., I am afraid I over-simplified the truth. I did so for
expository reasons, and to keep the closer to the classic mystical
tradition. The classic religious mysticism, it now must be confessed, is only a 'privileged case.' It is an *extract,* kept true to type

by the selection of the fittest specimens and their preservation in 'schools.' It is carved out from a much larger mass; and if we take the larger mass as seriously as religious mysticism has historically taken itself, we find that the supposed unanimity largely disappears. To begin with, even religious mysticism itself, the kind that accumulates traditions and makes schools, is much less unanimous than I have allowed. It has been both ascetic and antinomianly self-indulgent within the Christian church. It is dualistic in Sankhya, and monistic in Vedanta philosophy. I called it pantheistic; but the great Spanish mystics are anything but pantheists. They are with few exceptions non-metaphysical minds, for whom 'the category of personality' is absolute. The 'union' of man with God is for them much more like an occasional miracle than like an original identity. How different again, apart from the happiness common to all, is the mysticism of Walt Whitman, Edward Carpenter, Richard Jefferies, and other naturalistic pantheists, from the more distinctively Christian sort. The fact is that the mystical feeling of enlargement, union, and emancipation has no specific intellectual content whatever of its own. It is capable of forming matrimonial alliances with material furnished by the most diverse philosophies and theologies, provided only they can find a place in their framework for its peculiar emotional mood. We have no right, therefore, to invoke its prestige as distinctively in favor of any special belief, such as that in absolute idealism, or in the absolute monistic identity, or in the absolute goodness, of the world. It is only relatively in favor of all these things—it passes out of common human consciousness in the direction in which they lie.

So much for religious mysticism proper. But more remains to be told, for religious mysticism is only one half of mysticism. The other half has no accumulated traditions except those which the text-books on insanity supply. Open any one of these, and you will find abundant cases in which 'mystical ideas' are cited as characteristic symptoms of enfeebled or deluded states of mind. In delusional insanity, paranoia, as they sometimes call it, we may have a *diabolical* mysticism, a sort of religious mysticism turned upside down. The same sense of ineffable importance in the smallest events, the same texts and words coming with new meanings, the same voices and visions and leadings and missions, the same controlling by extraneous powers; only this time the emotion is pessimistic: instead of consolations we have desolations; the meanings are dreadful; and the powers are enemies to life. It is evident that from the point of view of their psychological mechanism, the classic mysticism and these lower mysticisms spring from the same mental level, from that great subliminal or transmarginal region of which science is beginning to admit the existence, but of which so little is really known. That region contains every kind of matter: 'seraph and snake' abide there side by side. To come from thence is no infallible credential. What comes must be sifted and tested, and run the gauntlet of confrontation with the total context of experience, just like what comes from the outer world of sense. Its value must be ascertained by empirical methods, so long as we are not mystics ourselves.

Once more, then, I repeat that non-mystics are under no obligation to acknowledge in mystical states a superior authority conferred on them by their intrinsic nature.

3.

Yet, I repeat once more, the existence of mystical states absolutely overthrows the pretension of non-mystical states to be the sole and ultimate dictators of what we may believe. As a rule, mystical states merely add a supersensuous meaning to the ordinary outward data of consciousness. They are excitements like the emotions of love or ambition, gifts to our spirit by means of which facts already objectively before us fall into a new expressiveness and make a new connection with our active life. They do not contradict these facts as such, or deny anything that our senses have immediately seized. It is the rationalistic critic rather who plays the part of denier in the controversy, and his denials have no strength, for there never can be a state of facts to which new meaning may not truthfully be added, provided the mind ascend to a more enveloping point of view. It must always remain an open question whether mystical states may not possibly be such superior points of view, windows through which the mind looks out upon ꓦ more extensive and inclusive world. The difference of the views seen from the different mystical windows need not prevent us from entertaining this supposition. The wider world would in that case prove to have a mixed constitution like that of this world, that is all. It would have its celestial and its infernal regions, its tempting and its saving moments, its valid experiences and its counterfeit ones, just as our world has them; but it would be a wider world all the same. We should have to use its experiences by selecting and subordinating and substituting just as is our custom in this ordinary naturalistic world; we should be liable to error just as we are now; yet the counting in of that wider world of meanings, and the serious dealing with it, might, in spite of all the perplexity, be indispensable stages in our approach to the final fullness of the truth.

In this shape, I think, we have to leave the subject. Mystical states indeed wield no authority due simply to their being mystical states. But the higher ones among them point in directions to which the religious sentiments even of non-mystical men incline. They tell of the supremacy of the ideal, of vastness, of union, of safety, and of rest. They offer us *hypotheses,* hypotheses which we may voluntarily ignore, but which as thinkers we cannot possibly upset. The supernaturalism and optimism to which they would persuade us may, interpreted in one way or another, be after all the truest of insights into the meaning of this life.

"Oh, the little more, and how much it is; and the little less, and what worlds away!" It may be that possibility and permission of this sort are all that the religious consciousness requires to live on. In my last lecture I shall have to try to persuade you that this is the case. Meanwhile, however, I am sure that for many of my readers this diet is too slender. If supernaturalism and inner union with the divine are true, you think, then not so much permission, as compulsion to believe, ought to be found. Philosophy has always professed to prove religious truth by coercive argument; and the construction of philosophies of this kind has always been one favorite function of the religious life, if we use this term in the large historic sense. . . .

F. Philosophy*

. . . In all sad sincerity I think we must conclude that the attempt to demonstrate by purely intellectual processes the truth of the deliverances of direct religious experience is absolutely hopeless.

* From Lecture XVIII of *The Varieties of Religious Experience.*

It would be unfair to philosophy, however, to leave her under this negative sentence. Let me close, then, by briefly enumerating what she *can* do for religion. If she will abandon metaphysics and deduction for criticism and induction, and frankly transform herself from theology into science of religions, she can make herself enormously useful.

The spontaneous intellect of man always defines the divine which it feels in ways that harmonize with its temporary intellectual prepossessions. Philosophy can by comparison eliminate the local and the accidental from these definitions. Both from dogma and from worship she can remove historic incrustations. By confronting the spontaneous religious constructions with the results of natural science, philosophy can also eliminate doctrines that are now known to be scientifically absurd or incongruous.

Sifting out in this way unworthy formulations, she can leave a residuum of conceptions that at least are possible. With these she can deal as *hypotheses,* testing them in all the manners, whether negative or positive, by which hypotheses are ever tested. She can reduce their number, as some are found more open to objection. She can perhaps become the champion of one which she picks out as being the most closely verified or verifiable. She can refine upon the definition of this hypothesis, distinguishing between what is innocent over-belief and symbolism in the expression of it, and what is to be literally taken. As a result, she can offer mediation between different believers, and help to bring about consensus of opinion. She can do this the more successfully, the better she discriminates the common and essential from the individual and local elements of the religious beliefs which she compares.

I do not see why a critical Science of Religions of this sort might not eventually command as general a public adhesion as is commanded by a physical science. Even the personally non-religious might accept its conclusions on trust, much as blind persons now accept the facts of optics—it might appear as foolish to refuse them. Yet as the science of optics has to be fed in the first instance, and continually verified later, by facts experienced by seeing persons; so the science of religions would depend for its original material on facts of personal experience, and would have to square itself with personal experience through all its critical reconstructions. It could never get away from concrete life, or work in a conceptual vacuum. It would forever have to confess, as every science confesses, that the subtlety of nature flies beyond it, and that its formulas are but approximations. Philosophy lives in words, but truth and fact well up into our lives in ways that exceed verbal formulation. There is in the living act of perception always something that glimmers and twinkles and will not be caught, and for which reflection comes too late. No one knows this as well as the philosopher. He must fire his volley of new vocables out of his conceptual shotgun, for his profession condemns him to this industry, but he secretly knows the hollowness and irrelevancy. His formulas are like stereoscopic or kinetoscopic photographs seen outside the instrument; they lack the depth, the motion, the vitality. In the religious sphere, in particular, belief that formulas are true can never wholly take the place of personal experience. . . .

G. Conclusions*

. . . You see now why I have been so individualistic throughout these lectures, and why I have seemed so bent on rehabilitating the element of feeling in religion and subordinating its intellectual part. Individuality is founded in feeling; and the recesses of feeling, the darker, blinder strata of character, are the only places in the world in which we catch real fact in the making, and directly perceive how events happen, and how work is actually done. Compared with this world of living individualized feelings, the world of generalized objects which the intellect contemplates is without solidity or life. As in stereoscopic or kinetoscopic pictures seen outside the instrument, the third dimension, the movement, the vital element are not there. We get a beautiful picture of an express train supposed to be moving, but where in the picture, as I have heard a friend say, is the energy or the fifty miles an hour?

Let us agree, then, that Religion, occupying herself with personal destinies and keeping thus in contact with the only absolute realities which we know, must necessarily play an eternal part in human history. The next thing to decide is what she reveals about those destinies, or whether indeed she reveals anything distinct

* From Lecture XX of *The Varieties of Religious Experience*.

enough to be considered a general message to mankind. We have done as you see, with our preliminaries, and our final summing up can now begin. . . .

We must next pass beyond the point of view of merely subjective utility, and make inquiry into the intellectual content itself.

First, is there, under all the discrepancies of the creeds, a common nucleus to which they bear their testimony unanimously?

And second, ought we to consider the testimony true?

I will take up the first question first, and answer it immediately in the affirmative. The warring gods and formulas of the various religions do indeed cancel each other, but there is a certain uniform deliverance in which religions all appear to meet. It consists of two parts:

1. An uneasiness; and
2. Its solution.

1. The uneasiness, reduced to its simplest terms, is a sense that there is *something wrong about us* as we naturally stand.

2. The solution is a sense that *we are saved from the wrongness* by making proper connection with the higher powers.

In those more developed minds which alone we are studying, the wrongness takes a moral character, and the salvation takes a mystical tinge. I think we shall keep well within the limits of what is common to all such minds if we formulate the essence of their religious experience in terms like these:

The individual, so far as he suffers from his wrongness and criticises it, is to that extent consciously beyond it, and in at least possible touch with something higher, if anything higher exist. Along with the wrong part there is thus a better part of him, even though it may be but a most helpless germ. With which part he should identify his real being is by no means obvious at this stage; but when stage 2 (the stage of solution or salvation) arrives, the man identifies his real being with the germinal higher part of himself; and does so in the following way. *He becomes conscious that this higher part is conterminous and continuous with a* MORE *of the same quality, which is operative in the universe outside of him, and which he can keep in working touch with, and in a fashion get on board of and save himself when all his lower being has gone to pieces in the wreck.*

It seems to me that all the phenomena are accurately describable in these very simple general terms. They allow for the divided self and the struggle; they involve the change of personal centre and the surrender of the lower self; they express the appearance of exteriority of the helping power and yet account for our sense of union with it; and they fully justify our feelings of security and joy. There is probably no autobiographic document, among all those which I have quoted, to which the description will not well apply. One need only add such specific details as will adapt it to various theologies and various personal temperaments, and one will then have the various experiences reconstructed in their individual forms.

So far, however, as this analysis goes, the experiences are only psychological phenomena. They possess, it is true, enormous biological worth. Spiritual strength really increases in the subject when he has them, a new life opens for him, and they seem to him a place of conflux where the forces of two universes meet; and yet this may be nothing but his subjective way of feeling things, a mood of his own fancy, in spite of the effects produced. I now turn to my second question: What is the objective 'truth' of their content?

The part of the content concerning which the question of truth most pertinently arises is that 'MORE of the same quality' with which our own higher self appears in the experience to come into harmonious working relation. Is such a 'more' merely our own notion, or does it really exist? If so, in what shape does it exist? Does it act, as well as exist? And in what form should we conceive of that 'union' with it of which religious geniuses are so convinced?

It is in answering these questions that the various theologies perform their theoretic work, and that their divergencies most come to light. They all agree that the 'more' really exists; though some of them hold it to exist in the shape of a personal god or gods, while others are satisfied to conceive it as a stream of ideal tendency embedded in the eternal structure of the world. They all agree, moreover, that it acts as well as exists, and that something really is effected for the better when you throw your life into its hands. It is when they treat of the experience of 'union' with it that their speculative differences appear most clearly. Over this point pantheism and theism, nature and second birth, works and grace and karma, immortality and reincarnation, rationalism and mysticism, carry on inveterate disputes.

At the end of my lecture on Philosophy, I held out the notion that an impartial science of religions might sift out from the midst of their discrepancies a common body of doctrine which she might also formulate in terms to which physical science need not object. This, I said, she might adopt as her own reconciling hypothesis, and recommend it for general belief. I also said that in my last lecture I should have to try my own hand at framing such an hypothesis.

The time has now come for this attempt. Who says 'hypothesis' renounces the ambition to be coercive in his arguments. The most I can do is, accordingly, to offer something that may fit the facts so easily that your scientific logic will find no plausible pretext for vetoing your impulse to welcome it as true.

The 'more,' as we called it, and the meaning of our 'union' with it, form the nucleus of our inquiry. Into what definite description can these words be translated, and for what definite facts do they stand? It would never do for us to place ourselves offhand at the position of a particular theology, the Christian theology, for example, and proceed immediately to define the 'more' as Jehovah, and the 'union' as his imputation to us of the righteousness of Christ. That would be unfair to other religions, and, from our present standpoint at least, would be an over-belief.

We must begin by using less particularized terms; and, since one of the duties of the science of religions is to keep religion in connection with the rest of science, we shall do well to seek first of all a way of describing the 'more,' which psychologists may also recognize as real. The *subconscious self* is nowadays a well-accredited psychological entity; and I believe that in it we have exactly the mediating term required. Apart from all religious considerations, there is actually and literally more life in our total soul than we are at any time aware of. The exploration of the transmarginal field has hardly yet been seriously undertaken, but what Mr.

Myers said in 1892 in his issay on the Subliminal Consciousness[1] is as true as when it was first written: "Each of us is in reality an abiding psychical entity far more extensive than he knows—an individuality which can never express itself completely through any corporeal manifestation. The Self manifests through the organism; but there is always some part of the Self unmanifested; and always, as it seems, some power of organic expression in abeyance or reserve." Much of the content of this larger background against which our conscious being stands out in relief is insignificant. Imperfect memories, silly jingles, inhibitive timidities, 'dissolutive' phenomena of various sorts, as Myers calls them, enter into it for a large part. But in it many of the performances of genius seem also to have their origin; and in our study of conversion, of mystical experiences, and of prayer, we have seen how striking a part invasions from this region play in the religious life.

Let me then propose, as an hypothesis, that whatever it may be on its *farther* side, the 'more' with which in religious experience we feel ourselves connected is on its *hither* side the subconscious continuation of our conscious life. Starting thus with a recognized psychological fact as our basis, we seem to preserve a contact with 'science' which the ordinary theologian lacks. At the same time the theologian's contention that the religious man is moved by an external power is vindicated, for it is one of the peculiarities of invasions from the subconscious region to take on objective appearances, and to suggest to the Subject an external control. In the religious life the control is felt as 'higher'; but since on our hypothesis it is primarily the higher faculties of our own hidden mind which are controlling, the sense of union with the power beyond us is a sense of something, not merely apparently, but literally true.

This doorway into the subject seems to me the best one for a science of religions, for it mediates between a number of different points of view. Yet it is only a doorway, and difficulties present themselves as soon as we step through it, and ask how far our transmarginal consciousness carries us if we follow it on its remoter side. Here the over-beliefs begin: here mysticism and the conversion-rapture and Vedantism and transcendental idealism

1. Proceedings of the Society for Psychical Research, vol. vii. p. 305.

bring in their monistic interpretations and tell us that the finite self rejoins the absolute self, for it was always one with God and identical with the soul of the world. Here the prophets of all the different religions come with their visions, voices, raptures, and other openings, supposed by each to authenticate his own peculiar faith.

Those of us who are not personally favored with such specific revelations must stand outside of them altogether and, for the present at least, decide that, since they corroborate incompatible theological doctrines, they neutralize one another and leave no fixed result. If we follow any one of them, or if we follow philo-sophical theory and embrace monistic pantheism on non-mystical grounds, we do so in the exercise of our individual freedom, and build out our religion in the way most congruous with our personal susceptibilities. Among these susceptibilities intellectual ones play a decisive part. Although the religious question is pri-marily a question of life, of living or not living in the higher union which opens itself to us as a gift, yet the spiritual excite-ment in which the gift appears a real one will often fail to be aroused in an individual until certain particular intellectual be-liefs or ideas which, as we say, come home to him, are touched. These ideas will thus be essential to that individual's religion— which is as much as to say that over-beliefs in various directions are absolutely indispensable, and that we should treat them with tenderness and tolerance so long as they are not intolerant them-selves. As I have elsewhere written, the most interesting and valuable things about a man are usually his over-beliefs.

Disregarding the over-beliefs, and confining ourselves to what is common and generic, we have in *the fact that the conscious person is continuous with a wider self through which saving experiences come,* a positive content of religious experience which, it seems to me, *is literally and objectively true as far as it goes.* If I now proceed to state my own hypothesis about the farther limits of this extension of our personality, I shall be offering my own over-belief—though I know it will appear a sorry under-belief to some of you—for which I can only bespeak the same indulgence which in a converse case I should accord to yours.

The further limits of our being plunge, it seems to me, into an altogether other dimension of existence from the sensible and merely 'understandable' world. Name it the mystical region, or the supernatural region, whichever you choose. So far as our ideal impulses originate in this region (and most of them do originate in it, for we find them possessing us in a way for which we cannot articulately account), we belong to it in a more intimate sense than that in which we belong to the visible world, for we belong in the most intimate sense wherever our ideals belong. Yet the unseen region in question is not merely ideal, for it produces effects in this world. When we commune with it, work is actually done upon our finite personality, for we are turned into new men, and consequences in the way of conduct follow in the natural world upon our regenerative change. But that which produces effects within another reality must be termed a reality itself, so I feel as if we had no philosophic excuse for calling the unseen or mystical world unreal.

God is the natural appellation, for us Christians at least, for the supreme reality, so I will call this higher part of the universe by the name of God. We and God have business with each other; and in opening ourselves to his influence our deepest destiny is fulfilled. The universe, at those parts of it which our personal being constitutes, takes a turn genuinely for the worse or for the better in proportion as each one of us fulfills or evades God's demands. As far as this goes I probably have you with me, for I only translate into schematic language what I may call the instinctive belief of mankind: God is real since he produces real effects.

The real effects in question, so far as I have as yet admitted them, are exerted on the personal centres of energy of the various subjects, but the spontaneous faith of most of the subjects is that they embrace a wider sphere than this. Most religious men believe (or 'know,' if they be mystical) that not only they themselves, but the whole universe of beings to whom the God is present, are secure in his parental hands. There is a sense, a dimension, they are sure, in which we are *all* saved, in spite of the gates of hell and all adverse terrestrial appearances. God's existence is the guarantee of an ideal order that shall be permanently preserved. This world may indeed, as science assures us, some day burn up or freeze; but if it is part of his order, the old ideals are sure to be brought elsewhere to fruition, so that where God is, tragedy is only provisional and partial, and shipwreck and dissolution are not the absolutely final things. Only when this farther step of faith concerning God is taken, and remote objective consequences are predicted, does religion, as it seems to me, get wholly free from the first immediate subjective experience, and bring a *real hypothesis* into play. A good hypothesis in science must have other properties than those of the phenomenon it is immediately invoked to explain, otherwise it is not prolific enough. God, meaning only what enters into the religious man's experience of union, falls short of being an hypothesis of this more useful order. He needs to enter into wider cosmic relations in order to justify the subject's absolute confidence and peace.

That the God with whom, starting from the hither side of our own extra-marginal self, we come at its remoter margin into commerce should be the absolute world-ruler, is of course a very considerable over-belief. Over-belief as it is, though, it is an article of almost every one's religion. Most of us pretend in some way to prop it upon our philosophy, but the philosophy itself is really propped upon this faith. What is this but to say that Religion, in her fullest exercise of function, is not a mere illumination of facts already elsewhere given, not a mere passion, like love, which views things in a rosier light. It is indeed that, as we have seen abundantly. But it is something more, namely, a postulator of new *facts* as well. The world interpreted religiously is not the materialistic world over again, with an altered expression; it must have, over and above the altered expression, *a natural constitution* different at some point from that which a materialistic world would have. It must be such that different events can be expected in it, different conduct must be required.

This thoroughly 'pragmatic' view of religion has usually been taken as a matter of course by common men. They have interpolated divine miracles into the field of nature, they have built a heaven out beyond the grave. It is only transcendentalist metaphysicians who think that, without adding any concrete details to Nature, or subtracting any, but by simply calling it the expression of absolute spirit, you make it more divine just as it stands. I believe the pragmatic way of taking religion to be the deeper way. It gives it body as well as soul, it makes it claim, as everything real must claim, some characteristic realm of fact as its very own. What the more characteristically divine facts are, apart from the actual inflow of energy in the faith-state and the prayer-state, I know not.

But the over-belief on which I am ready to make my personal venture is that they exist. The whole drift of my education goes to persuade me that the world of our present consciousness is only one out of many worlds of consciousness that exist, and that those other worlds must contain experiences which have a meaning for our life also; and that although in the main their experiences and those of this world keep discrete, yet the two become continuous at certain points, and higher energies filter in. By being faithful in my poor measure to this over-belief, I seem to myself to keep more sane and true. I *can*, of course, put myself into the sectarian scientist's attitude, and imagine vividly that the world of sensations and of scientific laws and objects may be all. But whenever I do this, I hear that inward monitor of which W. K. Clifford once wrote, whispering the word 'bosh!' Humbug is humbug, even though it bear the scientific name, and the total expression of human experience, as I view it objectively, invincibly urges me beyond the narrow 'scientific' bounds. Assuredly, the real world is of a different temperament—more intricately built than physical science allows. So my objective and my subjective conscience both hold me to the over-belief which I express. Who knows whether the faithfulness of individuals here below to their own poor over-beliefs may not actually help God in turn to be more effectively faithful to his own greater tasks?

8.

Humanism and Truth*

. . . First, as to the word 'pragmatism.' I myself have only used the term to indicate a method of carrying on abstract discussion. The serious meaning of a concept, says Mr. Peirce, lies in the concrete difference to some one which its being true will make. Strive to bring all debated conceptions to that 'pragmatic' test, and you will escape vain wrangling: if it can make no practical difference which of two statements be true, then they are really one statement in two verbal forms; if it can make no practical difference whether a given statement be true or false, then the statement has no real meaning. In neither case is there anything fit to quarrel about: we may save our breath, and pass to more important things.

All that the pragmatic method implies, then, is that truths should *have* practical[1] consequences. In England the word has been used more broadly still, to cover the notion that the truth of any statement *consists* in the consequences, and particularly in their being good consequences. Here we get beyond affairs of method altogether; and since my pragmatism and this wider pragmatism are so different, and both are important enough to have different names, I think that Mr. Schiller's proposal to call the wider pragmatism by the name of 'humanism' is excellent and ought to be adopted. The narrower pragmatism may still be spoken of as the 'pragmatic method.' . . .

As I understand the pragmatist way of seeing things, it owes its being to the break-down which the last fifty years have brought

* From *The Meaning of Truth: A Sequel to "Pragmatism"* (New York & London: Longmans, Green & Co., 1909). Consists in the main of an article in *Mind*, vol. xiii (1904). Portions of text and some footnotes have been deleted. [B.W.]

1. 'Practical' in the sense of *particular*, of course, not in the sense that the consequences may not be *mental* as well as physical.

about in the older notions of scientific truth. 'God geometrizes,' it used to be said; and it was believed that Euclid's elements literally reproduced his geometrizing. There is an eternal and unchangeable 'reason'; and its voice was supposed to reverberate in *Barbara* and *Celarent*. So also of the 'laws of nature,' physical and chemical, so of natural history classifications—all were supposed to be exact and exclusive duplicates of pre-human archetypes buried in the structure of things, to which the spark of divinity hidden in our intellect enables us to penetrate. The anatomy of the world is logical, and it logic is that of a university professor, it was thought. Up to about 1850 almost every one believed that sciences expressed truths that were exact copies of a definite code of non-human realities. But the enormously rapid multiplication of theories in these latter days has well-nigh upset the notion of any one of them being a more literally objective kind of thing than another. There are so many geometries, so many logics, so many physical and chemical hypotheses, so many classifications, each one of them good for so much and yet not good for everything, that the notion that even the truest formula may be a human device and not a literal transcript has dawned upon us. We hear scientific laws now treated as so much 'conceptual shorthand,' true so far as they are useful but no farther. Our mind has become tolerant of symbol instead of reproduction, of approximation instead of exactness, of plasticity instead of rigor. 'Energetics,' measuring the bare face of sensible phenomena so as to describe in a single formula all their changes of 'level,' is the last word of this scientific humanism, which indeed leaves queries enough outstanding as to the reason for so curious a congruence between the world and the mind, but which at any rate makes our whole notion of scientific truth more flexible and genial than it used to be.

It is to be doubted whether any theorizer to-day, either in mathematics, logic, physics or biology, conceives himself to be literally re-editing processes of nature or thoughts of God. The main forms of our thinking, the separation of subjects from predicates, the negative, hypothetic and disjunctive judgments, are purely human habits. The ether, as Lord Salisbury said, is only a noun for the verb to undulate; and many of our theological ideas are admitted, even by those who call them 'true,' to be humanistic in like degree.

I fancy that these changes in the current notions of truth are what originally gave the impulse to Messrs. Dewey's and Schiller's views. The suspicion is in the air nowadays that the superiority of one of our formulas to another may not consist so much in its literal 'objectivity,' as in subjective qualities like its usefulness, its 'elegance' or its congruity with our residual beliefs. Yielding to these suspicions, and generalizing, we fall into something like the humanistic state of mind. Truth we conceive to mean everywhere, not duplication, but addition; not the constructing of inner copies of already complete realities, but rather the collaborating with realities so as to bring about a clearer result. Obviously this state of mind is at first full of vagueness and ambiguity. 'Collaborating' is a vague term; it must at any rate cover conceptions and logical arrangements. 'Clearer' is vaguer still. Truth must bring clear thoughts, as well as clear the way to action. 'Reality' is the vaguest term of all. The only way to test such a programme at all is to apply it to the various types of truth, in the hope of reaching an account that shall be more precise. Any hypothesis that forces such a review upon one has one great merit, even if in the end it prove invalid: it gets us better acquainted with the total subject. To give the theory plenty of 'rope' and see if it hangs itself eventually is better tactics than to choke it off at the outset by abstract accusations of self-contradiction. I think therefore that a decided effort at sympathetic mental play with humanism is the provisional attitude to be recommended to the reader.

When I find myself playing sympathetically with humanism, something like what follows is what I end by conceiving it to mean.

Experience is a process that continually gives us new material to digest. We handle this intellectually by the mass of beliefs of which we find ourselves already possessed, assimilating, rejecting, or rearranging in different degrees. Some of the apperceiving ideas are recent acquisitions of our own, but most of them are common-sense traditions of the race. There is probably not a common-sense tradition, of all those which we now live by, that was not in the first instance a genuine discovery, an inductive generalization like those more recent ones of the atom, of inertia, of energy, of reflex action, or of fitness to survive. The notions of one Time and of one Space as single continuous receptacles; the distinction between thoughts and things, matter and mind; between permanent subjects and changing attributes; the conception of classes with sub-classes within them; the separation of fortuitous from regularly caused connections; surely all these were once definite conquests made at historic dates by our ancestors in their attempts to get the chaos of their crude individual experiences into a more shareable and manageable shape. They proved of such sovereign use as *denkmittel* that they are now a part of the very structure of our mind. We cannot play fast and loose with them. No experience can upset them. On the contrary, they apperceive every experience and assign it to its place.

To what effect? That we may the better foresee the course of our experiences, communicate with one another, and steer our lives by rule. Also that we may have a cleaner, clearer, more inclusive mental view.

The greatest common-sense achievement, after the discovery of one Time and one Space, is probably the concept of permanently existing things. When a rattle first drops out of the hand of a baby, he does not look to see where it has gone. Non-perception he accepts as annihilation until he finds a better belief. That our perceptions mean *beings,* rattles that are there whether we hold them in our hands or not, becomes an interpretation so luminous of what happens to us that, once employed, it never gets forgotten. It applies with equal felicity to things and persons, to the objective and to the ejective realm. However a Berkeley, a Mill, or a Cornelius may criticise it, it *works;* and in practical life we never think of 'going back' upon it, or reading our incoming experiences in any other terms. We may, indeed, speculatively imagine a state of 'pure' experience before the hypothesis of permanent objects behind its flux had been framed; and we can play with the idea that some primeval genius might have struck into a different hypothesis. But we cannot positively imagine today what the different hypothesis could have been, for the category of trans-perceptual reality is now one of the foundations of our life. Our thoughts must still employ it if they are to possess reasonableness and truth.

This notion of a *first* in the shape of a most chaotic pure experience which sets us questions, of a *second* in the way of fundamental categories, long ago wrought into the structure of our consciousness and practically irreversible, which define the general frame within which answers must fall, and of a *third* which gives the detail of the answers in the shapes most congruous with all our present needs, is, as I take it, the essence of the humanistic conception. It represents experience in its pristine purity to be now so enveloped in predicates historically worked out that we can think of it as little more than an *Other*, of a *That*, which the mind, in Mr. Bradley's phrase, 'encounters,' and to whose stimulating presence we respond by ways of thinking which we call 'true' in proportion as they facilitate our mental or physical activities and bring us outer power and inner peace. But whether the Other, the universal *That*, has itself any definite inner structure, or whether, if it have any, the structure resembles any of our predicated *whats*, this is a question which humanism leaves untouched. For us, at any rate, it insists, reality is an accumulation of our own intellectual inventions, and the struggle for 'truth' in our progressive dealings with it is always a struggle to work in new nouns and adjectives while altering as little as possible the old. . . .

The best way to discuss it would be to see what the alternative might be. What is it indeed? Its critics make no explicit statement, Professor Royce being the only one so far who has formulated anything definite. The first service of humanism to philosophy accordingly seems to be that it will probably oblige those who dislike it to search their own hearts and heads. It will force analysis to the front and make it the order of the day. At present the lazy tradition that truth is *adæquatio intellectûs et rei* seems all there is to contradict it with. Mr. Bradley's only suggestion is that true thought 'must correspond to a determinate being which it cannot be said to make,' and obviously that sheds no new light. What is the meaning of the word to 'correspond?' Where is the 'being?' What sort of things are 'determinations,' and what is meant in this particular case by 'not to make'?

Humanism proceeds immediately to refine upon the looseness of these epithets. We correspond in *some* way with anything with which we enter into any relations at all. If it be a thing, we may produce an exact copy of it, or we may simply feel it as an existent in a certain place. If it be a demand, we may obey it without knowing anything more about it than its push. If it be a proposition we may agree by not contradicting it, by letting it pass. If it be a relation between things, we may act on the first thing so as to bring ourselves out where the second will be. If it be something inaccessible, we may substitute a hypothetical object for it, which, having the same consequences, will cipher out for us real results. In a general way we may simply *add our thought to it;* and if it *suffers the addition,* and the whole situation harmoniously prolongs and enriches itself, the thought will pass for true.

As for the whereabouts of the beings thus corresponded to, although they may be outside of the present thought as well as in it, humanism sees no ground for saying they are outside of finite experience itself. Pragmatically, their reality means that we submit to them, take account of them, whether we like to or not, but this we must perpetually do with experiences other than our own. The whole system of what the present experience must correspond to 'adequately' may be continuous with the present experience itself. Reality, so taken as experience other than the present, might be either the legacy of past experience or the content of experience to come. Its determinations for *us* are in any case the adjectives which our acts of judging fit to it, and those are essentially humanistic things.

To say that our thought does not 'make' this reality means pragmatically that if our own particular thought were annihilated the reality would still be there in some shape, though possibly it might be a shape that would lack something that our thought supplies. That reality is 'independent' means that there is something in every experience that escapes our arbitrary control. If it be a sensible experience it coerces our attention; if a sequence, we cannot invert it; if we compare two terms we can come to only one result. There is a push, an urgency, within our very experience, against which we are on the whole powerless, and which drives us in a direction that is the destiny of our belief. That this drift of experience itself is in the last resort due to something independent of all possible experience may or may not be true. There may or may not be an extra-experiential 'ding an sich' that keeps the ball rolling, or an 'absolute' that lies eternally behind all the successive determinations which human thought has made. But within our experience *itself,* at any rate, humanism says, some determinations show themselves as being independent of others; some questions, if

we ever ask them, can only be answered in one way; some beings,
if we ever suppose them, must be supposed to have existed previously to the supposing; some relations, if they exist ever, must
exist as long as their terms exist.

Truth thus means, according to humanism, the relation of less
fixed parts of experience (predicates) to other relatively more
fixed parts (subjects); and we are not required to seek it in a
relation of experience as such to anything beyond itself. We can
stay at home, for our behavior as experients is hemmed in on every
side. The forces both of advance and of resistance are exerted by
our own objects, and the notion of truth as something opposed to
waywardness or license inevitably grows up solipsistically inside of
every human life.

So obvious is àll this that a common charge against the humanistic authors 'makes me tired.' "How can a deweyite discriminate
sincerity from bluff?" was a question asked at a philosophic meeting where I reported on Dewey's *Studies.* "How can the mere
pragmatist feel any duty to think truly?" is the objection urged by
Professor Royce. Mr. Bradley in turn says that if a humanist
understands his own doctrine, "he must hold any idea, however
mad, to be the truth, if any one will have it so." And Professor
Taylor describes pragmatism as believing anything one pleases
and calling it truth.

Such a shallow sense of the conditions under which men's thinking actually goes on seems to me most surprising. These critics
appear to suppose that, if left to itself, the rudderless raft of our
experience must be ready to drift anywhere or nowhere. Even tho
there were compasses on board, they seem to say, there would be
no pole for them to point to. There must be absolute sailing-
directions, they insist, decreed from outside, and an independent
chart of the voyage added to the 'mere' voyage itself, if we are ever
to make a port. But is it not obvious that even tho there be such
absolute sailing-directions in the shape of pre-human standards of
truth that we *ought* to follow, the only guarantee that we shall in
fact follow them must lie in our human equipment. The 'ought'
would be a *brutum fulmen* unless there were a felt grain inside of
our experience that conspired. As a matter of fact the devoutest
believers in absolute standards must admit that men fail to obey

them. Waywardness is here, in spite of the eternal prohibitions, and the existence of any amount of reality *ante rem* is no warrant against unlimited error *in rebus* being incurred. The only *real* guarantee we have against licentious thinking is the circumpressure of experience itself, which gets us sick of concrete errors, whether there be a trans-empirical reality or not. How does the partisan of absolute reality know what this orders him to think? He cannot get direct sight of the absolute; and he has no means of guessing what it wants of him except by following the humanistic clues. The only truth that he himself will ever practically *accept* will be that to which his finite experiences lead him of themselves. The state of mind which shudders at the idea of a lot of experiences left to themselves, and that augurs protection from the sheer name of an absolute, as if, however inoperative, that might still stand for a sort of ghostly security, is like the mood of those good people who, whenever they hear of a social tendency that is damnable, begin to redden and to puff, and say "Parliament or Congress ought to make a law against it," as if an impotent decree would give relief.

All the *sanctions* of a law of truth lie in the very texture of experience. Absolute or no absolute, the concrete truth *for us* will always be that way of thinking in which our various experiences most profitably combine.

And yet, the opponent obstinately urges, your humanist will always have a greater liberty to play fast and loose with truth than will your believer in an independent realm of reality that makes the standard rigid. If by this latter believer he means a man who pretends to know the standard and who fulminates it, the humanist will doubtless prove more flexible; but no more flexible than the absolutist himself if the latter follows (as fortunately our present-day absolutists do follow) empirical methods of inquiry in concrete affairs. To consider hypotheses is surely always better than to dogmatize *ins blaue hinein.*

Nevertheless this probable flexibility of temper in him has been used to convict the humanist of sin. Believing as he does, that truth lies *in rebus,* and is at every moment our own line of most propitious reaction, he stands forever debarred, as I have heard a learned colleague say, from trying to convert opponents, for does not their view, being *their* most propitious momentary reaction, already fill the bill? Only the believer in the *ante-rem* brand of truth can on this theory seek to make converts without self-stultification. But can there be self-stultification in urging any account whatever of truth? Can the definition ever contradict the deed? "Truth is what I feel like saying"—suppose that to be the definition. "Well, I feel like saying that, and I want you to feel like saying it, and shall continue to say it until I get you to agree." Where is there any contradiction? Whatever truth may be said to be, that is the kind of truth which the saying can be held to carry. The *temper* which a saying may comport is an extra-logical matter. It may indeed be hotter in some individual absolutist than in a humanist, but it need not be so in another. And the humanist, for his part, is perfectly consistent in compassing sea and land to make one proselyte, if his nature be enthusiastic enough.

"But how *can* you be enthusiastic over any view of things which you know to have been partly made by yourself, and which is liable to alter during the next minute? How is any heroic devotion to the ideal of truth possible under such paltry conditions?"

This is just another of those objections by which the anti-humanists show their own comparatively slack hold on the realities of the situation. If they would only follow the pragmatic method and ask: "What is truth *known* as? What does its existence stand for in the way of concrete goods?"—they would see that the name of it is the *inbegriff* of almost everything that is valuable in our lives. The true is the opposite of whatever is instable, of whatever is practically disappointing, of whatever is useless, of whatever is lying and unreliable, of whatever is unverifiable and unsupported, of whatever is inconsistent and contradictory, of whatever is artificial and eccentric, of whatever is unreal in the sense of being of no practical account. Here are pragmatic reasons with a vengeance why we should turn to truth—truth saves us from a world of that complexion. What wonder that its very name awakens loyal feelings! In particular what wonder that all little provisional fool's paradises of belief should appear contemptible in comparison with its bare pursuit! When absolutists reject humanism because they feel it to be untrue, that means that the whole habit of their mental needs is wedded already to a different view of reality, in comparison with which the humanistic world seems but the whim of a few irresponsible youths. Their own subjective apperceiving mass is what speaks here in the name of the eternal natures and bids them reject our humanism—as they apprehend it. Just so with us humanists, when we condemn all noble, clean-cut, fixed, eternal, rational, temple-like systems of philosophy. These contradict the *dramatic temperament* of nature, as our dealings with nature and our habits of thinking have so far brought us to conceive it. They seem oddly personal and artificial, even when not bureaucratic and professional in an absurd degree. We turn from them to the great unpent and unstayed wilderness of truth as we feel it to be constituted, with as good a conscience as rationalists are moved by when they turn from our wilderness into their neater and cleaner intellectual abodes.

This is surely enough to show that the humanist does not ignore the character of objectivity and independence in truth. Let me turn next to what his opponents mean when they say that to be true, our thoughts must 'correspond.'

The vulgar notion of correspondence here is that the thoughts must *copy* the reality—cognitio fit per *assimiliationem* cogniti et cognoscentis; and philosophy, without having ever fairly sat down to the question, seems to have instinctively accepted this idea: propositions are held true if they copy the eternal thought; terms are held true if they copy extra-mental realities. Implicitly, I think that the copy-theory has animated most of the criticisms that have been made on humanism.

A priori, however, it is not self-evident that the sole business of our mind with realities should be to copy them. Let my reader suppose himself to constitute for a time all the reality there is in the universe, and then to receive the announcement that another being is to be created who shall know him truly. How will he represent the knowing in advance? What will he hope it to be? I doubt extremely whether it could ever occur to him to fancy it as a mere copying. Of what use to him would an imperfect second edition of himself in the new comer's interior be? It would seem pure waste of a propitious opportunity. The demand would more probably be for something absolutely new. The reader would conceive the knowing humanistically, "the new comer," he would say, "must *take account of my presence by reacting on it in such a way that good would accrue to us both.* If copying be requisite to that end, let there be copying; otherwise not." The essence in any case would not be the copying, but the enrichment of the previous world. . . .

It seems obvious that the pragmatic account of all this routine of phenomenal knowledge is accurate. Truth here is a relation, not of our ideas to non-human realities, but of conceptual parts of our experience to sensational parts. Those thoughts are true which guide us to *beneficial interaction* with sensible particulars as they occur, whether they copy these in advance or not.

From the frequency of copying in the knowledge of phenomenal fact, copying has been supposed to be the essence of truth in matters rational also. Geometry and logic, it has been supposed, must copy archetypal thoughts in the Creator. But in these abstract spheres there is no need of assuming archetypes. The mind is free to carve so many figures out of space, to make so many numerical collections, to frame so many classes and series, and it can analyze and compare so endlessly, that the very superabundance of the resulting ideas makes us doubt the 'objective' pre-existence of their models. It would be plainly wrong to suppose a God whose thought consecrated rectangular but not polar co-ordinates, or Jevons's notation but not Boole's. Yet if, on the other hand, we assume God to have thought in advance of every *possible* flight of human fancy in these directions, his mind becomes too much like a Hindoo idol with three heads, eight arms and six breasts, too much made up of superfoetation and redundancy for us to wish to copy it, and the whole notion of copying tends to evaporate from these sciences. Their objects can be better interpreted as being created step by step by men, as fast as they successively conceive them.

If now it be asked how, if triangles, squares, square roots, genera, and the like, are but improvised human 'artefacts,' their properties and relations can be so promptly known to be 'eternal,' the humanistic answer is easy. If triangles and genera are of our own production we can keep them invariant. We can make them 'timeless' by expressly decreeing that on *the things we mean* time shall exert no altering effect, that they are intentionally and it may be fictitiously abstracted from every corrupting real associate and condition. But relations between invariant objects will themselves be invariant. Such relations cannot be happenings, for by hypothesis nothing shall happen to the objects. I have tried to show in the last chapter of my *Principles of Psychology* that they can only be relations of comparison. No one so far seems to have noticed my suggestion, and I am too ignorant of the development of mathematics to feel very confident of my own view. But if it were correct it would solve the difficulty perfectly. Relations of comparison are matters of direct inspection. As soon as mental objects are mentally compared, they are perceived to be either like or unlike. But once the same, always the same, once different, always different, under these timeless conditions. Which is as much as to say that truths concerning these man-made objects are necessary and eternal. We can change our conclusions only by changing our data first.

The whole fabric of the *a priori* sciences can thus be treated as a man-made product. As Locke long ago pointed out, these sciences have no immediate connection with fact. Only *if* a fact can be humanized by being identified with any of these ideal objects, is what was true of the objects now true also of the facts. The truth itself meanwhile was originally a copy of nothing; it was only a relation directly perceived to obtain between two artificial mental things.

We may now glance at some special types of knowing, so as to see better whether the humanistic account fits. On the mathematical and logical types we need not enlarge further, nor need we return at much length to the case of our descriptive knowledge of the course of nature. So far as this involves anticipation, tho that *may* mean copying, it need, as we saw, mean little more than 'getting ready' in advance. But with many distant and future objects, our practical relations are to the last degree potential and remote. In no sense can we now get ready for the arrest of the earth's revolution by the tidal brake, for instance; and with the past, tho we suppose ourselves to know it truly, we have no practical relations at all. It is obvious that, altho interests strictly practical have been the original starting-point of our search for true phenomenal descriptions, yet an intrinsic interest in the bare describing function has grown up. We wish accounts that shall be true, whether they bring collateral profit or not. The primitive function has developed its demand for mere exercise. This theoretic curiosity seems to be the characteristically human *differentia*, and humanism recognizes its enormous scope. A true idea now means not only one that prepares us for an actual perception. It means also one that might prepare us for a merely possible perception, or one that, if spoken, would suggest possible perceptions to others, or suggest actual perceptions which the speaker cannot share. The *ensemble* of perceptions thus thought of as either actual or possible form a system which it is obviously advantageous to us to get into a stable and consistent shape; and here it is that the common-sense notion of permanent beings finds triumphant use. Beings acting outside of the thinker explain, not only his actual perceptions, past and future, but his possible perceptions and those of every one else. Accordingly they gratify our theoretic need in a supremely beautiful way. We pass from our immediate actual through them into the foreign and the potential, and back again into the future actual, accounting for innumerable particulars by a single cause. As in those circular panoramas, where a real foreground of dirt, grass, bushes, rocks and a broken-down cannon is enveloped by a canvas picture of sky and earth and of a raging battle, continuing the foreground so cunningly that the spectator can detect no joint; so these conceptual objects, added to our present perceptual reality, fuse with it into the whole universe of our belief. In spite of all berkeleyan criticism, we do not doubt that they are really there. Tho our discovery of any one of them may only date from now, we unhesitatingly say that it not only *is*, but *was* there, if, by so saying, the past appears connected more consistently with what we feel the present to be. This is historic truth. Moses wrote the Pentateuch, we think, because if he didn't, all our religious habits will have to be undone. Julius Caesar was real, or we can never listen to history again. Trilobites were once alive, or all our thought about the strata is at sea. Radium, discovered only yesterday, must always have existed, or its analogy with other natural elements, which are permanent, fails. In all this, it is but one portion of our beliefs reacting on another so as to yield the most satisfactory total state of mind. That state of mind, we say, sees truth, and the content of its deliverances we believe.

Of course, if you take the satisfactoriness concretely, as something felt by you now, and if, by truth, you mean truth taken abstractly and verified in the long run, you cannot make them equate, for it is notorious that the temporarily satisfactory is often false. Yet at each and every concrete moment, truth for each man is what that man 'troweth' at that moment with the maximum of satisfaction to himself; and similarly, abstract truth, truth verified by the long run, and abstract satisfactoriness, long-run satisfactoriness, coincide. If, in short, we compare concrete with concrete and abstract with abstract, the true and the satisfactory do mean the same thing. I suspect that a certain muddling of matters hereabouts is what makes the general philosophic public so impervious to humanism's claims.

The fundamental fact about our experience is that it is a process of change. For the 'trower' at any moment, truth, like the visible area round a man walking in a fog, or like what George Eliot calls "the wall of dark seen by small fishes' eyes that pierce a span in the wide Ocean," is an objective field which the next moment enlarges and of which it is the critic, and which then either suffers alteration or is continued unchanged. The critic sees both the first trower's truth and his own truth, compares them with each other, and verifies or confutes. *His* field of view is the reality independent of that earlier trower's thinking with which that thinking ought to correspond. But the critic is himself only a trower; and if the whole process of experience should terminate at that instant, there would be no otherwise known independent reality with which *his* thought might be compared.

The immediate in experience is always provisionally in this situation. The humanism, for instance, which I see and try so hard to defend, is the completest truth attained from my point of view up to date. But, owing to the fact that all experience is a process, no point of view can ever be *the* last one. Every one is insufficient and off its balance, and responsible to later points of view than itself. You, occupying some of these later points in your own person, and believing in the reality of others, will not agree that my point of view sees truth positive, truth timeless, truth that counts, unless they verify and confirm what it sees.

You generalize this by saying that any opinion, however satisfactory, can count positively and absolutely as true only so far as it agrees with a standard beyond itself; and if you then forget that this standard perpetually grows up endogenously inside the web of the experiences, you may carelessly go on to say that what distributively holds of each experience, holds also collectively of all experience, and that experience as such and in its totality owes whatever truth it may be possessed-of to its correspondence with absolute realities outside of its own being. This evidently is the popular and traditional position. From the fact that finite experiences must draw support from one another, philosophers pass to the notion that experience *überhaupt* must need an absolute support. The denial of such a notion by humanism lies probably at the root of most of the dislike which it incurs.

But is this not the globe, the elephant and the tortoise over again? Must not something end by supporting itself? Humanism is willing to let finite experience be self-supporting. Somewhere being must immediately breast nonentity. Why may not the advancing front of experience, carrying its immanent satisfactions and dissatisfactions, cut against the black inane as the luminous orb of the moon cuts the caerulean abyss? Why should anywhere the world be absolutely fixed and finished? And if reality genuinely grows, why may it not grow in these very determinations which here and now are made?

In point of fact it actually seems to grow by our mental determinations, be these never so 'true.' Take the 'great bear' or 'dipper' constellation in the heavens. We call it by that name, we count the stars and call them seven, we say they were seven before they were counted, and we say that whether any one had ever noted the fact or not, the dim resemblance to a long-tailed (or long-necked?) animal was always truly there. But what do we mean by this projection into past eternity of recent human ways of thinking? Did an 'absolute' thinker actually do the counting, tell off the stars upon his standing number-tally, and make the bear-comparison, silly as the latter is? Were they explicitly seven, explicitly bear-like, before the human witness came? Surely nothing in the truth of the attributions drives us to think this. They were only implicitly or virtually what we call them, and we human witnesses first explicated them and made them 'real.' A fact virtually pre-exists when every condition of its realization save one is already there. In this case the condition lacking is the act of the counting and comparing mind. But the stars (once the mind considers them) themselves dictate the result. The counting in no wise modifies their previous nature, and, they being what and where they are, the count cannot fall out differently. It could then *always* be made. *Never* could the number seven be questioned, *if the question once were raised.*

We have here a quasi-paradox. Undeniably something comes by the counting that was not there before. And yet that something was *always true.* In one sense you create it, and in another sense you *find* it. You have to treat your count as being true beforehand, the moment you come to treat the matter at all.

Our stellar attributes must always be called true, then, yet none the less are they genuine additions made by our intellect to the world of fact. Not additions of consciousness only, but additions of 'content.' They copy nothing that pre-existed, yet they agree with what pre-existed, fit it, amplify it, relate and connect it with a 'wain,' a number-tally, or what not, and build it out. It seems to me that humanism is the only theory that builds this case out in the good direction, and this case stands for innumerable other kinds of case. In all such cases, odd as it may sound, our judgment may actually be said to retroact and to enrich the past.

Our judgments at any rate change the character of *future* reality by the acts to which they lead. Where these acts are acts expressive of trust—trust, *e.g.,* that a man is honest, that our health is good enough, or that we can make a successful effort—which acts may be a needed antecedent of the trusted things becoming true, Professor Taylor says that our trust is at any rate *untrue when it is made, i.e.,* before the action; and I seem to remember that he disposes of anything like a faith in the general excellence of the universe (making the faithful person's part in it at any rate more excellent) as a 'lie in the soul.' But the pathos of this expression should not blind us to the complication of the facts. I doubt whether Professor Taylor would himself be in favor of practically handling trusters of these kinds as liars. Future and present really mix in such emergencies, and one can always escape lies in them by using hypothetic forms. But Mr. Taylor's attitude suggests such absurd possibilities of practice that it seems to me to illustrate beautifully how self-stultifying the conception of a truth that shall merely register a standing fixture may become. Theoretic truth, truth of passive copying, sought in the sole interests of copying as such, not because copying is *good for something*, but because copying ought *schlechthin* to be, seems, if you look at it coldly, to be an almost preposterous ideal. Why should the universe, existing in itself, also exist in copies? How *can* it be copied in the solidity of its objective fulness? And even if it could, what would the motive be? "Even the hairs of your head are numbered." Doubtless they are, virtually; but why, as an absolute proposition, *ought* the number to become copied and known? Surely knowing is only one way of interacting with reality and adding to its effect.

The opponent here will ask: "Has not the knowing of truth any substantive value on its own account, apart from the collateral advantages it may bring? And if you allow theoretic satisfactions to exist at all, do they not crowd the collateral satisfactions out of house and home, and must not pragmatism go into bankruptcy, if she admits them at all?" The destructive force of such talk disappears as soon as we use words concretely instead of abstractly, and ask, in our quality of good pragmatists, just what the famous theoretic needs are known-as and in what the intellectual satisfactions consist.

Are they not all mere matters of *consistency*—and emphatically *not* of consistency between an absolute reality and the mind's copies of it, but of actually felt consistency among judgments, objects, and habits of reacting, in the mind's own experienceable world? And are not both our need of such consistency and our pleasure in it conceivable as outcomes of the natural fact that we are beings that do develop mental *habits*—habit itself proving adaptively beneficial in an environment where the same objects, or the same kinds of objects, recur and follow 'law'? If this were so, what would have come first would have been the collateral profits of habit as such, and the theoretic life would have grown up in aid of these. In point of fact, this seems to have been the probable case. At life's origin, any present perception may have been 'true' —if such a word could then be applicable. Later, when reactions became organized, the reactions became 'true' whenever expectation was fulfilled by them. Otherwise they were 'false' or 'mistaken' reactions. But the same class of objects needs the same kind of reaction, so the impulse to react consistently must gradually have been established, and a disappointment felt whenever the results frustrated expectation. Here is a perfectly plausible germ for all our higher consistencies. Nowadays, if an object claims from us a reaction of the kind habitually accorded only to the opposite class of objects, our mental machinery refuses to run smoothly. The situation is intellectually unsatisfactory.

Theoretic truth thus falls *within* the mind, being the accord of some of its processes and objects with other processes and objects— 'accord' consisting here in well-definable relations. So long as the satisfaction of feeling such an accord is denied us, whatever collateral profits may seem to inure from what we believe in are but as dust in the balance—provided always that we are highly organized intellectually, which the majority of us are not. The amount of accord which satisfies most men and women is merely the absence of violent clash between their usual thoughts and statements and the limited sphere of sense-perceptions in which their lives are cast. The theoretic truth that most of us think we 'ought' to attain to is thus the possession of a set of predicates that do not explicitly contradict their subjects. We preserve it as often as not by leaving other predicates and subjects out.

In some men theory is a passion, just as music is in others. The form of inner consistency is pursued far beyond the line at which collateral profits stop. Such men systematize and classify and schematize and make synoptical tables and invent ideal objects for the pure love of unifying. Too often the results, glowing with 'truth' for the inventors, seem pathetically personal and artificial to bystanders. Which is as much as to say that the purely theoretic criterion of truth can leave us in the lurch as easily as any other criterion, and that the absolutists, for all their pretensions, are 'in the same boat' concretely with those whom they attack.

I am well aware that this paper has been rambling in the extreme. But the whole subject is inductive, and sharp logic is hardly yet in order. My great trammel has been the non-existence of any definitely stated alternative on my opponents' part. It may conduce to clearness if I recapitulate, in closing, what I conceive the main points of humanism to be. They are these:

1. An experience, perceptual or conceptual, must conform to reality in order to be true.

2. By 'reality' humanism means nothing more than the other conceptual or perceptual experiences with which a given present experience may find itself in point of fact mixed up.[2]

3. By 'conforming,' humanism means taking account-of in such a way as to gain any intellectually and practically satisfactory result.

4. To 'take account-of' and to be 'satisfactory' are terms that admit of no definition, so many are the ways in which these requirements can practically be worked out.

5. Vaguely and in general, we take account of a reality by *preserving* it in as unmodified a form as possible. But, to be then satisfactory, it must not contradict other realities outside of it which claim also to be preserved. That we must preserve all the experience we can and minimize contradiction in what we preserve, is about all that can be said in advance.

6. The truth which the conforming experience embodies may be a positive addition to the previous reality, and later judgments may have to conform to *it*. Yet, virtually at least, it may have been true previously. Pragmatically, virtual and actual truth mean the same thing: the possibility of only one answer, *when once the question is raised.*

2. This is meant merely to exclude reality of an 'unknowable' sort, of which no account in either perceptual or conceptual terms can be given. It includes of course any amount of empirical reality independent of the knower. Pragmatism is thus 'epistemologically' realistic in its account.

9.

A Dialogue*

I imagine a residual state of mind on the part of my reader which
may still keep him unconvinced, and which it may be my duty to
try at least to dispel. I can perhaps be briefer if I put what I have
to say in dialogue form. Let then the anti-pragmatist begin:

Anti-Pragmatist:—You say that the truth of an idea is constituted by its workings. Now suppose a certain state of facts, facts for
example of antediluvian planetary history, concerning which the
question may be asked: "Shall the truth about them ever be
known?" And suppose (leaving the hypothesis of an omniscient
absolute out of the account) that we assume that the truth is never
to be known. I ask you now, brother pragmatist, whether according to you there can be said to be any truth at all about such a
state of facts. Is there a truth, or is there not a truth, in cases where
at any rate it never comes to be known?

Pragmatist:—Why do you ask me such a question?

Anti-Prag.:—Because I think it puts you in a bad dilemma.

Prag.:—How so?

Anti-Prag.:—Why, because if on the one hand you elect to say
that there is a truth, you thereby surrender your whole pragmatist
theory. According to that theory, truth requires ideas and workings to constitute it; but in the present instance there is supposed
to be no knower, and consequently neither ideas nor workings can
exist. What then remains for you to make your truth of?

Prag.:—Do you wish, like so many of my enemies, to force me to
make the truth out of the reality itself? I cannot: the truth is
something known, thought or said about the reality, and consequently numerically additional to it. But probably your intent is
something different; so before I say which horn of your dilemma I
choose, I ask you to let me hear what the other horn may be.

* From *The Meaning of Truth.*

Anti-Prag.:—The other horn is this, that if you elect to say that there is *no* truth under the conditions assumed, because there are no ideas or workings, then you fly in the face of common sense. Doesn't common sense believe that every state of facts must in the nature of things be truly statable in some kind of a proposition, even tho in point of fact the proposition should never be propounded by a living soul?

Prag.:—Unquestionably common sense believes this, and so do I. There have been innumerable events in the history of our planet of which nobody ever has been or ever will be able to give an account, yet of which it can already be said abstractly that only one sort of possible account can ever be true. The truth about any such event is thus already generically predetermined by the event's nature; and one may accordingly say with a perfectly good conscience that it virtually pre-exists. Common sense is thus right in its instinctive contention.

Anti-Prag.:—Is this then the horn of the dilemma which you stand for? Do you say that there is a truth even in cases where it shall never be known?

Prag.:—Indeed I do, provided you let me hold consistently to my own conception of truth, and do not ask me to abandon it for something which I find impossible to comprehend. You also believe, do you not, that there is a truth, even in cases where it never shall be known?

Anti-Prag.:—I do indeed believe so.

Prag.:—Pray then inform me in what, according to you, this truth regarding the unknown consists.

Anti-Prag.:—Consists?—pray what do you mean by 'consists'? It consists in nothing but itself, or more properly speaking it has neither consistence nor existence, it obtains, it *holds*.

Prag.:—Well, what relation does it bear to the reality of which it holds?

Anti-Prag.:—How do you mean, 'what relation'? It holds *of* it, of course; it knows it, it represents it.

Prag.:—Who knows it? What represents it?

Anti-Prag.:—The truth does; the truth knows it; or rather not exactly that, but any one knows it who *possesses* the truth. Any true idea of the reality *represents* the truth concerning it.

Prag.:—But I thought that we had agreed that no knower of it, nor any idea representing it was to be supposed.

Anti-Prag.:—Sure enough!

Prag.:—Then I beg you again to tell me in what this truth consists, all by itself, this *tertium quid* intermediate between the facts *per se,* on the one hand, and all knowledge of them, actual or potential, on the other. What is the shape of it in this third estate? Of what stuff, mental, physical, or 'epistemological,' is it built? What metaphysical region of reality does it inhabit?

Anti-Prag.:—What absurd questions! Isn't it enough to say that it *is true* that the facts are so-and-so, and false that they are otherwise?

Prag.:—'*It*' is true that the facts are so-and-so—I won't yield to the temptation of asking you *what* is true; but I do ask you whether your phrase that 'it is true that' the facts are so-and-so really means anything really additional to the bare *being* so-and-so of the facts themselves.

Anti-Prag.:—It seems to mean more than the bare being of the facts. It is a sort of mental equivalent for them, their epistemological function, their value in noetic terms.

Prag.:—A sort of spiritual double or ghost of them, apparently! If so, may I ask you *where* this truth is found.

Anti-Prag.:—Where? where? There is no 'where'—it simply obtains, absolutely obtains.

Prag.:—Not in any one's mind?

Anti-Prag.:—No, for we agreed that no actual knower of the truth should be assumed.

Prag.:—No actual knower, I agree. But are you sure that no notion of a potential or ideal knower has anything to do with forming this strangely elusive idea of the truth of the facts in your mind?

Anti-Prag.:—Of course if there be a truth concerning the facts, that truth is what the ideal knower would know. To that extent you can't keep the notion of it and the notion of him separate. But it is not him first and then it; it is it first and then him, in my opinion.

Prag.:—But you still leave me terribly puzzled as to the status of this so-called truth, hanging as it does between earth and heaven, between reality and knowledge, grounded in the reality, yet numerically additional to it, and at the same time antecedent to any knower's opinion and entirely independent thereof. Is it as independent of the knower as you suppose? It looks to me terribly dubious, as if it might be only another name for a potential as distinguished from an actual knowledge of the reality. Isn't your truth, after all, simply what any successful knower *would* have to know *in case he existed?* And in a universe where no knowers were even conceivable would any truth about the facts there as something numerically distinguishable from the facts themselves, find a place to exist in? To me such truth would not only be non-existent, it would be unimaginable, inconceivable.

Anti-Prag.:—But I thought you said a while ago that there *is* a truth of past events, even tho no one shall ever know it.

Prag.:—Yes, but you must remember that I also stipulated for permission to define the word in my own fashion. The truth of an event, past, present, or future, is for me only another name for the fact that *if* the event ever *does* get known, the nature of the knowledge is already to some degree predetermined. The truth which precedes actual knowledge of a fact means only what any possible knower of the fact will eventually find himself necessitated to believe about it. He must believe something that will bring him into satisfactory relations with it, that will prove a decent mental substitute for it. What this something may be is of course partly fixed already by the nature of the fact and by the sphere of its associations.

This seems to me all that you can clearly mean when you say that truth pre-exists to knowledge. It is knowledge anticipated, knowledge in the form of possibility merely.

Anti-Prag.:—But what does the knowledge know when it comes? Doesn't it know the *truth?* And, if so, mustn't the truth be distinct from either the fact or the knowledge?

Prag.:—It seems to me that what the knowledge knows is the fact itself, the event, or whatever the reality may be. Where you see three distinct entities in the field, the reality, the knowing, and the truth, I see only two. Moreover, I can see what each of my two entities is *known-as,* but when I ask myself what your third entity, the truth, is known-as, I can find nothing distinct from the reality on the one hand, and the ways in which it may be known on the other. Are you not probably misled by common language, which has found it convenient to introduce a hybrid name, meaning sometimes a kind of knowing and sometimes a reality known, to apply to either of these things interchangeably? And has philosophy anything to gain by perpetuating and consecrating the ambiguity? If you call the object of knowledge 'reality,' and call the manner of its being cognized 'truth,' cognized moreover on particular occasions, and variously, by particular human beings who have their various businesses with it, and if you hold consistently to this nomenclature, it seems to me that you escape all sorts of trouble.

Anti-Prag.:—Do you mean that you think you escape from my dilemma?

Prag.:—Assuredly I escape; for if truth and knowledge are terms correlative and interdependent, as I maintain they are, then wherever knowledge is conceivable truth is conceivable, wherever knowledge is possible truth is possible, wherever knowledge is actual truth is actual. Therefore when you point your first horn at me, I think of truth *actual,* and say it doesn't exist. It doesn't; for by hypothesis there is no knower, no ideas, no workings. I agree, however, that truth *possible* or *virtual* might exist, for a knower might possibly be brought to birth; and truth *conceivable* certainly exists, for, abstractly taken, there is nothing in the nature of antediluvian events that should make the application of knowledge to them inconceivable. Therefore when you try to impale me on your second horn, I think of the truth in question as a mere abstract possibility, so I say it does exist, and side with common sense.

Do not these distinctions rightly relieve me from embarrassment? And don't you think it might help you to make them yourself?

Anti-Prag.:—Never!—so avaunt with your abominable hair-splitting and sophistry! Truth is truth; and never will I degrade it by identifying it with low pragmatic particulars in the way you propose.

Prag.:—Well, my dear antagonist, I hardly hoped to convert an eminent intellectualist and logician like you; so enjoy, as long as you live, your own ineffable conception. Perhaps the rising generation will grow up more accustomed than you are to that concrete and empirical interpretation of terms in which the pragmatic method consists. Perhaps they may then wonder how so harmless and natural an account of truth as mine could have found such difficulty in entering the minds of men far more intelligent than I can ever hope to become, but wedded by education and tradition to the abstractionist manner of thought.

10.

Address at the Emerson Centenary in Concord*

The pathos of death is this, that when the days of one's life are
ended, those days that were so crowded with business and felt so
heavy in their passing, what remains of one in memory should
usually be so slight a thing. The phantom of an attitude, the echo
of a certain mode of thought, a few pages of print, some invention,
or some victory we gained in a brief critical hour, are all that can
survive the best of us. It is as if the whole of a man's significance
had now shrunk into the phantom of an attitude, into a mere
musical note or phrase suggestive of his singularity—happy are
those whose singularity gives a note so clear as to be victorious
over the inevitable pity of such a diminution and abridgment.

An ideal wraith like this, of Emerson's personality, hovers over
all Concord to-day, taking, in the minds of those of you who were
his neighbors and intimates a somewhat fuller shape, remaining
more abstract in the younger generation, but bringing home to all
of us the notion of a spirit indescribably precious. The form that
so lately moved upon these streets and country roads, or awaited
in these fields and woods the beloved Muse's visits, is now dust;
but the soul's note, the spiritual voice, rises strong and clear above
the uproar of the times, and seems securely destined to exert an
ennobling influence over future generations.

What gave a flavor so matchless to Emerson's individuality was,
even more than his rich mental gifts, their singularly harmonious
combination. Rarely has a man so accurately known the limits of
his genius or so unfailingly kept within them. "Stand by your
order," he used to say to youthful students; and perhaps the
paramount impression one gets of his life is of his loyalty to his

---

* An Address delivered at the Centenary of the Birth of Ralph Waldo
Emerson in Concord, Mass., May 25, 1903, and printed in the published proceedings of that meeting.

own personal type and mission. The type was that of what he liked
to call the scholar, the perceiver of pure truth; and the mission was
that of the reporter in worthy form of each perception. The day is
good, he said, in which we have the most perceptions. There are
times when the cawing of a crow, a weed, a snowflake, or a farmer
planting in his field become symbols to the intellect of truths
equal to those which the most majestic phenomena can open. Let
me mind my own charge, then, walk alone, consult the sky, the
field and forest, sedulously waiting every morning for the news
concerning the structure of the universe which the good Spirit will
give me.

This was the first half of Emerson, but only half; for genius, as
he said, is insatiate for expression, and truth has to be clad in the
right verbal garment. The form of the garment was so vital with
Emerson that it is impossible to separate it from the matter. They
form a chemical combination—thoughts which would be trivial
expressed otherwise, are important through the nouns and verbs to
which he married them. The style is the man, it has been said; the
man Emerson's mission culminated in his style, and if we must
define him in one word, we have to call him Artist. He was an
artist whose medium was verbal and who wrought in spiritual
material.

This duty of spiritual seeing and reporting determined the
whole tenor of his life. It was to shield this duty from invasion and
distraction that he dwelt in the country, that he consistently de-
clined to entangle himself with associations or to encumber himself with functions which, however he might believe in them, he
felt were duties for other men and not for him. Even the care of
his garden, "with its stoopings and fingerings in a few yards of
space," he found "narrowing and poisoning," and took to long
free walks and saunterings instead, without apology. "Causes"
innumerable sought to enlist him as their "worker"—all got his
smile and word of sympathy, but none entrapped him into service.
The struggle against slavery itself, deeply as it appealed to him,
found him firm: "God must govern his own world, and knows his
way out of this pit without my desertion of my post, which has
none to guard it but me. I have quite other slaves to face than
those Negroes, to wit, imprisoned thoughts far back in the brain of
man, and which have no watchman or lover or defender but me."

This in reply to the possible questions of his own conscience. To hot-blooded moralists with more objective ideas of duty, such a fidelity to the limits of his genius must often have made him seem provokingly remote and unavailable; but we, who can see things in more liberal perspective, must unqualifiably approve the results. The faultless tact with which he kept his safe limits while he so dauntlessly asserted himself within them, is an example fitted to give heart to other theorists and artists the world over.

The insight and creed from which Emerson's life followed can be best summed up in his own verses:

> So nigh is grandeur to our dust,
> So near is God to man!

Through the individual fact there ever shone for him the effulgence of the Universal Reason. The great Cosmic Intellect terminates and houses itself in mortal men and passing hours. Each of us is an angle of its eternal vision, and the only way to be true to our Maker is to be loyal to ourselves. "O rich and various Man!" he cries, "thou palace of sight and sound, carrying in thy senses the morning and the night and the unfathomable galaxy; in thy brain the geometry of the city of God; in thy heart the bower of love and the realms of right and wrong."

If the individual open thus directly into the Absolute, it follows that there is something in each and all of us, even the lowliest, that ought not to consent to borrowing traditions and living at second hand. "If John was perfect, why are you and I alive?" Emerson writes; "As long as any man exists there is some need of him; let him fight for his own." This faith that in a life at first hand there is something sacred is perhaps the most characteristic note in Emerson's writings. The hottest side of him is this nonconformist persuasion, and if his temper could ever verge on common irascibility, it would be by reason of the passionate character of his feelings on this point. The world is still new and untried. In seeing freshly, and not in hearing of what others saw, shall a man find what truth is. "Each one of us can bask in the great morning which rises out of the Eastern Sea, and be himself one of the children of the light." "Trust thyself, every heart vibrates to that iron string. There is a time in each man's education when he must arrive at the conviction that imitation is suicide; when he must take himself for better or worse as his portion; and know that though the wide universe is full of good, no kernel of nourishing corn can come to him but through his toil bestowed on that plot of ground which it was given him to till."

The matchless eloquence with which Emerson proclaimed the sovereignty of the living individual electrified and emancipated his generation, and his bugle-blast will doubtless be regarded by future critics as the soul of his message. The present man is the aboriginal reality, the Institution is derivative, and the past man is irrelevant and obliterate for present issues. "If anyone would lay an axe to your tree with a text from 1 John, v, 7, or a sentence from Saint Paul, say to him," Emerson wrote, " 'My tree is Yggdrasil, the tree of life.' Let him know by your security that your conviction is clear and sufficient, and, if he were Paul himself, that you also are here and with your Creator." "Cleave ever to God," he insisted, "against the name of God"; and so, in spite of the intensely religious character of his total thought, when he began his career it seemed to many of his brethren in the clerical profession that he was little more than an iconoclast and desecrator.

Emerson's belief that the individual must in reason be adequate to the vocation for which the Spirit of the world has called him into being, is the source of those sublime pages, hearteners and sustainers of our youth, in which he urges his hearers to be incorruptibly true to their own private conscience. Nothing can harm the man who rests in his appointed place and character. Such a man is invulnerable; he balances the universe, balances it as much by keeping small when he is small, as by being great and spreading when he is great. "I love and honor Epaminondas," said Emerson, "but I do not wish to be Epaminondas. I hold it more just to love the world of this hour than the world of his hour. Nor can you, if I am true, excite me to the least uneasiness by saying, 'He acted and thou sittest still.' I see action to be good when the need is, and sitting still to be also good. Epaminondas, if he was the man I take him for, would have sat still with joy and peace, if his lot had been mine. Heaven is large, and affords space for all modes of love and fortitude." "The fact that I am here certainly shows me that the Soul has need of an organ here, and shall I not assume the post?"

The vanity of all superserviceableness and pretence was never more happily set forth than by Emerson in the many passages in which he develops this aspect of his philosophy. Character infallibly proclaims itself. "Hide your thoughts!—hide the sun and moon. They publish themselves to the universe. They will speak through you though you were dumb. They will flow out of your actions, your manners and your face. . . . Don't say things: What you are stands over you the while and thunders so that I cannot say what you say to the contrary. . . . What a man *is* engraves itself upon him in letters of light. Concealment avails him nothing, boasting nothing. There is confession in the glances of our eyes; in our smiles; in salutations; and the grasp of hands. His sin bedaubs him, mars all his good impression. Men know not why they do not trust him, but they do not trust him. His vice glasses the eye, casts lines of mean expression in the cheek, pinches the nose, sets the mark of the beast upon the back of the head, and writes, O fool! fool! on the forehead of a king. If you would not be known to do a thing, never do it; a man may play the fool in the drifts of a desert, but every grain of sand shall seem to see.—How can a man be concealed? How can he be concealed?"

On the other hand, never was a sincere word or a sincere thought utterly lost. "Never a magnanimity fell to the ground but there is some heart to greet and accept it unexpectedly. . . . The hero fears not that if he withstood the avowal of a just and brave act, it will go unwitnessed and unloved. One knows it—himself—and is pledged by it to sweetness of peace and to nobleness of aim, which will prove in the end a better proclamation than the relating of the incident."

The same indefeasible right to be exactly what one is, provided one only be authentic, spreads itself, in Emerson's way of thinking, from persons to things and to times and places. No date, no position is insignificant, if the life that fills it out be only genuine:

"In solitude, in a remote village, the ardent youth loiters and mourns. With inflamed eye, in this sleeping wilderness, he has read the story of the Emperor, Charles the Fifth, until his fancy has brought home to the surrounding woods the faint roar of cannonades in the Milanese, and marches in Germany. He is curious concerning that man's day. What filled it? The crowded orders, the stern decisions, the foreign despatches, the Castilian etiquette? The soul answers—Behold his day here! In the sighing of these woods, in the quiet of these gray fields, in the cool breeze that sings out of these northern mountains; in the workmen, the boys, the maidens you meet—in the hopes of the morning, the *ennui* of noon, and sauntering of the afternoon; in the disquieting comparisons; in the regrets at want of vigor; in the great idea and the puny execution—behold Charles the Fifth's day; another, yet the same; behold Chatham's, Hampden's, Bayard's, Alfred's, Scipio's, Pericles's day—day of all that are born of women. The difference of circumstance is merely costume. I am tasting the self-same life—its sweetness, its greatness, its pain, which I so admire in other men. Do not foolishly ask of the inscrutable, obliterated past what it cannot tell—the details of that nature, of that day, called Byron or Burke; but ask it of the enveloping Now. . . . Be lord of a day, and you can put up your history books."

"The deep to-day which all men scorn" receives thus from Emerson superb revindication. "Other world! there is no other world." All God's life opens into the individual particular, and here and now, or nowhere, is reality. "The present hour is the decisive hour, and every day is doomsday."

Such a conviction that Divinity is everywhere may easily make of one an optimist of the sentimental type that refuses to speak ill of anything. Emerson's drastic perception of differences kept him at the opposite pole from this weakness. After you have seen men a few times, he could say, you find most of them as alike as their barns and pantries, and soon as musty and as dreary. Never was such a fastidious lover of significance and distinction, and never an eye so keen for their discovery. His optimism had nothing in common with that indiscriminate hurrahing for the Universe with which Walt Whitman has made us familiar. For Emerson, the individual fact and moment were indeed suffused with absolute radiance, but it was upon a condition that saved the situation— they must be worthy specimens—sincere, authentic, archetypal; they must have made connection with what he calls the Moral Sentiment, they must in some way act as symbolic mouthpieces of the Universe's meaning. To know just which thing does act in this way, and which thing fails to make the true connection, is the secret (somewhat incommunicable, it must be confessed) of seer-ship, and doubtless we must not expect of the seer too rigorous a consistency. Emerson himself was a real seer. He could perceive the full squalor of the individual fact, but he could also see the transfiguration. He might easily have found himself saying of some present-day agitator against our Philippine conquest what he said of this or that reformer of his own time. He might have called him, as a private person, a tedious bore and canter. But he would infallibly have added what he then added: "It is strange and horrible to say this, for I feel that under him and his partiality and exclusiveness is the earth and the sea, and all that in them is, and the axis round which the Universe revolves passes through his body where he stands."

Be it how it may, then, this is Emerson's revelation: The point of any pen can be an epitome of reality; the commonest person's act, if genuinely actuated, can lay hold on eternity. This vision is the headspring of all his outpourings; and it is for this truth, given to no previous literary artist to express in such penetratingly persuasive tones, that posterity will reckon him a prophet, and, perhaps neglecting other pages, piously turn to those that convey this message. His life was one long conversation with the invisible divine, expressing itself through individuals and particulars: "So nigh is grandeur to our dust, so near is God to man!"

I spoke of how shrunken the wraith, how thin the echo, of men is after they are departed. Emerson's wraith comes to me now as if it were but the very voice of this victorious argument. His words to this effect are certain to be quoted and extracted more and more as time goes on, and to take their place among the Scriptures of humanity. " 'Gainst death and all oblivious enmity, shall you pace forth," beloved Master. As long as our English language lasts men's hearts will be cheered and their souls strengthened and liberated by the noble and musical pages with which you have enriched it.

11.

The Moral Philosopher and the Moral Life*

The main purpose of this paper is to show that there is no such thing possible as an ethical philosophy dogmatically made up in advance. We all help to determine the content of ethical philosophy so far as we contribute to the race's moral life. In other words, there can be no final truth in ethics any more than in physics, until the last man has had his experience and said his say. In the one case as in the other, however, the hypotheses which we now make while waiting, and the acts to which they prompt us, are among the indispensable conditions which determine what that 'say' shall be.

First of all, what is the position of him who seeks an ethical philosophy? To begin with, he must be distinguished from all those who are satisfied to be ethical sceptics. He *will* not be a sceptic; therefore so far from ethical scepticism being one possible fruit of ethical philosophizing, it can only be regarded as that residual alternative to all philosophy which from the outset menaces every would-be philosopher who may give up the quest discouraged, and renounce his original aim. That aim is to find an account of the moral relations that obtain among things, which will weave them into the unity of a stable system, and make of the world what one may call a genuine universe from the ethical point of view. So far as the world resists reduction to the form of unity, so far as ethical propositions seem unstable, so far does the philosopher fail of his ideal. The subject-matter of his study is the ideals he finds existing in the world; the purpose which guides him is this ideal of his own, of getting them into a certain form. This

* An address to the Yale Philosophical Club, published in the *International Journal of Ethics* (April, 1891). Reprinted in *The Will to Believe*. Section III on casuistry is here deleted. [B.W.]

ideal is thus a factor in ethical philosophy whose legitimate presence must never be overlooked; it is a positive contribution which the philosopher himself necessarily makes to the problem. But it is his only positive contribution. At the outset of his inquiry he ought to have no other ideals. Were he interested peculiarly in the triumph of any one kind of good, he would *pro tanto* cease to be a judicial investigator, and become an advocate for some limited element of the case.

There are three questions in ethics which must be kept apart. Let them be called respectively the *psychological* question, the *metaphysical* question, and the *casuistic* question. The psychological question asks after the historical *origin* of our moral ideas and judgments; the metaphysical question asks what the very *meaning* of the words 'good,' 'ill,' and 'obligation' are; the casuistic question asks what is the *measure* of the various goods and ills which men recognize, so that the philosopher may settle the true order of human obligations.

I

The psychological question is for most disputants the only question. When your ordinary doctor of divinity has proved to his own satisfaction that an altogether unique faculty called 'conscience' must be postulated to tell us what is right and what is wrong, or when your popular-science enthusiast has proclaimed that 'apriorism' is an exploded superstition, and that our moral judgments have gradually resulted from the teaching of the environment, each of these persons thinks that ethics is settled and nothing more is to be said. The familiar pair of names, Intuitionist and Evolutionist, so commonly used now to connote all possible differences in ethical opinion, really refer to the psychological question alone. The discussion of this question hinges so much upon particular details that it is impossible to enter upon it at all within the limits of this paper. I will therefore only express dogmatically my own belief, which is this—that the Benthams, the Mills, and the Bains have done a lasting service in taking so many of our human ideals and showing how they must have arisen from the association with acts of simple bodily pleasures and reliefs from pain. Association with many remote pleasures will unquestionably make a thing significant of goodness in our minds; and the more vaguely the goodness is conceived of, the more mysterious will its source appear to be. But it is surely impossible to explain all our sentiments and preferences in this simple way. The more minutely psychology studies human nature, the more clearly it finds there traces of secondary affections, relating the impressions of the environment with one another and with our impulses in quite different ways from those mere associations of coexistence and succession which are practically all that pure empiricism can admit. Take the love of drunkenness; take bashfulness, the terror of high places, the tendency to seasickness, to faint at the sight of blood, the susceptibility to musical sounds; take the emotion of the comical, the passion for poetry, for mathematics, or for metaphysics—no one of these things can be wholly explained by either association or utility. They *go with* other things that can be so explained, no doubt; and some of them are prophetic of future utilities, since there is nothing in us for which some use may not be found. But their origin is in incidental complications to our cerebral structure, a structure whose original features arose with no reference to the perception of such discords and harmonies as these.

Well, a vast number of our moral perceptions also are certainly of this secondary and brain-born kind. They deal with directly felt fitnesses between things, and often fly in the teeth of all the prepossessions of habit and presumptions of utility. The moment you get beyond the coarser and more commonplace moral maxims, the Decalogues and Poor Richard's Almanacs, you fall into schemes and positions which to the eye of common-sense are fantastic and over-strained. The sense for abstract justice which some persons have is as excentric a variation, from the natural-history point of view, as is the passion for music or for the higher philosophical consistencies which consumes the soul of others. The feeling of the inward dignity of certain spiritual attitudes, as peace, serenity, simplicity, veracity; and of the essential vulgarity of others, as querulousness, anxiety, egoistic fussiness, etc., are quite inexplicable except by an innate preference of the more ideal attitude for its own pure sake. The nobler thing *tastes* better, and that is all that we can say. 'Experience' of consequences may truly teach us what things are *wicked,* but what have consequences to do with what is *mean* and *vulgar?* If a man has shot his wife's paramour, by reason of what subtle repugnancy in things is it that we are so disgusted when we hear that the wife and the husband have made it up and are living comfortably together again? Or if the hypothesis were offered us of a world in which Messrs. Fourier's and Bellamy's and Morris's utopias should all be outdone, and millions kept permanently happy on the one simple condition that a certain lost soul on the far-off edge of things should lead a life of lonely torture, what except a specific and independent sort of emotion can it be which would make us immediately feel, even though an impulse arose within us to clutch at the happiness so offered, how hideous a thing would be its enjoyment when deliberately accepted as the fruit of such a bargain? To what, once more, but subtle brain-born feelings of discord can be due all these recent protests against the entire race-tradition of retributive justice? I refer to Tolstoï with his ideas of non-resistance, to Mr. Bellamy with his substitution of oblivion for repentance (in his novel of Dr. Heidenhain's Process), to M. Guyau with his radical condemnation of the punitive ideal. All these subtileties of the moral sensibility go as much beyond what can be ciphered out from the 'laws of association' as the delicacies of sentiment possible between a pair of young lovers go beyond such precepts of the "etiquette to be observed during engagement" as are printed in manuals of social form.

No! Purely inward forces are certainly at work here. All the higher, more penetrating ideals are revolutionary. They present themselves far less in the guise of effects of past experience than in that of probable causes of future experience, factors to which the environment and the lessons it has so far taught us must learn to bend.

This is all I can say of the psychological question now. In the last chapter of a recent work,[1] I have sought to prove in a general way the existence, in our thought, of relations which do not merely repeat the couplings of experience. Our ideals have certainly many sources. They are not all explicable as signifying

1. *The Principles of Psychology.*

corporeal pleasures to be gained, and pains to be escaped. And for having so constantly perceived this psychological fact, we must applaud the intuitionist school. Whether or not such applause must be extended to that school's other characteristics will appear as we take up the following questions.

The next one in order is the metaphysical question, of what we mean by the words 'obligation,' 'good,' and 'ill.'

II

First of all, it appears that such words can have no application or relevancy in a world in which no sentient life exists. Imagine an absolutely material world, containing only physical and chemical facts, and existing from eternity without a God, without even an interested spectator: would there be any sense in saying of that world that one of its states is better than another? Or if there were two such worlds possible, would there be any rhyme or reason in calling one good and the other bad—good or bad positively, I mean, and apart from the fact that one might relate itself better than the other to the philosopher's private interests? But we must leave these private interests out of the account, for the philosopher is a mental fact, and we are asking whether goods and evils and obligations exist in physical facts *per se.* Surely there is no *status* for good and evil to exist in, in a purely insentient world. How can one physical fact, considered simply as a physical fact, be 'better' than another? Betterness is not a physical relation. In its mere material capacity, a thing can no more be good or bad than it can be pleasant or painful. Good for what? Good for the production of another physical fact, do you say? But what in a purely physical universe demands the production of that other fact? Physical facts simply *are* or are *not;* and neither when present or absent, can they be supposed to make demands. If they do, they can only do so by having desires; and then they have ceased to be purely physical facts, and have become facts of conscious sensibility. Goodness, badness, and obligation must be *realized* somewhere in order really to exist; and the first step in ethical philosophy is to see that no merely inorganic 'nature of things' can realize them. Neither moral relations nor the moral law can swing *in vacuo.*

Their only habitat can be a mind which feels them; and no world composed of merely physical facts can possibly be a world to which ethical propositions apply.

The moment one sentient being, however, is made a part of the universe, there is a chance for goods and evils really to exist. Moral relations now have their *status*, in that being's consciousness. So far as he feels anything to be good, he *makes* it good. It *is* good, for him; and being good for him, is absolutely good, for he is the sole creator of values in that universe, and outside of his opinion things have no moral character at all.

In such a universe as that it would of course be absurd to raise the question of whether the solitary thinker's judgments of good and ill are true or not. Truth supposes a standard outside of the thinker to which he must conform; but here the thinker is a sort of divinity, subject to no higher judge. Let us call the supposed universe which he inhabits a *moral solitude*. In such a moral solitude it is clear that there can be no outward obligation, and that the only trouble the god-like thinker is liable to have will be over the consistency of his own several ideals with one another. Some of these will no doubt be more pungent and appealing than the rest, their goodness will have a profounder, more penetrating taste; they will return to haunt him with more obstinate regrets if violated. So the thinker will have to order his life with them as its chief determinants, or else remain inwardly discordant and unhappy. Into whatever equilibrium he may settle, though, and however he may straighten out his system, it will be a right system; for beyond the facts of his own subjectivity there is nothing moral in the world.

If now we introduce a second thinker with his likes and dislikes into the universe, the ethical situation becomes much more complex, and several possibilities are immediately seen to obtain.

One of these is that the thinkers may ignore each other's attitude about good and evil altogether, and each continue to indulge his own preferences, indifferent to what the other may feel or do. In such a case we have a world with twice as much of the ethical quality in it as our moral solitude, only it is without ethical unity. The same object is good or bad there, according as you measure it by the view which this one or that one of the thinkers takes. Nor can you find any possible ground in such a world for saying that one thinker's opinion is more correct than the other's, or that either has the truer moral sense. Such a world, in short, is not a moral universe but a moral dualism. Not only is there no single point of view within it from which the values of things can be unequivocally judged, but there is not even a demand for such a point of view, since the two thinkers are supposed to be indifferent to each other's thoughts and acts. Multiply the thinkers into a pluralism, and we find realized for us in the ethical sphere something like that world which the antique sceptics conceived of—in which individual minds are the measures of all things, and in which no one 'objective' truth, but only a multitude of 'subjective' opinions, can be found.

But this is the kind of world with which the philosopher, so long as he holds to the hope of a philosophy, will not put up. Among the various ideals represented, there must be, he thinks, some which have the more truth or authority; and to these the others *ought* to yield, so that system and subordination may reign. Here in the word 'ought' the notion of *obligation* comes emphatically into view, and the next thing in order must be to make its meaning clear.

Since the outcome of the discussion so far has been to show us that nothing can be good or right except so far as some consciousness feels it to be good or thinks it to be right, we perceive on the very threshold that the real superiority and authority which are postulated by the philosopher to reside in some of the opinions, and the really inferior character which he supposes must belong to others, cannot be explained by any abstract moral 'nature of things' existing antecedently to the concrete thinkers themselves with their ideals. Like the positive attributes good and bad, the comparative ones better and worse must be *realized* in order to be real. If one ideal judgment be objectively better than another, that betterness must be made flesh by being lodged concretely in some one's actual perception. It cannot float in the atmosphere, for it is not a sort of meteorological phenomenon, like the aurora borealis or the zodiacal light. Its *esse* is *percipi*, like the *esse* of the ideals themselves between which it obtains. The philosopher, therefore, who seeks to know which ideal ought to have supreme weight and which one ought to be subordinated, must trace the *ought* itself to the *de facto* constitution of some existing consciousness, behind which, as one of the data of the universe, he as a purely ethical philosopher is unable to go. This consciousness must make the one ideal right by feeling it to be right, the other wrong by feeling it to be wrong. But now what particular consciousness in the universe *can* enjoy this prerogative of obliging others to conform to a rule which it lays down?

If one of the thinkers were obviously divine, while all the rest were human, there would probably be no practical dispute about the matter. The divine thought would be the model, to which the others should conform. But still the theoretic question would remain, What is the ground of the obligation, even here?

In our first essays at answering this question, there is an inevitable tendency to slip into an assumption which ordinary men follow when they are disputing with one another about questions of good and bad. They imagine an abstract moral order in which the objective truth resides; and each tries to prove that this pre-existing order is more accurately reflected in his own ideas than in those of his adversary. It is because one disputant is backed by this overarching abstract order that we think the other should submit. Even so, when it is a question no longer of two finite thinkers, but of God and ourselves—we follow our usual habit, and imagine a sort of *de jure* relation, which antedates and overarches the mere facts, and would make it right that we should conform our thoughts to God's thoughts, even though he made no claim to that effect, and though we preferred *de facto* to go on thinking for ourselves.

But the moment we take a steady look at the question, *we see not only that without a claim actually made by some concrete person there can be no obligation, but that there is some obligation wherever there is a claim.* Claim and obligation are, in fact, coextensive terms; they cover each other exactly. Our ordinary attitude of regarding ourselves as subject to an overarching system of moral relations, true 'in themselves,' is therefore either an out-and-out superstition, or else it must be treated as a merely provisional abstraction from that real Thinker in whose actual demand upon us to think as he does our obligation must be ultimately based. In a theistic-ethical philosophy that Thinker in question is, of course, the Deity to whom the existence of the universe is due.

I know well how hard it is for those who are accustomed to what I have called the superstitious view, to realize that every *de facto* claim creates in so far forth an obligation. We inveterately think that something which we call the 'validity' of the claim is what gives to it its obligatory character, and that this validity is something outside of the claim's mere existence as a matter of fact. It rains down upon the claim, we think, from some sublime dimension of being, which the moral law inhabits, much as upon the steel of the compass-needle the influence of the Pole rains down from out of the starry heavens. But again, how can such an inorganic abstract character of imperativeness, additional to the imperativeness which is in the concrete claim itself, *exist?* Take any demand, however slight, which any creature, however weak, may make. Ought it not, for its own sole sake, to be satisfied? If not, prove why not. The only possible kind of proof you could adduce would be the exhibition of another creature who should make a demand that ran the other way. The only possible reason there can be why any phenomenon ought to exist is that such a phenomenon actually is desired. Any desire is imperative to the extent of its amount; it *makes* itself valid by the fact that it exists at all. Some desires, truly enough, are small desires; they are put forward by insignificant persons, and we customarily make light of the obligations which they bring. But the fact that such personal demands as these impose small obligations does not keep the largest obligations from being personal demands.

If we must talk impersonally, to be sure we can say that 'the universe' requires, exacts, or makes obligatory such or such an action, whenever it expresses itself through the desires of such or such a creature. But it is better not to talk about the universe in this personified way, unless we believe in a universal or divine consciousness which actually exists. If there be such a consciousness, then its demands carry the most of obligation simply because they are the greatest in amount. But it is even then not *abstractly* right that we should respect them. It is only *concretely* right—or right after the fact, and by virtue of the fact, that they are actually made. Suppose we do not respect them, as seems largely to be the case in this queer world. That ought not to be, we say; that is wrong. But in what way is this fact of wrongness made more acceptable or intelligible when we imagine it to consist rather in

the laceration of an *a priori* ideal order than in the disappointment of a living personal God? Do we, perhaps, think that we
cover God and protect him and make his impotence over us less
ultimate, when we back him up with this *a priori* blanket from
which he may draw some warmth of further appeal? But the only
force of appeal to *us*, which either a living God or an abstract
ideal order can wield, is found in the 'everlasting ruby vaults' of
our own human hearts, as they happen to beat responsive and not
irresponsive to the claim. So far as they do feel it when made by a
living consciousness, it is life answering to life. A claim thus
livingly acknowledged is acknowledged with a solidity and fulness
which no thought of an 'ideal' backing can render more complete;
while if, on the other hand, the heart's response is withheld, the
stubborn phenomenon is there of an impotence in the claims
which the universe embodies, which no talk about an eternal
nature of things can gloze over or dispel. An ineffective *a priori*
order is as impotent a thing as an ineffective God; and in the eye
of philosophy, it is as hard a thing to explain.

We may now consider that what we distinguished as the metaphysical question in ethical philosophy is sufficiently answered,
and that we have learned what the words 'good,' 'bad,' and 'obligation' severally mean. They mean no absolute natures, independent of personal support. They are objects of feeling and desire,
which have no foothold or anchorage in Being, apart from the
existence of actually living minds.

Wherever such minds exist, with judgments of good and ill, and
demands upon one another, there is an ethical world in its essential features. Were all other things, gods and men and starry
heavens, blotted out from this universe, and were there left but
one rock with two loving souls upon it, that rock would have as
thoroughly moral a constitution as any possible world which the
eternities and immensities could harbor. It would be a tragic
constitution, because the rock's inhabitants would die. But while
they lived, there would be real good things and real bad things in
the universe; there would be obligations, claims, and expectations;
obediences, refusals, and disappointments; compunctions and
longings for harmony to come again, and inward peace of conscience when it was restored; there would, in short, be a moral life,

whose active energy would have no limit but the intensity of interest in each other with which the hero and heroine might be endowed.

We, on this terrestrial globe, so far as the visible facts go, are just like the inhabitants of such a rock. Whether a God exist, or whether no God exist, in yon blue heaven above us bent, we form at any rate an ethical republic here below. And the first reflection which this leads to is that ethics have as genuine and real a foothold in a universe where the highest consciousness is human, as in a universe where there is a God as well. 'The religion of humanity' affords a basis for ethics as well as theism does. Whether the purely human system can gratify the philosopher's demand as well as the other is a different question, which we ourselves must answer ere we close. . . .

IV

. . . On the whole, then, we must conclude that no philosophy of ethics is possible in the old-fashioned absolute sense of the term. Everywhere the ethical philosopher must wait on facts. The thinkers who create the ideals come he knows not whence, their sensibilities are evolved he knows not how; and the question as to which of two conflicting ideals will give the best universe then and there, can be answered by him only through the aid of the experience of other men. I said some time ago, in treating of the 'first' question, that the intuitional moralists deserve credit for keeping most clearly to the psychological facts. They do much to spoil this merit on the whole, however, by mixing with it that dogmatic temper which, by absolute distinctions and unconditional 'thou shalt nots,' changes a growing, elastic, and continuous life into a superstitious system of relics and dead bones. In point of fact, there are no absolute evils, and there are no non-moral goods; and the *highest* ethical life—however few may be called to bear its burdens—consists at all times in the breaking of rules which have grown too narrow for the actual case. There is but one unconditional commandment, which is that we should seek incessantly, with fear and trembling, so to vote and to act as to bring about the very largest total universe of good which we can see. Abstract rules indeed can help; but they help the less in proportion as our intuitions are more piercing, and our vocation is the stronger for the moral life. For every real dilemma is in literal strictness a unique situation; and the exact combination of ideals realized and ideals disappointed which each decision creates is always a universe without a precedent, and for which no adequate previous rule exists. The philosopher, then, *qua* philosopher, is no better able to determine the best universe in the concrete emergency than other men. He sees, indeed, somewhat better than most men what the question always is—not a question of this good or that good simply taken, but of the two total universes with which these goods respectively belong. He knows that he must vote always for the richer universe, for the good which seems most organizable, most fit to enter into complex combinations, most apt to be a member of a more inclusive whole. But which particular universe this is he cannot know for certain in advance; he only knows that if he makes a bad mistake the cries of the wounded will soon inform him of the fact. In all this the philosopher is just like the rest of us non-philosophers, so far as we are just and sympathetic instinctively, and so far as we are open to the voice of complaint. His function is in fact indistinguishable from that of the best kind of statesman at the present day. His books upon ethics, therefore, so far as they truly touch the moral life, must more and more ally themselves with a literature which is confessedly tentative and suggestive rather than dogmatic—I mean with novels and dramas of the deeper sort, with sermons, with books on statecraft and philanthropy and social and economical reform. Treated in this way ethical treatises may be voluminous and luminous as well; but they never can be *final,* except in their abstractest and vaguest features; and they must more and more abandon the old-fashioned, clear-cut, and would-be 'scientific' form.

V

The chief of all the reasons why concrete ethics cannot be final is that they have to wait on metaphysical and theological beliefs. I said some time back that real ethical relations existed in a purely human world. They would exist even in what we called a moral solitude if the thinker had various ideals which took hold of him in turn. His self of one day would make demands on his self of another; and some of the demands might be urgent and tyrannical, while others were gentle and easily put aside. We call the tyrannical demands *imperatives*. If we ignore these we do not hear the last of it. The good which we have wounded returns to plague us with interminable crops of consequential damages, compunctions, and regrets. Obligation can thus exist inside a single thinker's consciousness; and perfect peace can abide with him only so far as he lives according to some sort of a casuistic scale which keeps his more imperative goods on top. It is the nature of these goods to be cruel to their rivals. Nothing shall avail when weighed in the balance against them. They call out all the mercilessness in our disposition, and do not easily forgive us if we are so soft-hearted as to shrink from sacrifice in their behalf.

The deepest difference, practically, in the moral life of man is the difference between the easy-going and the strenuous mood. When in the easy-going mood the shrinking from present ill is our ruling consideration. The strenuous mood, on the contrary, makes us quite indifferent to present ill, if only the greater ideal be attained. The capacity for the strenuous mood probably lies slumbering in every man, but it has more difficulty in some than in others in waking up. It needs the wilder passions to arouse it, the big fears, loves, and indignations; or else the deeply penetrating appeal of some one of the higher fidelities, like justice, truth, or freedom. Strong relief is a necessity of its vision; and a world where all the mountains are brought down and all the valleys are exalted is no congenial place for its habitation. This is why in a solitary thinker this mood might slumber on forever without waking. His various ideals, known to him to be mere preferences of his own, are too nearly of the same denominational value: he can play fast or loose with them at will. This too is why, in a merely human world without a God, the appeal to our moral energy falls short of its maximal stimulating power. Life, to be sure, is even in such a world a genuinely ethical symphony; but it is played in the compass of a couple of poor octaves, and the infinite scale of values fails to open up. Many of us, indeed—like Sir James Stephen in those eloquent "Essays by a Barrister"—would openly laugh at the very idea of the strenuous mood being

awakened in us by those claims of remote posterity which constitute the last appeal of the religion of humanity. We do not love
these men of the future keenly enough; and we love them perhaps
the less the more we hear of their evolutionized perfection, their
high average longevity and education, their freedom from war and
crime, their relative immunity from pain and zymotic disease, and
all their other negative superiorities. This is all too finite, we say;
we see too well the vacuum beyond. It lacks the note of infinitude
and mystery, and may all be dealt with in the don't-care mood. No
need of agonizing ourselves or making others agonize for these
good creatures just at present.

When, however, we believe that a God is there, and that he is
one of the claimants, the infinite perspective opens out. The scale
of the symphony is incalculably prolonged. The more imperative
ideals now begin to speak with an altogether new objectivity and
significance, and to utter the penetrating, shattering, tragically
challenging note of appeal. They ring out like the call of Victor
Hugo's alpine eagle, "qui parle au précipice et que le gouffre
entend," and the strenuous mood awakens at the sound. It saith
among the trumpets, ha, ha! it smelleth the battle afar off, the
thunder of the captains and the shouting. Its blood is up; and
cruelty to the lesser claims, so far from being a deterrent element,
does but add to the stern joy with which it leaps to answer to the
greater. All through history, in the periodical conflicts of puri-
tanism with the don't-care temper, we see the antagonism of the
strenuous and genial moods, and the contrast between the ethics
of infinite and mysterious obligation from on high, and those of
prudence and the satisfaction of merely finite need.

The capacity of the strenuous mood lies so deep down among
our natural human possibilities that even if there were no metaphysical or traditional grounds for believing in a God, men would
postulate one simply as a pretext for living hard, and getting out
of the game of existence its keenest possibilities of zest. Our attitude towards concrete evils is entirely different in a world where
we believe there are none but finite demanders, from what it is in
one where we joyously face tragedy for an infinite demander's
sake. Every sort of energy and endurance, of courage and capacity
for handling life's evils, is set free in those who have religious
faith. For this reason the strenuous type of character will on the

battle-field of human history always outwear the easy-going type, and religion will drive irreligion to the wall.

It would seem, too—and this is my final conclusion—that the stable and systematic moral universe for which the ethical philosopher asks is fully possible only in a world where there is a divine thinker with all-enveloping demands. If such a thinker existed, his way of subordinating the demands to one another would be the finally valid casuistic scale; his claims would be the most appealing; his ideal universe would be the most inclusive realizable whole. If he now exist, then actualized in his thought already must be that ethical philosophy which we seek as the pattern which our own must evermore approach.[2] In the interests of our own ideal of systematically unified moral truth, therefore, we, as would-be philosophers, must postulate a divine thinker, and pray for the victory of the religious cause. Meanwhile, exactly what the thought of the infinite thinker may be is hidden from us even were we sure of his existence; so that our postulation of him after all serves only to let loose in us the strenuous mood. But this is what it does in all men, even those who have no interest in philosophy. The ethical philosopher, therefore, whenever he ventures to say which course of action is the best, is on no essentially different level from the common man. "See, I have set before thee this day life and good, and death and evil; therefore, choose life that thou and thy seed may live"—when this challenge comes to us, it is simply our total character and personal genius that are on trial; and if we invoke any so-called philosophy, our choice and use of that also are but revelations of our personal aptitude or incapacity for moral life. From this unsparing practical ordeal no professor's lectures and no array of books can save us. The solving word, for the learned and the unlearned man alike, lies in the last resort in the dumb willingnesses and unwillingnesses of their interior characters, and nowhere else. It is not in heaven, neither is it beyond the sea; but the word is very nigh unto thee, in thy mouth and in thy heart, that thou mayest do it.

2. All this is set forth with great freshness and force in the work of my colleague, Professor Josiah Royce: *The Religious Aspect of Philosophy*, Boston, 1885.

12.

The Will to Believe*

I

. . . Let us give the name of *hypothesis* to anything that may be
proposed to our belief; and just as the electricians speak of live
and dead wires, let us speak of any hypothesis as either *live* or
dead. A live hypothesis is one which appeals as a real possibility to
him to whom it is proposed. If I ask you to believe in the Mahdi,
the notion makes no electric connection with your nature—it refuses to scintillate with any credibility at all. As an hypothesis it is
completely dead. To an Arab, however (even if he be not one of
the Mahdi's followers), the hypothesis is among the mind's possibilities: it is alive. This shows that deadness and liveness in an
hypothesis are not intrinsic properties, but relations to the individual thinker. They are measured by his willingness to act. The
maximum of liveness in an hypothesis means willingness to act
irrevocably. Practically, that means belief; but there is some
believing tendency wherever there is willingness to act at all.

Next, let us call the decision between two hypotheses an *option*.
Options may be of several kinds. They may be—1. *living* or *dead;*
2. *forced* or *avoidable;* 3. *momentous* or *trivial;* and for our
purposes we may call an option a *genuine* option when it is of the
forced, living, and momentous kind.

1. A living option is one in which both hypotheses are live ones.
If I say to you: "Be a theosophist or be a Mohammedan," it is
probably a dead option, because for you neither hypothesis is
likely to be alive. But if I say: "Be an agnostic or be a Christian,"
it is otherwise: trained as you are, each hypothesis makes some
appeal, however small, to your belief.

* An address to the Philosophical Clubs of Yale and Brown Universities. Published in the *New World* (June, 1896). Republished in the book of this title.
Sections have been deleted. [B.W.]

2. Next, if I say to you: "Choose between going out with your umbrella or without it," I do not offer you a genuine option, for it is not forced. You can easily avoid it by not going out at all. Similarly, if I say, "Either love me or hate me," "Either call my theory true or call it false," your option is avoidable. You may remain indifferent to me, neither loving nor hating, and you may decline to offer any judgment as to my theory. But if I say, "Either accept this truth or go without it," I put on you a forced option, for there is no standing place outside of the alternative. Every dilemma based on a complete logical disjunction, with no possibility of not choosing, is an option of this forced kind.

3. Finally, if I were Dr. Nansen and proposed to you to join my North Pole expedition, your option would be momentous; for this would probably be your only similar opportunity, and your choice now would either exclude you from the North Pole sort of immortality altogether or put at least the chance of it into your hands. He who refuses to embrace a unique opportunity loses the prize as surely as if he tried and failed. *Per contra,* the option is trivial when the opportunity is not unique, when the stake is insignificant, or when the decision is reversible if it later prove unwise. Such trivial options abound in the scientific life. A chemist finds an hypothesis live enough to spend a year in its verification: he believes in it to that extent. But if his experiments prove inconclusive either way, he is quit for his loss of time, no vital harm being done.

It will facilitate our discussion if we keep all these distinctions well in mind.

II

The next matter to consider is the actual psychology of human opinion. When we look at certain facts, it seems as if our passional and volitional nature lay at the root of all our convictions. When we look at others, it seems as if they could do nothing when the intellect had once said its say. Let us take the latter facts up first.

Does it not seem preposterous on the very face of it to talk of our opinions being modifiable at will? Can our will either help or hinder our intellect in its perceptions of truth? Can we, by just willing it, believe that Abraham Lincoln's existence is a myth, and that the portraits of him in McClure's Magazine are all of some one else? Can we, by any effort of our will, or by any strength of wish that it were true, believe ourselves well and about when we are roaring with rheumatism in bed, or feel certain that the sum of the two one-dollar bills in our pocket must be a hundred dollars? We can *say* any of these things, but we are absolutely impotent to believe them; and of just such things is the whole fabric of the truths that we do believe in made up—matters of fact, immediate or remote, as Hume said, and relations between ideas, which are either there or not there for us if we see them so, and which if not there cannot be put there by any action of our own.

In Pascal's *Thoughts* there is a celebrated passage known in literature as Pascal's wager. In it he tries to force us into Christianity by reasoning as if our concern with truth resembled our concern with the stakes in a game of chance. Translated freely his words are these: You must either believe or not believe that God is—which will you do? Your human reason cannot say. A game is going on between you and the nature of things which at the day of judgment will bring out either heads or tails. Weigh what your gains and your losses would be if you should stake all you have on heads, or God's existence: if you win in such case, you gain eternal beatitude; if you lose, you lose nothing at all. If there were an infinity of chances, and only one for God in this wager, still you ought to stake your all on God; for though you surely risk a finite loss by this procedure, any finite loss is reasonable, even a certain one is reasonable, if there is but the possibility of infinite gain. Go, then, and take holy water, and have masses said; belief will come and stupefy your scruples—*Cela vous fera croire et vous abêtira.* Why should you not? At bottom, what have you to lose?

You probably feel that when religious faith expresses itself thus, in the language of the gaming-table, it is put to its last trumps. Surely Pascal's own personal belief in masses and holy water had far other springs; and this celebrated page of his is but an argument for others, a last desperate snatch at a weapon against the hardness of the unbelieving heart. We feel that a faith in masses and holy water adopted wilfully after such a mechanical calculation would lack the inner soul of faith's reality; and if we were ourselves in the place of the Deity, we should probably take particular pleasure in cutting off believers of this pattern from their infinite reward. It is evident that unless there be some pre-existing tendency to believe in masses and holy water, the option offered to the will by Pascal is not a living option. Certainly no Turk ever took to masses and holy water on its account; and even to us Protestants these means of salvation seem such foregone impossibilities that Pascal's logic, invoked for them specifically, leaves us unmoved. As well might the Mahdi write to us, saying, "I am the Expected One whom God has created in his effulgence. You shall be infinitely happy if you confess me; otherwise you shall be cut off from the light of the sun. Weigh, then, your infinite gain if I am genuine against your finite sacrifice if I am not!" His logic would be that of Pascal; but he would vainly use it on us, for the hypothesis he offers us is dead. No tendency to act on it exists in us to any degree.

The talk of believing by our volition seems, then, from one point of view, simply silly. From another point of view it is worse than silly, it is vile. When one turns to the magnificent edifice of the physical sciences, and sees how it was reared; what thousands of disinterested moral lives of men lie buried in its mere foundations; what patience and postponement, what choking down of preference, what submission to the icy laws of outer fact are wrought into its very stones and mortar; how absolutely impersonal it stands in its vast augustness—then how besotted and contemptible seems every little sentimentalist who comes blowing his voluntary smoke-wreaths, and pretending to decide things from out of his private dream! Can we wonder if those bred in the rugged and manly school of science should feel like spewing such subjectivism out of their mouths? The whole system of loyalties which grow up in the schools of science go dead against its toleration; so that it is only natural that those who have caught the scientific fever should pass over to the opposite extreme, and write sometimes as if the incorruptibly truthful intellect ought positively to prefer bitterness and unacceptableness to the heart in its cup.

> It fortifies my soul to know
> That, though I perish, Truth is so—

sings Clough, while Huxley exclaims: "My only consolation lies in the reflection that, however bad our posterity may become, so far as they hold by the plain rule of not pretending to believe what they have no reason to believe, because it may be to their advantage so to pretend [the word 'pretend' is surely here redundant], they will not have reached the lowest depth of immorality." And that delicious *enfant terrible* Clifford writes: "Belief is desecrated when given to unproved and unquestioned statements for the solace and private pleasure of the believer. . . . Whoso would deserve well of his fellows in this matter will guard the purity of his belief with a very fanaticism of jealous care, lest at any time it should rest on an unworthy object, and catch a stain which can never be wiped away. . . . If [a] belief has been accepted on insufficient evidence [even though the belief be true, as Clifford on the same page explains] the pleasure is a stolen one. . . . It is sinful because it is stolen in defiance of our duty to mankind. That duty is to guard ourselves from such beliefs as from a pestilence which may shortly master our own body and then spread to the rest of the town. . . . It is wrong always, everywhere, and for every one, to believe anything upon insufficient evidence."

III

All this strikes one as healthy, even when expressed, as by Clifford, with somewhat too much of robustious pathos in the voice. Free-will and simple wishing do seem, in the matter of our credences, to be only fifth wheels to the coach. Yet if any one should thereupon assume that intellectual insight is what remains after wish and will and sentimental preference have taken wing, or that pure reason is what then settles our opinions, he would fly quite as directly in the teeth of the facts.

It is only our already dead hypotheses that our willing nature is unable to bring to life again. But what has made them dead for us is for the most part a previous action of our willing nature of an antagonistic kind. When I say 'willing nature,' I do not mean only such deliberate volitions as may have set up habits of belief that we cannot now escape from—I mean all such factors of belief as fear and hope, prejudice and passion, imitation and partisanship, the circumpressure of our caste and set. As a matter of fact we find ourselves believing, we hardly know how or why. Mr. Balfour gives the name of 'authority' to all those influences, born of the intellectual climate, that make hypotheses possible or impossible for us, alive or dead. Here in this room, we all of us believe in molecules and the conservation of energy, in democracy and necessary progress, in Protestant Christianity and the duty of fighting for 'the doctrine of the immortal Monroe,' all for no reasons worthy of the name. We see into these matters with no more inner clearness, and probably with much less, than any disbeliever in them might possess. His unconventionality would probably have some grounds to show for its conclusions; but for us, not insight, but the *prestige* of the opinions, is what makes the spark shoot from them and light up our sleeping magazines of faith. Our reason is quite satisfied, in nine hundred and ninety-nine cases out of every thousand of us, if it can find a few arguments that will do to recite in case our credulity is criticised by some one else. Our faith is faith in some one else's faith, and in the greatest matters this is most the case. Our belief in truth itself, for instance, that there is a truth, and that our minds and it are made for each other—what is it but a passionate affirmation of desire, in which our social system backs us up? We want to have a truth; we want to believe that our experiments and studies and discussions must put us in a continually better and better position towards it; and on this line we agree to fight out our thinking lives. But if a pyrrhonistic sceptic asks us *how we know* all this, can our logic find a reply? No! certainly it cannot. It is just one volition against another—we willing to go in for life upon a trust or assumption which he, for his part, does not care to make.[1]

As a rule we disbelieve all facts and theories for which we have no use. Clifford's cosmic emotions find no use for Christian feelings. Huxley belabors the bishops because there is no use for sacerdotalism in his scheme of life. Newman, on the contrary, goes over to Romanism, and finds all sorts of reasons good for staying there, because a priestly system is for him an organic need and

1. Compare the admirable page 310 in S. H. Hodgson's *Time and Space,* London, 1865.

delight. Why do so few 'scientists' even look at the evidence for telepathy, so called? Because they think, as a leading biologist, now dead, once said to me, that even if such a thing were true, scientists ought to band together to keep it suppressed and concealed. It would undo the uniformity of Nature and all sorts of other things without which scientists cannot carry on their pursuits. But if this very man had been shown something which as a scientist he might *do* with telepathy, he might not only have examined the evidence, but even have found it good enough. This very law which the logicians would impose upon us—if I may give the name of logicians to those who would rule out our willing nature here—is based on nothing but their own natural wish to exclude all elements for which they, in their professional quality of logicians, can find no use.

Evidently, then, our non-intellectual nature does influence our convictions. There are passional tendencies and volitions which run before and others which come after belief, and it is only the latter that are too late for the fair; and they are not too late when the previous passional work has been already in their own direction. Pascal's argument, instead of being powerless, then seems a regular clincher, and is the last stroke needed to make our faith in masses and holy water complete. The state of things is evidently far from simple; and pure insight and logic, whatever they might do ideally, are not the only things that really do produce our creeds.

IV

Our next duty, having recognized this mixed-up state of affairs, is to ask whether it be simply reprehensible and pathological, or whether, on the contrary, we must treat it as a normal element in making up our minds. The thesis I defend is, briefly stated, this: *Our passional nature not only lawfully may, but must, decide an option between propositions, whenever it is a genuine option that cannot by its nature be decided on intellectual grounds; for to say, under such circumstances, "Do not decide, but leave the question open," is itself a passional decision—just like deciding yes or no—and is attended with the same risk of losing the truth. . . .*

VI

. . . No concrete test of what is really true has ever been agreed upon. Some make the criterion external to the moment of perception, putting it either in revelation, the *consensus gentium,* the instincts of the heart, or the systematized experience of the race. Others make the perceptive moment its own test—Descartes, for instance, with his clear and distinct ideas guaranteed by the veracity of God; Reid with his 'common-sense'; and Kant with his forms of synthetic judgment *a priori.* The inconceivability of the opposite; the capacity to be verified by sense; the possession of complete organic unity or self-relation, realized when a thing is its own other—are standards which, in turn, have been used. The much lauded objective evidence is never triumphantly there; it is a mere aspiration of *Grenzbegriff,* marking the infinitely remote ideal of our thinking life. To claim that certain truths now possess it, is simply to say that when you think them true and they *are* true, then their evidence is objective, otherwise it is not. But practically one's conviction that the evidence one goes by is of the real objective brand, is only one more subjective opinion added to the lot. For what a contradictory array of opinions have objective evidence and absolute certitude been claimed! The world is rational through and through—its existence is an ultimate brute fact; there is a personal God—a personal God is inconceivable; there is an extra-mental physical world immediately known—the mind can only know its own ideas; a moral imperative exists— obligation is only the resultant of desires; a permanent spiritual principle is in every one—there are only shifting states of mind; there is an endless chain of causes—there is an absolute first cause; an eternal necessity—a freedom; a purpose—no purpose; a primal One—a primal Many; a universal continuity—an essential discontinuity in things; an infinity—no infinity. There is this—there is that; there is indeed nothing which some one has not thought absolutely true, while his neighbor deemed it absolutely false; and not an absolutist among them seems ever to have considered that the trouble may all the time be essential, and that the intellect, even with truth directly in its grasp, may have no infallible signal for knowing whether it be truth or no. When, indeed, one remembers that the most striking practical application to life of the doctrine of objective certitude has been the conscientious labors of the Holy Office of the Inquisition, one feels less tempted than ever to lend the doctrine a respectful ear.

But please observe, now, that when as empiricists we give up the doctrine of objective certitude, we do not thereby give up the quest or hope of truth itself. We still pin our faith on its existence, and still believe that we gain an ever better position towards it by systematically continuing to roll up experiences and think. Our great difference from the scholastic lies in the way we face. The strength of his system lies in the principles, the origin, the *terminus a quo* of his thought; for us the strength is in the outcome, the upshot, the *terminus ad quem*. Not where it comes from but what it leads to is to decide. It matters not to an empiricist from what quarter an hypothesis may come to him: he may have acquired it by fair means or by foul; passion may have whispered or accident suggested it; but if the total drift of thinking continues to confirm it, that is what he means by its being true.

VII

One more point, small but important, and our preliminaries are done. There are two ways of looking at our duty in the matter of opinion—ways entirely different, and yet ways about whose difference the theory of knowledge seems hitherto to have shown very little concern. *We must know the truth;* and *we must avoid error*—these are our first and great commandments as would-be knowers; but they are not two ways of stating an identical commandment, they are two separable laws. Although it may indeed happen that when we believe the truth *A,* we escape as an incidental consequence from believing the falsehood *B,* it hardly ever happens that by merely disbelieving *B* we necessarily believe *A.* We may in escaping *B* fall into believing other falsehoods, *C* or *D,* just as bad as *B;* or we may escape *B* by not believing anything at all, not even *A.*

Believe truth! Shun error!—these, we see, are two materially different laws; and by choosing between them we may end by coloring differently our whole intellectual life. We may regard the chase for truth as paramount, and the avoidance of error as secondary; or we may, on the other hand, treat the avoidance of error as more imperative, and let truth take its chance. Clifford, in the instructive passage which I have quoted, exhorts us to the latter course. Believe nothing, he tells us, keep your mind in suspense forever, rather than by closing it on insufficient evidence incur the awful risk of believing lies. You, on the other hand, may think that the risk of being in error is a very small matter when compared with the blessings of real knowledge, and be ready to be duped many times in your investigation rather than postpone indefinitely the chance of guessing true. I myself find it impossible to go with Clifford. We must remember that these feelings of our duty about either truth or error are in any case only expressions of our passional life. Biologically considered, our minds are as ready to grind out falsehood as veracity, and he who says, "Better go without belief forever than believe a lie!" merely shows his own preponderant private horror of becoming a dupe. He may be critical of many of his desires and fears, but this fear he slavishly obeys. He cannot imagine any one questioning its binding force. For my own part, I have also a horror of being duped; but I can believe that worse things than being duped may happen to a man in this world: so Clifford's exhortation has to my ears a thoroughly fantastic sound. It is like a general informing his soldiers that it is better to keep out of battle forever than to risk a single wound. Not so are victories either over enemies or over nature gained. Our errors are surely not such awfully solemn things. In a world where we are so certain to incur them in spite of all our caution, a certain lightness of heart seems healthier than this excessive nervousness on their behalf. At any rate, it seems the fittest thing for the empiricist philosopher.

VIII

And now, after all this introduction, let us go straight at our question. I have said, and now repeat it, that not only as a matter of fact do we find our passional nature influencing us in our opinions, but that there are some options between opinions in which this influence must be regarded both as an inevitable and as a lawful determinant of our choice.

I fear here that some of you my hearers will begin to scent danger, and lend an inhospitable ear. Two first steps of passion you have indeed had to admit as necessary—we must think so as to avoid dupery, and we must think so as to gain truth; but the surest path to those ideal consummations, you will probably consider, is from now onwards to take no further passional step.

Well, of course, I agree as far as the facts will allow. Wherever the option between losing truth and gaining it is not momentous, we can throw the chance of *gaining truth* away, and at any rate save ourselves from any chance of *believing falsehood,* by not making up our minds at all till objective evidence has come. In scientific questions, this is almost always the case; and even in human affairs in general, the need of acting is seldom so urgent that a false belief to act on is better than no belief at all. Law courts, indeed, have to decide on the best evidence attainable for the moment, because a judge's duty is to make law as well as to ascertain it, and (as a learned judge once said to me) few cases are worth spending much time over: the great thing is to have them decided on *any* acceptable principle, and got out of the way. But in our dealings with objective nature we obviously are recorders, not makers, of the truth; and decisions for the mere sake of deciding promptly and getting on to the next business would be wholly out of place. Throughout the breadth of physical nature facts are what they are quite independently of us, and seldom is there any such hurry about them that the risks of being duped by believing a premature theory need be faced. The questions here are always trivial options, the hypotheses are hardly living (at any rate not living for us spectators), the choice between believing truth or falsehood is seldom forced. The attitude of sceptical balance is therefore the absolutely wise one if we would escape mistakes. What difference, indeed, does it make to most of us whether we have or have not a theory of the Röntgen rays, whether we believe or not in mind-stuff, or have a conviction about the causality of conscious states? It makes no difference. Such options are not forced on us. On every account it is better not to make them, but still keep weighing reasons *pro et contra* with an indifferent hand.

I speak, of course, here of the purely judging mind. For purposes of discovery such indifference is to be less highly recommended, and science would be far less advanced than she is if the passionate desires of individuals to get their own faiths confirmed had been kept out of the game. See for example the sagacity which Spencer and Weismann now display. On the other hand, if you want an absolute duffer in an investigation, you must, after all, take the man who has no interest whatever in its results: he is the warranted incapable, the positive fool. The most useful investigator, because the most sensitive observer, is always he whose eager interest in one side of the question is balanced by an equally keen nervousness lest he become deceived.[2] Science has organized this nervousness into a regular *technique,* her so-called method of verification; and she has fallen so deeply in love with the method that one may even say she has ceased to care for truth by itself at all. It is only truth as technically verified that interests her. The truth of truths might come in merely affirmative form, and she would decline to touch it. Such truth as that, she might repeat with Clifford, would be stolen in defiance of her duty to mankind. Human passions, however, are stronger than technical rules. "Le cœur a ses raisons," as Pascal says, "que la raison ne connaît pas"; and however indifferent to all but the bare rules of the game the umpire, the abstract intellect, may be, the concrete players who furnish him the materials to judge of are usually, each one of them, in love with some pet 'live hypothesis' of his own. Let us agree, however, that wherever there is no forced option, the dispassionately judicial intellect with no pet hypothesis, saving us, as it does, from dupery at any rate, ought to be our ideal.

The question next arises: Are there not somewhere forced options in our speculative questions, and can we (as men who may be interested at least as much in positively gaining truth as in merely escaping dupery) always wait with impunity till the coercive evidence shall have arrived? It seems *a priori* improbable that the truth should be so nicely adjusted to our needs and powers as that. In the great boarding-house of nature, the cakes and the butter and the syrup seldom come out so even and leave

2. Compare Wilfrid Ward's essay, "The Wish to Believe," in his *Witnesses to the Unseen,* Macmillan & Co., 1893.

the plates so clean. Indeed, we should view them with scientific suspicion if they did.

IX

Moral questions immediately present themselves as questions *forced* whose solution cannot wait for sensible proof. A moral question is a question not of what sensibly exists, but of what is good, or would be good if it did exist. Science can tell us what exists; but to compare the *worths,* both of what exists and of what does not exist, we must consult not science, but what Pascal calls our heart. Science herself consults her heart when she lays it down that the infinite ascertainment of fact and correction of false belief are the supreme goods for man. Challenge the statement, and science can only repeat it oracularly, or else prove it by showing that such ascertainment and correction bring man all sorts of other goods which man's heart in turn declares. The question of having moral beliefs at all or not having them is decided by our will. Are our moral preferences true or false, or are they only odd biological phenomena, making things good or bad for *us,* but in themselves indifferent? How can your pure intellect decide? If your heart does not *want* a world of moral reality, your head will assuredly never make you believe in one. Mephistophelian scepticism, indeed, will satisfy the head's play-instincts much better than any rigorous idealism can. Some men (even at the student age) are so naturally cool-hearted that the moralistic hypothesis never has for them any pungent life, and in their supercilious presence the hot young moralist always feels strangely ill at ease. The appearance of knowingness is on their side, of *naïveté* and gullibility on his. Yet, in the inarticulate heart of him, he clings to it that he is not a dupe, and that there is a realm in which (as Emerson says) all their wit and intellectual superiority is no better than the cunning of a fox. Moral scepticism can no more be refuted or proved by logic than intellectual scepticism can. When we stick to it that there *is* truth (be it of either kind), we do so with our whole nature, and resolve to stand or fall by the results. The sceptic with his whole nature adopts the doubting attitude; but which of us is the wiser, Omniscience only knows.

Turn now from these wide questions of good to a certain class of questions of fact, questions concerning personal relations, states of mind between one man and another. <u>*Do you like me or not?*</u>—for example. Whether you do or not depends, in countless instances, on whether I meet you half-way, am willing to assume that you must like me, and show you trust and expectation. The previous faith on my part in your liking's existence is in such cases what makes your liking come. But if I stand aloof, and refuse to budge an inch until I have objective evidence, until you shall have done something apt, as the absolutists say, *ad extorquendum assensum meum,* ten to one your liking never comes. How many women's hearts are vanquished by the mere sanguine insistence of some man that they *must* love him! he will not consent to the hypothesis that they cannot. The desire for a certain kind of truth here brings about that special truth's existence; and so it is in innumerable cases of other sorts. Who gains promotions, boons, appointments, but the man in whose life they are seen to play the part of live hypotheses, who discounts them, sacrifices other things for their sake before they have come, and takes risks for them in advance? His faith acts on the powers above him as a claim, and creates its own verification.

A social organism of any sort whatever, large or small, is what it is because each member proceeds to his own duty with a trust that the other members will simultaneously do theirs. Wherever a desired result is achieved by the co-operation of many independent persons, its existence as a fact is a pure consequence of the precursive faith on one another of those immediately concerned. A government, an army, a commercial system, a ship, a college, an athletic team, all exist on this condition, without which not only is nothing achieved, but nothing is even attempted. A whole train of passengers (individually brave enough) will be looted by a few highwaymen, simply because the latter can count on one another, while each passenger fears that if he makes a movement of resistance, he will be shot before any one else backs him up. If we believed that the whole car-full would rise at once with us, we should each severally rise, and train robbing would never even be attempted. There are, then, cases where a fact cannot come at all unless a preliminary faith exists in its coming. *And where faith in a fact can help create the fact,* that would be an insane logic which should say that faith running ahead of scientific evidence is the 'lowest kind of immorality' into which a thinking being can fall. Yet such is the logic by which our scientific absolutists pretend to regulate our lives!

X

In truths dependent on our personal action, then, faith based on desire is certainly a lawful and possibly an indispensable thing.

But now, it will be said, these are all childish human cases, and have nothing to do with great cosmical matters, like the question of religious faith. Let us then pass on to that. Religions differ so much in their accidents that in discussing the religious question we must make it very generic and broad. What then do we now mean by the religious hypothesis? Science says things are; morality says some things are better than other things; and religion says essentially two things.

First, she says that the best things are the more eternal things, the overlapping things, the things in the universe that throw the last stone, so to speak, and say the final word. "Perfection is eternal"—this phrase of Charles Secrétan seems a good way of putting this first affirmation of religion, an affirmation which obviously cannot yet be verified scientifically at all.

The second affirmation of religion is that we are better off even now if we believe her first affirmation to be true.

Now, let us consider what the logical elements of this situation are *in case the religious hypothesis in both its branches be really true.* (Of course, we must admit that possibility at the outset. If we are to discuss the question at all, it must involve a living option. If for any of you religion be a hypothesis that cannot, by any living possibility be true, then you need go no farther. I speak to the 'saving remnant' alone.) So proceeding, we see, first, that religion offers itself as a *momentous* option. We are supposed to gain, even now, by our belief, and to lose by our non-belief, a certain vital good. Secondly, religion is a *forced* option, so far as that good goes. We cannot escape the issue by remaining sceptical and waiting for more light, because, although we do avoid error in that way *if religion be untrue,* we lose the good, *if it be true,* just as certainly as if we positively chose to disbelieve. It is as if a man should hesitate indefinitely to ask a certain woman to marry him because he was not perfectly sure that she would prove an angel after he brought her home. Would he not cut himself off from that particular angel-possibility as decisively as if he went and married some one else? Scepticism, then, is not avoidance of option; it is option of a certain particular kind of risk. *Better risk loss of truth than chance of error*—that is your faith-vetoer's exact position. He is actively playing his stake as much as the believer is; he is backing the field against the religious hypothesis, just as the believer is backing the religious hypothesis against the field. To preach scepticism to us as a duty until 'sufficient evidence' for religion be found, is tantamount therefore to telling us, when in presence of the religious hypothesis, that to yield to our fear of its being error is wiser and better than to yield to our hope that it may be true. It is not intellect against all passions, then; it is only intellect with one passion laying down its law. And by what, forsooth, is the supreme wisdom of this passion warranted? Dupery for dupery, what proof is there that dupery through hope is so much worse than dupery through fear? I, for one, can see no proof; and I simply refuse obedience to the scientist's command to imitate his kind of option, in a case where my own stake is important enough to give me the right to choose my own form of risk. If religion be true and the evidence for it be still insufficient, I do not wish, by putting your extinguisher upon my nature (which feels to me as if it had after all some business in this matter), to forfeit my sole chance in life of getting upon the winning side—that chance depending, of course, on my willingness to run the risk of acting as if my passional need of taking the world religiously might be prophetic and right.

All this is on the supposition that it really may be prophetic and right, and that, even to us who are discussing the matter, religion is a live hypothesis which may be true. Now, to most of us religion comes in a still further way that makes a veto on our active faith even more illogical. The more perfect and more eternal aspect of the universe is represented in our religions as having personal form. The universe is no longer a mere *It* to us, but a *Thou*, if we are religious; and any relation that may be possible from person to person might be possible here. For instance, although in one sense

Buber

we are passive portions of the universe, in another we show a curious autonomy, as if we were small active centres on our own account. We feel, too, as if the appeal of religion to us were made to our own active good-will, as if evidence might be forever withheld from us unless we met the hypothesis half-way. To take a trivial illustration: just as a man who in a company of gentlemen made no advances, asked a warrant for every concession, and believed no one's word without proof, would cut himself off by such churlishness from all the social rewards that a more trusting spirit would earn—so here, one who should shut himself up in snarling logicality and try to make the gods extort his recognition willy-nilly, or not get it at all, might cut himself off forever from his only opportunity of making the gods' acquaintance. This feeling, forced on us we know not whence, that by obstinately believing that there are gods (although not to do so would be so easy both for our logic and our life) we are doing the universe the deepest service we can, seems part of the living essence of the religious hypothesis. If the hypothesis *were* true in all its parts, including this one, then pure intellectualism, with its veto on our making willing advances, would be an absurdity; and some participation of our sympathetic nature would be logically required. I, therefore, for one, cannot see my way to accepting the agnostic rules for truth-seeking, or wilfully agree to keep my willing nature out of the game. I cannot do so for this plain reason, that *a rule of thinking which would absolutely prevent me from acknowledging certain kinds of truth if those kinds of truth were really there, would be an irrational rule.* That for me is the long and short of the formal logic of the situation, no matter what the kinds of truth might materially be. . . .

13.

On a Certain Blindness in Human Beings*

Our judgments concerning the worth of things, big or little, depend on the *feelings* the things arouse in us. Where we judge a thing to be precious in consequence of the *idea* we frame of it, this is only because the idea is itself associated already with a feeling. If we were radically feelingless, and if ideas were the only things our mind could entertain, we should lose all our likes and dislikes at a stroke, and be unable to point to any one situation or experience in life more valuable or significant than any other.

Now the blindness in human beings, of which this discourse will treat, is the blindness with which we all are afflicted in regard to the feelings of creatures and people different from ourselves.

We are practical beings, each of us with limited functions and duties to perform. Each is bound to feel intensely the importance of his own duties and the significance of the situations that call these forth. But this feeling is in each of us a vital secret, for sympathy with which we vainly look to others. The others are too much absorbed in their own vital secrets to take an interest in ours. Hence the stupidity and injustice of our opinions, so far as they deal with the significance of alien lives. Hence the falsity of our judgments, so far as they presume to decide in an absolute way on the value of other persons' conditions or ideals.

Take our dogs and ourselves, connected as we are by a tie more intimate than most ties in this world; and yet, outside of that tie of friendly fondness, how insensible, each of us, to all that makes life significant for the other!—we to the rapture of bones under hedges, or smells of trees and lamp-posts, they to the delights of literature and art. As you sit reading the most moving romance you ever fell upon, what sort of a judge is your fox-terrier of your

* From *Talks to Teachers on Psychology and to Students on Some of Life's Ideals*. A short section deleted. [B.W.]

behavior? With all his good will toward you, the nature of your conduct is absolutely excluded from his comprehension. To sit there like a senseless statue, when you might be taking him to walk and throwing sticks for him to catch! What queer disease is this that comes over you every day, of holding things and staring at them like that for hours together, paralyzed of motion and vacant of all conscious life? The African savages came nearer the truth; but they, too, missed it, when they gathered wonderingly round one of our American travellers who, in the interior, had just come into possession of a stray copy of the New York *Commercial Advertiser,* and was devouring it column by column. When he got through, they offered him a high price for the mysterious object; and, being asked for what they wanted it, they said: "For an eye medicine"—that being the only reason they could conceive of for the protracted bath which he had given his eyes upon its surface.

The spectator's judgment is sure to miss the root of the matter, and to possess no truth. The subject judged knows a part of the world of reality which the judging spectator fails to see, knows more while the spectator knows less; and, wherever there is conflict of opinion and difference of vision, we are bound to believe that the truer side is the side that feels the more, and not the side that feels the less.

Let me take a personal example of the kind that befalls each one of us daily:

Some years ago, while journeying in the mountains of North Carolina, I passed by a large number of 'coves,' as they call them there, or heads of small valleys between the hills, which had been newly cleared and planted. The impression on my mind was one of unmitigated squalor. The settler had in every case cut down the more manageable trees, and left their charred stumps standing. The larger trees he had girdled and killed, in order that their foliage should not cast a shade. He had then built a log cabin, plastering its chinks with clay, and had set up a tall zigzag rail fence around the scene of his havoc, to keep the pigs and cattle out. Finally, he had irregularly planted the intervals between the stumps and trees with Indian corn, which grew among the chips; and there he dwelt with his wife and babes—an axe, a gun, a few utensils, and some pigs and chickens feeding in the woods, being the sum total of his possessions.

The forest had been destroyed; and what had 'improved' it out of existence was hideous, a sort of ulcer, without a single element of artificial grace to make up for the loss of Nature's beauty. Ugly, indeed, seemed the life of the squatter, scudding, as the sailors say, under bare poles, beginning again away back where our first ancestors started, and by hardly a single item the better off for all the achievements of the intervening generations.

Talk about going back to nature! I said to myself, oppressed by the dreariness, as I drove by. Talk of a country life for one's old age and for one's children! Never thus, with nothing but the bare ground and one's bare hands to fight the battle! Never, without the best spoils of culture woven in! The beauties and commodities gained by the centuries are sacred. They are our heritage and birthright. No modern person ought to be willing to live a day in such a state of rudimentariness and denudation.

Then I said to the mountaineer who was driving me, "What sort of people are they who have to make these new clearings?" "All of us," he replied. "Why, we ain't happy here, unless we are getting one of these coves under cultivation." I instantly felt that I had been losing the whole inward significance of the situation. Because to me the clearings spoke of naught but denudation, I thought that to those whose sturdy arms and obedient axes had made them they could tell no other story. But, when *they* looked on the hideous stumps, what they thought of was personal victory. The chips, the girdled trees, and the vile split rails spoke of honest sweat, persistent toil and final reward. The cabin was a warrant of safety for self and wife and babes. In short, the clearing, which to me was a mere ugly picture on the retina, was to them a symbol redolent with moral memories and sang a very pæan of duty, struggle, and success.

I had been as blind to the peculiar ideality of their conditions as they certainly would also have been to the ideality of mine, had they had a peep at my strange indoor academic ways of life at Cambridge.

Wherever a process of life communicates an eagerness to him who lives it, there the life becomes genuinely significant. Sometimes the eagerness is more knit up with the motor activities, sometimes with the perceptions, sometimes with the imagination, sometimes with reflective thought. But, wherever it is found, there is the zest, the tingle, the excitement of reality; and there *is* 'importance' in the only real and positive sense in which importance ever anywhere can be.

Robert Louis Stevenson has illustrated this by a case, drawn from the sphere of the imagination, in an essay which I really think deserves to become immortal, both for the truth of its matter and the excellence of its form.

"Toward the end of September," Stevenson writes, "when school-time was drawing near, and the nights were already black, we would begin to sally from our respective villas, each equipped with a tin bull's-eye lantern. The thing was so well known that it had worn a rut in the commerce of Great Britain; and the grocers, about the due time, began to garnish their windows with our particular brand of luminary. We wore them buckled to the waist upon a cricket belt, and over them, such was the rigor of the game, a buttoned top-coat. They smelled noisomely of blistered tin. They never burned aright, though they would always burn our fingers. Their use was naught, the pleasure of them merely fanci-ful, and yet a boy with a bull's-eye under his top-coat asked for nothing more. The fishermen used lanterns about their boats, and it was from them, I suppose, that we had got the hint; but theirs were not bull's-eyes, nor did we ever play at being fishermen. The police carried them at their belts, and we had plainly copied them in that; yet we did not pretend to be policemen. Burglars, indeed, we may have had some haunting thought of; and we had certainly an eye to past ages when lanterns were more common, and to certain story-books in which we had found them to figure very largely. But take it for all in all, the pleasure of the thing was substantive; and to be a boy with a bull's-eye under his top-coat was good enough for us.

"When two of these asses met, there would be an anxious 'Have you got your lantern?' and a gratified 'Yes!' That was the shib-boleth, and very needful, too; for, as it was the rule to keep our glory contained, none could recognize a lantern-bearer unless (like the polecat) by the smell. Four or five would sometimes climb into the belly of a ten-man lugger, with nothing but the thwarts above them—for the cabin was usually locked—or chose out some hollow of the links where the wind might whistle overhead. Then the coats would be unbuttoned, and the bull's-eyes discovered; and in the chequering glimmer, under the huge, windy hall of the night, and cheered by a rich steam of toasting tinware, these fortunate young gentlemen would crouch together in the cold sand of the links, or on the scaly bilges of the fishing-boat, and delight them with inappropriate talk. Woe is me that I cannot give some specimens! . . . But the talk was but a condiment, and these gatherings themselves only accidents in the career of the lantern-bearer. The essence of this bliss was to walk by yourself in the black night, the slide shut, the top-coat buttoned, not a ray escaping, whether to conduct your footsteps or to make your glory public—a mere pillar of darkness in the dark; and all the while, deep down in the privacy of your fool's heart, to know you had a bull's-eye at your belt, and to exult and sing over the knowledge.

"It is said that a poet has died young in the breast of the most stolid. It may be contended rather that a (somewhat minor) bard in almost every case survives, and is the spice of life to his possessor. Justice is not done to the versatility and the unplumbed childishness of man's imagination. His life from without may seem but a rude mound of mud: there will be some golden chamber at the heart of it, in which he dwells delighted; and for as dark as his pathway seems to the observer, he will have some kind of bull's-eye at his belt.

. . . "There is one fable that touches very near the quick of life—the fable of the monk who passed into the woods, heard a bird break into song, hearkened for a trill or two, and found himself at his return a stranger at his convent gates; for he had been absent fifty years, and of all his comrades there survived but one to recognize him. It is not only in the woods that this enchanter carols, though perhaps he is native there. He sings in the most doleful places. The miser hears him and chuckles, and his days are moments. With no more apparatus than an evil-smelling lantern, I have evoked him on the naked links. All life that is not merely mechanical is spun out of two strands—seeking for that bird and hearing him. And it is just this that makes life so hard to value, and the delight of each so incommunicable. And it is just a knowledge of this, and a remembrance of those fortunate hours in which the bird *has* sung to *us*, that fills us with such wonder when we turn to the pages of the realist. There, to be sure, we find a picture of life in so far as it consists of mud and of old iron, cheap desires and cheap fears, that which we are ashamed to remember and that which we are careless whether we forget; but of the note of that time-devouring nightingale we hear no news.

. . . "Say that we came [in such a realistic romance] on some such business as that of my lantern-bearers on the links, and described the boys as very cold, spat upon by flurries of rain, and drearily surrounded, all of which they were; and their talk as silly and indecent, which it certainly was. To the eye of the observer they *are* wet and cold and drearily surrounded; but ask themselves, and they are in the heaven of a recondite pleasure, the ground of which is an ill-smelling lantern.

"For, to repeat, the ground of a man's joy is often hard to hit. It may hinge at times upon a mere accessory, like the lantern; it may reside in the mysterious inwards of psychology. . . . It has so little bond with externals . . . that it may even touch them not, and the man's true life, for which he consents to live, lie together in the field of fancy. . . . In such a case the poetry runs underground. The observer (poor soul, with his documents!) is all abroad. For to look at the man is but to court deception. We shall see the trunk from which he draws his nourishment; but he himself is above and abroad in the green dome of foliage, hummed through by winds and nested in by nightingales. And the true realism were that of the poets, to climb after him like a squirrel, and catch some glimpse of the heaven in which he lives. And the true realism, always and everywhere, is that of the poets: to find out where joy resides, and give it a voice far beyond singing.

"For to miss the joy is to miss all. In the joy of the actors lies the sense of any action. That is the explanation, that the excuse. To one who has not the secret of the lanterns the scene upon the links is meaningless. And hence the haunting and truly spectral unreality of realistic books. . . . In each we miss the personal poetry, the enchanted atmosphere, that rainbow work of fancy that clothes what is naked and seems to ennoble what is base; in each, life falls dead like dough, instead of soaring away like a balloon into the colors of the sunset; each is true, each inconceivable; for no man lives in the external truth among salts and acids, but in the warm, phantasmagoric chamber of his brain, with the painted windows and the storied wall."[1]

These paragraphs are the best thing I know in all Stevenson. "To miss the joy is to miss all." Indeed, it is. Yet we are but finite, and each one of us has some single specialized vocation of his own. And it seems as if energy in the service of its particular duties might be got only by hardening the heart toward everything unlike them. Our deadness toward all but one particular kind of joy would thus be the price we inevitably have to pay for being practical creatures. Only in some pitiful dreamer, some philosopher, poet, or romancer, or when the common practical man becomes a lover, does the hard externality give way, and a gleam of insight into the ejective world, as Clifford called it, the vast world of inner life beyond us, so different from that of outer seeming, illuminate our mind. Then the whole scheme of our customary values gets confounded, then our self is riven and its narrow interests fly to pieces, then a new centre and a new perspective must be found. . . .

Richard Jefferies has written a remarkable autobiographic document entitled *The Story of my Heart*. It tells, in many pages, of the rapture with which in youth the sense of the life of Nature filled him. On a certain hill-top he says:

"I was utterly alone with the sun and the earth. Lying down on the grass, I spoke in my soul to the earth, the sun, the air, and the distant sea, far beyond sight. . . . With all the intensity of feeling which exalted me, all the intense communion I held with the earth, the sun and sky, the stars hidden by the light, with the ocean—in no manner can the thrilling depth of these feelings be written—with these I prayed as if they were the keys of an instrument. . . . The great sun, burning with light, the strong earth—dear earth—the warm sky, the pure air, the thought of ocean, the inexpressible beauty of all filled me with a rapture, an ecstasy, an inflatus. With this inflatus, too, I prayed. . . . The prayer, this soul-emotion, was in itself, not for an object: it was a passion. I

---

1. "The Lantern-Bearers," in the volume entitled *Across the Plains*. Abridged in the quotation.

hid my face in the grass. I was wholly prostrated, I lost myself in the wrestle, I was rapt and carried away. . . . Had any shepherd accidentally seen me lying on the turf, he would only have thought I was resting a few minutes. I made no outward show. Who could have imagined the whirlwind of passion that was going on in me as I reclined there!"[2]

Surely, a worthless hour of life, when measured by the usual standards of commercial value. Yet in what other *kind* of value can the preciousness of any hour, made precious by any standard, consist, if it consist not in feelings of excited significance like these, engendered in some one, by what the hour contains?

Yet so blind and dead does the clamor of our own practical interests make us to all other things, that it seems almost as if it were necessary to become worthless as a practical being, if one is to hope to attain to any breadth of insight into the impersonal world of worths as such, to have any perception of life's meaning on a large objective scale. Only your mystic, your dreamer, or your insolvent tramp or loafer, can afford so sympathetic an occupation, an occupation which will change the usual standards of human value in the twinkling of an eye, giving to foolishness a place ahead of power, and laying low in a minute the distinctions which it takes a hard-working conventional man a lifetime to build up. You may be a prophet, at this rate; but you cannot be a worldly success.

Walt Whitman, for instance, is accounted by many of us a contemporary prophet. He abolishes the usual human distinctions, brings all conventionalisms into solution, and loves and celebrates hardly any human attributes save those elementary ones common to all members of the race. For this he becomes a sort of ideal tramp, a rider on omnibus-tops and ferry-boats, and, considered either practically or academically, a worthless, unproductive being. His verses are but ejaculations—things mostly without subject or verb, a succession of interjections on an immense scale. He felt the human crowd as rapturously as Wordsworth felt the mountains, felt it as an overpoweringly significant presence, simply to absorb one's mind in which should be business sufficient and

2. *Op. cit.*, Boston, Roberts, 1883, pp. 5, 6.

worthy to fill the days of a serious man. As he crosses Brooklyn ferry, this is what he feels:

> Flood-tide below me! I watch you, face to face;
> Clouds of the west! sun there half an hour high! I see you also face to face.
> Crowds of men and women attired in the usual costumes! how curious you are to me!
> On the ferry-boats, the hundreds and hundreds that cross, returning home, are more curious to me than you suppose;
> And you that shall cross from shore to shore years hence, are more to me, and more in my meditations, than you might suppose.
> Others will enter the gates of the ferry, and cross from shore to shore;
> Others will watch the run of the flood-tide;
> Others will see the shipping of Manhattan north and west, and the heights of Brooklyn to the south and east;
> Others will see the islands large and small;
> Fifty years hence, others will see them as they cross, the sun half an hour high.
> A hundred years hence, or ever so many hundred years hence, others will see them,
> Will enjoy the sunset, the pouring in of the flood-tide, the falling back to the sea of the ebb-tide.
> It avails not, neither time or place—distance avails not.
> Just as you feel when you look on the river and sky, so I felt;
> Just as any of you is one of a living crowd, I was one of a crowd;
> Just as you are refresh'd by the gladness of the river and the bright flow, I was refresh'd;
> Just as you stand and lean on the rail, yet hurry with the swift current, I stood, yet was hurried;
> Just as you look on the numberless masts of ships, and the thick-stemmed pipes of steamboats, I looked.
> I too many and many a time cross'd the river, the sun half an hour high;
> I watched the Twelfth-month sea-gulls—I saw them high in the air, with motionless wings, oscillating their bodies,

I saw how the glistening yellow lit up parts of their bodies,
and left the rest in strong shadow,
I saw the slow-wheeling circles, and the gradual edging
toward the south.
Saw the white sails of schooners and sloops, saw the ships
at anchor,
The sailors at work in the rigging, or out astride the spars;
The scallop-edged waves in the twilight, the ladled cups,
the frolicsome crests and glistening;
The stretch afar growing dimmer and dimmer, the gray
walls of the granite store-houses by the docks;
On the neighboring shores, the fires from the foundry
chimneys burning high . . . into the night,
Casting their flicker of black . . . into the clefts of
streets.
These, and all else, were to me the same as they are to
you.[3]

And so on, through the rest of a divinely beautiful poem. And,
if you wish to see what this hoary loafer considered the most
worthy way of profiting by life's heaven-sent opportunities, read
the delicious volume of his letters to a young car-conductor who
had become his friend:

"NEW YORK, Oct. 9, 1868.

"dear Pete—It is splendid here this forenoon—bright and cool.
I was out early taking a short walk by the river only two squares
from where I live. . . . Shall I tell you about [my life] just to fill
up? I generally spend the forenoon in my room writing, etc., then
take a bath fix up and go out about twelve and loafe somewhere or
call on someone down town or on business, or perhaps if it is very
pleasant and I feel like it ride a trip with some driver friend on
Broadway from 23rd Street to Bowling Green, three miles each
way. (Every day I find I have plenty to do, every hour is occupied
with something.) You know it is a never ending amusement and
study and recreation for me to ride a couple of hours on a pleasant
afternoon on a Broadway stage in this way. You see everything as
you pass, a sort of living, endless panorama—shops and splendid

3. *Crossing Brooklyn Ferry* (abridged).

buildings and great windows: on the broad sidewalks crowds of
women richly dressed continually passing, altogether different,
superior in style and looks, from any to be seen anywhere else—in
fact a perfect stream of people—men too dressed in high style, and
plenty of foreigners—and then in the streets the thick crowd of
carriages, stages, carts, hotel and private coaches, and in fact all
sorts of vehicles and many first class teams, mile after mile, and the
splendor of such a great street and so many tall, ornamental, noble
buildings many of them of white marble, and the gayety and
motion on every side: you will not wonder how much attraction
all this is on a fine day, to a great loafer like me, who enjoys so
much seeing the busy world move by him, and exhibiting itself for
his amusement, while he takes it easy and just looks on and
observes."[4]

Truly a futile way of passing the time, some of you may say, and
not altogether creditable to a grown-up man. And yet, from the
deepest point of view, who knows the more of truth, and who
knows the less—Whitman on his omnibus-top, full of the inner joy
with which the spectacle inspires him, or you, full of the disdain
which the futility of his occupation excites?

When your ordinary Brooklynite or New Yorker, leading a life
replete with too much luxury, or tired and careworn about his
personal affairs, crosses the ferry or goes up Broadway, *his* fancy
does not thus 'soar away into the colors of the sunset' as did
Whitman's, nor does he inwardly realize at all the indisputable
fact that this world never did anywhere or at any time contain
more of essential divinity, or of eternal meaning, than is embodied
in the fields of vision over which his eyes so carelessly pass. There
is life; and there, a step away, is death. There is the only kind of
beauty there ever was. There is the old human struggle and its
fruits together. There is the text and the sermon, the real and the
ideal in one. But to the jaded and unquickened eye it is all dead
and common, pure vulgarism, flatness, and disgust. "Hech! it is a
sad sight!" says Carlyle, walking at night with some one who
appeals to him to note the splendor of the stars. And that very
repetition of the scene to new generations of men *in secula
seculorum,* that eternal recurrence of the common order, which so

4. *Calamus,* Boston, 1897, pp. 41, 42.

fills a Whitman with mystic satisfaction, is to a Schopenhauer, with the emotional anæsthesia, the feeling of 'awful inner emptiness' from out of which he views it all, the chief ingredient of the tedium it instils. What is life on the largest scale, he asks, but the same recurrent inanities, the same dog barking, the same fly buzzing, forevermore? Yet of the kind of fibre of which such inanities consist is the material woven of all the excitements, joys, and meanings that ever were, or ever shall be, in this world.

To be rapt with satisfied attention, like Whitman, to the mere spectacle of the world's presence, is one way, and the most fundamental way, of confessing one's sense of its unfathomable significance and importance. But how can one attain to the feeling of the vital significance of an experience, if one have it not to begin with? There is no receipt which one can follow. Being a secret and a mystery, it often comes in mysteriously unexpected ways. It blossoms sometimes from out of the very grave wherein we imagined that our happiness was buried. Benvenuto Cellini, after a life all in the outer sunshine, made of adventures and artistic excitements, suddenly finds himself cast into a dungeon in the Castle of San Angelo. The place is horrible. Rats and wet and mould possess it. His leg is broken and his teeth fall out, apparently with scurvy. But his thoughts turn to God as they have never turned before. He gets a Bible, which he reads during the one hour in the twenty-four in which a wandering ray of daylight penetrates his cavern. He has religious visions. He sings psalms to himself, and composes hymns. And thinking, on the last day of July, of the festivities customary on the morrow in Rome, he says to himself: "All these past years I celebrated this holiday with the vanities of the world: from this year henceforward I will do it with the divinity of God. And then I said to myself, 'Oh, how much more happy I am for this present life of mine than for all those remembered!' "[5]

But the great understander of these mysterious ebbs and flows is Tolstoï. They throb all through his novels. In his 'War and Peace,' the hero, Peter, is supposed to be the richest man in the Russian empire. During the French invasion he is taken prisoner, and dragged through much of the retreat. Cold, vermin, hunger, and every form of misery assail him, the result being a revelation to

5. *Vita*, lib. 2, chap. iv.

him of the real scale of life's values. "Here only, and for the first time, he appreciated, because he was deprived of it, the happiness of eating when he was hungry, of drinking when he was thirsty, of sleeping when he was sleepy, and of talking when he felt the desire to exchange some words. . . . Later in life he always recurred with joy to this month of captivity, and never failed to speak with enthusiasm of the powerful and ineffaceable sensations, and especially of the moral calm which he had experienced at this epoch. When at daybreak, on the morrow of his imprisonment, he saw [I abridge here Tolstoï's description] the mountains with their wooded slopes disappearing in the grayish mist; when he felt the cool breeze caress him; when he saw the light drive away the vapors, and the sun rise majestically behind the clouds and cupolas, and the crosses, the dew, the distance, the river, sparkle in the splendid, cheerful rays—his heart overflowed with emotion. This emotion kept continually with him, and increased a hundredfold as the difficulties of his situation grew graver. . . . He learnt that man is meant for happiness, and that this happiness is in him, in the satisfaction of the daily needs of existence, and that unhappiness is the fatal result, not of our need, but of our abundance. . . . When calm reigned in the camp, and the embers paled, and little by little went out, the full moon had reached the zenith. The woods and the fields roundabout lay clearly visible; and, beyond the inundation of light which filled them, the view plunged into the limitless horizon. Then Peter cast his eyes upon the firmament, filled at that hour with myriads of stars. 'All that is mine,' he thought. 'All that is in me, is me! And that is what they think they have taken prisoner! That is what they have shut up in a cabin!' So he smiled, and turned in to sleep among his comrades."[6]

The occasion and the experience, then, are nothing. It all depends on the capacity of the soul to be grasped, to have its life-currents absorbed by what is given. "Crossing a bare common," says Emerson, "in snow puddles, at twilight, under a clouded sky, without having in my thoughts any occurrence of special good fortune, I have enjoyed a perfect exhilaration. I am glad to the brink of fear."

6. *La Guerre et la Paix*, Paris, 1884, vol. iii. pp. 268, 275, 316.

Life is always worth living, if one have such responsive sensibilities. But we of the highly educated classes (so called) have most of us got far, far away from Nature. We are trained to seek the choice, the rare, the exquisite exclusively, and to overlook the common. We are stuffed with abstract conceptions, and glib with verbalities and verbosities; and in the culture of these higher functions the peculiar sources of joy connected with our simpler functions often dry up, and we grow stone-blind and insensible to life's more elementary and general goods and joys.

The remedy under such conditions is to descend to a more profound and primitive level. To be imprisoned or shipwrecked or forced into the army would permanently show the good of life to many an over-educated pessimist. Living in the open air and on the ground, the lop-sided beam of the balance slowly rises to the level line; and the over-sensibilities and insensibilities even themselves out. The good of all the artificial schemes and fevers fades and pales; and that of seeing, smelling, tasting, sleeping, and daring and doing with one's body, grows and grows. The savages and children of Nature, to whom we deem ourselves so much superior, certainly are alive where we are often dead, along these lines; and, could they write as glibly as we do, they would read us impressive lectures on our impatience for improvement and on our blindness to the fundamental static goods of life. "Ah! my brother," said a chieftain to his white guest, "thou wilt never know the happiness of both thinking of nothing and doing nothing. This, next to sleep, is the most enchanting of all things. Thus we were before our birth, and thus we shall be after death. Thy people, . . . when they have finished reaping one field, they begin to plough another; and, if the day were not enough, I have seen them plough by moonlight. What is their life to ours—the life that is as naught to them? Blind that they are, they lose it all! But we live in the present."[7]

The intense interest that life can assume when brought down to the non-thinking level, the level of pure sensorial perception, has been beautifully described by a man who *can* write—Mr. W. H. Hudson, in his volume, "Idle Days in Patagonia."

7. Quoted by Lotze, *Microcosmus*, English translation, vol. ii. p. 240.

"I spent the greater part of one winter," says this admirable author, "at a point on the Rio Negro, seventy or eighty miles from the sea.

. . . "It was my custom to go out every morning on horseback with my gun, and, followed by one dog, to ride away from the valley; and no sooner would I climb the terrace, and plunge into the gray, universal thicket, than I would find myself as completely alone as if five hundred instead of only five miles separated me from the valley and river. So wild and solitary and remote seemed that gray waste, stretching away into infinitude, a waste untrodden by man, and where the wild animals are so few that they have made no discoverable path in the wilderness of thorns. . . . Not once nor twice nor thrice, but day after day I returned to this solitude, going to it in the morning as if to attend a festival, and leaving it only when hunger and thirst and the westering sun compelled me. And yet I had no object in going—no motive which could be put into words; for, although I carried a gun, there was nothing to shoot—the shooting was all left behind in the valley. . . . Sometimes I would pass a whole day without seeing one mammal, and perhaps not more than a dozen birds of any size. The weather at that time was cheerless, generally with a gray film of cloud spread over the sky, and a bleak wind, often cold enough to make my bridle-hand quite numb. . . . At a slow pace, which would have seemed intolerable under other circumstances, I would ride about for hours together at a stretch. On arriving at a hill, I would slowly ride to its summit, and stand there to survey the prospect. On every side it stretched away in great undulations, wild and irregular. How gray it all was! Hardly less so near at hand than on the haze-wrapped horizon where the hills were dim and the outline obscured by distance. Descending from my outlook, I would take up my aimless wanderings again, and visit other elevations to gaze on the same landscape from another point; and so on for hours. And at noon I would dismount, and sit or lie on my folded poncho for an hour or longer. One day in these rambles I discovered a small grove composed of twenty or thirty trees, growing at a convenient distance apart, that had evidently been resorted to by a herd of deer or other wild animals. This grove was on a hill differing in shape from other hills in its neighborhood; and, after a time, I made a point of finding and using it as a resting-place every day at noon. I did not ask myself why I made choice of that one spot, sometimes going out of my way to sit there, instead of sitting down under any one of the millions of trees and bushes on any other hillside. I thought nothing about it, but acted unconsciously. Only afterward it seemed to me that, after having rested there once, each time I wished to rest again, the wish came associated with the image of that particular clump of trees, with polished stems and clean bed of sand beneath; and in a short time I formed a habit of return-ing, animal like, to repose at that same spot.

"It was, perhaps, a mistake to say that I would sit down and rest, since I was never tired; and yet, without being tired, that noon-day pause, during which I sat for an hour without moving, was strangely grateful. All day there would be no sound, not even the rustling of a leaf. One day, while *listening* to the silence, it occurred to my mind to wonder what the effect would be if I were to shout aloud. This seemed at the time a horrible suggestion, which almost made me shudder. But during those solitary days it was a rare thing for any thought to cross my mind. In the state of mind I was in, thought had become impossible. My state was one of *suspense* and *watchfulness;* yet I had no expectation of meeting an adventure, and felt as free from apprehension as I feel now while sitting in a room in London. The state seemed familiar rather than strange, and accompanied by a strong feeling of ela-tion; and I did not know that something had come between me and my intellect until I returned to my former self—to thinking, and the old insipid existence [again].

"I had undoubtedly *gone back;* and that state of intense watch-fulness or alertness, rather, with suspension of the higher intellec-tual faculties, represented the mental state of the pure savage. He thinks little, reasons little, having a surer guide in his [mere sensory perceptions]. He is in perfect harmony with nature, and is nearly on a level, mentally, with the wild animals he preys on, and which in their turn sometimes prey on him."[8]

For the spectator, such hours as Mr. Hudson writes of form a mere tale of emptiness, in which nothing happens, nothing is gained, and there is nothing to describe. They are meaningless

8. *Op. cit.,* pp. 210–222 (abridged).

and vacant tracts of time. To him who feels their inner secret, they tingle with an importance that unutterably vouches for itself. I am sorry for the boy or girl, or man or woman, who has never been touched by the spell of this mysterious sensorial life, with its irrationality, if so you like to call it, but its vigilance and its supreme felicity. The holidays of life are its most vitally significant portions, because they are, or at least should be, covered with just this kind of magically irresponsible spell.

And now what is the result of all these considerations and quotations? It is negative in one sense, but positive in another. It absolutely forbids us to be forward in pronouncing on the meaninglessness of forms of existence other than our own; and it commands us to tolerate, respect, and indulge those whom we see harmlessly interested and happy in their own ways, however unintelligible these may be to us. Hands off: neither the whole of truth nor the whole of good is revealed to any single observer, although each observer gains a partial superiority of insight from the peculiar position in which he stands. Even prisons and sickrooms have their special revelations. It is enough to ask of each of us that he should be faithful to his own opportunities and make the most of his own blessings, without presuming to regulate the rest of the vast field.

14.

The Ph.D. Octopus*

. . . Human nature is once for all so childish that every reality becomes a sham somewhere, and in the minds of Presidents and Trustees the Ph.D. degree is in point of fact already looked upon as a mere advertising resource, a manner of throwing dust in the Public's eyes. "No instructor who is not a Doctor" has become a maxim in the smaller institutions which represent demand; and in each of the larger ones which represent supply, the same belief in decorated scholarship expresses itself in two antagonistic passions, one for multiplying as much as possible the annual output of doctors, the other for raising the standard of difficulty in passing, so that the Ph.D. of the special institution shall carry a higher blaze of distinction than it does elsewhere. Thus we at Harvard are proud of the number of candidates whom we reject, and of the inability of men who are not *distingués* in intellect to pass our tests.

America is thus as a nation rapidly drifting towards a state of things in which no man of science or letters will be accounted respectable unless some kind of badge or diploma is stamped upon him, and in which bare personality will be a mark of outcast estate. It seems to me high time to rouse ourselves to consciousness, and to cast a critical eye upon this decidedly grotesque tendency. Other nations suffer terribly from the Mandarin disease. Are we doomed to suffer like the rest?

Our higher degrees were instituted for the laudable purpose of stimulating scholarship, especially in the form of "original research." Experience has proved that great as the love of truth may be among men, it can be made still greater by adventitious rewards. The winning of a diploma certifying mastery and marking

* Published in the *Harvard Monthly* (March, 1903). Initial and final anecdotal pages have been deleted. [B.W.]

a barrier successfully passed, acts as a challenge to the ambitious; and if the diploma will help to gain bread-winning positions also, its power as a stimulus to work is tremendously increased. So far, we are on innocent ground; it is well for a country to have research in abundance, and our graduate schools do but apply a normal psychological spur. But the institutionizing on a large scale of any natural combination of need and motive always tends to run into technicality and to develop a tyrannical Machine with unforeseen powers of exclusion and corruption. Observation of the workings of our Harvard system for twenty years past has brought some of these drawbacks home to my consciousness, and I should like to call the attention of my readers to this disadvantageous aspect of the picture, and to make a couple of remedial suggestions, if I may.

In the first place, it would seem that to stimulate study, and to increase the *gelehrtes Publikum,* the class of highly educated men in our country, is the only positive good, and consequently the sole direct end at which our graduate schools, with their diploma-giving powers, should aim. If other results have developed they should be deemed secondary incidents, and if not desirable in themselves, they should be carefully guarded against.

To interfere with the free development of talent, to obstruct the natural play of supply and demand in the teaching profession, to foster academic snobbery by the prestige of certain privileged institutions, to transfer accredited value from essential manhood to an outward badge, to blight hopes and promote invidious sentiments, to divert the attention of aspiring youth from direct dealings with truth to the passing of examinations—such consequences, if they exist, ought surely to be regarded as drawbacks to the system, and an enlightened public consciousness ought to be keenly alive to the importance of reducing their amount. Candidates themselves do seem to be keenly conscious of some of these evils, but outside of their ranks or in the general public no such consciousness, so far as I can see, exists; or if it does exist, it fails to express itself aloud. Schools, Colleges, and Universities, appear enthusiastic over the entire system, just as it stands, and unanimously applaud all its developments.

I beg the reader to consider some of the secondary evils which I have enumerated. First of all, is not our growing tendency to appoint no instructors who are not also doctors an instance of pure sham? Will any one pretend for a moment that the doctor's degree is a guarantee that its possessor will be successful as a teacher? Notoriously his moral, social and personal characteristics may utterly disqualify him for success in the class-room; and of these characteristics his doctor's examination is unable to take any account whatever. Certain bare human beings will always be better candidates for a given place than all the doctor-applicants on hand; and to exclude the former by a rigid rule, and in the end to have to sift the latter by private inquiry into their personal peculiarities among those who know them, just as if they were not doctors at all, is to stultify one's own procedure. You may say that at least you guard against ignorance of the subject by considering only the candidates who are doctors; but how then about making doctors in one subject teach a different subject? This happened in the instance by which I introduced this article, and it happens daily and hourly in all our colleges. The truth is that the Doctor-Monopoly in teaching, which is becoming so rooted an American custom, can show no serious grounds whatsoever for itself in reason. As it actually prevails and grows in vogue among us, it is due to childish motives exclusively. In reality it is but a sham, a bauble, a dodge, whereby to decorate the catalogues of schools and colleges.

Next, let us turn from the general promotion of a spirit of academic snobbery to the particular damage done to individuals by the system.

There are plenty of individuals so well endowed by nature that they pass with ease all the ordeals with which life confronts them. Such persons are born for professional success. Examinations have no terrors for them, and interfere in no way with their spiritual or worldly interests. There are others, not so gifted, who nevertheless rise to the challenge, get a stimulus from the difficulty, and become doctors, not without some baleful nervous wear and tear and retardation of their purely inner life, but on the whole successfully, and with advantage. These two classes form the natural Ph.D.'s for whom the degree is legitimately instituted. To be sure, the degree is of no consequence one way or the other for the first sort of man, for in him the personal worth obviously outshines the title. To the second set of persons, however, the doctor ordeal may contribute a touch of energy and solidity of scholarship which otherwise they might have lacked, and were our candidates all drawn from these classes, no oppression would result from the institution.

But there is a third class of persons who are genuinely, and in the most pathetic sense, the institution's victims. For this type of character the academic life may become, after a certain point, a virulent poison. Men without marked originality or native force, but fond of truth and especially of books and study, ambitious of reward and recognition, poor often, and needing a degree to get a teaching position, weak in the eyes of their examiners—among these we find the veritable *chair à canon* of the wars of learning, the unfit in the academic struggle for existence. There are individuals of this sort for whom to pass one degree after another seems the limit of earthly aspiration. Your private advice does not discourage them. They will fail, and go away to recuperate, and then present themselves for another ordeal, and sometimes prolong the process into middle life. Or else, if they are less heroic morally they will accept the failure as a sentence of doom that they are not fit, and are broken-spirited men thereafter.

We of the university faculties are responsible for deliberately creating this new class of American social failures, and heavy is the responsibility. We advertise our "schools" and send out our degree-requirements, knowing well that aspirants of all sorts will be attracted, and at the same time we set a standard which intends to pass no man who has not native intellectual distinction. We know that there is no test, however absurd, by which, if a title or decoration, a public badge or mark, were to be won by it, some weakly suggestible or hauntable persons would not feel challenged, and remain unhappy if they went without it. We dangle our three magic letters before the eyes of these predestined victims, and they swarm to us like moths to an electric light. They come at a time when failure can no longer be repaired easily and when the wounds it leaves are permanent; and we say deliberately that mere work faithfully performed, as they perform it, will not by itself save them; they must in addition put in evidence the one thing they have not got, namely this quality of intellectual distinction. Occasionally, out of sheer human pity, we ignore our high and mighty standard and pass them. Usually, however, the standard, and not the candidate, commands our fidelity. The result is caprice, majorities of one on the jury, and on the whole a confession that our pretensions about the degree cannot be lived up to consistently. Thus, partiality in the favored cases; in the unfavored, blood on our hands; and in both a bad conscience—are the results of our administration.

The more widespread becomes the popular belief that our diplomas are indispensable hall-marks to show the sterling metal of their holders, the more widespread these corruptions will become. We ought to look to the future carefully, for it takes generations for a national custom, once rooted, to be grown away from. All the European countries are seeking to diminish the check upon individual spontaneity which state examinations with their tyrannous growth have brought in their train. We have had to institute state examinations too; and it will perhaps be fortunate if some day hereafter our descendants, comparing machine with machine, do not sigh with regret for old times and American freedom, and wish that the *régime* of the dear old bosses might be reinstalled, with plain human nature, the glad hand and the marble heart, liking and disliking, and man-to-man relations grown possible again. Meanwhile, whatever evolution our state-examinations are destined to undergo, our universities at least should never cease to regard themselves as the jealous custodians of personal and spiritual spontaneity. They are indeed its only organized and recognized custodians in America to-day. They ought to guard against contributing to the increase of officialism and snobbery and insincerity as against a pestilence; they ought to keep truth and disinterested labor always in the foreground, treat degrees as secondary incidents, and in season and out of season make it plain that what they live for is to help men's souls, and not to decorate their persons with diplomas.

There seem to be three obvious ways in which the increasing hold of the Ph.D. Octopus upon American life can be kept in check.

The first way lies with the universities. They can lower their fantastic standards (which here at Harvard we are so proud of) and give the doctorate as a matter of course, just as they give the bachelor's degree, for a due amount of time spent in patient labor in a special department of learning, whether the man be a brilliantly gifted individual or not. Surely native distinction needs no official stamp, and should disdain to ask for one. On the other hand, faithful labor, however commonplace, and years devoted to a subject, always deserve to be acknowledged and requited.

The second way lies with both the universities and colleges. Let them give up their unspeakably silly ambition to bespangle their lists of officers with these doctorial titles. Let them look more to substance and less to vanity and sham.

The third way lies with the individual student, and with his personal advisers in the faculties. Every man of native power, who might take a higher degree, and refuses to do so, because examinations interfere with the free following out of his more immediate intellectual aims, deserves well of his country, and in a rightly organized community, would not be made to suffer for his independence. With many men the passing of these extraneous tests is a very grievous interference indeed. Private letters of recommendation from their instructors, which in any event are ultimately needful, ought, in these cases, completely to offset the lack of the bread-winning degree; and instructors ought to be ready to advise students against it upon occasion, and to pledge themselves to back them later personally, in the market-struggle which they have to face.

It is indeed odd to see this love of titles—and such titles—growing up in a country of which the recognition of individuality and bare manhood have so long been supposed to be the very soul. . . .

15.

The Moral Equivalent of War*

The war against war is going to be no holiday excursion or camping party. The military feelings are too deeply grounded to abdicate their place among our ideals until better substitutes are offered than the glory and shame that come to nations as well as to individuals from the ups and downs of politics and the vicissitudes of trade. There is something highly paradoxical in the modern man's relation to war. Ask all our millions, north and south, whether they would vote now (were such a thing possible) to have our war for the Union expunged from history, and the record of a peaceful transition to the present time substituted for that of its marches and battles, and probably hardly a handful of eccentrics would say yes. Those ancestors, those efforts, those memories and legends, are the most ideal part of what we now own together, a sacred spiritual possession worth more than all the blood poured out. Yet ask those same people whether they would be willing in cold blood to start another civil war now to gain another similar possession, and not one man or woman would vote for the proposition. In modern eyes, precious though wars may be, they must not be waged solely for the sake of the ideal harvest. Only when forced upon one, only when an enemy's injustice leaves us no alternative, is a war now thought permissible.

It was not thus in ancient times. The earlier men were hunting men, and to hunt a neighboring tribe, kill the males, loot the village and possess the females, was the most profitable, as well as the most exciting, way of living. Thus were the more martial tribes selected, and in chiefs and peoples a pure pugnacity and love of glory came to mingle with the more fundamental appetite for plunder.

* Written for and first published by the Association for International Conciliation (Leaflet No. 27) and also published in *McClure's Magazine* (August, 1910) and the *Popular Science Monthly* (October, 1910).

Modern war is so expensive that we feel trade to be a better avenue to plunder; but modern man inherits all the innate pugnacity and all the love of glory of his ancestors. Showing war's irrationality and horror is of no effect upon him. The horrors make the fascination. War is the *strong* life; it is life *in extremis;* war-taxes are the only ones men never hesitate to pay, as the budgets of all nations show us.

History is a bath of blood. The Iliad is one long recital of how Diomedes and Ajax, Sarpedon and Hector *killed.* No detail of the wounds they made is spared us, and the Greek mind fed upon the story. Greek history is a panorama of jingoism and imperialism— war for war's sake, all the citizens being warriors. It is horrible reading, because of the irrationality of it all—save for the purpose of making "history"—and the history is that of the utter ruin of a civilization in intellectual respects perhaps the highest the earth has ever seen.

Those wars were purely piratical. Pride, gold, women, slaves, excitement, were their only motives. In the Peloponnesian war for example, the Athenians ask the inhabitants of Melos (the island where the "Venus of Milo" was found), hitherto neutral, to own their lordship. The envoys meet, and hold a debate which Thucydides gives in full, and which, for sweet reasonableness of form, would have satisfied Matthew Arnold. "The powerful exact what they can," said the Athenians, "and the weak grant what they must." When the Meleans say that sooner than be slaves they will appeal to the gods, the Athenians reply: "Of the gods we believe and of men we know that, by a law of their nature, wherever they can rule they will. This law was not made by us, and we are not the first to have acted upon it; we did but inherit it, and we know that you and all mankind, if you were as strong as we are, would do as we do. So much for the gods; we have told you why we expect to stand as high in their opinion as you." Well, the Meleans still refused, and their town was taken. "The Athenians," Thucydides quietly says, "thereupon put to death all who were of military age and made slaves of the women and children. They then colonized the island, sending thither five hundred settlers of their own."

Alexander's career was piracy pure and simple, nothing but an orgy of power and plunder, made romantic by the character of the hero. There was no rational principle in it, and the moment he died his generals and governors attacked one another. The cruelty of those times is incredible. When Rome finally conquered Greece, Paulus Æmilius was told by the Roman Senate to reward his soldiers for their toil by "giving" them the old kingdom of Epirus. They sacked seventy cities and carried off a hundred and fifty thousand inhabitants as slaves. How many they killed I know not; but in Etolia they killed all the senators, five hundred and fifty in number. Brutus was "the noblest Roman of them all," but to reanimate his soldiers on the eve of Philippi he similarly promises to give them the cities of Sparta and Thessalonica to ravage, if they win the fight.

Such was the gory nurse that trained societies to cohesiveness. We inherit the warlike type; and for most of the capacities of heroism that the human race is full of we have to thank this cruel history. Dead men tell no tales, and if there were any tribes of other type than this they have left no survivors. Our ancestors have bred pugnacity into our bone and marrow, and thousands of years of peace won't breed it out of us. The popular imagination fairly fattens on the thought of wars. Let public opinion once reach a certain fighting pitch, and no ruler can withstand it. In the Boer war both governments began with bluff but couldn't stay there, the military tension was too much for them. In 1898 our people had read the word "war" in letters three inches high for three months in every newspaper. The pliant politician McKinley was swept away by their eagerness, and our squalid war with Spain became a necessity.

At the present day, civilized opinion is a curious mental mixture. The military instincts and ideals are as strong as ever, but are confronted by reflective criticisms which sorely curb their ancient freedom. Innumerable writers are showing up the bestial side of military service. Pure loot and mastery seem no longer morally avowable motives, and pretexts must be found for attributing them solely to the enemy. England and we, our army and navy authorities repeat without ceasing, arm solely for "peace," Germany and Japan it is who are bent on loot and glory. "Peace" in military mouths to-day is a synonym for "war expected." The word has become a pure provocative, and no government wishing peace sincerely should allow it ever to be printed in a newspaper.

Every up-to-date dictionary should say that "peace" and "war" mean the same thing, now *in posse*, now *in actu*. It may even reasonably be said that the intensely sharp competitive *preparation* for war by the nations *is the real war*, permanent, unceasing; and that the battles are only a sort of public verification of the mastery gained during the "peace" interval.

It is plain that on this subject civilized man has developed a sort of double personality. If we take European nations, no legitimate interest of any one of them would seem to justify the tremendous destructions which a war to compass it would necessarily entail. It would seem as though common sense and reason ought to find a way to reach agreement in every conflict of honest interests. I myself think it our bounden duty to believe in such international rationality as possible. But, as things stand, I see how desperately hard it is to bring the peace-party and the war-party together, and I believe that the difficulty is due to certain deficiencies in the program of pacificism which set the militarist imagination strongly, and to a certain extent justifiably, against it. In the whole discussion both sides are on imaginative and sentimental ground. It is but one utopia against another, and everything one says must be abstract and hypothetical. Subject to this criticism and caution, I will try to characterize in abstract strokes the opposite imaginative forces, and point out what to my own very fallible mind seems the best utopian hypothesis, the most promising line of conciliation.

In my remarks, pacificist though I am, I will refuse to speak of the bestial side of the war-*régime* (already done justice to by many writers) and consider only the higher aspects of militaristic sentiment. Patriotism no one thinks discreditable; nor does any one deny that war is the romance of history. But inordinate ambitions are the soul of every patriotism, and the possibility of violent death the soul of all romance. The militarily patriotic and romantic-minded everywhere, and especially the professional military class, refuse to admit for a moment that war may be a transitory phenomenon in social evolution. The notion of a sheep's paradise like that revolts, they say, our higher imagination. Where then would be the steeps of life? If war had ever stopped, we should have to re-invent it, on this view, to redeem life from flat degeneration.

Reflective apologists for war at the present day all take it religiously. It is a sort of sacrament. Its profits are to the vanquished as well as to the victor; and quite apart from any question of profit, it is an absolute good, we are told, for it is human nature at its highest dynamic. Its "horrors" are a cheap price to pay for rescue from the only alternative supposed, of a world of clerks and teachers, of co-education and zo-ophily, of "consumer's leagues" and "associated charities," of industrialism unlimited, and femininism unabashed. No scorn, no hardness, no valor any more! Fie upon such a cattleyard of a planet!

So far as the central essence of this feeling goes, no healthy-minded person, it seems to me, can help to some degree partaking of it. Militarism is the great preserver of our ideals of hardihood, and human life with no use for hardihood would be contemptible. Without risks or prizes for the darer, history would be insipid indeed; and there is a type of military character which every one feels that the race should never cease to breed, for every one is sensitive to its superiority. The duty is incumbent on mankind, of keeping military characters in stock—of keeping them, if not for use, then as ends in themselves and as pure pieces of perfection—so that Roosevelt's weaklings and mollycoddles may not end by making everything else disappear from the face of nature.

This natural sort of feeling forms, I think, the innermost soul of army-writings. Without any exception known to me, militarist authors take a highly mystical view of their subject, and regard war as a biological or sociological necessity, uncontrolled by ordinary psychological checks and motives. When the time of development is ripe the war must come, reason or no reason, for the justifications pleaded are invariably fictitious. War is, in short, a permanent human *obligation*. General Homer Lea, in his recent book "The Valor of Ignorance," plants himself squarely on this ground. Readiness for war is for him the essence of nationality, and ability in it the supreme measure of the health of nations.

Nations, General Lea says, are never stationary—they must necessarily expand or shrink, according to their vitality or decrepitude. Japan now is culminating; and by the fatal law in question it is impossible that her statesmen should not long since have entered, with extraordinary foresight, upon a vast policy of conquest—the game in which the first moves were her wars with

China and Russia and her treaty with England, and of which the final objective is the capture of the Philippines, the Hawaiian Islands, Alaska, and the whole of our Coast west of the Sierra Passes. This will give Japan what her ineluctable vocation as a state absolutely forces her to claim, the possession of the entire Pacific Ocean; and to oppose these deep designs we Americans have, according to our author, nothing but our conceit, our ignorance, our commercialism, our corruption, and our feminism. General Lea makes a minute technical comparison of the military strength which we at present could oppose to the strength of Japan, and concludes that the islands, Alaska, Oregon, and Southern California, would fall almost without resistance, that San Francisco must surrender in a fortnight to a Japanese investment, that in three or four months the war would be over, and our republic, unable to regain what it had heedlessly neglected to protect sufficiently, would then "disintegrate," until perhaps some Cæsar should arise to weld us again into a nation.

A dismal forecast indeed! Yet not unplausible, if the mentality of Japan's statesmen be of the Cæsarian type of which history shows so many examples, and which is all that General Lea seems able to imagine. But there is no reason to think that women can no longer be the mothers of Napoleonic or Alexandrian characters; and if these come in Japan and find their opportunity, just such surprises as "The Valor of Ignorance" paints may lurk in ambush for us. Ignorant as we still are of the innermost recesses of Japanese mentality, we may be foolhardy to disregard such possibilities.

Other militarists are more complex and more moral in their considerations. The "Philosophie des Krieges," by S. R. Steinmetz is a good example. War, according to this author, is an ordeal instituted by God, who weighs the nations in its balance. It is the essential form of the State, and the only function in which peoples can employ all their powers at once and convergently. No victory is possible save as the resultant of a totality of virtues, no defeat for which some vice or weakness is not responsible. Fidelity, cohesiveness, tenacity, heroism, conscience, education, inventiveness, economy, wealth, physical health and vigor—there isn't a moral or intellectual point of superiority that doesn't tell, when God holds his assizes and hurls the peoples upon one another. *Die*

Weltgeschichte ist das Weltgericht; and Dr. Steinmetz does not believe that in the long run chance and luck play any part in apportioning the issues.

The virtues that prevail, it must be noted, are virtues anyhow, superiorities that count in peaceful as well as in military competition; but the strain on them, being infinitely intenser in the latter case, makes war infinitely more searching as a trial. No ordeal is comparable to its winnowings. Its dread hammer is the welder of men into cohesive states, and nowhere but in such states can human nature adequately develop its capacity. The only alternative is "degeneration."

Dr. Steinmetz is a conscientious thinker, and his book, short as it is, takes much into account. Its upshot can, it seems to me, be summed up in Simon Patten's word, that mankind was nursed in pain and fear, and that the transition to a "pleasure-economy" may be fatal to a being wielding no powers of defence against its disintegrative influences. If we speak of the *fear of emancipation from the fear-régime,* we put the whole situation into a single phrase; fear regarding ourselves now taking the place of the ancient fear of the enemy.

Turn the fear over as I will in my mind, it all seems to lead back to two unwillingnesses of the imagination, one æsthetic, and the other moral; unwillingness, first to envisage a future in which army-life, with its many elements of charm, shall be forever impossible, and in which the destinies of peoples shall nevermore be decided quickly, thrillingly, and tragically, by force, but only gradually and insipidly by "evolution"; and, secondly, unwillingness to see the supreme theatre of human strenuousness closed, and the splendid military aptitudes of men doomed to keep always in a state of latency and never show themselves in action. These insistent unwillingnesses, no less than other æsthetic and ethical insistencies, have, it seems to me, to be listened to and respected. One cannot meet them effectively by mere counter-insistency on war's expensiveness and horror. The horror makes the thrill; and when the question is of getting the extremest and supremest out of human nature, talk of expense sounds ignominious. The weakness of so much merely negative criticism is evident—pacificism makes no converts from the military party. The military party denies neither the bestiality nor the horror, nor the expense; it only says that these things tell but half the story. It only says that war is *worth* them; that, taking human nature as a whole, its wars are its best protection against its weaker and more cowardly self, and that mankind cannot *afford* to adopt a peace-economy.

Pacificists ought to enter more deeply into the æsthetical and ethical point of view of their opponents. Do that first in any controversy, says J. J. Chapman, *then move the point,* and your opponent will follow. So long as anti-militarists propose no substitute for war's disciplinary function, no *moral equivalent* of war, analogous, as one might say, to the mechanical equivalent of heat, so long they fail to realize the full inwardness of the situation. And as a rule they do fail. The duties, penalties, and sanctions pictured in the utopias they paint are all too weak and tame to touch the military-minded. Tolstoï's pacificism is the only exception to this rule, for it is profoundly pessimistic as regards all this world's values, and makes the fear of the Lord furnish the moral spur provided elsewhere by the fear of the enemy. But our socialistic peace-advocates all believe absolutely in this world's values; and instead of the fear of the Lord and the fear of the enemy, the only fear they reckon with is the fear of poverty if one be lazy. This weakness pervades all the socialistic literature with which I am acquainted. Even in Lowes Dickinson's exquisite dialogue,[1] high wages and short hours are the only forces invoked for overcoming man's distaste for repulsive kinds of labor. Meanwhile men at large still live as they always have lived, under a pain-and-fear economy—for those of us who live in an ease-economy are but an island in the stormy ocean—and the whole atmosphere of present-day utopian literature tastes mawkish and dishwatery to people who still keep a sense for life's more bitter flavors. It suggests, in truth, ubiquitous inferiority.

Inferiority is always with us, and merciless scorn of it is the keynote of the military temper. "Dogs, would you live forever?" shouted Frederick the Great. "Yes," say our utopians, "let us live forever, and raise our level gradually." The best thing about our "inferiors" to-day is that they are as tough as nails, and physically and morally almost as insensitive. Utopianism would see them soft and squeamish, while militarism would keep their callousness, but

1. *Justice and Liberty,* N.Y., 1909.

transfigure it into a meritorious characteristic, needed by "the service," and redeemed by that from the suspicion of inferiority. All the qualities of a man acquire dignity when he knows that the service of the collectivity that owns him needs them. If proud of the collectivity, his own pride rises in proportion. No collectivity is like an army for nourishing such pride; but it has to be confessed that the only sentiment which the image of pacific cosmopolitan industrialism is capable of arousing in countless worthy breasts is shame at the idea of belonging to *such* a collectivity. It is obvious that the United States of America as they exist to-day impress a mind like General Lea's as so much human blubber. Where is the sharpness and precipitousness, the contempt for life, whether one's own, or another's? Where is the savage "yes" and "no," the unconditional duty? Where is the conscription? Where is the blood-tax? Where is anything that one feels honored by belonging to?

Having said thus much in preparation, I will now confess my own utopia. I devoutly believe in the reign of peace and in the gradual advent of some sort of a socialistic equilibrium. The fatalistic view of the war-function is to me nonsense, for I know that war-making is due to definite motives and subject to prudential checks and reasonable criticisms, just like any other form of enterprise. And when whole nations are the armies, and the science of destruction vies in intellectual refinement with the sciences of production, I see that war becomes absurd and impossible from its own monstrosity. Extravagant ambitions will have to be replaced by reasonable claims, and nations must make common cause against them. I see no reason why all this should not apply to yellow as well as to white countries, and I look forward to a future when acts of war shall be formally outlawed as between civilized peoples.

All these beliefs of mine put me squarely into the anti-militarist party. But I do not believe that peace either ought to be or will be permanent on this globe, unless the states pacifically organized preserve some of the old elements of army-discipline. A permanently successful peace-economy cannot be a simple pleasure-economy. In the more or less socialistic future towards which mankind seems drifting we must still subject ourselves collectively to those severities which answer to our real position upon this only

partly hospitable globe. We must make new energies and hardi-
hoods continue the manliness to which the military mind so faithfully clings. Martial virtues must be the enduring cement;
intrepidity, contempt of softness, surrender of private interest,
obedience to command, must still remain the rock upon which
states are built—unless, indeed, we wish for dangerous reactions
against commonwealths fit only for contempt, and liable to invite
attack whenever a centre of crystallization for military-minded
enterprise gets formed anywhere in their neighborhood.

The war-party is assuredly right in affirming and reaffirming
that the martial virtues, although originally gained by the race
through war, are absolute and permanent human goods. Patriotic
price and ambition in their military form are, after all, only
specifications of a more general competitive passion. They are its
first form, but that is no reason for supposing them to be its last
form. Men now are proud of belonging to a conquering nation,
and without a murmur they lay down their persons and their
wealth, if by so doing they may fend off subjection. But who can
be sure that *other aspects of one's country* may not, with time and
education and suggestion enough, come to be regarded with similarly effective feelings of pride and shame? Why should men not
some day feel that it is worth a blood-tax to belong to a collectivity
superior in *any* ideal respect? Why should they not blush with
indignant shame if the community that owns them is vile in
any way whatsoever? Individuals, daily more numerous, now feel
this civic passion. It is only a question of blowing on the spark till
the whole population gets incandescent, and on the ruins of the
old morals of military honor, a stable system of morals of civic
honor builds itself up. What the whole community comes to believe in grasps the individual as in a vise. The war-function has
grasped us so far; but constructive interests may some day seem no
less imperative, and impose on the individual a hardly lighter
burden.

Let me illustrate my idea more concretely. There is nothing to
make one indignant in the mere fact that life is hard, that men
should toil and suffer pain. The planetary conditions once for all
are such, and we can stand it. But that so many men, by mere
accidents of birth and opportunity, should have a life of *nothing*

else but toil and pain and hardness and inferiority imposed upon them, should have *no* vacation, while others natively no more deserving never get any taste of this campaigning life at all—*this* is capable of arousing indignation in reflective minds. It may end by seeming shameful to all of us that some of us have nothing but campaigning, and others nothing but unmanly ease. If now—and this is my idea—there were, instead of military conscription, a conscription of the whole youthful population to form for a certain number of years a part of the army enlisted against *Nature*, the injustice would tend to be evened out, and numerous other goods to the commonwealth would follow. The military ideals of hardihood and discipline would be wrought into the growing fibre of the people; no one would remain blind as the luxurious classes now are blind, to man's relations to the globe he lives on, and to the permanently sour and hard foundations of his higher life. To coal and iron mines, to freight trains, to fishing fleets in December, to dish-washing, clothes-washing, and window-washing, to road-building and tunnel-making, to foundries and stoke-holes, and to the frames of sky-scrapers, would our gilded youths be drafted off, according to their choice, to get the childishness knocked out of them, and to come back into society with healthier sympathies and soberer ideas. They would have paid their blood-tax, done their own part in the immemorial human warfare against nature; they would tread the earth more proudly, the women would value them more highly, they would be better fathers and teachers of the following generation.

Such a conscription, with the state of public opinion that would have required it, and the many moral fruits it would bear, would preserve in the midst of a pacific civilization the manly virtues which the military party is so afraid of seeing disappear in peace. We should get toughness without callousness, authority with as little criminal cruelty as possible, and painful work done cheerily because the duty is temporary, and threatens not, as now, to degrade the whole remainder of one's life. I spoke of the "moral equivalent" of war. So far, war has been the only force that can discipline a whole community, and until an equivalent discipline is organized, I believe that war must have its way. But I have no serious doubt that the ordinary prides and shames of social man, once developed to a certain intensity, are capable of organizing such a moral equivalent as I have sketched, or some other just as effective for preserving manliness of type. It is but a question of time, of skilful propagandism, and of opinion-making men seizing historic opportunities.

The martial type of character can be bred without war. Strenuous honor and disinterestedness abound elsewhere. Priests and medical men are in a fashion educated to it, and we should all feel some degree of it imperative if we were conscious of our work as an obligatory service to the state. We should be *owned*, as soldiers are by the army, and our pride would rise accordingly. We could be poor, then, without humiliation, as army officers now are. The only thing needed henceforward is to inflame the civic temper as past history has inflamed the military temper. H. G. Wells, as usual, sees the centre of the situation. "In many ways," he says, "military organization is the most peaceful of activities. When the contemporary man steps from the street, of clamorous insincere advertisement, push, adulteration, underselling and intermittent employment into the barrack-yard, he steps on to a higher social plane, into an atmosphere of service and cooperation and of infinitely more honorable emulations. Here at least men are not flung out of employment to degenerate because there is no immediate work for them to do. They are fed and drilled and trained for better services. Here at least a man is supposed to win promotion by self-forgetfulness and not by self-seeking. And beside the feeble and irregular endowment of research by commercialism, its little short-sighted snatches at profit by innovation and scientific economy, see how remarkable is the steady and rapid development of method and appliances in naval and military affairs! Nothing is more striking than to compare the progress of civil conveniences which has been left almost entirely to the trader, to the progress in military apparatus during the last few decades. The house-appliances of to-day for example, are little better than they were fifty years ago. A house of to-day is still almost as ill-ventilated, badly heated by wasteful fires, clumsily arranged and furnished as the house of 1858. Houses a couple of hundred years old are still satisfactory places of residence, so little have our standards risen. But the rifle or battleship of fifty years ago was beyond all comparison inferior to those we possess; in power, in speed, in convenience alike. No one has a use now for such superannuated things."[2]

Wells adds[3] that he thinks that the conceptions of order and discipline, the tradition of service and devotion, of physical fitness, unstinted exertion, and universal responsibility, which universal military duty is now teaching European nations, will remain a permanent acquisition, when the last ammunition has been used in the fireworks that celebrate the final peace. I believe as he does. It would be simply preposterous if the only force that could work ideals of honor and standards of efficiency into English or American natures should be the fear of being killed by the Germans or the Japanese. Great indeed is Fear; but it is not, as our military enthusiasts believe and try to make us believe, the only stimulus known for awakening the higher ranges of men's spiritual energy. The amount of alteration in public opinion which my utopia postulates is vastly less than the difference between the mentality of those black warriors who pursued Stanley's party on the Congo with their cannibal war-cry of "Meat! Meat!" and that of the "general-staff" of any civilized nation. History has seen the latter interval bridged over: the former one can be bridged over much more easily.

2. *First and Last Things*, 1908, p. 215.
3. *Ibid.*, p. 226.

16.

From *A Pluralistic Universe*

A. The Continuity of Experience*

. . . Not only the absolute is its own other, but the simplest bits of immediate experience are their own other, if that hegelian phrase be once for all allowed. The concrete pulses of experience appear pent in by no such definite limits as our conceptual substitutes for them are confined by. They run into one another continuously and seem to interpenetrate. What in them is relation and what is matter related is hard to discern. You feel no one of them as inwardly simple, and no two as wholly without confluence where they touch. There is no datum so small as not to show this mystery, if mystery it be. The tiniest feeling that we can possibly have comes with an earlier and a later part and with a sense of their continuous procession. Mr. Shadworth Hodgson showed long ago that there is literally no such object as the present moment except as an unreal postulate of abstract thought. The 'passing' moment is, as I already have reminded you, the minimal fact, with the 'apparition of difference' inside of it as well as outside. If we do not feel both past and present in one field of feeling, we feel them not at all. We have the same many-in-one in the matter that fills the passing time. The rush of our thought forward through its fringes is the everlasting peculiarity of its life. We realize that life as something always off its balance, something in transition, something that shoots out of a darkness through a dawn into a brightness that we feel to be the dawn fulfilled. In the very midst of the continuity our experience comes as an alteration. "Yes," we say at the full brightness, *"this* is what I just meant." "No," we feel at the dawning, "this is not yet the full meaning, there is more to come." In every crescendo of sensation, in every effort to recall,

* Lecture VII of the Hibbert Lectures of 1909, published as *A Pluralistic Universe* (New York & London: Longmans, Green & Co., 1909). Portions of text and some footnotes have been deleted. [B.W.]

in every progress towards the satisfaction of desire, this succession of an emptiness and fulness that have reference to each other and are one flesh is the essence of the phenomenon. In every hindrance of desire the sense of an ideal presence which is absent in fact, of an absent, in a word, which the only function of the present is to *mean*, is even more notoriously there. And in the movement of pure thought we have the same phenomenon. When I say *Socrates is mortal*, the moment *Socrates* is incomplete; it falls forward through the *is* which is pure movement, into the *mortal* which is indeed bare mortal on the tongue, but for the mind is *that mortal*, the *mortal Socrates*, at last satisfactorily disposed of and told off.

Here, then, inside of the minimal pulses of experience, is realized that very inner complexity which the transcendentalists say only the absolute can genuinely possess. The gist of the matter is always the same—something ever goes indissolubly with something else. You cannot separate the same from its other, except by abandoning the real altogether and taking to the conceptual system. What is immediately given in the single and particular instance is always something pooled and mutual, something with no dark spot, no point of ignorance. No one elementary bit of reality is eclipsed from the next bit's point of view, if only we take reality sensibly and in small enough pulses—and by us it has to be taken pulse-wise, for our span of consciousness is too short to grasp the larger collectivity of things except nominally and abstractly. No more of reality collected together at once is extant anywhere, perhaps, than in my experience of reading this page, or in yours of listening; yet within those bits of experience as they come to pass we get a fulness of content that no conceptual description can equal. Sensational experiences *are* their 'own others,' then, both internally and externally. Inwardly they are one with their parts, and outwardly they pass continuously into their next neighbors, so that events separated by years of time in a man's life hang together unbrokenly by the intermediary events. Their *names*, to be sure, cut them into separate conceptual entities, but no cuts existed in the continuum in which they originally came.

If, with all this in our mind, we turn to our own particular predicament, we see that our old objection to the self-compounding of states of consciousness, our accusation that it was impossible for purely logical reasons, is unfounded in principle. Every smallest state of consciousness, concretely taken, overflows its own definition. Only concepts are self-identical; only 'reason' deals with closed equations; nature is but a name for excess; every point in her opens out and runs into the more; and the only question, with reference to any point we may be considering, is how far into the rest of nature we may have to go in order to get entirely beyond its overflow. In the pulse of inner life immediately present now in each of us is a little past, a little future, a little awareness of our own body, of each other's persons, of these sublimities we are trying to talk about, of the earth's geography and the direction of history, of truth and error, of good and bad, and of who knows how much more? Feeling, however dimly and subconsciously, all these things, your pulse of inner life is continuous with them, belongs to them and they to it. You can't identify it with either one of them rather than with the others, for if you let it develop into no matter which of those directions, what it develops into will look back on it and say, "That was the original germ of me."

In *principle,* then, the real units of our immediately-felt life are unlike the units that intellectualist logic holds to and makes its calculations with. They are not separate from their own others, and you have to take them at widely separated dates to find any two of them that seem unblent. Then indeed they do appear separate even as their concepts are separate; a chasm yawns between them; but the chasm itself is but an intellectualist fiction, got by abstracting from the coninuous sheet of experiences with which the intermediary time was filled. It is like the log carried first by William and Henry, then by William, Henry, and John, then by Henry and John, then by John and Peter, and so on. All real units of experience *overlap.* Let a row of equidistant dots on a sheet of paper symbolize the concepts by which we intellectualize the world. Let a ruler long enough to cover at least three dots stand for our sensible experience. Then the conceived changes of the sensible experience can be symbolized by sliding the ruler along the line of dots. One concept after another will apply to it, one after another drop away, but it will always cover at least two of them, and no dots less than three will ever adequately cover *it.* You falsify it if you treat it conceptually, or by the law of dots.

What is true here of successive states must also be true of simultaneous characters. They also overlap each other with their being. My present field of consciousness is a centre surrounded by a fringe that shades insensibly into a subconscious more. I use three separate terms here to describe this fact; but I might as well use three hundred, for the fact is all shades and no boundaries. Which part of it properly is in my consciousness, which out? If I name what is out, it already has come in. The centre works in one way while the margins work in another, and presently overpower the centre and are central themselves. What we conceptually identify ourselves with and say we are thinking of at any time is the centre; but our *full* self is the whole field, with all those indefinitely radiating subconscious possibilities of increase that we can only feel without conceiving, and can hardly begin to analyze. The collective and the distributive ways of being coexist here, for each part functions distinctly, makes connexion with its own peculiar region in the still wider rest of experience and tends to draw us into that line, and yet the whole is somehow felt as one pulse of our life—not conceived so, but felt so.

In principle, then, as I said, intellectualism's edge is broken; it can only approximate to reality, and its logic is inapplicable to our inner life, which spurns its vetoes and mocks at its impossibilities. Every bit of us at every moment is part and parcel of a wider self, it quivers along various radii like the wind-rose on a compass, and the actual in it is continuously one with possibles not yet in our present sight. And just as we are co-conscious with our own momentary margin, may not we ourselves form the margin of some more really central self in things which is co-conscious with the whole of us? May not you and I be confluent in a higher consciousness, and confluently active there, tho we now know it not?

I am tiring myself and you, I know, by vainly seeking to describe by concepts and words what I say at the same time exceeds either conceptualization or verbalization. As long as one continues *talking*, intellectualism remains in undisturbed possession of the field. The return to life can't come about by talking. It is an *act;* to make you return to life, I must set an example for your imitation, I must deafen you to talk, or to the importance of talk, by showing you, as Bergson does, that the concepts we talk with are made for purposes of *practice* and not for purposes of insight. Or I must *point*, point to the mere *that* of life, and you by inner sympathy must fill out the *what* for yourselves. The minds of some of you, I know, will absolutely refuse to do so, refuse to think in non-conceptualized terms. I myself absolutely refused to do so for years together, even after I knew that the denial of manyness-in-oneness by intellectualism must be false, for the same reality does perform the most various functions at once. But I hoped ever for a revised intellectualist way round the difficulty and it was only after reading Bergson that I saw that to continue using the intellectualist method was itself the fault. I saw that philosophy had been on a false scent ever since, the days of Socrates and Plato, that an *intellectual* answer to the intellectualist's difficulties will never come, and that the real way out of them, far from consisting in the discovery of such an answer, consists in simply closing one's ears to the question. When conceptualism summons life to justify itself in conceptual terms, it is like a challenge addressed in a foreign language to some one who is absorbed in his own business; it is irrelevant to him altogether—he may let it lie unnoticed. I went thus through the 'inner catastrophe' of which I spoke in the last lecture; I had literally come to the end of my conceptual stock-in-trade, I was bankrupt intellectualistically, and had to change my base. No words of mine will probably convert you, for words can be the names only of concepts. But if any of you try sincerely and pertinaciously on your own separate accounts to intellectualize reality, you may be similarly driven to a change of front. I say no more: I must leave life to teach the lesson.

We have now reached a point of view from which the self-compounding of mind in its smaller and more accessible portions seems a certain fact, and in which the speculative assumption of a similar but wider compounding in remoter regions must be reckoned with as a legitimate hypothesis. The absolute is not the impossible being I once thought it. Mental facts do function both singly and together, at once, and we finite minds may simultaneously be co-conscious with one another in a superhuman intelligence. It is only the extravagant claims of coercive necessity on the absolute's part that have to be denied by *a priori* logic. As an hypothesis trying to make itself probable on analogical and inductive grounds, the absolute is entitled to a patient hearing. Which is as much as to say that our serious business from now onward lies with Fechner and his method, rather than with Hegel, Royce, or Bradley. Fechner treats the superhuman consciousness he so fervently believes in as an hypothesis only, which he then recommends by all the resources of induction and persuasion. . . .

B. Conclusions*

. . . Pragmatically interpreted, pluralism or the doctrine that [reality] is many means only that the sundry parts of reality *may be externally related*. Everything you can think of, however vast or inclusive, has on the pluralistic view a genuinely 'external' environment of some sort or amount. Things are 'with' one another in many ways, but nothing includes everything, or dominates over everything. The word 'and' trails along after every sentence. Something always escapes. 'Ever not quite' has to be said of the best attempts made anywhere in the universe at attaining all-inclusiveness. The pluralistic world is thus more like a federal republic than like an empire or a kingdom. However much may be collected, however much may report itself as present at any effective centre of consciousness or action, something else is self-governed and absent and unreduced to unity.

Monism, on the other hand, insists that when you come down to reality as such, to the reality of realities, everything is present to *everything* else in one vast instantaneous co-implicated completeness—nothing can in *any* sense, functional or substantial, be really absent from anything else, all things interpenetrate and telescope together in the great total conflux.

For pluralism, all that we are required to admit as the constitution of reality is what we ourselves find empirically realized in every minimum of finite life. Briefly it is this, that nothing real is absolutely simple, that every smallest bit of experience is a *multum in parvo* plurally related, that each relation is one aspect, character, or function, way of its being taken, or way of its taking something else; and that a bit of reality when actively engaged in one of these relations is not *by that very fact* engaged in all the other relations simultaneously. The relations are not *all* what the French call *solidaires* with one another. Without losing its identity a thing can either take up or drop another thing, like the log I

* From Lecture VIII of *A Pluralistic Universe*.

spoke of, which by taking up new carriers and dropping old ones can travel anywhere with a light escort.

For monism, on the contrary, everything, whether we realize it or not, drags the whole universe along with itself and drops nothing. The log starts and arrives with all its carriers supporting it. If a thing were once disconnected, it could never be connected again, according to monism. The pragmatic difference between the two systems is thus a definite one. It is just thus, that if *a* is once out of sight of *b* or out of touch with it, or, more briefly, 'out' of it at all, then, according to monism, it must always remain so, they can never get together; whereas pluralism admits that on another occasion they may work together, or in some way be connected again. Monism allows for no such things as 'other occasions' in reality—in *real* or absolute reality, that is.

The difference I try to describe amounts, you see, to nothing more than the difference between what I formerly called the each-form and the all-form of reality. Pluralism lets things really exist in the each-form or distributively. Monism thinks that the all-form or collective-unit form is the only form that is rational. The all-form allows of no taking up and dropping of connexions, for in the all the parts are essentially and eternally co-implicated. In the each-form, on the contrary, a thing may be connected by inter-mediary things, with a thing with which it has no immediate or essential connexion. It is thus at all times in many possible connexions which are not necessarily actualized at the moment. They depend on which actual path of intermediation it may functionally strike into: the word 'or' names a genuine reality. Thus, as I speak here, I may look ahead *or* to the right *or* to the left, and in either case the intervening space and air and ether enable me to see the faces of a different portion of this audience. My being here is independent of any one set of these facts.

If the each-form be the eternal form of reality no less than it is the form of temporal appearance, we still have a coherent world, and not an incarnate incoherence, as is charged by so many absolutists. Our 'multiverse' still makes a 'universe'; for every part, tho it may not be in actual or immediate connexion, is neverthe-less in some possible or mediated connexion, with every other part however remote, through the fact that each part hangs together with its very next neighbors in inextricable interfusion. The type of union, it is true, is different here from the monistic type of *alleinheit*. It is not a universal co-implication, or integration of all things *durcheinander*. It is what I call the strung-along type, the type of continuity, contiguity, or concatenation. If you prefer greek words, you may call it the synechistic type. At all events, you see that it forms a definitely conceivable alternative to the through-and-through unity of all things at once, which is the type opposed to it by monism. You see also that it stands or falls with the notion I have taken such pains to defend, of the through-and-through union of adjacent minima of experience, of the confluence of every passing moment of concretely felt experience with its immediately next neighbors. The recognition of this fact of coalescence of next with next in concrete experience, so that all the insulating cuts we make there are artificial products of the conceptualizing faculty, is what distinguishes the empiricism which I call 'radical,' from the bugaboo empiricism of the traditional rationalist critics, which (rightly or wrongly) is accused of chopping up experience into atomistic sensations, incapable of union with one another until a purely intellectual principle has swooped down upon them from on high and folded them in its own conjunctive categories.

Here, then, you have the plain alternative, and the full mystery of the difference between pluralism and monism, as clearly as I can set it forth on this occasion. It packs up into a nutshell: Is the manyness in oneness that indubitably characterizes the world we inhabit, a property only of the absolute whole of things, so that you must postulate that one-enormous-whole indivisibly as the *prius* of there being any many at all—in other words, start with the rationalistic block-universe, entire, unmitigated, and complete?—or can the finite elements have their own aboriginal forms of manyness in oneness, and where they have no immediate oneness still be continued into one another by intermediary terms—each one of these terms being one with its next neighbors, and yet the total 'oneness' never getting absolutely complete?

The alternative is definite. It seems to me, moreover, that the two horns of it make pragmatically different ethical appeals—at least they *may* do so, to certain individuals. But if you consider the pluralistic horn to be intrinsically irrational, self-contradictory, and absurd, I can now say no more in its defence. . . .